Xuedou's *100 Odes to Old Cases*

Xuedou's *100 Odes to Old Cases*

A Translation with Commentary

STEVEN HEINE

OXFORD
UNIVERSITY PRESS

Oxford University Press is a department of the University of Oxford. It furthers the University's objective of excellence in research, scholarship, and education by publishing worldwide. Oxford is a registered trade mark of Oxford University Press in the UK and certain other countries.

Published in the United States of America by Oxford University Press
198 Madison Avenue, New York, NY 10016, United States of America.

Library of Congress Cataloging-in-Publication Data
Names: Xuedou, 980–1052, author. | Heine, Steven, 1950– translator.
Title: Xuedou's 100 odes to old cases : a translation with commentary / Steven Heine.
Other titles: Xuedou bai ze song gu. English
Description: New York : Oxford University Press, 2024. |
Includes bibliographical references and index.
Identifiers: LCCN 2023040363 (print) | LCCN 2023040364 (ebook) |
ISBN 9780197676998 (paperback) | ISBN 9780197676561 (hardback) |
ISBN 9780197677001 (epub)
Subjects: LCSH: Koan—Early works to 1800. |
Spiritual life—Zen Buddhism. | Zen Buddhism—Doctrines.
Classification: LCC BQ9289 .H79513 2024 (print) | LCC BQ9289 (ebook) |
DDC 294.3/927—dc23/eng/20230925
LC record available at https://lccn.loc.gov/2023040363
LC ebook record available at https://lccn.loc.gov/2023040364

DOI: 10.1093/oso/9780197676561.001.0001

Paperback printed by Marquis Book Printing, Canada
Hardback printed by Bridgeport National Bindery, Inc., United States of America

Contents

Preface

The idea for writing this book, a translation with my interpretative comments of one hundred odes or verse comments (*songgu*) on gong'an cases by the eleventh-century poet-monk Xuedou, began to form after I completed the volume, *Chan Rhetoric of Uncertainty in the Blue Cliff Record* (Oxford University Press, 2016). At that time, I started to realize that the core ingredient of the *Blue Cliff Record*, which was compiled with extensive annotations in the 1110s by Yuanwu, was not necessarily the gong'an themselves but, rather, the poetry by Xuedou that was originally composed and presented to his assembly as dharma hall sermons nearly a century before Yuanwu's intricate prose and capping-phrase remarks were added. The component of Xuedou's odes, long eclipsed by Yuanwu's interpretations and for the most part neglected by scholars for many centuries, remains generally overlooked in contemporary studies. Nevertheless, it was becoming clear to me this core text represents the seminal discourse that helped form the content and style of the gong'an tradition during the Northern Song dynasty and has greatly influenced so many major Chan rhetorical and theoretical developments ever since.

As the fifteenth-century Japanese Zen poet-monk Ikkyū once remarked in a verse that was, in turn, inspired by a similar poem written in China a couple of hundred years earlier, "Scriptural scrolls have always been nothing more than paper to remove filth," an ironic form of praise alluding to the Buddha's own words. In that vein, regrettably yet perhaps from a certain perspective providentially because periods of absence highlighted its importance, Xuedou's text and the *Blue Cliff Record* were both initially left out of the vast Buddhist canon included in the *Great Treasury of Sūtras* (大蔵經, C. *Dazang jing*, J. *Daizōkyō*) that was produced in Song China and transported to Kamakura-period Japan. Therefore, Ikkyū recommends, "One must read carefully [Xuedou's] comments on one hundred cases, / These inspired the assembly at Mount Xuedou temple prior to the flowing of breezes or the glow of moonlight." The final phrase refers to the proliferation of diverse Chan/Zen lineages with their respective and sometimes conflicting teaching methods.

During a research trip in the summer of 2019, which took place well before I knew it would be my last visit to Japan for four COVID-19-afflicted years, while perusing the shelves in the Toyodo Buddhist bookstore in the Jimbocho bookshops section of Tokyo, I fortuitously stumbled on a reprint of a critical edition of Xuedou's original text. This version, known in Japanese as the *Setchō juko* (雪竇頌古, C. *Xuedou songgu*), was first released in 1981 by the premier Zen scholars of the postwar era, Yanagida Seizan and Iriya Yoshitaka. Purchasing this tome furthered my research path, since I already had gathered many other Chinese and Japanese scholarly materials from the previous project. But I also understood that I needed to delve more thoroughly into Xuedou's life and writings, as well as the context of Northern Song literati culture, especially with regard to assessing how innovative developments in the Chan approach to doctrinal notions and meditative practices were intimately connected to explicating gong'an cases through the composition of poetic along with other kinds of commentaries.

The two background chapters examine the origins and significance of Xuedou's work in terms of its religious and cultural as well as ritual and rhetorical foundations. This section of the book also discusses the rationale for my translation method that highlights the author's use of diverse discursive devices, such as lyrical flourishes and interjected exclamations, to exhort his followers to heed the basic spiritual message of overcoming delusions to attain genuine Chan realization. This shows, to cite a Japanese maxim, that poetry "makes what's invisible to the eye visible to the eye" (目に見えないものを目に見えるようにする).

Next, the main section of the book in Chapter 3 provides translations with explanations of Xuedou's verse comments, in addition to a critical summary of the source gong'an dialogues as well as selected capping phrases that were appended by two leading commentators: Yuanwu from the Song dynasty, who also wrote introductions and prose remarks; and Tianqi from the Ming dynasty, who composed only capping phrases. My brief discussions of each case's poem composed by Xuedou integrate the perspectives of these premodern annotations with current scholarly research and literary reflections concerning eleventh-century Chan thought.

There are many people to thank for their helpful feedback or assistance while writing this book, but I will just mention a few: Kevin Buckelew, Chris Byrne, Xiaohuan Cao, George Keyworth, Zuzana Kubovčáková, Taigen Dan Leighton, Li Ma, Michaela Mross, Jason Protass, Morten Schlütter, Albert Welter, Julie Zeng, Aihua Zheng, and the anonymous reader for Oxford University Press, in addition to Maria Sol Echarren for creating the images and Rachel Levine for preparing the index.

PART I
BACKGROUND

1

Historical and Rhetorical Foundations of Xuedou's *100 Odes*

A thousand soldiers are easy to recruit, but one superb general is hard to find (千兵易得. 一將難求).

—Ode 54 (capping phrase on Xuedou's verse, by Yuanwu)

Aims of This Volume

The single most important element in the tradition of voluminous Chan Buddhist gong'an (公案, J. kōan) compilations that contain various kinds of interpretative remarks is not necessarily the records of encounter dialogues (機緣問答, *jiyuan wenda*) but, rather, the eloquent yet enigmatic verses commenting on one hundred cases composed in 1038 by the master Xuedou Chongxian (雪竇重顯, 980–1052).[1] A representative of the Yunmen (雲門) branch of Chan that he helped revive and bring to prominence during the Northern Song dynasty (960–1127), before its impact declined with the fall of the capital in Kaifeng, Xuedou demonstrates a unique literary flair for explicating gong'an that is evident in numerous writings included in his recorded sayings.[2] In particular, *Xuedou's 100 Odes to Old Cases* (雪竇百則頌古, C. *Xuedou baize songgu*, J. *Setchō hyakusoku juko*; hereafter *Odes*) is recognized as the seminal discourse that has greatly influenced the way stories of former teachers (古則, *guze*) have been appreciated and appropriated for the past thousand years. This text continues to exert a profound impact on the overall legacy of East Asian Buddhist intellectual history and religious literature.[3]

According to numerous interpreters, the greatness of Xuedou's work lies in his ability to transform the role of literature from conveying ornamental imagery to disclosing didactic injunctions and instructions while remaining eminently lyrical through utilizing a variety of discursive techniques that admonish yet inspire disciples about disabling self-deceptions to attain a

Xuedou's 100 Odes to Old Cases. Steven Heine, Oxford University Press.
DOI: 10.1093/oso/9780197676561.003.0001

spontaneous realization of the dharma. Xuedou relies on metaphors and allusions to symbolize the Chan quest and uses irregular meter and vernacular interjections by inserting exclamations, exhortations, proclamations, and personal reflections that help stimulate the reader's reactions.

These devices are designed to disrupt typical literary expectations for the purpose of promoting interior realization. Xuedou thereby demonstrates a knack for "taming the mind with elegance" (yongdian xunyun, 用典雅馴) by challenging and overcoming the drawbacks of the normally disturbed or obstructed mental state of his followers through recasting various sayings and maxims drawn from gong'an and a vast body Chinese cultural resources to articulate seamlessly the pursuit of Chan awakening. This approach to cultivating self-awareness recalls the notion of "taming the ox," according to the famous Song Chan series of *10 Oxherding Pictures* (十牛圖) that features poems inscribed to depict each stage of this spiritual process.

Xuedou was the second main teacher to utilize the genre of odes following the *Fenyang songgu* (汾陽頌古), the initial collection written a decade or more earlier, also with one hundred cases, by Linji (臨済, J. Rinzai) school master Fenyang Shanzhao (汾陽善昭, 947–1022).[4] As will be explained in Chapter 2, Fenyang's poetry tends to express straightforward remarks regarding the doctrinal implications of cases through using conventional poetic syntax. However, because of its extraordinarily innovative rhetorical skill and rich philosophical content articulated in an indirect or roundabout and oblique approach to Chan discourse (繞路說禪, *raolu shuo Chan*) that often bends or takes a detour from the rules of composition, the *Odes* is considered "the key to learning the ways of meditative practice" (叢林學道詮要), as noted by contemporary Chinese scholar Zhou Yukai.[5] Xuedou's text thereby surpasses the work of his predecessor and deserves to be seen as the primary guide for the unfolding of subsequent gong'an commentaries.

According to a premodern interpreter, the *Odes* conveys "the very heart and lifeblood of the buddhas and patriarchs" (是佛祖心肝, 蒼生命脈), because it "unravels mysteries in fine detail through probing their uttermost depths" (剖決玄微, 抉剔幽邃). This is accomplished by "displaying marvelous knowledge of pure emptiness and the fundamental source of true silence" (妙智虛凝, 神機默運).[6] Furthermore, the prominent modern Japanese Buddhist studies scholar Nukariya Kaiten (忽滑谷快天, 1867–1934) has admired Xuedou's work for being concise, elegant, and aesthetic.

As Nukariya notes according to a Chinese summary, "Xuedou shows the splendor of his thought, as if adding embroidery to a brocade [an image mentioned in Ode 12] by skillfully writing poems that explicate the ways of our ancestors" (顯錦想繡囊, 巧打詩偈, 以述祖道). Furthermore, "his verse comments have a marvelous quality . . . by transforming language into exquisite phrasings as an expansive yet succinct form of expression. In fact, through his lyrical commentary Xuedou has constructed a special form of versification enabling others to grasp the essential point of the one hundred cases" (尤於頌古發揮其妙 . . . 變平實之語為浮華之詞, 化簡勁之語為森茫之辭. 事實上, 雪竇禪師正是以此特點構建了他的頌古百則).[7]

My aim in this book is to provide the first complete translation of Xuedou's *100 Odes*. For each verse, I offer a critical summary of the gong'an case that is treated by Xuedou and explanations of religious symbolism by drawing out various explicit or implicit connections linking the poetry's allusions to Chan lore, Buddhist theories, and other examples of the Sinitic cultural legacy that Xuedou conjures to amplify yet go beyond the meaning of the source dialogue. To complement Xuedou's verses on cases, I also translate selected samples of traditional commentaries, including the capping phrases (着語) and evaluative prose annotations (評唱) proffered by prominent classical and early modern pundits.

These works mainly include (a) the remarks of Yuanwu Keqin (圜悟克勤, 1063–1135), a prominent Linji school master, contained in the *Blue Cliff Record* (碧巖錄, C. *Biyanlu*, J. *Hekiganroku*, T.48.2003, 10 vols.) that was first published in 1128; and (b) the comments by Tianqi Benrui (天奇本瑞, d. 1508), also of the Linji school, in his late fifteenth-century work, *Elder Qiongjue Tianqi's Capping Remarks on Xuedou Chongxian's Odes to Old Cases* (煢絕老人天奇直註雪竇顯和尚頌古, C. *Qiongjue Laoren Tianqi zhizhu Xuedou Xian heshang songgu*, J. *Keizei Tōjin Tenki choku Setchō Ken oshō juko*, X.67.1302, 2 vols.).[8]

For both Yuanwu and Tianqi, I have chosen those examples of capping phrases that seem particularly relevant to interpreting Xuedou's cases and odes. I also occasionally cite examples of Yuanwu's prose remarks, a style of commentary that was not used by Tianqi.[9] It is noteworthy that Yuanwu's recorded sayings (語錄, *yulu*) include a section of *songgu*, although this group of poems did not become an independent collection, apparently because of Yuanwu's discursive preferences.[10] Additionally, I have consulted two major Edo-period Japanese commentaries on the *Blue Cliff Record* by famous scholar-monks representing the Rinzai and Sōtō (曹洞, C. Caodong, J. Sōtō) sects, respectively: Hakuin (白隠, 1686–1769) in *Hekiganroku hisshō*

(碧巖錄秘抄); and Tenkei (天桂, 1648–1735) in *Hekiganroku kōgi* (碧巖錄講義).[11]

Figure 1.1 shows a woodblock edition of Xuedou's *Odes*, which was originally an independent work that, by the mid-twelfth century, was incorporated into the *Blue Cliff Record* as part of a complex seven-part commentarial structure created by Yuanwu.[12] Although this textual association lent the *Odes* a great sense of esteem, it also caused the autonomy of Xuedou's work as a separate body of writing to become overlooked or lost over the centuries. Despite its overwhelming significance, for diverse and intricate textual and historical reasons, Xuedou's text is usually considered a component of the larger commentary, which has had its own rocky textual history. Therefore, one of my goals is to recover and rediscover the enduring value of the *Odes* when seen in a way that is both free from and enhanced by Yuanwu's contributions.

The rest of this chapter examines the significance of Xuedou's lyrical approach to gong'an commentary by exploring the origins of *songgu* as a distinct Chan genre in comparison to other typical poetic styles, which developed at a fruitful juncture of interactions between Buddhism and literature that transpired during the Northern Song. I also briefly describe the history of the formation of Xuedou's *Odes*, in addition to the considerable controversies surrounding its circulation over the centuries, to demonstrate why this text should be read today as an autonomous work. The second chapter presents a theory I have devised about a way of reading the *Odes* by examining the sources for its encounter dialogues, the metrical experimentation used by Xuedou, and the role of extensive allusions and abrupt intrusions employed by the poet to inspire his readers.

Significance of Odes as Gong'an Comments

The *songgu* or odes is a category of brief "eulogies" or "encomia" (頌, *song*) offering stirring remarks on "established" or "precedent" (古, *gu*; literally "old" or "ancient") stories concerning the spiritual exploits of iconic teachers, usually but not always drawn from accounts of the Tang-dynasty leaders included in Chan transmission of the lamp records. Many other types of poetic and prose commentaries on gong'an that were produced from the eleventh through thirteenth centuries in China and Japan remain important, including additional styles composed by Xuedou. Yet the *Odes* stands out

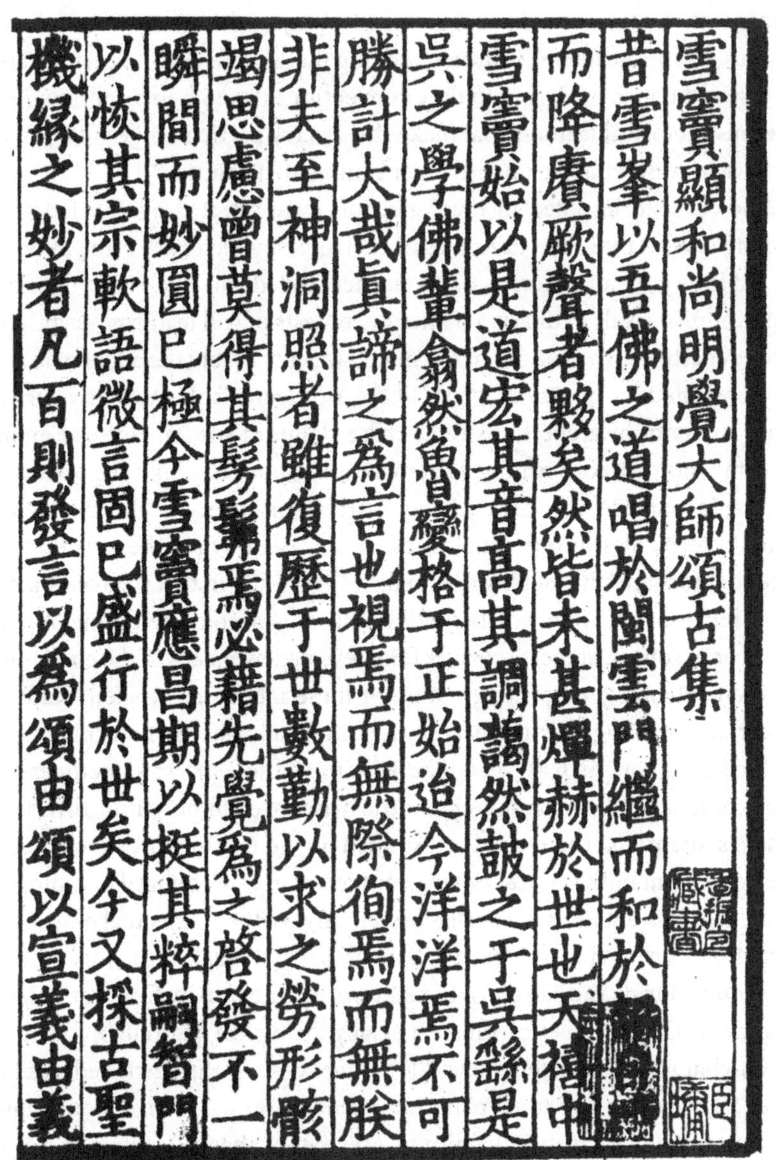

雪竇顯和尚明覺大師頌古集

昔雪峯以吾佛之道唱於閩雲門繼而和於
而降賡歌聲者夥矣然皆未甚燀赫於世也天禧中
雪竇始以是道宏其音高其調藹然鼓之于吳谿是
吳之學佛輩翕然魯變格于正始迨今洋洋焉不可
勝計大哉眞諦之爲言也視焉而無際徇焉而無朕
非夫至神洞照者雖復歷于世數勤以求之勞形骸
竭思慮曾莫得其髣髴焉必藉先覺爲之啓發不一
瞬間而妙圓已極今雪竇應昌期以挺其粹嗣智門
以恢其宗軟語微言固已盛行於世矣今又採古聖
機緣之妙者凡一百則發言以爲頌由頌以宣義由義

Figure 1.1 Woodblock edition of Xuedou's *songgu* collection.

because its verses are said to express the fluency of the literature of the prestigious Hanlin Academy, while embodying the savviness of the performance of a sword dance by daring to defy conventions through incorporating numerous rhetorical features that make this poetry particularly vivid and persuasive in conveying the underlying meaning of dialogues.[13]

The core stories cited in the collection were selected by Xuedou from among several thousand examples of exchanges, which later came to be referred to as gong'an, whereby Chan teachers tested and challenged their disciples and/or rivals in dharma battles or contests of will featuring cryptic yet witty repartee.[14] The winner of the match was invariably the adept who best demonstrated the quality of *jifeng* (機鋒), or the ineffable capability derived from authentic awareness, instead of false claims of wisdom, to seize an opportune moment for creating a dramatic turnabout enabling the winner to gain an advantage over his exchange partner or adversary. Xuedou sometimes interpolates into the dialogues, as in case 4, where he says that the interlocutors are "thoroughly exposed!" (勘破了也) in that the true state of their religious situation, whether admirably advanced or deserving of criticism, or in some instances scorn, is fully revealed by means of the encounter.

The deliberately perplexing nature of these interactions, often featuring uncertain or ambiguous and paradoxical implications, begs for explanations by commentators such as Xuedou, even if the verse remarks sometimes further complicate the meaning or, contrariwise, oversimplify it or divert the reader's attention. The *Odes*, long studied as the preeminent exposition of the genre containing lyrical poetry composed in a specialized yet idiosyncratic discursive style, is a crucial representative of the intellectual movement sometimes referred to as literary Chan (文字禪, *wenzi* Chan). This outlook developed during the Northern Song by borrowing heavily from yet altering traditional Chinese poetic forms, especially the typical quatrain or four-line, seven-character truncated verse (绝句, *jueju*) style that included various rules for rhyming and tonal patterns. Xuedou uses this convention primarily for edifying or instructional purposes rather than aesthetics or art for art's sake.

The text was compiled by Xuedou's disciple, Yuanchen (遠塵, n. d.), probably in the 1060s. According to the preface by Tanyu (曇玉, n. d.), Xuedou "selects the most sublime examples of stories from records of the dialogues of ancient sages" (今又採古聖機緣). Furthermore, "through verses he captures their fundamental moral message and thus transmits essential Chan teachings. Xuedou hopes that those who are ignorant will be enlightened, those with blockages will be illumined, those stymied by delusion will be extricated, and those stuck in the mire and unable to reach beyond it will gain liberation" (由頌以宣義. 由義以垂裕, 俾夫昧者明, 窒者通, 泥而不能致遠者咸, 有所救焉.[15]

To convey the mysterious quality of an enlightenment experience through writing poems, Tanyu explains, Xuedou expresses much more than praise for the sayings of prior masters. He conveys concisely and critically his own unique understanding of the objectives underpinning their interactions, often by alluding to images drawn from legends or folklore or conveying the splendor of the natural environment to provide appropriate counterpoint that ironically highlights an emphasis on attaining authentic subjective awareness.

The *Odes* conveys in beguiling pedagogical fashion the value of penetrating misconceptions and defusing attachments by disclosing the roots of human afflictions and adopting transcendent, nondual perspectives to overcome the mind's troubles, thus opening the path to insight in a way that epitomizes but goes beyond the implications of the original case record. The effectiveness of the work derives from the way Xuedou combines the formal rules of truncated verse with the irregular meters of folksongs and the cadences of tropes drawn from popular culture. This modifies the basic literary elements and introduces new discursive features reflecting the author's distinctive religious stance.

One of Xuedou's most acclaimed verse comments is Ode 37, which consists of four lines, including two with eight characters (both are 4 + 4) and a final couplet with seven characters per line, thus varying from the usual pattern. The opening passage repeats the keyword of the dialogue, a philosophical saying associated with the Huayan school, but the poem ends with a set of natural and musical images that are both alluring and melancholic by evoking contemplative awareness in a way that overtakes any possible preoccupation with an individual's false sense of intellect or focus on ordinary logic and language:

> "Since the triple world is without things, where can you find the mind?"
> White clouds create a canopy, streaming waters form a lute,
> Playing one or more tunes no one gets.
> After an autumn evening rain passes, waters deepen in the pond.
> 三界無法. 何處求心 / 白雲為蓋. 流泉作琴 / 一曲兩曲無人會 / 雨過夜塘秋水深.

Xuedou's main interpreter, Yuanwu, maintains that the poet is "overly kind in the first line, but then goes on to challenge his readers" (雪竇忒殺慈悲. 更向爾道). Furthermore, "This verse has been discussed and judged by literary critics who've deemed Xuedou worthy of the talent of an imperial academy scholar. . . . So, you must set your eyes attentively on this poem; if you linger in doubt, you'll look without seeing" (却似雨過夜塘秋水深. 此一頌曾有人論量. 美雪竇有翰林之才. . . 也須是急著眼看. 更若遲疑. 即討不見).[16]

According to the discursive analysis of Zhou Yukai, Xuedou's verse comments exemplify yet eclipse the significance of encounter dialogues by incorporating three main literary methods that were becoming prevalent in the Northern Song: indirect communication (不道破), the transformation of phenomena (轉物), and reversals of meaning (翻案法).[17] In Ode 37, these techniques are evoked respectively in lines two ("canopy" and "lute," using nature as a symbol for human emotions), three ("one or more tunes," highlighting the musical quality of the environment), and four ("waters deepen," showing the mystery of self-awareness).

The device of indirection or circuitous, metaphorical writing, which is tortuous but revelatory through the twists and turns, is dependent on the use of implied (隱語), inferred (曲喻), and inexplicit (側筆) images. These metaphors conjure a profound existential impression that cannot be adequately described by concepts because it escapes the limits of usual perception. For example, the poet makes an analogy to spirituality by evoking a concrete object but without identifying the underlying connection (言其用不言其名), thereby leaving that task up to the reader's imagination. Words are thereby functional based on their literary context, rather than holding a fixed or static association (言用勿言體).

Next, the technique of transforming phenomena was, as Zhou points out, first suggested by Southern Song-dynasty (1127–1279) poet Yang Wanli (楊萬里, 1127–1206), who said that all things can serve as material for composing poetry since they symbolize or are reflective of levels of interior awareness based on the author's ability to recognize or endow objective scenery with human reactions and emotions. The literary critic Yan Yu (嚴羽, 1191–1241) remarked that the way of Chan is found only in enlightenment, and the way of poetry is also seen through enlightenment.[18] He cites as an example of phenomenal imagery a passage from the works of a Tang-dynasty poet, "The winding path leads one to a secluded place, where a Chan cloister is replete with flowers and trees" (曲徑通幽處, 禪房花木深).[19]

The third technique mentioned by Zhou consists of a pattern of overturning typical meanings to undermine misleading assumptions and assertions proposed by preceding commentators on a case in order to establish a new paradigm, which usually incorporates ongoing examples of reversal, or upending views, and often results in a double reversal. This quality makes the poems full of creative tension and vividness, especially because Xuedou challenges readers with his own opinions and commands, as when he says in line three of Ode 37, "no one gets (that tune)." Also, in another gong'an commentary, Xuedou confronts doubters by brashly demanding that "they should step forward so we can see one another face-to-face!" (出來與雪竇相見).[20]

Xuedou's approach to reversal is evident in Ode 20A when, with feigned impatience, he tells the interlocutors fighting over a meditation cushion and bench, "Just hand these over to me!" (只應分付與盧公). Xuedou complains that the contesting parties "only know how to let go, but not how to hold firm" (只解放不解收). However, he starts Ode 20B with "Why would I ever need these, anyway?" (盧公付了亦何憑), thus casting off a final attachment of his own making, and he concludes with a serenely transcendent view of "distant mountains stretching endlessly with layer upon layer of azure" (遠山無限碧層層).

However, as part of the reversal process, Xuedou himself is not immune to receiving criticism and putdowns by subsequent interpreters, including both Yuanwu and Tianqi, as seen in numerous instances translated in Chapter 3. Another example occurs when the master Fayong (法湧, n. d.) asserts in regard to Odes 20A and B, "Xuedou only sees others' faults" (雪竇要且只見他非), but while reproaching their wrong, "he's unaware of his own flaws and always ends up supporting Yunmen (the patriarch of his school)" (不知自己有過, 扶起雲門也). Furthermore, Xuedou and his ilk, another commentator says, "are just like the praying mantis that, while trying to catch the cicada sitting in front, doesn't realize a goldfinch is lurking right behind" (者幾箇漢, 恰似螗蜋捕蟬于前, 不知黃雀在其後).[21]

Furthermore, even though Yuanwu very much admires and often lavishly praises the *Odes*, as part of his evaluative approach that demands an even-handed, albeit subjective, investigation and appraisal of all sources and perspectives, on some occasions in typical Chan fashion he is playfully critical of certain standpoints that Xuedou propagates. Indeed, Yuanwu remarks now and then that Xuedou "falls into secondary status" (落在第二) by "carrying a board across his shoulder" (只為他擔板), or failing to rise to the occasion and, therefore, "he deserves thirty blows" (也好與三十棒) from Yuanwu's staff. Such comments are part of the disingenuously competitive repartee displaying an emphasis on ongoing reversals that characterizes the gong'an tradition.

Origins of *Songgu*

How and why did the composition of *songgu* develop as a crucial literary genre for assessing source cases? This style was initiated by Fenyang and Xuedou and, thereafter, it was considered de rigueur for leading Song Chan teachers to compose *songgu* along with other kinds of poetry. A related question, to be discussed in Chapter 2, concerns the reasons Xuedou's collection is considered special when seen in relation to other examples of the genre. The *Odes* takes a rhetorical path of indirection that moves beyond the realm of conventional logic and language but without resorting to excessive pedagogical devices, such as the "sticks and shouts" (棒喝) used by Tang teachers Deshan (德山, 780–865) and Linji (臨済, d. 866).

Songgu originated as part of a remarkable period of cross-fertilization when the Chan monastic institution flourished in Chinese society while enjoying government support largely because of productive collaborations involving the literati class of scholar-officials intrigued with methods of contemplative learning. At this time, skeptical of scriptures and analytic works as well as more informal records, journals, and notebooks or any kind of rote learning or recitation, Chan teachers used poetic creativity to capture the imagination and transport the reader to a realm beyond words. The gong'an cases were thereby eclipsed by the literary content of verse comments that, through the strategic use of innovative rhetorical techniques, at once represented and exceeded the didactic message embedded in encounter dialogues.

To briefly mention some prior Chan literary trends, poetry was a valuable discursive tool used in the Tang dynasty for composing doctrinal rhymes by sixth patriarch Huineng (惠能, 638–713), whose *gāthā* about the dust-free mirror won a poetry contest that led to his exalted status, as well as by leading Chan teachers Yongjia (永嘉, 665–713), Shitou (石頭, 700–790), and Dongshan (洞山, 807–869), among others. Lyrical verse was also the primary form of expression crafted by the enigmatic, reclusive monk Hanshan (寒山, fl. ninth century). In addition, the nonclerical poet Wang Wei (王維,

692–761) often playfully expressed nondual ideals, as in the following verse titled, "Reflections" (書事): "A mist hangs over Qingyin Pavilion. / Inside the courtyard on an idle afternoon, / I sit watching the bright green moss, / That feels like clothes I'm wearing" (輕陰閣小雨 / 深院晝慵開 / 坐看蒼苔色 / 欲上人衣來).

The legacy of those literary activities greatly influenced the writings of many Northern Song poet-monks (詩僧, *shiseng*), a category of practitioner revered for demonstrating extraordinary aesthetic ingenuity in composing rather than simply appreciating poetry, but also at times they were criticized for turning into a cliché when their verses seemed mannered instead of genuinely imaginative.[22] Then, the first few decades of the eleventh century saw the profuse production of Chan transmission of the lamp records, or genealogical histories based in part on the style of traditional Chinese Buddhist monk biographies summarizing the lives and deeds of diverse adepts who were grouped into multibranched lineages. The lamp records were the major repository of anecdotes of encounter dialogues that were selected by Fenyang and Xuedou for inclusion in their respective gong'an collections.

Additional new genres that started appearing were the recorded sayings of individual teachers, monastic rules for guiding temple communities, contemplative essays, poetic reflections on reclusion, other kinds of verse and prose works on gong'an and related topics, verses composed for ceremonies and memorials, and assorted anthologies or digests of reference materials, including comments on various traditional Buddhist texts. The flow of publications rapidly accelerated so that a veritable torrent of literary activity continued to expand during the next several hundred years that captivated literati and was widely studied by clerics in training. The former group, including Su Shi (蘇軾, 1037–1101) and Huang Tingjian (黄庭坚, 1045–1105), often interacted with eminent clergy while pursuing Buddhist ideas expressed through poetry.

Although some Northern Song Chan adepts were involved in analyzing poetry, their main motivation was not to critique verses but to create transcendent insight through literary form.[23] Xuedou and other leading teachers routinely wrote various kinds of poetry that were grouped into the category of "general verse" (偈頌, *jisong*, J. *geju*), which included works to bid farewell to departing visiting monks or to commemorate funerals and other communal occasions, such as seasonal festivals or Buddhist holidays. Adepts also composed inscriptions for portraits or paintings, lyrical reflections on meditation, verses presented to lay followers who "rhymed in unison" by writing ritual couplets on a particular topic of personal or philosophical interest, poetic instructions for monastic practice, and celebratory hymns.

Xuedou's non-*songgu* poetry collections have been highly praised for their originality. A few decades after his death, Zhang Boduan (張伯端, 987?–1082), a scholar who advocated the "unity of the three teachings" and is often linked with Daoism although he studied for a time under Xuedou, wrote the verse "On Reading Chan Master Xuedou's *Zuying ji*" (讀雪竇禪師祖英集). This refers to an anthology of letters, essays, and poems collected by a disciple of Xuedou with a preface from 1032. Zhang compares the works of other Buddhist leaders to mere puddles, whereas Xuedou represents the great ocean of knowledge:

> Old Master Xuedou reached the true meaning, / Great bursts of thunder sound as he beats the drum of the dharma. / When the lion king's roar emerges from his cave, / All beasts and monsters alike are fearful. / Whether in verse or with pithy sayings, / He persistently guides those who are lost with his words. / His teachings are direct, and their meanings reach the depths, / Like striking jade [chimes] and sounding bronze [bells], they echo from antiquity (雪竇老師達真趣 / 大震雷音推法鼓 / 獅王哮吼出窟來 / 百獸千邪皆恐懼 / 或歌詩或語句丁 / 寧指引迷人路言 / 詞磊落義高深擊 / 玉敲金響千古爭).[24]

Xuedou and others also composed different kinds of remarks on cases, including prose comments (拈古, *niangu*) that are contained in *Xuedou's Prose Comments on Old Cases* (*Xuedou heshang niangu ji*, 雪竇和尚拈古集), a collection of one hundred gong'an that was further interpreted by Yuanwu in *Keeping the Beat* (擊節錄, *Jijielu*), a work that complements the *Blue Cliff Record*. Additional kinds of nonpoetic remarks on gong'an were citations (舉古, *jugu*), annotations (徵古, *zhenggu*), alternative phrases (代語, *daiyu*), replacement phrases (別語, *bieyu*), evaluative examinations (評唱, *pingchang*), further investigations (請益, *qingyi*), and capping phrases (着語, *zheyu* or 著語, *zhuoyu*, or 下語, *xiayu*).[25] Comments on cases additionally became a key part of monastic ritual and teaching functions, such as dharma hall sermons (上堂, *shangtang*), informal homilies (小參, *xiaocan*), dharma talks (法語, *fayu*), letters (普說, *pushuo*) to literati or other lay followers, or raising cases in the abbot's quarter (室中, *shizhong*).

Despite the variety of genres, it seems clear that to attain high status in the Chan institution adepts were expected to express their poetic understanding of cases. While other styles of poetry were a regular part of a temple abbot's assigned oratory, it was the *songgu* that showed most effectively his distinctive level of insight into the essential teachings of Chan. Foguo Weibai (fl. eleventh century), a monk of the Yunmen lineage, suggests in his *Jianzhong jingguo xudenglu mulu* (建中靖國續燈錄) that the main purpose of odes is not to appeal to higher standards of poetry through artistic craft, unlike the *jisong* styles that both proclaim Buddhist truth and participate in Chinese culture. Rather, gong'an verses serve as a vehicle for propagating Chan principles to illustrate the awakened intentions of lineal ancestors. According to Foguo, "The gateway of odes discloses the moral depths of former worthies through eulogies, whose expressions follow literary guidelines, yet their spiritual import is unerring" (頌古門. 先德淵奧, 頌以發揮, 詞意有規, 宗旨無忒).[26]

Also, *songgu* showed "no disparity between words and letters" (不离文字) as a key element of literary Chan in that "poetry and dharma are not disconnected" (詩法不相妨), according to a verse by Su Shi written near the end of the eleventh century. Su further said, "Words that are never discordant are like a potted plant with shimmering blossoms flourishing in their own way" (語不必煩. 似盆花灼灼, 自有生趣).[27]

As Christopher Byrne points out, Fenyang and, to a greater extent, Xuedou developed the view that the verse is the main component of a gong'an collection, rather than the case or other kinds of remarks.[28] Thus, the focus of a *songgu* collection is chiefly on the poems (*song*), which are eminently creative expressions, and less so on the stories (*gu*) that would have been well known to the audience from other sources but get brought to life through versification. Song teachers, therefore, did not generally produce new gong'an cases, although the main exception to this rule is Fenyang, who crafted his own group of one hundred dialogues (詰問, *jiewen*). Also, Xuedou includes two cases attributed to his teacher, Zhimen Guanzuo (智門光祚, d. 1031), numbers 21 and 93 (or 90 in the variant *Blue Cliff Record* numbering).

It is notable that there are nine prominent Song-dynasty masters who produced major collections of *songgu*. In addition to four compilations by Hongzhi Zhengjue (宏智正覺, 1091–1157), Xuedou, Touzi Yiqing (投子義青, 1032–1083), and Danxia Zichun (丹霞子淳, 1064–1117), which are often grouped together in a single compilation, other authors include Fenyang, Baiyun Shouduan (白雲守端, 1025–1072), Dahui Zonggao (大慧宗杲, 1089–1163), Donglin Daoyan (東林道顏, 1094–1164), and Xutang Zhiyu (虛堂智愚, 1185–1269).

The overall significance of *songgu* in Chan literature during the Song dynasty is further indicated by a couple of poetry anthologies organized in terms of either authors or gong'an cases. A main example is the *Gemlike Verse Comments Collection* (禪宗頌古聯珠集, *Chanzong songgu lianzhu ji*, X.65.1295) compiled in 1175, which contains *songgu* written by numerous adepts; an expanded version from 1318 arranges the poetry by author based on listing 325 cases with 2,100 commentarial verses from 122 masters. Also, the *Jiatai pudeng lu* (嘉泰普燈錄, X.79.1559) compiled in 1202 features two volumes of verses selected from the works of sixty-nine teachers.[29] Furthermore, the popularity of composing odes spread to Kamakura-period Japan through the Sōtō master Dōgen (道元, 1200–1253), whose *Extensive Record* (永平廣録, *Eihei kōroku*) includes a volume (no. 9) with 102 verse comments on ninety cases, in addition to the writings of the eminent Rinzai school master, Daitō (大燈, 1282–1337), among many other Zen teachers.

Formation and Controversies Concerning Xuedou's *Odes*

Xuedou's text was first published in 1038 (alternatively, 1028) as a pioneering approach to construing gong'an discourse at a time when several sorts of voluminous Chan writings were beginning to flourish and get distributed widely to both monks and literati. Honored as a dharma successor of Zhimen, who helped "revive the Yunmen school" (*Yunmen zhongxing*, 雲門中興) in the Northern Song, Xuedou was a native of Sichuan province from an obscure family that provided him a Confucian education, including a focus on literature and fine arts. He first joined a monastery around age twenty after both his parents passed away, and he studied with numerous Buddhist teachers. One of his early instructors named Yuanying (元瑩, n. d.) could not adequately respond to Xuedou's probing inquiries about awakening and recommended that he follow the Chan school. Xuedou achieved enlightenment under Zhimen's mentorship, and in 1019 he was invited to become the abbot of Cuifeng temple (翠峯寺) located beside lake Dongting (洞庭) in the town of Suzhou in Jiangsu province.

In 1031, when he was fifty-two years old and had been living and teaching for ten years at Zisheng temple (資聖寺) (see Figure 1.2) on Mount Xuedou in current Zhejiang province south of the port city of Ningbo, Xuedou finished compiling the *Record of Chan Master Zhimen Zuo* (智門祚禪師語錄, *Zhimen Zuo chanshi yulu*). The preface begins by emphasizing the

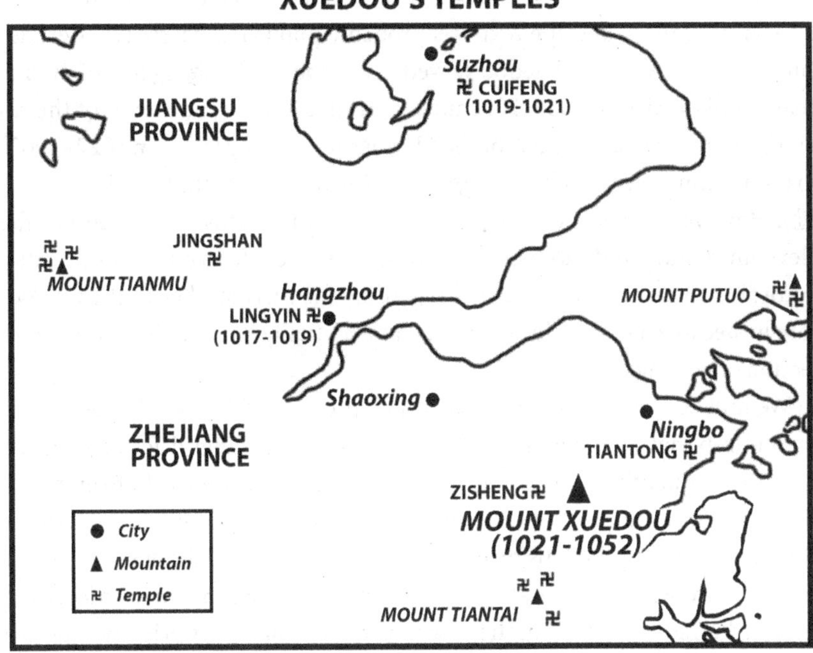

Figure 1.2 Temple locations where Xuedou taught: Cuifeng, Lingyin, and Xuedou.
(Drawn by Maria Sol Echarren and Steven Heine)

pedagogical qualities of any Chan teacher's work, "To benefit sentient beings who possess varying faculties, one must compose words with wisdom and compassion."[30] However, Xuedou criticized as "giant woodworms" (*judu*, 巨蠹) those monks who tried to show off their knowledge and mislead followers by seeking fame and fortune through the composition of elaborate writings.

After he died, Xuedou's disciples compiled seven of his texts. In addition to the *Odes* with commentarial verses and *Xuedou's Prose Comments on Old Cases* with nonpoetic remarks, the five works include *Dongting yulu* (洞庭語錄), *Xuedou kaitang lu* (雪竇開堂錄), *Puquan ji* (瀑泉集), *Zuying ji* (祖英集), and *Xuedou houlu* (雪竇後錄). Among these writings, Xuedou's *songgu* had the greatest impact on Chan poetry and helped foster an amplified level of engagement by monks with local powerful literati that, in turn, encouraged the involvement of social elites with the activities of monastic institutions.

The composition of the *Odes* started sometime between 1017 and 1021, when Xuedou was first studying at Lingyin temple (靈隱寺) in Hangzhou for a couple of years and soon after gave lectures as head of Cuifeng temple in nearby Suzhou, and the text was probably published nearly two decades later at Mount Xuedou. Xuedou served as the abbot of Zisheng for thirty-one years until he died in 1052. He enjoyed prestige among the literati of the region and their recommendations led Emperor Renzong (仁宗, r. 1022–1062) to award him a purple robe with the title "Clear Enlightenment" (*Mingjue* 明覺). However, it seems that the *Odes* fell out of favor toward the end of the eleventh century and was banned by the government for a couple of decades, according to Yuanwu's comments regarding his early studies of the text before he became a major abbot, and it was eventually left out of Xuedou's collection of writings.

We must consider that the publication of diverse Chan works took place under imperial sanction that also brought strict supervision, especially if these frequently iconoclastic teachings were considered subversive to the state. For example, the *Odes* opens with the story of how first patriarch Bodhidharma thumbed his nose at the emperor's queries about sacrality and merit before withdrawing altogether from societal engagement. Moreover, the third verse indicates that the authority of buddhas takes priority over that of emperors. A common understanding is that Xuedou's text was banned for a couple of decades in the late eleventh century and was examined surreptitiously by Yuanwu and others during that period.

Yuanwu tells his readers in occasional self-reflections in the *Blue Cliff Record* that, while studying under the master Wuzu Fayan (五祖法演, 1024–1104) at a temple in his native city of Chengdu in Sichuan province, along with other novices, including some very knowledgeable colleagues, he deliberated on the *Odes* for more than a decade through the 1090s. Once he became an abbot at Jiashan temple (夾山寺) in Hunan province, Yuanwu lectured on Xuedou's work for nearly ten years before his lectures that became the *Blue Cliff Record* were presented at Jiashan, also known for its venerable history of integrating Chan practicing with preparing and imbibing tea. These talks were transcribed and, over a decade later, were edited, published, and distributed by monks at Jiashan, even though Yuanwu no longer led the temple.

Nevertheless, Xuedou's *Odes* along with many Song-dynasty writings was transported and published anew in Japan during the late thirteenth and fourteenth centuries. The *Odes* was included in the early Japanese Five Mountains publications (五山版, Gozan-ban) of accumulated Chinese Chan works, in addition to Mahāyāna scriptures, and some secular Chinese books and Japanese writings, which were printed with a new technology beginning in

1289. The Five Mountains continued to produce well-distributed editions of Chan/Zen classics, some of which were sent back to China, where they rekindled waning interest. In many instances, the editing and preservation of manuscripts was kept alive more so in Japan than on the mainland. Numerous versions of the Five Mountains publications are held today in the National Museum of Japanese History.

Despite its prodigious importance, Xuedou's work has endured numerous ups and downs in terms of its reception and availability because it was banned or left out of print for lengthy periods, and some degree of this unfortunate trend persists today.[31] The *Odes* is best known for being inserted in and forming the basis of the *Blue Cliff Record*, with Yuanwu providing extensive prose and capping phrase remarks in addition to introductions. This larger text, constructed almost a hundred years after the original composition and with its own complicated trajectory involving phases of destruction or neglect mixed with rejuvenation and acclaim, usually surpasses in reputation the component of Xuedou's poetry, so that the *Odes* has rarely been treated as an autonomous work.

The intertextual connections with the *Blue Cliff Record* greatly enhance the *Odes*' prestige, but an ill-fated byproduct of the complicated text-historical situation is that Xuedou's work is usually seen as an appendage or just one of numerous factors contributing to the magnitude of Yuanwu's commentary. Furthermore, the *Blue Cliff Record* was kept out of circulation for a century and a half beginning in 1140, apparently incinerated by his disciple Dahui, and it was not included in the first Japanese Five Mountains edition, even though some of Yuanwu's other records were published therein.[32] In any event, the *Odes* has been overlooked or seen through a lens that tends to misrepresent or diminish its significance as a self-sufficient work. A general historical pattern is that when the *Odes* was prominent in China during the twelfth and thirteenth centuries, the *Blue Cliff Record* was suppressed. But when the latter text came to the fore in the Japanese Zen setting in the fourteenth century, for the most part the *Odes* became far less visible as a discrete entity.

Xuedou's *songgu* was traditionally included in the compilation of prominent gong'an poems known as the *Odes to Old Cases of Four Lineages* (四家頌古, *Sijia songgu*), first published in 1342 (and no longer extant) with four collections in the following sequence that is not in chronological order: *Collection of Odes to Old Cases of Monk Hongzhi Jue at Tiantong* (天童宏智覺和尚頌古集, *Tiantong Hongzhi Jue heshang songgu ji*); *Collection of*

Odes to Old Cases of Monk Xuedou Mingjue (雪竇明覺和尚頌古集, *Mingjue heshang songgu ji*); *Collection of Odes to Old Cases of Monk Touzi at Touzi Mount* (投子山青和尚頌古集, *Touzi Shan Qing heshang songgu ji*); and *Collection of Odes to Old Cases of Chan Master Danxia Chun* (丹霞淳禪師頌古集, *Danxia Chun Chanshi songgu ji*).[33]

Probably the earliest extant Song-dynasty version of Xuedou's records was printed in China in 1195 and appears in a 1935 Shanghai edition under the title *Xuedou siji* (雪竇四集), which covers four of the master's seven main works, including the *songgu* collection. The three texts not entered are the *Xuedou heshang niangu ji*, *Puquan ji*, and *Zuying ji*. However, the most popular version of Xuedou's overall records is the Ming-dynasty edition, which contains six of the seven texts that appear in the modern *Taishō* canon under the title *Mingjue chanshi yulu* (明覺禪師語錄, T.47.1996). The *Taishō* version of Xuedou's record is based on a printed edition from 1634 that is stored at Zōjōji temple (增上寺) in Japan. This compilation inexplicably does not contain the *Odes*, a trend showing that Xuedou's *songgu* collection deserves our attention.

An indication that the *Odes* is no longer held in as high regard today as might be expected is its diminished role at Mount Xuedou, which currently houses a devotional temple rather than a Chan monastery. As shown in Figure 1.3, this site, which is located across the road from ancestral home of Chiang Kai-shek, features a huge golden statue of Maitreya overlooking a magnificent waterfall.

Also, Figure 1.4 features a calligraphic copy of the first case of the *Odes* that was published in a brochure circulated in the late 2010s, when I visited the temple several times; Xuedou's text is still being studied there but in limited fashion. A monk explained that the text is seen primarily as an historical artifact sometimes memorized or copied, and it does not constitute a major feature of the temple curriculum.

To conclude, my translation of Xuedou' *Odes* seen here as an independent body of writing highlights how a superbly creative Chan thinker produced an innovative set of verses that inspired the venerable legacy of gong'an commentaries. The primary aim is to foreground Xuedou's profound contributions and promote a recognition of his *songgu* position as the seminal Chan discourse. In addition, I feature the Southern-Song dynasty comments in capping phrase and prose by Yuanwu, in addition to Ming-dynasty capping phrase comments of Tianqi, which have not previously been translated into a Western language.

Figure 1.3 Today's Mount Xuedou in northeastern Zhejiang Province.

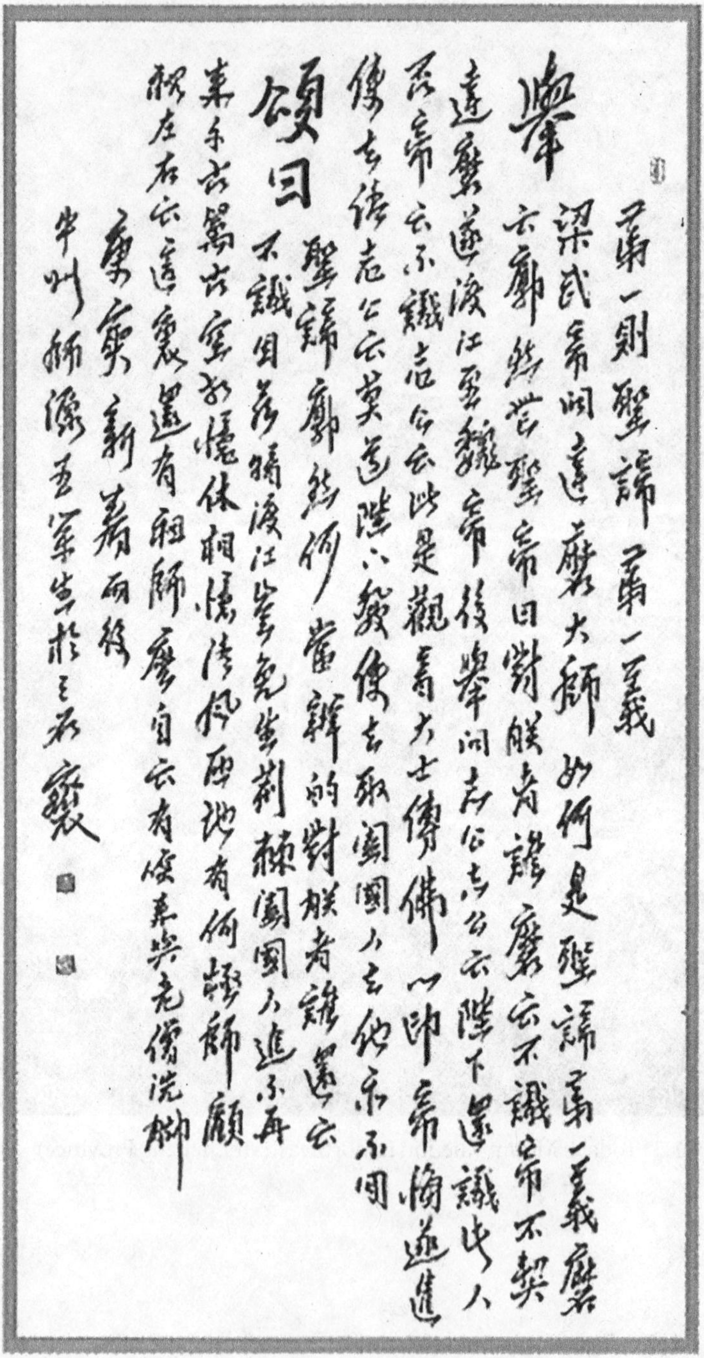

Figure 1.4 A calligraphy of case 1 of the *Odes* at modern Mount Xuedou.

2

On Reading the Text

Literary Qualities with Didactic Objectives

Xuedou's *Odes* emerged in conjunction with a remarkably fertile cultural ethos in the early phase of the Northern Song dynasty largely based on the government policy of "promoting learning and lessening military force" (重文輕武, *zhongwen qingwu*), which was characterized by the fusion of the lyrical eye with dharmic insight, or the integration of literary flair with a Chan realization. As Ding-hwa Hsieh notes of the era, "poetic exercise complemented the experience of enlightenment, and enlightenment was manifested through the composition of poetry."[1] In this intricate socio-religious environment, prominent literati such as Yang Yi (楊億, 976–1020), a member of the Hanlin Academy who edited and wrote the preface for the first Chan transmission of the lamp record, the *Jingde Era Record of the Transmission of the Lamp* (景德傳燈錄, *Jingde chuandeng lu*), were very much supportive of polished and refined poetic efforts.[2] This included verses produced by monks demonstrating they "attained total command of words and phrases" (得言句之總持).[3]

Such a standpoint of unifying Chan with poetry helped foster techniques for indirectly disclosing the truth of spiritual attainment by using allusions, metaphors, and deliberately obtuse sayings based on paradoxes and puns, as evoked by Xuedou, to distract and disarm the reader from lapsing into stereotypical interpretations of encounter dialogues without first gaining a genuinely personal understanding. At the same time, Xuedou's verse interjects intrusive or exclamatory phrases that further disrupt and disassemble conventional meter and rhyming patterns to induce a deeper level of self-reflection and self-awareness that is experienced ontologically prior to usual forms of judgment or comparative investigation. According to Zhou Yukai and other interpreters, by adopting approaches that are "sometimes rustic and sometimes graceful, or sometimes lighthearted and sometimes solemn" (或村樸, 或典雅, 或輕靈, 或凝重), Xuedou's verses reflect the author's unique capacity for taming through elegance the undisciplined and deluded

Xuedou's 100 Odes to Old Cases. Steven Heine, Oxford University Press. © Oxford University Press 2024.
DOI: 10.1093/oso/9780197676561.003.0002

minds of followers struggling with self-imposed obstacles to discern reality and thereby discover inner peace.

In response to the question of why Xuedou's text is considered to have made such a significant contribution to the gong'an tradition, I will first briefly contrast his work with Fenyang's *songgu* collection, and then present an approach to reading and deciphering the *Odes* by considering three interrelated rhetorical aspects of the construction of the *songgu*, with each section of the chapter accompanied by a table illustrating how the key theme can be examined for all one hundred cases. The first aspect concerns how the gong'an selected by Xuedou are cited from previous Chan texts, particularly transmission of the lamp records published in the early Northern Song. The second element refers to the irregular meter embedded in many odes that shows the author's distinctive approach to merging literature with didactic Buddhist discourse.

The third and most important element of my analysis involves a method for understanding the allusive and intrusive qualities of Xuedou's fundamentally instructive rhetoric. This discussion is carried out through decoding and cataloging examples of ambiguous imagery that feature how phenomenal existence can be seen as emblematic of human experience, in addition to highlighting unequivocally emphatic interjections that suggest Xuedou's subjective evaluations of the levels of Buddhist insight attained by interlocutors of the dialogues. His exclamations are tendered to enjoin followers to overcome self-imposed obstacles and to strengthen their efforts of contemplative cultivation in pursuit of spontaneous realization.

Xuedou's *Odes* vis-à-vis Fenyang's Collection

Although Fenyang and Xuedou wrote compendia of odes just a few years apart and their approaches share many similarities in utilizing the quatrain style for religious purposes, some basic discrepancies in the ways the poetry was composed highlight different literary values.[4] One key point is that Fenyang seems more traditional from a formal standpoint in adhering to the rules for truncated verse. For example, his *songgu* uniformly consist of seven or occasionally five characters, although the total number of lines often exceeds four (with a range of five to eight). Xuedou, however, experiments in many instances with the number of both lines and characters, and he also includes several follow-up passages that help exhibit a freewheeling approach.

A second difference involves the author's goal in writing *songgu*. For Fenyang, this is done primarily for the purpose of explicating Chan doctrine expressed in gong'an cases from a neutral or nonjudgmental standpoint, and in a way that is relatively simple and straightforward to comprehend. In a "coda" (都頌) discussing the aim of his collection, Fenyang offers the following verse consisting of eight five-character lines:

My record of one-hundred cases of former sages,
Is transmitted throughout the Chan world.
Covering dialogues that are difficult to discern and easy to understand—
Both kinds are elucidated in my odes.
A flower in the sky (emptiness) bears fruit in thin air,
That occurs without before or after.
Whoever wishes to attain awakening,
Must realize the profound meaning (of these cases).
先賢一百則 / 天下錄來傳 / 難知與易會 / 汾陽頌皎然 / 空花結空果 / 非後亦非先 / 普告諸開士 / 同明第一玄.[5]

By contrast, the elliptical, winding discourse of Xuedou's versifications seeks primarily through complicated rhetorical maneuverings to trigger a transformation in the reader. Even if the gist of Fenyang's coda may seem compatible with the preface written for Xuedou's collection by Tanyu that was mentioned in Chapter 1, we can see a wide gap separating the aims of the two Chan teachers by considering their respective verses on the same case. One example involves a dialogue (number 30 in the *Odes*) in which the master Zhaozhou (趙州, 778–897) responds to a monk's query about studying with his own teacher by referring mysteriously to a concrete object from a nearby village. He replies, "Zhen county produces big radishes" (鎮州出大蘿蔔頭). According to Fenyang's ode:

When asked about the time he first attained dharma,
[Zhaozhou] didn't speak of China (eastern land) or India (western sky).
He said that in Zhen County, there's a vegetable called a radish,
That's already rescued hundreds of thousands of hungry and wounded people.
因問當初得法緣 / 不言東土及西天 / 鎮州有菜名蘿蔔 / 濟却飢瘡幾萬千.[6]

Fenyang makes an interesting point about the teaching capacity of the vegetable, with a minor ambiguity indicated in the last line leaving it unclear whether the healing is performed by the radishes or by Zhaozhou's utterance about them. Xuedou's verse starts by citing the key phrase of the case and then utilizes several innovative rhetorical features that move the discourse beyond the conceptual realm of the source dialogue:

> "Zhen County produces big radishes,"
> Patch-robed monks all over the world cling to this example.
> Since they know only their own past and present,
> How can they distinguish between a white swan and a black crow?
> [Zhaozhou's] such a thief!
> Grabbing the nostrils of patch-robed monks.
> 鎮州出大蘿蔔 / 天下衲僧取則 / 只知自古自今 / 爭辯鵠白烏黑 / 賊賊 /
> 衲僧鼻孔曾拈得.

In lines two through four, Xuedou criticizes typical monks who cling to Zhaozhou's words, rather than comprehending the ideas behind them, and are incapable of making basic distinctions between before and after or black and white. Then, following the first four lines with seven characters, Xuedou interjects that Zhaozhou is a "thief" as a disingenuous form of praise because stealth is what it takes to stir followers from their spiritual slumber so they will appreciate the true meaning of the dialogue.

For Xuedou, crafting a verse expands and intensifies the literary dimensions of the case by drawing on a broad repertoire of images and expressions culled from Chan writings, and allusions to the Chinese cultural tradition at large, including vernacular Song locutions. The *Odes* quotes or suggests passages from Buddhist scriptures, anecdotes from the classics, Confucian ethical virtues, Daoist metaphysical ideals, and notions from mythology or folklore proverbs. An additional feature pertains to Xuedou's eclectic observations connecting human behavior, based on perceptions of phenomena via eyes and ears, to its underlying experiential relation with natural surroundings that reflect the possibilities and limits of perspective and emotion. The risk of evoking these diverse references is that later generations would not easily understand their targets and thus need to depend on voluminous but at times contradictory or incomplete annotations for clarification.[7]

Yuanwu points out Xuedou's literary prowess evident in the four lines of Ode 72. After an opening passage that comments ironically on a case about speaking with lips shut, Xuedou concludes by referring to a legendary site where balminess eventually dwindles and, paradoxically, it is only under water that the sun continues to shine: "Over the ten continents, springtime ends as flowers fade and wither, / Yet coral reefs are lit up by dazzling sunlight" (十洲春盡花凋殘 / 珊瑚樹林日杲杲). Yuanwu notes, "Although Xuedou completes the verse in the first couplet, he has enough skill to turnaround by changing direction in the next" (雪竇只一句頌了也. 他有轉變餘才). Moreover, "Xuedou's words exude a graceful refinement that is subtle yet majestic" (雪竇語帶風措. 宛轉盤礴).[8]

Another interesting example is Ode 7 that comments on, but without making any direct reference to, a cryptic case in which the master overturns the deficient thinking of his disciple:

> Near the beautiful river, spring breezes blow without stirring,
> Partridges sing while nesting amid myriad flowers.
> At the three-tiered gate, where waves leap high, fish are transformed
> into dragons,
> Yet foolish ones still draw water from a ditch at night.
> 江國春風吹不起 / 鷓鴣啼在深花裏 / 三級浪高魚化龍 / 癡人猶戽夜塘水.

Line two evokes a famous poetic saying about the vitality of the Jiangnan region as a symbol of rebirth, and the next line alludes to the legend of fish swimming upstream in a mighty storm that symbolizes passing civil examinations but, here, refers to the path to Chan awakening that is beyond ordinary logic and rational explanations. The verse concludes with a reprimand for those whose stubborn ignorance and arrogance prevent them from reaching the goal of passing through the proverbial dragon's gate.

Next, Ode 34 is enhanced by a subtle reference (暗用) to the lyricism (詩句) of the Tang hermit Hanshan, while commenting on an encounter dialogue that is referred to as a "conversation held in the weeds":

> Whether this suggests getting out or entering the weeds, who can tell?
> White clouds gather, yet the fiery sun shines clear.
> Looking to the left, nothing's lost; glancing to the right, everything's
> ripened.
> Don't you know that the revered recluse Hanshan (Cold Mountain),

> Traveled to places so far away, it took him ten years to return?
> He said at that point he'd forgotten his way home.
> 出草入草. 誰解尋討 / 白雲重重. 紅日杲杲 / 左顧無暇. 右盻已老 /
> 君不見. 寒山子 / 行太早. 十年歸不得 / 忘却來時道.

Xuedou first evokes a lofty natural setting that contrasts with weediness, and then cites the story of Hanshan's extensive travels that left him blissfully lost as a reminder to appreciate the journey without reifying a projected goal.

Additionally, Ode 12 comments on the cryptic phrase, "Three measures of hemp," the reply given by a master in response to a query about the Buddha, with an inventive nine-line verse that does not refer to the source dialogue. In the last half, Xuedou uses beautiful yet simple natural images and evokes a legend in which an official laughed inappropriately during a funeral. He concludes by chuckling aloud as an apparent rebuke of various levels of misunderstanding:

> Abundant flowers adorn a luxuriant brocade,
> Bamboos in the south and evergreens to the north.
> I recall that during the exchange between Changqing and Officer Lu,
> It was explained that one should laugh rather than cry.
> Ha!
> 花簇簇. 錦簇簇 / 南地竹兮北地木 / 因思長慶陸大夫 / 解道合笑不
> 合哭 / 咦.

Compared to Fenyang's more one-dimensional literary style, Xuedou's poetics "abides in the *samādhi* of joyful play" (住游戲之三昧) by using brilliant literary conceits. His work is no doubt more compatible with the imaginative verse of Hongzhi, a subsequent poet-monk in the Caodong lineage. Known for his own remarkable *songgu* collection, Hongzhi also wrote the following poem as part of a dharma hall sermon on the significance of nonduality: "By candlelight as dawn breaks in the desolate hall, / A seamstress shuttles a loom to weave fine yarn. / At a windless lake on a clear night, / An old fisherman clings to a straw raincoat while standing alone under the cool moonlight" (燭曉堂虛. 織婦轉機梭路細. 水明夜靜. 漁老擁蓑舡月寒). After these two parallel couplets that alternate four and seven characters, with the first concerning brightness during morning activities and the second depicting a moonlit nighttime scene, Hongzhi concludes with an admonition emphasizing the virtue of suitability: "Ye Chan worthies: Do you know when to go back to the rice paddy? If it's not yet the time, then don't rush ahead" (諸禪德. 還曾到箇田地箇時節麼. 其或未然. 不要亂舉).[9]

The following sections of this chapter, each with a table covering all cases, examine examples of three main discursive elements that characterize Xuedou's odes: gong'an sources, irregular meter, and poetic allusions with exclamatory intrusions.

Feature 1: Sources for Xuedou's Cases

The first feature helpful for understanding the construction of the *Odes* considers the various sources of the gong'an that are cited by Xuedou. From which writings does he cull the dialogues, and what does this process indicate about his sense of Chan lineal history? Yanagida Seizan points out five main types of sources for the *songgu*: (1) transmission of the lamp histories, (2) the recorded sayings of individual masters, (3) sūtras, (4) contemporary texts, and (5) unknown sources. As shown in Table 2.1, the vast majority of cases were drawn from transmission records, especially the *Jingde Era Record* published around 1008 and the *Tiansheng Era Record of the Transmission of the Lamp* (*Tiansheng guangdeng lu*, 天聖廣燈錄) from 1036. Another possible source is the earlier *Patriarchs' Hall Collection* (祖堂集, *Zutangji*) from 952, which was long lost until a modern recovery of it in Korea, so it is not clear whether Xuedou would have read this work.

Eighteen dialogues in all are taken from the records of or feature Yunmen (雲門文演 864–949), the founder of Xuedou's lineage that was far more prominent during the Northern Song than in the Southern Song after its main temples in Kaifeng, which had been supported by the imperium, were demolished by Jin invaders. With seven other stories focusing on members of this branch of Chan, including Xuedou's teacher Zhimen, the Yunmen lineal component comprises a quarter of the cases. Furthermore, in comparing the wording used for cases by Fenyang and Xuedou to the *Jingde Era Record* and another influential transmission of the lamp text from the era, the *Chan Gate True Lamp Record* (*Zongmeng zhengdeng lu*, 宗

Table 2.1 Masters and Possible Sources for Cases Selected by Xuedou from Chan Chronicles

Abbreviations
JCL *Jingde chuandeng lu* 景德傳燈錄 (1008)
TGL *Tiansheng guangdeng lu* 天聖廣燈錄 (1036)
YG *Yunmen guang lu* 雲門廣錄 (1120s?)
ZL *Zhaozhou lu* 趙州錄 (mid-1100s?)
ZTJ *Zutang ji* 祖堂集 (952)

Case No.	Master	Source
1.	Bodhidharma	JCL 3
2.	Zhaozhou	uncertain
3.	Mazu	TGL 8, ZTJ 14
4.	Deshan	JCL 15
5.	Xuefeng	YG 3
6.	Yunmen	YG 2
7.	Fayan	JCL 25
8.	Cuiyan	JCL 18, YG 2
9.	Zhaozhou	ZL 1
10.	Muzhou	*Muzhou yulu* 2
11.	Huangbo	ZTJ 16, JCL 9, TGL 8
12.	Dongshan Shouchu	JCL 22
13.	Baling	JCL 22?
14.	Yunmen	YG 1
15.	Yunmen	YG 1
16.	Jingqing	ZTJ 10, JCL 18
17.	Xianglin	JCL 22?
18.	National Teacher	JCL 5
19.	Gutei	JCL 11
20.	Longya	JCL 17
21.	Zhimen	*Zhimen yulu* 1, TGL 22?
22.	Xuefeng	JCL 18
23.	Xuefeng	JCL 18
24.	Liu Tiemo	*Chanmen niansong ji* 10
25.	Hermit of Lotus Peak	*Zuting shiyuan*?
26.	Baizhang	TGL 10
27.	Yunmen	YG 1
28.	Nanquan	JCL 6
29.	Dasui	JCL 11
30.	Zhaozhou	ZL

Table 2.1 Continued

Case No.	Master	Source
31.	Magu	JCL 7
32.	Linji	*Linji lu*
33.	Zifu	*Zongmen tongyao ji* 6?
34.	Yangshan	YG 2
35.	Wuzhuo	(Buddhist legend)
36.	Changsha	ZTJ 17, JCL 10?
37.	Panshan	JCL 7
38.	Fengxue	JCL 13, TGL 15
39.	Yunmen	YG 1
40.	Nanquan	JCL 8
41.	Zhaozhou	ZTJ 6, JCL 10
42.	Layman Pang	*Pangyan ji*?
43.	Dongshan Liangjie	*Dongshan lu*?
44.	Heshan	YG?
45.	Zhaozhou	JCL 10, ZL 2
46.	Jingqing	ZTJ 10, JCL 18
47.	Yunmen	YG 2
48.	Senior Monk Lang	JCL 18
49.	Sansheng	*Fenyang songgu*
50.	Yunmen	YG 1
51.	Yantou	ZTJ 1
52.	Zhaozhou	ZL 1, JCL 10
53.	Mazu	TGL 8
54.	Yunmen	YG 3
55.	Daowu	ZTJ 6, JCL 15
56.	Qinshan	JCL 17
57.	Zhaozhou	ZL 2
58.	Zhaozhou	Zl 1
59.	Zhaozhou	ZL 1
60.	Yunmen	YG 2
61.	Fengxue	TGL 15
62.	Yunmen	YG 2
63.	Nanquan	ZTJ 5
64.	Zhaozhou	JCL 18, ZL 1
65.	Non-Buddhist	ZTJ 11, JCL 27
66 (82).	Dalong	JCL 23?

(*continued*)

Table 2.1 Continued

Case No.	Master	Source
67 (83).	Yunmen	YG 2
68 (66).	Yantou	JCL 16
69 (67).	Mahāsattva Fu	*Fenyang songgu*
70 (68).	Guishan	JCL 20
71 (69).	Nanquan	JCL 8
72 (70).	Baizhang	JCL 6
73 (71).	Baizhang	JCL 6
74 (72).	Baizhang	JCL 6
75 (73).	Mazu	ZTJ 10, JCL 7, TGL 8
76 (74).	Jinnui	ZTJ 10, JCL 8
77 (93).	Daguang	ZTJ 10, JCL 8
78 (91).	Yanguan	JCL 7
79 (92).	World-Honored One	ZTJ 12
80 (75).	Wujiu	JCL 4?
81 (76).	Danxia	ZTJ 4, JCL 14
82 (77).	Yunmen	YG 1
83 (78).	16 Bodhisattvas	*Śūraṅgama sūtra* ch. 5
84 (79).	Touzi	uncertain
85 (80).	Zhaozhou	ZL 1
86 (81).	Yaoshan	*Xuefeng lu* 3?
87 (84).	Vimalakīrti	*Vimalakīrti sūtra*, ch. 8
88 (85).	Tongfeng	JCL 12, TGL 13
89 (86).	Yunmen	YG 2
90 (87).	Yunmen	YG 2
91 (88).	Xuansha	JCL 18
92 (89).	Yunyan	JCL 14
93 (90).	Zhimen	*Zhimen lu* 1
94.	Buddha	*Śūraṅgama sūtra* ch. 2
95.	Changqing	JCL 19
96.	Zhaozhou	JCL 28
97.	Diamond Sūtra	JCL 29
98.	Tianping	JCL 21, TGL 14
99.	National Teacher	ZTJ 13, JCL 5
100.	Baling	uncertain

Note: In compiling this list, I relied on the annotations in *Setchō Juko*, eds. Yanagida Seizan, Iriya Yoshitaka, Kajitani Kōjin (Tokyo: Chikuma shobō, 1981). Most entries are speculative since it is not clear which sources—or, more importantly, which versions or editions of these—were available to Xuedou at the time he produced his collection between 1028 and 1038.

門正燈錄), Nagai Masashi argues that the gong'an diction in Xuedou's *Odes* is much closer to Fenyang's collection than to the lamp histories. Both poets generally use shortened versions of cases that do not try to duplicate the original accounts of transmission records but instead offer a kind of critical summary.[10]

Table 2.1 lists the main interlocutor of the dialogue and the source text with volume number, and texts additional to those mentioned in the abbreviations are occasionally cited. Also, question marks in the list suggest a higher than usual degree of uncertainty. Moreover, for cases 66 through 93, where the numbering system in the original *Odes* collection varies from the numbering in the *Blue Cliff Record*, the latter text's numbers are indicated in parenthesis (but this information is not included in the second and third tables).

Feature 2: Examples of Irregular Meter

The second main feature in my analysis, as shown by Table 2.2, is that Xuedou's poetry demonstrates originality in handling literary structure by frequently varying from the standard use of four lines with seven characters. Xuedou composes some lines with five, six, or eight characters, or as little as two, and he also often extends some poems beyond four lines. A majority of the total of 103 odes in the collection, when we consider that case 20 has two verses and case 96 has three, are examples of irregular meter. Xuedou's inventive discursive techniques enable shifts of thematic emphasis and expressions of his own opinions about Chan breakthrough experiences, which help stimulate the reader's sense of self-reliance and self-awakening based on the moral injunctions inserted between poetic images.

Note that six-character lines indicated in the table generally refer to two three-character phrases (an exception is Ode 60, which has one such line of three with six characters), and eight-character lines generally refer to two four-character phrases. Also, forty-one poems feature the conventional format of four lines with seven characters, thirty-two have six or eight characters in the opening line, and twenty-two include lines with five characters, among other examples of irregular meter.

Table 2.2 Literary Structures of Xuedou's Collection

1.	2 lines with 8 characters, 2 with 5, 2 with 7, 1 with 3, 1 with 7 (follow-up)
2.	2 lines with 8 characters, 2 with 6, 2 with 7, 1 with 2, 1 with 7
3.	1 line with 6 characters, 3 with 7, 1 with 3, 1 with 7
4.	1 line with 8 characters (3 + 5), 1 with 3, 4 with 7, 1 with 1
5.	1 line with 6 characters, 3 with 7
6.	1 line with 6 characters, 3 with 7, 1 with 6, 2 with 7, 1 with 3, 1 with 5
7.	4 lines with 7 characters
8.	6 lines with 8 characters
9.	4 lines with 7 characters
10.	4 lines with 5 characters, 1 with 3, 1 with 7
11.	4 lines with 7 characters
12.	1 line with 6 characters, 3 with 7, 1 with 6, 3 with 7, 1 with 1
13.	1 line with 6 characters, 3 with 7, 1 with 6, 1 with 7
14.	1 line with 6 characters, 3 with 7, 1 with 2, 1 with 7
15.	1 line with 6 characters, 3 with 7, 1 with 2, 1 with 7
16.	4 lines with 5 characters, 1 with 8, 1 with 7
17.	4 lines with 7 characters
18.	1 line with 6 characters, 1 with 7, 1 with 6, 1 with 7
19.	4 lines with 7 characters
20.A	4 lines with 7 characters
20.B.	4 lines with 7 characters
21.	4 lines with 7 characters
22.	4 lines with 7 characters, 1 with 6, 7 with 7 (follow-up)
23.	4 lines with 7 characters
24.	4 lines with 7 characters
25.	4 lines with 7 characters
26.	4 lines with 7 characters
27.	2 lines with 8 characters, 2 with 7, 1 with 3, 2 with 7
28.	4 lines with 7 characters
29.	4 lines with 7 characters
30.	4 lines with 6 characters, 1 with 2, 1 with 7
31.	4 lines with 4 characters, 2 with 7, 1 with 3, 1 with 7
32.	4 lines with 7 characters
33.	4 lines with 7 characters (follow-up)
34.	3 lines with 8 characters, 1 with 6, 1 with 8 (3+5), 1 with 5
35.	4 lines with 7 characters
36.	6 lines with 5 characters, 1 with 6 (5+1)
37.	2 lines with 8 characters, 2 with 7
38.	4 lines with 7 characters

Table 2.2 Continued

39.	1 line with 6 characters, 1 with 7, 1 with 6, 1 with 7
40.	4 lines with 7 characters
41.	4 lines with 7 characters
42.	1 line with 6 characters, 3 with 7, 1 with 3, 1 with 7
43.	4 lines with 7 characters
44.	1 line with 6 characters, 3 with 7, 1 with 6, 1 with 7
45.	4 lines with 7 characters
46.	4 lines with 5 characters, 1 with 3, 1 with 7
47.	1 line with 6 characters, 5 with 7
48.	4 lines with 5 characters, 1 with 6, 1 with 7
49.	2 lines with 8 characters, 2 with 7, 2 with 5
50.	1 line with 6 characters, 3 with 7, 1 with 6, 1 with 7
51.	1 line with 6 characters, 3 with 7, 1 with 3, 3 with 7
52.	4 lines with 7 characters
53.	1 line with 6 characters, 3 with 7, 1 with 6, 1 with 2
54.	3 lines with 7 characters, 1with 5 (1+4)
55.	2 lines with 8 characters, 2 with 7, 1 with 3, 1 with 7
56.	6 lines with 7 characters, 2 with 8 (3+5)
57.	2 lines with 8 characters, 2 with 7, 2 with 4
58.	3 lines with 8 characters
59.	2 lines with 8 characters, 2 with 7
60.	2 lines with 6 characters, 2 with 9, 1 with 6 (3+3), 2 with 6, 2 with 7 (follow-up)
61.	4 lines with 7 characters
62.	1 line with 2 characters, 1 with 7, 1 with 6, 1 with 7
63.	4 lines with 7 characters
64.	4 lines with 7 characters
65.	4 lines with 5 characters, 4 with 7, 1 with 7 (3+4)
66.	2 lines with 8 characters, 1 with 7, 3 with 5, 1 with 6, 1 with 8
67.	1 line with 6 characters, 3 with 7, 1 with 6, 1 with 7
68.	4 lines with 7 characters
69.	4 lines with 7 characters
70.	4 lines with 7 characters
71.	4 lines with 5 characters, 2 with 7 (follow-up)
72.	1 line with 5 characters, 3 with 7
73.	Line with 5 characters, 3 with 7
74.	1 line with 5 characters, 3 with 7
75.	1 line with 6 characters, 3 with 7, 1 with 6, 1 with 7
76.	4 lines with 7 characters

(continued)

Table 2.2 Continued

77.	4 lines with 7 characters
78.	4 lines with 7 characters (follow-up)
79.	4 lines with 7 characters
80.	1 line with 6 characters, 3 with 7, 1 with 9 (3+3+3), 1 with 7
81.	2 lines with 5 characters, 2 with 7, 1 with 6, 1 with 7
82	4 lines with 7 characters
83.	4 lines with 7 characters
84.	1 line with 8 characters, 3 with 7, 1 with 3, 1 with 7
85.	4 lines with 7 characters
86.	2 lines with 6 characters, 2 with 5, 1 with 7 (follow-up)
87.	1 line with 5 characters (1+4), 7 with 5, 1 with 3, 1 with 7
88.	2 lines with 8 characters, 1 with 10 (3+7), 1 with 7, 1 with 6, 1 with 7
89.	4 lines with 5 characters, 1 with 3, 1 with 7
90.	4 lines with 5 characters, 1 with 2, 1 with 7
91.	4 lines with 4 characters, 4 with 7 (follow-up)
92.	1 line with 6 characters, 5 with 7, 1 with 3, 2 with 7, 1 with 1
93.	4 lines with 7 characters
94.	4 lines with 7 characters
95.	4 lines with 6 characters, 1 with 6 (3+3), 1 with 7
96.A.	4 lines with 5 characters
96.B.	4 lines with 5 characters
96.C.	4 lines with 5 characters
97.	8 lines with 4 characters (follow-up)
98.	1 line with 6 characters, 3 with 7, 1 with 2, 1 with 7 (follow-up)
99.	8 lines with 7 characters
100.	2 lines with 8 characters, 2 with 7, 1 with 2, 1 with 7

Feature 3: Allusive and Intrusive Elements

The third main feature, illustrated by Table 2.3, highlights the role of various rhetorical elements to suggest that Xuedou is especially resourceful based on two qualities that underscore every verse: allusiveness, regarding the symbolism of traditional legends and lore for understanding Chan awakening; and intrusiveness, through interjecting his own attitudes in an abrupt fashion to trigger a sudden reaction that leads to realization. Both elements in turn encompass two key aspects. Allusions include references to the case through quoting, summing up, or epitomizing its meaning as well as to Buddhist or Chinese myths or customs that are cited or mentioned indirectly to buttress the poem's didactic message. Also, the element of intrusiveness indicates that Xuedou interjects diverse kinds of exclamations, unexpected utterances, or critical rejoinders to arouse the authentic pursuit of dharma among his followers. He concludes most verses with animated phrasing that supports a spiritual missive, whether by exhortation, instruction, admonition, or inspiration, about how to overcome delusion to attain a realization of nonduality.

As indicated in the table's final column, Xuedou often makes use of inventive lyrical images to evoke natural scenery or landscapes that highlight a standpoint beyond human affairs yet are intimately related to the depths of genuine subjectivity. Enlightened awareness is further refined through Xuedou's use of intimate reflections and pronouncements; this component is occasionally buttressed by the performative quality of the oral delivery of the poems that were no doubt written in advance but presented as sermons during dharma hall convocations.

There are ten instances in the collection of a follow-up remark or comments added after the verse; these instances stand in addition to fifteen examples in which Xuedou interjects capping phrases or similar asides into the source dialogue, including cases 4, 18, 23, 31, 34, 36, 42, 48, 55, 61, 74 (72 in the *Blue Cliff Record*), 81 (76), 84 (79), 85 (80), and 91 (88). All those additional remarks are included in my translations. Modern editors agree that earlier versions of the text incorporated many more examples of Xuedou inserting his own capping phrases or supplementary remarks, but these were lost as manuscript copies underwent alterations.

Ode 46 is an example of how diverse rhetorical elements can be identified to interpret the significance of Xuedou's verse:

> "Sound of raindrops," in the desolate hall,
> Even an adept has a hard time responding.
> If he says his understanding is one with the flux,
> That's not really an understanding.
> Whether there's an understanding or not,
> Southern and northern mountains are drenched by driving rain.
> 虛堂雨滴聲 / 作者難酬對 / 若謂曾入流 / 依前還不會 / 會不會 /
> 南山北山轉霶霈.

This poem includes four lines with five characters, an interjection in the fifth line with three characters, and a seven-character conclusion. It starts by quoting a passage from the encounter dialogue and then comments on the (in)capacity of a Chan teacher, challenges the audience's ability to comprehend the key point, and ends with a simple yet stunning natural image capturing the essential meaning of the case beyond yet encompassing individuated viewpoints.

The next example, Ode 60, is an irregular poem that contains two lines with six characters (3 + 3), two with nine, one with six (3 + 3), two more lines with six characters featuring reduplicative phrasings, and two lines with seven characters, plus a rejoinder:

"This staff swallows the whole universe!"
> Don't waste your time speaking about peach blossoms floating on the water.
> A fish that singes its tail doesn't grasp clouds or seize the mist,
> But those with gills exposed need not lose heart.
> I've spoken, but do you understand me?
> You should let your spirit soar freely,
> And stay apart from turbulence and turmoil.
> If seventy-two blows aren't enough,
> Even a hundred-fifty wouldn't be sufficient.
> 拄杖子. 吞乾坤 / 徒說桃. 花浪奔 / 燒尾者不在拏雲攫霧 / 曝腮者何必喪膽忘魂 / 拈了也. 聞不聞 / 直須洒洒落落 / 休更紛紛紜紜 / 七十二棒且輕恕 / 一百五十難放君.

Follow-up: Xuedou, wielding his staff, steps down from his seat, and the whole assembly all at once runs away in fright (師驀拈拄杖下座. 大眾一時走散).

The verse begins by quoting the source dialogue and then elaborates on the legend (also cited in Ode 7) of fish swimming upstream to cross the proverbial dragon gate during a fierce storm. Xuedou concludes with the threat of blows from his staff, and after this, he chases his assembly members from their seats as well as their ingrained self-deceptions.

A third example is Ode 45, a regular verse with four lines of seven characters that opens by epitomizing a dialogue in which Zhaozhou talks incongruously about a seven-pound shirt, which Xuedou abruptly says he tosses into a nearby waterway as symbolic of casting aside attachments while challenging his audience to grasp the deeper import of this bold act:

> The ancient awl (Zhaozhou) is challenged in his understanding,
> But how many people know the "seven-pound shirt"?
> Right now, I'll toss it into West Lake,
> Thrown into the untainted breeze, who'll fetch it?
> 編辟曾挨老古錐 / 七斤衫重幾人知 / 如今拋擲西湖裏 / 下載清風付與誰.

Table 2.3 provides a flexible guideline that can be used as a provisional interpretative tool for deciphering the primary rhetorical elements of Xuedou's *Odes*. The table includes several categories highlighting key examples for each verse regarding the structural innovation, functional creativity, primary moral message, lyrical ingenuity, and performative qualities that characterize Xuedou's approach to developing a unique style of *songgu* poetics. In this table:

- "Dialogue" indicates whether the source case is quoted, summarized, or epitomized.
- "Lore" pertains to the inclusion of religious symbols or cultural legends.
- "X's Interjection" points to how Xuedou interpolates an abrupt or emphatic comment.
- "Moral Message" specifies my assessment of the principal edifying theme of the verse.
- "Additional Element" designates another key rhetorical feature, including in ten instances a follow-up or added comment (1, 22, 33, 60, 71, 78, 86, 91, 97, 98); or, in other examples, the pronounced use of natural imagery featuring concrete particularities, such as mountain mists or rushing rivers, or a deeply personal standpoint based on Xuedou's reactions that reinforce the case's basic spiritual injunction. Capitalization in the right-hand column indicates that aspect represents the poem's main discursive feature.

Table 2.3 Main Rhetorical Elements in Xuedou's Collection

	Allusiveness		Intrusiveness		
	Dialogue	**Lore**	**X's Interjection**	**Moral Message**	**Additional Element**
1.	quotes	futile chase	"Stop thoughts"	"limitless	follow-up
2.	quotes	dragons howl	"It's so difficult"	self-reliance	nature
3.	quotes	dragon cave	"So hard to explain"	dedication	Personal
4.	quotes	General	"Nah!"	solitude	
5.	epitomizes	mirror	"For whom?"	renewal	Nature
6.	summarizes	Subhūti	"Snaps fingers"	demythology	Personal
7.	epitomizes	dragon gate	"Yet foolish ones"	admonition	nature
8.	summarizes	precious jade	"Only Changqing"	authenticity	
9.	summarizes	city gates	"The heaviest blows"	impenetrable	
10.	summarizes	riding tiger	"Blind fools"	self-deception	Personal
11.	summarizes	Xuanzong	"Held firmly"	dignity	
12.	epitomizes	flowers-trees	"Ha!"	unconventional	nature
13.	quotes	96 schools	"Kanadeva school"	nonduality	
14.	quotes	Jambu tree	"How extraordinary"	paradox	
15.	quotes	phoenix	"How extraordinary"	equanimity	Nature
16.	epitomizes	tap and peck	"Try in vain"	admonition	
17.	epitomizes	female hermit	"Had no choice"	endurance	
18.	quotes	dragon coils	"It's been seen	"endlessness	nature
19.	summarizes	blind turtle	"Who else like him"	salvation	personal
20A.	epitomizes	still water	"Hand to me"	self-sufficiency	Personal
20B.	summarizes	transmission	"Even if I"	serenity	Nature
21.	quotes	foxlike	"But that leads"	admonition	
22.	summarizes	snake	"Today it abides"	immediacy	Personal
23.	epitomizes	skulls	"Who knows"	insight	
24.	epitomizes	imperial	"Who'll travel"	exceptional	
25.	epitomizes	countryside	"Where's he gone?"	reclusion	nature
26.	summarizes	flash-sparks	"A laughingstock"	adaptable	nature
27.	epitomizes	arrowpoint	"Haven't you heard"	renewal	nature
28.	epitomizes	Big Dipper	"No place to grasp"	self-deception	
29.	summarizes	checkpoint	"What a pity"	admonition	
30.	quotes	swan/crow	"Such a thief"	determination	
31.	quotes	ancient rod	"Not forsaken"	nonduality	nature
32.	epitomizes	Juling	"Why expect Linji"	spontaneous	
33.	epitomizes	fishing	"Lets down cage"	compassion	Follow-up
34.	epitomizes	Hanshan	"Don't you know"	transcendence	nature

Table 2.3 Continued

	Allusiveness		Intrusiveness		
	Dialogue	Lore	X's Interjection	Moral Message	Additional Element
35.	quotes	bodhisattva	"I can only laugh"	mystery	nature
36.	epitomizes	wildlife	"Nah!"	practicality	nature
37.	quotes	music	"Waters deepen"	harmony	Nature
38.	epitomizes	shield	"One great shout"	insight	nature
39.	quotes	steelyard	"Pointless!"	inscrutable	
40.	epitomizes	mirror	"Whose silhouette?"	reflective	nature
41.	epitomizes	buddhas	"I'm not sure"	inexpressible	
42.	epitomizes	purity	"Even Bodhidharma"	activity	
43.	epitomizes	jade pavilion	"Hunting hound"	unfathomable	nature
44.	epitomizes	long bow	"Let me remind"	as-it-isness	
45.	epitomizes	ancient awl	"I toss it"	ungraspable	Personal
46.	quotes	flux	"Whether or not"	contemplation	Nature
47.	epitomizes	Shaolin	"At night"	immediacy	Personal
48.	summarizes	fangs-claw	"How many times"	dedication	Personal
49.	quotes	golden carp	"How many people"	purity	nature
50.	quotes	*Lotus* parable	"Whether or not"	admonition	nature
51.	quotes	patriarchs	"Let us return"	contemplation	Nature
52.	summarizes	Guanxi's folly	"It's laughable"	admonition	personal
53.	quotes	encounter	"Speak up!"	instruction	nature
54.	epitomizes	dignity	"Didn't the monk"	release	Personal
55.	epitomizes	paradox	"Nowhere at all!"	ungraspable	personal
56.	quotes	arrow	"Don't you know"	skillfulness	
57.	epitomizes	insects	"What is picking"	nonduality	nature
58.	epitomizes	animals	"All over south"	flavorless	
59.	epitomizes	gods-spirits	"Who's the one"	skillful	
60.	quotes	fish at gate	"Seventy-two blows"	admonition	Follow-up
61.	epitomizes	martial tactics	"I alone feel"	purity	Personal
62.	epitomizes	bucolic	"See for yourself"	nonduality	Nature
63.	summarizes	cats	"Without regard"	impartiality	
64.	summarizes	Chang'an	"No one understands"	tranquility	
65.	epitomizes	mirror	"Snap my fingers"	self-control	
66.	epitomizes	jade whip	"The country's laws"	flawless	nature
67.	quotes	transmission	"Who'd ever say"	discernment	
68.	summarizes	punishment	"Lose an advantage"	even-handed	

(*continued*)

Table 2.3 Continued

	Allusiveness		Intrusiveness		
	Dialogue	**Lore**	**X's Interjection**	**Moral Message**	**Additional Element**
69.	summarizes	hermitage	"If it weren't for"	silence	
70.	epitomizes	laughter	"No one knows"	regret	
71.	quotes	arrow	"The path to Caoxi"	unremitting	Follow-up
72.	quotes	tiger's horn	"Springtime ends"	nonduality	Nature
73.	quotes	arrow	"Recall General Li"	self-confidence	
74.	quotes	lions	"Fruitlessly snaps"	impenetrable	
75.	quotes	colt	"I alone know"	self-reliance	Personal
76.	summarizes	golden lion	"Those who're cubs"	genuine	
77.	epitomizes	Caoxi	"Who says yellow"	variable	
78.	summarizes	breeze	"Just like clouds"	untraceable	follow-up
79.	epitomizes	Saindhava	"Wouldn't have"	responsive	
80.	epitomizes	swords	"Is there anyone"	equality	
81.	quotes	ox head	"Once missing"	inscrutable	
82.	epitomizes	itinerancy	"Even Yunmen"	silence	
83.	epitomizes	dream	"I'll spit"	admonition	Personal
84.	epitomizes	tides	"What if they come"	exhortation	
85.	summarizes	rapids	"Does anyone see"	impermanence	
86.	quotes	elk herd	"Look out for arrow"	admonition	Follow-up
87.	summarizes	illness	"He doesn't fall!"	silence	
88.	epitomizes	tigers	"Grab the tail"	savvy	
89.	summarizes	flowers	"Rides backwards"	self-reliance	nature
90.	quotes	carriage	"Mistakes!"	discipline	
91.	summarizes	perceptions	"Do you or not"	suitability	Follow-up
92.	quotes	phoenix	"Nah!"	practicality	
93.	epitomizes	Subhūti	"Oyster engulfing"	inscrutable	
94.	epitomizes	buddha	"Halfway there"	perspectivism	
95.	epitomizes	dragons	"You've failed"	admonition	
96A.	quotes	Huike	"Who wouldn't"	symbolism	
96B.	quotes	Zifu	"Is there any place"	universality	
96C.	quotes	oven god	"He'd betrayed"	awakening	
97.	summarizes	jewel	"O Gautama"	imperceptible	follow-up
98.	epitomizes	learning	"Quickly disposes"	unknowable	follow-up
99.	quotes	iron hammer	"Who'll be able"	reprimand	Personal
100.	epitomizes	sword	"So extraordinary"	paradox	

Conclusion: A Transformative Poetic Path

The *Odes*, along with other poetic and prose writings by Xuedou on *gongan* cases or related topics concerning Chan realization, is celebrated primarily for forging an inventive spiritual vision that displays but ultimately does not depend on the author's elegant literary skills. Xuedou's poetry challenges and edifies yet also, in a constructive sense, entices and motivates clerical practitioners of meditation as well as literati pursuing an experience of awakening, in part because it is thought-provoking and eminently engaging on a deeply personal level. This quality derives from the intricate use of references to religious lore or legends accompanied by exquisite lyrical imagery, in addition to extensive wordplay and other rhetorical devices, including exhortations and exclamations that inspire but also foster an emphasis on irony and contradiction. All these qualities promote a transcendental teaching tinged with purposeful ambiguity yet applicable to carrying out daily activities.

To evoke the terminology used in James J. Y. Liu's categorization of four approaches of traditional Sinitic poetry, Xuedou is an "intuitionalist," who explicates subjective perceptions that capture the essence of diverse experiences, situations, and natural settings. He also draws on the moral urgency characteristic of the "didacticist" standpoint, as well as the self-expressiveness of "individualists." Often, though not always, Xuedou eagerly breaks basic rhetorical rules adhered to by the "technicians" in support of his fundamental message.[11]

The source exchanges are often marked by abrupt or dramatic gestures, such as a master striking a disciple or feigning to be hit by an arrow, in addition to obscure phrasings that defy logical categorization. Xuedou's verse comments are designed to capture vividly the intentions underlying the actions of the participants at the time these transpired during the encounters—or are so imagined. Therefore, the goal of the *Odes* is not to explicate the meaning of the accounts of ancient teachers by offering a point-by-point examination of their doctrinal content, an outlook provided by Fenyang and prose commentaries, including the *Blue Cliff Record*.

Poetry for Xuedou is deliberately abstruse and elusive in wording and syntax to place responsibility for achieving a breakthrough on the part of trainees, but without causing a solipsistic syndrome that lapses into relativism or nihilism. Indeed, false negation, as the flip side of unbridled idealism, is thought to reflect all-too-human self-deceptions that must be overcome at every juncture. Instead, Xuedou's verses conjure an attitude often referred to in Chinese poetry criticism as a "spiritual resonance" (神韻, *shenyun*, literally, "marvelous cadence"). This was originally an auditory term indicating harmonious rhythm but later was connected to experiential qualities involved in creating or viewing nonaural arts as well, such as ink-brush painting and calligraphy.[12] The concept of resonance indicates that an adept offers an efficacious expression of the depths of personal realization that is inexpressible yet needs to be conveyed in a compelling and persuasive verbal fashion. Although Xuedou was not alone in treating gong'an cases this way, with Hongzhi representing another important exponent, his poetry is revered for its literary prowess and lyrical acumen that has been compared to the finest writings of the imperial academy yet constitutes an essentially transformative form of Chan discourse.

PART II
THE TEXT

3

A Translation of Xuedou's *100 Odes* with Interpretative Comments

Introduction

This chapter contains translations with annotations of Xuedou's collection of one hundred odes (actually, there are 103 in total since case 20 has two verses and case 96 features three). These translations integrate remarks by two main Chan commentators: Yuanwu and Tianqi. The former incorporates Xuedou's work from 1038 into the comprehensive *Blue Cliff Record* published in 1128 with a seven-part structure featuring (1) introduction (lost in twenty-one cases), (2) case with (3) capping phrases and (4) prose remarks, and (5) Xuedou's ode with (6) capping phrases and (7) prose remarks. Tianqi, however, uses capping phrases only to interpret the cases and verses, without providing either introductions or prose comments.

Each section of this chapter is divided into four components:

Title, which encapsulates the main theme of the dialogue in characters and English;

Case, a critical summary of gong'an selected by Xuedou with selected capping phrases by Yuanwu and Tianqi;

Verse, Xuedou's ode and selected capping phrases in parenthesis between lines of the verse, with authorship designated by "Y" for Yuanwu and "T" for Tianqi; and

Comments, brief assessments of the primary levels of meaning and significance of the poetry as seen in light of the traditional commentaries as well as various influences from Buddhist thought or Chinese culture, in addition to contemporary theoretical outlooks.

Since the numbering of cases 66 through 93 in Xuedou's original text varies from the numbering in the *Blue Cliff Record* (BCR), as listed in Table 3.1; for

Xuedou's 100 Odes to Old Cases. Steven Heine, Oxford University Press. © Oxford University Press 2024.
DOI: 10.1093/oso/9780197676561.003.0003

Table 3.1 Numbering Discrepancies between the *Odes* and the BCR

Odes	BCR	*Odes*	BCR	*Odes*	BCR	*Odes*	BCR
66	82	73	71	80	75	87	84
67	83	74	72	81	76	88	85
68	66	75	73	82	77	89	86
69	67	76	74	83	78	90	87
70	68	77	93	84	79	91	88
71	69	78	92	85	80	92	89
72	70	79	92	86	81	93	90

those twenty-eight odes the latter text's sequence is cited in parenthesis for readers who are used to that order.

There are also a few minor but interesting textual discrepancies between the Yuanwu and Tianqi versions of the text. These include, among other examples, case 6 involving the wording of the dialogue; case 64, which for Tianqi does not refer to shoes placed on Zhaozhou's head; case 71, which for Tianqi does not mention a midway course in the journey; and case 72, in which Tianqi leaves out the first sentence. Also the Tianqi cases do not begin with the character 舉, which Yuanwu uses in each instance to indicate the "raising" of the dialogue by Xuedou.

Moreover, Yuanwu's approach is voluble by capping every line of each case and verse with relatively lengthy remarks, in addition to his prose comments, and he generally tends to be playfully skeptical or even disingenuously scornful of Xuedou as well as the dialogue interlocutors. Tianqi, however, does not offer prose comments and tends to be taciturn in that his capping phrases do not refer to every phrase of the original text, are often a bit repetitious, and are usually but not always respectful of Xuedou. Also, Tianqi completes each dialogue with a "concluding note" (主意) and a "wrapping" (總結) remark, both of which are included in my translation.

Ode 1

Bodhidharma Says, "I Don't Know" 達磨云不識

Case: The opening case of Xuedou's *Odes* involves a dialogue between Bodhidharma (菩提達磨, d. 532), who had recently arrived from the west (i.e., India or South Asia), and Emperor Wu (武帝, 502–550), founder of the Liang (梁) dynasty in southern China known for building new temples, translating sūtras, and giving lectures on doctrine as expressions of his intense interest in spreading the dharma. Yuanwu's introduction highlights the pedagogical method of the first Chan patriarch by indicating, "If one corner [of a room] is shown, then the other three should be clear" (舉一明三), which recalls the notion of open-ended learning expressed in Confucius's *Analects* (舉一隅不以三隅反. 則不復也 in chapter 7.8).

According to the intricate narrative, Bodhidharma responds negatively to two basic questions posed by Emperor Wu. Regarding the query, "What's the main meaning of the noble truths?" (如何是聖諦第一義), the first patriarch replies, "They're unrestricted and not necessarily noble" (廓然無聖); and in reply to "Who's standing before me?" (對朕者誰), he says, "I don't know" (不識). In another version, Bodhidharma also tells the emperor "there's no merit" (無功德) to be gained from charitable Buddhist activities.

Bodhidharma then leaves and crosses the Yangzi River (in legend, by floating on a single leaf) to reach the northern kingdom of Wei (魏). Later, the emperor admits to the priest Zhigong (志公) that he "didn't know" (不識) to whom he had spoken, thus answering with the same words Bodhidharma used concerning his own identity. Zhigong tells Wu that the patriarch represents an appearance of the bodhisattva Guanyin (觀音), so that all the king's horses and men would never be able to fetch and persuade him to come back again.

Yuanwu's capping phrases refer to Bodhidharma playfully as a "wild fox spirit" (野狐精), who can't avoid feeling ashamed. Tianqi remarks of the emperor's admission, "What a confession!" (實供). Tianqi's concluding note says, "[Bodhidharma] making his case forcefully points to clarity by using an utterance with a hidden blade" (急處一提. 旨明句裏藏鋒); and his wrapping phrase reads, "The second teacher (Zhigong) didn't know [Bodhidharma] intimately, so the emperor should've chased after him!" (二師不遇知音. 武帝頭頭蹉過).

Verse: The noble truths "are unrestricted," how does one discern its meaning?
(T: The gong'an is raised before us, 拈前公案)
"Who are you?"—in response Bodhidharma answers, "I don't know,"
But fleeing across the river,
He couldn't avoid entering a thicket of thorns.
Although chased by nearly everyone in the country, he never returned,

Yet the emperor continued to reminisce about him in vain.
Stop those thoughts!
Is there any limit to the purity of Chan teachings?
(Y: He makes his living in a demon's cave, 向鬼窟裏作活計)
聖諦廓然. 何當辨的 / 對朕者誰. 還云不識 / 因茲暗渡江 / 豈免生荊棘 / 闔國人追不再來 / 千古萬古空相憶 / 休相憶 / 清風匝地有何極.

Follow-up: Xuedou asks while looking left and right, "Is there a patriarch among us?" He himself answers, "There is" (師顧視左右云. 這裏還有祖師麼. 自云. 有) (T: Both needle and hook are in his hands, and he sheds light by using them in unison, 鈎錐在手. 照用同時). Xuedou also says, "Then bring him here to wash my feet" (喚來與老僧洗脚) (Y: Thirty blows of the staff to drive him away wouldn't be too many, 更與三十棒趕出. 也未為分外) (T: Seeing that he doesn't understand how to punish people, this must be the only way he can clean his feet, 見不領旨所以點罰. 似恁般人只堪洗脚).

Comments: There are several key stylistic features throughout the *Odes* that are evident in the verse on Bodhidharma's dialogue and departure from the emperor, who remains rueful about his failure to have appreciated the patriarch at the time of their encounter. Xuedou begins by using two eight-character and two five-character phrases but concludes with three seven-character lines, with the last line preceded by an interjection consisting of three characters. This discursive element enables him express an evaluation relevant for teaching a lesson about how to overcome deluded thinking.

The account of the follow-up demonstrates vividly that the *Odes* were probably delivered in an oral setting, which included opportunities for live interactions between Xuedou as the teacher-poet and his assembly of monks. Tianqi's initial comment regarding the sequel suggests that a needle stitches together various levels of understanding while a hook productively tears them apart; used together, these devices fulfill a Chan leader's approach that at once gently prods and harshly scolds a diverse body of learners to help them advance with their respective levels of awareness. Yuanwu's final remark shows he is willing to critique Xuedou's verse in a spirited way when he considers it appropriate, just as he often admonishes the interlocutors who Xuedou takes to task for their deficiencies. Tianqi concludes with an ironic comment that offers an additional jab at the poet.

Ode 2

Zhaoshou's "Attaining the Way Isn't Difficult" 趙州至道無難

Case: Whereas the first case represents a complicated chronicle with sociopolitical significance in that Bodhidharma's ability to outsmart and defy imperial authority demonstrates the priority of Buddhist teachings over and above the strictures of civil society, the second case is a more typical Chan dialogue concerning the meaning of nonduality. The story involves the master Zhaozhou (趙州, 778–897), who is the subject of twelve gong'an in Xuedou's *Odes*, including three examples (57, 58, 59) that are variations of the main theme featured here based on interpreting the phrase "Attaining the way isn't difficult" (至道無難). This saying is, in turn, culled from the opening couplet in the *Inscription of the Faithful Mind* (*Xinxin ming*, 信心銘) by third Chan patriarch Sengcan (僧璨, fl. sixth century). Yuanwu says in the introduction that Zhaozhou's style of instruction is beyond "the canon of sūtras and commentaries" (一大藏教詮注) and shows that "even insightful patch-robed monks can't save themselves" (明眼衲僧自救不了).

In the dialogue Zhaozhou tells his assembly during an informal sermon (示眾) that the key to attaining the way is to "simply avoid picking and choosing" (唯嫌揀擇). He emphasizes that "difficulty" (難), which stands in contrast to "clarity" (明白), occurs "as soon as words are spoken" (纔有語言). Zhaozhou also stresses the need to overcome any subtle trace of duality between discriminatory thinking and detachment by suggesting, "I (literally, "this old monk," 老僧) don't abide within clarity" (老僧不在明白裏). An anonymous novice asks him about the meaning of that statement and Zhaozhou replies, "I don't know" (不知). The teacher abruptly dismisses the monk's follow-up query by remarking, "Asking one question is enough; now bow and go away" (問事即得. 禮拜了退).

Yuanwu writes of Zhaozhou's citation, "Truth is right in front of your eyes as the third patriarch lives on" (眼前是什麼. 三祖猶在), and of the monk's second challenge, "He chases him up a tree" (逐教上樹去). Tianqi comments on Zhaozhou's basic assertion, "Originally, everyone knows what to take in and what to let go" (人人本分. 何有取捨). Tianqi's final note says, "Casting a pole to help people points clearly to great merit that has no limit"

(垂釣為人. 旨明大功不宰); and his wrapping phrase reads, "There's no fall from his status" (不落階級).

Verse: "Attaining the way isn't difficult," as all words are provisional,
(T: Annotations aren't needed to sing along with this tune, 註無委曲)
Identity contains difference, but differentiation holds no distinctions.
In the sky, the sun rises and the moon sets.
Past the barrier, mountains deepen while rivers run cold.
How can joy arise in an empty skull that lacks true awareness?
Dragons howling on a withered tree are never drowned out.
It's so difficult!
(Y: Unprincipled methods are difficult to support. He gives a deliberately inappropriate teaching, but is this really the place to talk about what's difficult versus what's easy? 邪法難扶. 倒一說. 這裏是什麼所在. 說難說易)
(T: It's difficult to tell who hasn't fallen into the usual distinction between an ordinary person and a sage, 不落凡聖極難分訴)
Picking and choosing, or pure clarity? You must see for yourself!
(Y: It's not up to me (山僧, literarlly, "this mountain monk")
(T: Don't rely on others, you must use your own eyes, 莫靠他人. 應自着眼)
至道無難. 言端語端 / 一有多種. 二無兩般 / 天際日上月下 / 檻前山深水寒 / 髑髏識盡喜何立 / 枯木龍吟消未乾 / 難難 / 揀擇明白君自看.

Comments: The case concerns the classic Chan conundrum about overcoming all manner of polarization without succumbing to any subtle attachment to nonduality that may turn into a preoccupation with delusion and attachment. According to a saying, "If there's a hairbreadth of difference, heaven and earth are set asunder" (毫釐有差. 天地懸隔). In the first four lines of the verse, Xuedou seems to resolve the dilemma by pointing to the magnificence of nature in which heavenly bodies rise and set, and the landscape consistently maintains vigor and beauty.

In the second half, Xuedou evokes traditional Chan expressions to highlight the role of pure meditative consciousness or samādhi that represents the only mental state authentically attuned to the sounds of dragons droning on withered trees, which symbolize absolute nonduality. However, he also suggests that those who experience this condition may become overly detached and are, therefore, in need of being prodded from their torpor by a final injunction that compels followers to think through for themselves the endlessly challenging matter of clarifying the meaning of human experience. The capping phrases offered by Yuanwu and Tianqi praise the way the poet highlights the need to embrace, while at the same time overcoming, the realm of differences and distinctions by finding a balance between impartiality and engagement. This is accomplished through the ongoing process of self-discovery and self-realization that Zhaozhou encourages when he sends away the inquiring monk.

Ode 3

Mazu's "Sun-Face Buddha, Moon-Face Buddha" 馬祖日面佛月面佛

Case: Yuanwu's introduction emphasizes the inevitable dilemma in that "each activity and situation, each word and phrase enables everyone to enter into the place [of realization] (一機一境. 一言一句. 且圖有箇入處), but this is like cutting into a wound of a healthy body that turns into a nest of entanglements" (好肉上剜瘡. 成窠成窟). Therefore, "the great function is manifested right here without following a set of principles" (大用現前不存軌則).

The dialogue involves the master Mazu (馬祖, 709–788), who, after falling seriously ill (不安), is asked by the head monk (院主), "How're you feeling?" (尊候如何). How sick is Mazu? According to another version, this story occurs when the teacher is about to die and is visited by the temple superintendent late at night. On his deathbed Mazu responds to the monk's query, "Sun-face buddha, Moon-face buddha" (日面佛. 月面佛). This refers to the *Sūtra of Buddha's Names Explained by the Buddha* (佛說佛名經, *Foshuo foming jing*), which lists twelve hundred designations of buddhas and bodhisattvas. The Sun-face buddha lasts eighteen hundred years, a number suggesting an endless period, whereas the Moon-face buddha lasts one day and night or a phase as fleeting as a drop of morning dew. Thus, the two names indicate the unity of boundless and infinitesimal time.

Tianqi says that Mazu's response reflects "a kind heart caring for a son" (養子之心). His final note reads, "Directly revealing the radiant source points clearly to there being no fixed path" (直下明宗. 旨明無有意路); and his wrapping phrase says, "The question is based on human feeling, but the answer points directly (to truth)" (問以人情. 答以直指).

Verse: "Sun-face buddha, Moon-face buddha,"
(Y: When they open their mouths the guts [of Mazu and Xuedou] are evident, like two mirrors that face each other by shining from within rather than reflection, 開口見膽. 如兩面鏡相照於中無影像).
What about the Five Emperors and Three Sovereigns?
(T: For you to understand the Sun-face and Moon-face buddha, you must know that traditional rulers were exemplary social leaders, 若會日面月面. 便會五帝三皇. 舉一例請)
For more than twenty years, enduring pain and suffering,
I've delved so many times into the dragon's lair for your sake.
So hard to explain!
(Y: Whoever tells their troubles to troubled people troubles them to death, 向阿誰說. 說與愁人愁殺人).
If you want to become an insightful practitioner, don't take this lightly.
(Y: Will they pay close attention? Nah! They'll fall back three thousand paces, 更須子細. 咄. 倒退三千).
(T: In the end they won't understand two words, while still claiming they don't take him lightly" (末後雙收二字. 總言不得輕忽).
日面佛. 月面佛 / 五帝三皇是何物 / 二十年來曾苦辛 / 為君幾下蒼龍窟 / 屈堪述 / 明眼衲僧莫輕忽.

Comments: Xuedou opens the verse by repeating Mazu's key phrase in line one, and Yuanwu comments approvingly. Xuedou then adds a line recalling the mythical rulers of ancient China who apparently lived in harmony with the populace, an image that could imply a sense of affinity linking Buddhist and civil leaders. However, Yuanwu's prose comments suggest that Xuedou's verse reflects a stark contrast between deficient secular sovereigns and the unobstructed universal illumination of buddhas and patriarchs in a way that recalls poems of dissent during earlier dynasties when people were suppressed by unjust political authority.

Xuedou's poem, drawing from a Tang-dynasty verse by the poet Chanyue (禪月, 832–912), who is also cited in Odes 67 and 100, proved to be controversial and the primary reason his work was proscribed by the imperium for several decades in the late eleventh century. Yuanwu notes that during the rule of Emperor Shenzong (神宗, r. 1068–1085), known for publishing a comprehensive Buddhist canon, it was decided that "since this verse ridicules the state, the whole text should not be included" (自謂此頌諷國. 所以不肯入藏), although the ban was later lifted.

The rest of the verse consists of four lines featuring typical as well as deliberately atypical stylistic elements, as Xuedou reflects ironically on his own lifelong bodhisattva mission of sacrificing personal comfort to attain a high level of wisdom through struggles with adversity that ultimately enabled him to lead followers toward experiences of awakening. In the second couplet, Xuedou evokes a popular Chinese legend concerning how dragons that lurk in underwater lairs protect the dharma and other treasures. This underlines some of the challenges Xuedou wrestled with while plunging into deep, obscure realms that helped him develop idiosyncratic teaching methods. The fifth line is a three-character interjection augmenting his personal sentiment, followed by a final seven-character plea for disciples to remain attentive to each aspect of his preaching. The term "insightful" (literally, "clear-eyed," 明眼) alludes to Confucian moral injunctions and perhaps also to customs associated with the annual tomb-sweeping festival (Qingming, 睛明).

Ode 4

Xuedou's "Thoroughly Exposed!" 雪竇勘破了也

Case: This case is a complex narrative concerning monastic decorum and intrigue that Yuanwu's introduction says is an example of "administering medicine to the sick when the time is right" (時節因緣. 亦須應病與藥). The story involves the brash young monk, Deshan (德山, 780–865), who charges unceremoniously into the headquarters of an established leader, Guishan (溈山, 771–853), once an aspiring junior cleric who had become the abbot of a major monastery.

At first Deshan looks all around the dharma hall (法堂) and scornfully says, "There's nothing at all here" (無無)," and he abruptly leaves. Thinking better of this hasty action, Deshan reenters the building and in a highly dignified way greets Guishan by kneeling and calling out "Teacher!" (和尚). Guishan responds by silently holding up his flywhisk (拂子) as a symbol of authority, but the intruder shouts and walks away, shaking his sleeves in disdain. Later that night Guishan comments, "From now on, that fellow will go off and seclude himself by sitting on top of a solitary peak, building a grass-thatched hut, and scolding buddhas while reviling patriarchs" (此子已後.向孤峰頂上.盤結草庵.呵佛罵祖去在).

The story emulates Guishan's own remarkable career development, as portrayed in case 40 of *Wumen's Barrier* (*Wumenguan*, 無門關). Meanwhile, Xuedou interjects three observations: the phrase, "Thoroughly exposed!" (勘破了也), is cited both times Deshan leaves the hall (this saying is also used in cases 87 and 97); and "Adds frost to snow" (雪上加霜) is evoked in regard to Guishan's final utterance.

Yuanwu praises Guishan's silence, "Only he could act this way by setting strategy in motion while staying inside his tent" (須是那漢始得.運籌帷幄之中), but he is ambivalent toward Deshan: "His understanding is that of a wild fox spirit . . . but his shout is remarkable among all those who grasp clouds and mist" (野狐精見解.這一喝 . . . 一等是拏雲攫霧者,就中奇特). For all three notes by Xuedou, Yuanwu says, "Wrong! The point's clear" (錯.果然.點).

Tianqi says of Xuedou's first interjection, "He hits the nail on the head, so there's no need to gallop away" (當頭一點. 不必馳騁), of the second, "Without showing off, the point's made another time" (不過如此不須賣弄.一點二拈), and of the third, "Once again, he walks and talks like that" (他又如此行. 你又如此說他). Tianqi's final note reads, "Showing that [Deshan and Guishan] see through each other's activities points clearly to the great function manifest right here" (呈機相勘.旨明大用現前); and his wrapping phrase says, "Host and guest investigate one another" (主賓互驗).

Verse: At first "Thoroughly exposed" [twice], then "Adding frost to snow,"
This became a slippery slope!
(Y: The three sayings aren't the same, what's his point? 三段不同.在什麼處)
It's like General Guang, who once rode a flying steed after he was captured—
But could such an escape ever happen again?
[Deshan] rushes past, yet [Guishan] doesn't let him go.
He's said to abide amid the weeds, "Sitting on top of a solitary peak."
Nah!
(Y: Understand how two blades cut each other . . . while singing and clapping in unison. I'll strike! 會麼.兩刃相傷 . . . 唱拍相隨.便打)

(T: After initially being afraid of falling, now he sits precariously alone, at least that's what Guishan proclaims, 恐陷後人坐在孤危. 故責令出須當稟命)

一勘破. 二勘雪上加霜 / 曾險墮 / 飛騎將軍入虜庭 / 再得完全能幾箇 / 急走過不放過 / 孤峰頂上草裏坐 / 咄.

Comments: Xuedou uses several uneven lines in this verse that features two main interjections by the poet: in the first exclamation referring to a slippery slope, he critiques his own remarks that lead to a dead end, and in the second exclamation, "Nah!" (咄), he casts doubt on both interlocutors. That character is used at the end of verses 36 and 89 and at the beginning of verse 84, and elsewhere in the *Odes*, and it is also evoked by Yuanwu and Tianqi. Here, Tianqi's capping phrase rehabilitates the role of Deshan.

Another main image compares Deshan's exploits in dharma combat with Guishan to the legend of a great strategist, who was once captured by the Huns and stuck in a desperate situation as he was tied down between two horses. Weakened by his wounds, Guang played dead, but then suddenly and stealthily leapt onto the fastest steed while seizing hold of the rider's bow and arrows. As the horse galloped off, the general drew his bow and shot the riders chasing him.

As Yuanwu notes about Deshan, "This fellow has the ability to wrest life from the midst of death" (這漢有這般手段. 死中得活). Xuedou and his commentators do not conclude with an emphasis on quietude or detachment, since all those who attain enlightenment cannot rest on their laurels in solitude but must instead endlessly test and renew their teaching efforts.

Ode 5

Xuefeng's "As Big as a Grain of Rice" 雪峰 we 如粟米大

Case: Yuanwu introduces this case by suggesting of Xuefeng (雪峰, 822–908), one of the teachers of Yunmen (雲門, 864–949) and several other important Chan leaders, that "his illumination and function unfold at the moment he speaks, and he embraces and liberates with equal vigor. He shows that truth and phenomena are nondual, and that the provisional and real work together" (所以照用同時卷舒齊唱. 理事不二. 權實並行).

Furthermore, "Letting go of the main principle, he establishes secondary meaning because if he were to cut off entanglements too brusquely, it wouldn't be possible for neophyte students unfamiliar with the Chan pivot to find their footing" (放過一著. 建立第二義門. 直下截斷葛藤. 後學初機難為湊泊).

Xuefeng is featured in five cases in the *Odes* and his overall lineage, including Yunmen and his disciples, is found in over forty cases since, in some instances, more than one teacher appears in a case. In this dialogue Xuefeng tells his assembly during a sermon, "If you pick up the entire great earth, it's as big as a grain of rice that's tossed down right in front of you" (盡大地撮來如粟米大拋向面前). Then, Xuefeng calls his followers "lacquer buckets" (漆桶) as a typical Chan putdown for those who fail to understand the analogy because they are limitlessly ignorant and stubbornly foolish. However, in certain contexts, the same term indicates an ironic form of praise for profound and marvelous teaching devices that effectively address the needs of learners. Finally, Xuefeng admonishes, "I'll beat the drum to invite everyone to come here and see the grain" (打鼓普請看).

Yuanwu says of Xuefeng's opening comment, "This is the blind leading the blind" (一盲引眾盲). Tianqi says of the blockheads, "Ultimately there's no difference between emotion and detachment, but that doesn't mean you can just spit out all your emotions" (情與無情一切無別. 盡情吐出你又不會). He writes of Xuefeng's final remark, "Today's a special meeting of the assembly, so let's have everyone's attention!" (今特聚眾. 大家着眼).

Tianqi's concluding note reads, "Fishing with a pole to help people points clearly to the function of returning to phenomena" (垂釣為人. 旨明攝用歸體); and his wrapping phrase says, "Grandmotherly kindness!" (老婆心切).

Verse: "An ox's head disappears, and a horse's head appears,"
But Huineng's mirror never collects dust.
(T: An extraordinary statement. Chan preached at Mount Ling continues to live with no decline whatsoever, 會得上句. 靈山少室盡古盡今. 一切無漏)
Beating the drum summons people to look, but they still can't see [the grain].
For whom do myriad flowers bloom with the arrival of spring?
(Y: Things are disorderly but, even amid chaos, you can escape a cave of entanglements, 法不相饒. 一場狼籍. 葛藤窟裏出頭來)

(T: Why not engage fully with the situation since the path, after all, is for those who embrace countless distinctions and differentiations, 使盡其情因何不會. 且道萬別千差畢竟是誰)

牛頭沒. 馬頭回 / 曹溪鏡裏絕塵埃 / 打鼓看來君不見 / 百花春至為誰開.

Comments: Yuanwu notes that while many other Xuedou poems begin in a simple way by repeating part of the case's dialogue, thus perhaps indulging his disciples as Tianqi suggests in his wrapping phrase, this verse "shatters all with one hammer blow at the outset and settles the matter with a single phrase" (當頭一鎚擊碎一句截斷). For Yuanwu, "[Xuedou] is undeniably solitary and lofty, like flying sparks or a flash of lightning. Since he doesn't reveal his sword's edge, there's no place to find one's footing" (當頭一鎚擊碎一句截斷. 只是不妨孤峻, 如擊石火似閃電光. 不露鋒鋩無爾湊泊處).

The symbolism of the ox-head vanishing and the horsehead emerging is based on a passage from the *Heroic March Sūtra* (楞嚴經, *Lengyan jing*, Skr. *Śūraṅgama sūtra*), a Mahāyāna text drawing on Indian Buddhist philosophical principles embraced by Chan commentators. The saying suggests that everything is at stake when a deceased person's consciousness envisions a vast iron city leading to hell with fiery snakes and fierce dogs, wolves, lions, ox-headed jailkeepers and horse-headed man-eating demons brandishing spears to herd people along.

In the next two lines Xuedou softens his approach by using the familiar yet perplexing image from the famous verse by sixth patriarch Huineng (惠能, 638–713) about the lack of dust collecting on a mirror, an expression that helped him defeat rivals for receiving transmission and transform himself from an illiterate novice into a venerable abbot. Tianqi's capping phrase compares the Huineng allusion to Lingshan (靈山; literally, "spiritual mountain"), where it is said the Buddha's initial Chan sermon was preached when he silently held up a flower. Xuedou also curtly denies that casual observers will be able to find the single grain of rice representing the whole world.

The final line evokes a simple but endlessly mysterious view of everyday reality that needs no rationale or explanation but, if fully appreciated without hesitation or reservation, highlights an experience of awakening while being fully immersed in the ever-renewable present moment. Yuanwu's capping phrase is tinged with a bit of skepticism about the possibility of avoiding complications, whereas Tianqi emphasizes the merit of Xuedou's lyrical outlook concerning the realm of multiplicities.

Ode 6

Yunmen's "Every Day Is a Good Day" 雲門日日是好日

Case: This is the first of eighteen cases in the *Odes* featuring the master Yunmen, known for his pithy sayings rife with a plenitude of meanings, and the narrative is thematically linked to cases 14 and 15 that similarly deal with Yunmen's approach to explicating with ironic and paradoxical results the role of Chan awakening in relation to temporality and particular spans of time.

The dialogue begins in Tianqi's version by referring to the master as a "great teacher" (大師) who, according to both texts, was "giving his assembly an instruction" (垂語) in a temple hall. The setting suggests that members of the audience are knowledgeable and responsive, but it turns out they are unable to answer Yunmen's cryptic query, "I'm not asking you about the days before the fifteenth [of the month], but about the days after the fifteenth. Come here now and give us a word" (十五日已前不問汝. 十五日已後. 道將一句來). When nobody speaks up, Yunmen offers "his own substitute phrase" (自代云) as a typical Chan discursive technique by proclaiming, "Every day is a good day" (日日是好日).

Yunmen's division of the monthly cycle into two fortnight periods refers to the lunar calendar, during which temple monks routinely offered confessions to their colleagues and also wrote verses celebrating three nights around the time of the full moon. He further evokes a broader sense of separation between ordinary and monumental events, such as prior to and following ordination or the attaining of realization. Yuanwu says of the case's main phrase, "Still, a shrimp can't leap over the Big Dipper" (收. 鰕跳不出斗).

In prose comments, Yuanwu points out that Yunmen's teaching style is exceptional because he frequently expresses "three-leveled Chan" (三字禪), or investigating by oneself (顧), by following patterns (鑒), and by expressing surprise (咦), as well as "one-level Chan" (一字禪), such as saying "Universal" (普) in response to the question, "What's the treasury of the true dharma eye?" (如何正法眼藏). According to Yuanwu, Yunmen's approach "doesn't allow for straightforward explanations. Even in ordinary situations, he scolds people and every phrase uttered feels like an iron spear" (直是不容擬議. 到平鋪處. 又却罵人若下一句語. 如鐵橛子相似). Yuanwu further notes that Xuedou once said, "I like the fresh devices of Shaoyang [another moniker for Yunmen], who spent his life pulling out nails and pegs to help people" (我愛韶陽新定機. 一生與人抽釘拔楔).

Tianqi writes of the master's query, "Its meaning already abides in daily functions, as everything is relative" (既居日用. 一切任意). His concluding note reads, "Fishing with a pole points clearly to a hidden blade" (垂釣旨明藏鋒), and his wrapping phrase, as for case 5 and several other instances, says, "Grandmotherly kindness!" (老婆心切).

Verse: [Yunmen] lets go of one and picks up seven,
 (Y: Whatever can't be picked up, he lets go, 拈不出. 却不放過)
No one anywhere is his equal.
Slowly treading along, he cuts off the sounds of flowing water,
And calmly observes the traces of birds flying by.
 (T: Making use of nonduality, he's naturally detached within brightness yet stands alone within darkness, 若能了法不二. 明中自然踏斷. 暗中自然獨露)
Yet weeds spread and mists thicken.
 (T: That rule covers everything but without resorting to "this" versus "that,"一律平懷了無彼此)
Flowers scatter while Subhūti sits on the edge of a cliff,
I snap my fingers to put an end to the pitiful multitude of blossoms.
 (Y: You'll get what you deserve when I strike! 自領出去. 便打)
 (T: Two wrongs don't make a right, 今行法令莫犯二病)
Don't be bewildered; those who're bewildered get thirty blows from my stick!
去却一. 拈得七 / 上下四維無等匹 / 徐行踏斷流水聲 / 縱觀寫出飛禽迹 / 草茸茸烟羃羃 / 空生巖畔花狼藉 / 彈指堪悲舜若多 / 莫動著 / 動著三十棒.

Comments: The poem opens obliquely with a six-character line referring to Yunmen's capabilities, although Yuanwu is typically a bit more reserved in his reaction than Tianqi. The next couplet offers praise for Yunmen's power of concentration, but the fifth line acknowledges that even he cannot escape the messiness of ordinary life. The last couplet criticizes Subhūti, a follower of a primordial buddha so immersed in emptiness that birds dropped flowers from the sky. Although this sounds auspicious, for Xuedou and Chan discourse more generally, it is instead a sure sign that Subhūti's awareness is not genuinely traceless since true enlightenment avoids the extremes of naïve affirmation and nihilistic negation. In contrast to the image of flowers used in the previous verse that are emblematic of everyday reality without judgment or one-sidedness, here the blossoms represent something superfluous and therefore are detrimental to awakening.

In the final line that functions as a kind of capping phrase, Xuedou playfully threatens his disciples with corporal punishment if they are unable to avoid Subhūti's mistakes, but the comments by Yuanwu and Tianqi are a bit cynical. In prose Yuanwu remarks, "What does it mean to be bewildered? Sleeping with your eyes wide open while the bright sun shines in the clear sky" (動著時如何. 白日青天. 開眼瞌睡).

Ode 7

Fayan Says, "You're Huichao" 法眼云汝是慧超

Case: For Yuanwu this case captures the merits of the teaching method of Fayan (法眼, 885–958), founder of one of the five main houses of Chan who, like Yunmen, was a member of the larger lineage stemming from Xuefeng. Yuanwu says of Fayan's approach, "When no buddha is present and you alone are the worthy one, that's your first time playing a crucial role. But if you aren't yet ready, you must start by realizing that even the tip of a hair releases the great illumination in all directions [literally, "seven vertical and eight horizontal"]" (無佛處獨稱尊. 始較些子. 其或未然. 於一毫頭上透得. 放大光明七縱八横). Then, "You'll enjoy true freedom in the midst of phenomena and trust that whatever's held in your fingertips doesn't lack truth" (於法自在自由. 信手拈來無有不是).

In the brief dialogue, Fayan is approached by a monk who says, "I, Huichao, ask you, who's buddha?" (慧超咨和尚. 如何是佛), and the teacher responds, "You're Huichao" (汝是慧超).

Yuanwu's prose comments suggest that the "total dynamism" (全機) of Fayan's pedagogical device is based on repeating the saying he is asked about. When his response mimics and thereby cuts off the student's self-introduction, Huichao is awakened as "someone who doesn't flinch when struck, with teeth like sword trees and a mouth like a blood bowl, who can decipher meaning beyond words" (除非是一棒打不回頭底漢. 牙如劍樹. 口似血盆. 向言外知歸). This method, which Yuanwu says is different from the Caodong (曹洞) school's "five positions" (五位) or the Linji (臨濟) school's "four propositions" (四料簡), reflects the therapeutic view, "There're no sores, so don't inflict a wound" (所謂彼既無瘡. 勿傷之也).

Tianqi says of the monk's question, "He probes deeply" (請益), and of Fayan's response, "He had a head start" (當頭一提). Tianqi's final remark reads, "Speak urgently of the matter of a rabbit falling into a ditch, 急處一提. 旨明就窩打兔), which refers to a legend also mentioned in a Yuanwu capping phrase (守株待兔) of how a starving person accidentally came across a dead hare that ran into a tree stump and, after eating it, kept returning to the same spot every day expecting to find new food. Tianqi's wrapping phrase says, "Two arrowheads meeting in midair" (箭鋒相拄), another encapsulation of Fayan's instructional approach drawn from a Daoist classic that is cited briefly in Yuanwu's prose comments and is also mentioned in cases 44, 82, and 99.

Verse: Near the beautiful river, spring breezes blow without stirring,
(T: Everyone in the country calls out but doesn't understand why, 盡國人呼.未曾着意)
Partridges sing while nesting amid myriad flowers.
(T: This is probing further of a regular occurrence, 今日請益. 平常一提)
At the three-tiered gate, where waves leap high, fish are transformed into dragons,
(T: Huichao's enlightened, on hearing thunder he's transformed, 慧超悟處. 聞雷而化)
Yet foolish ones still draw water from a muddy ditch at night.
(Y: That's the same as standing by a stump waiting for a rabbit, 守株待兔)
江國春風吹不起 / 鷓鴣啼在深花裏 / 三級浪高魚化龍 / 癡人猶戽夜塘水.

Comments: Xuedou takes the path of indirection in the opening couplet. He turns from addressing the exchange in a straightforward way to conveying sublime natural imagery that alludes to a traditional song, also evoked in case 24 of *Wumen's Barrier*, about the culturally and economically prestigious Jiangnan (江南) region near the Yangzi River encompassing the area of Xuedou's temple. Xuedou indicates the breeze is moving rather than standing still, unlike the original saying, but it does not disrupt the serene environment. Tianqi's capping phrases, like Yuanwu's prose comments, caution readers against trying to interpret literally the symbolism of this image.

In the final lines, Xuedou casts in a Chan context another legend about dragons in which fish swimming upstream during a mighty storm are transformed into the auspicious mythical creature when they reach the top of a waterfall. Yuanwu's prose remarks offer praise by maintaining, "Whereas the sayings of ancients are difficult to chew, digest, penetrate, or see, like listening to an indecipherable tongue, Xuedou's verse teaches people how to look. Isn't this extraordinary?" (於古人難咬難嚼難透難見節角誵訛處. 頌出教人見. 不妨奇特). In agreement with Tianqi's phrase confirming Huichao's awakening, Yuanwu further notes that Xuedou feared people would misapprehend Fayan's severe barrier (關棙子) by "mistakenly claiming to understand, so instead he composed this verse" (錯作解會. 所以頌出這僧如此問).

Yuanwu's prose comments also cite a poem by the famous follower of Fayan, Tiantai Deshao (天台德韶, 891–972), who wrote at the time of his awakening about a beautiful summit: "Tongxuan Peak, / Isn't of the human world. / There's nothing outside the mind, / Blue mountains fill the eyes" (通玄峯頂 / 不是人間 / 心外無法 / 滿目青山). This verse was admired by the Neo-Confucian philosopher Zhu Xi (朱熹, 1130–1200), and a Song-dynasty monk Shi Wenjun (釋文珦) wrote a similar eight-line poem with the concluding passage: "Originally there's no perception outside mind, / So poems become demons. / A Chan practitioner should clean his ears, / Rather than listen to opaque songs" (心外元無境 / 詩成亦是魔 / 禪翁清淨耳 / 渾不聽笙歌).

Ode 8

Are Cuiyan's Eyebrows Still There? 翠巖眉毛在麼

Case: Yuanwu introduces this case by contrasting the skill of an enlightened person, whose capacity "resembles the power of a dragon in water or the savvy of a tiger in the mountains" (如龍得水. 似虎靠山), with the incapacity of an unenlightened person, "who's like an antelope getting its horns caught in a tree or an ignoramus waiting foolishly for a dead hare to show" (羝羊觸藩守株待兔); the latter analogy is also mentioned in case 7. Furthermore, he says, "Sometimes a phrase cuts off the tongues of everyone on earth, and sometimes a phrase follows the waves and pursues the currents" (有時一句. 坐斷天下人舌頭. 有時一句. 隨波逐浪).

The dialogue involves Cuiyan (翠巖, fl. ninth–tenth century), who is head monk of Xuefeng's temple where he speaks to the assembly about sermons offered during the annual three-month summer intensive retreat. Cuiyan asks if his colleagues would confirm that his eyebrows (眉毛) are still intact, since it is said in Chan circles that deficient teaching causes one's brows to fall off prematurely. Terse reactions to this rhetorical question are presented by three dharma brothers who also serve under Xuefeng: Baofu (保福, d.928) says, "He has the heart of a thief" (作賊人心虛); Changqing (長慶, 854–932), who also appears with Baofu in cases 23 and 95, responds, "They've grown!" (生也); and Yunmen remarks, "Checkpoint (or barrier)!" (關).

In a prose comment Yuanwu says of Cuiyan, "He was without doubt alone in his loftiness, as nothing stopped him from astonishing the heavens and shaking the earth. Now tell me, among the great treasury of teachings in five thousand and forty-eight volumes, whether explaining mind and nature or preaching sudden and gradual paths, has anyone else ever accomplished this?" (然而不妨孤峻. 不妨驚天動地. 且道. 一大藏教. 五千四十八卷. 不免說心說性. 說頓說漸. 還有這箇消息麼). But his capping remarks are typically cynical when he says of Changqing, "His tongue falls on the floor and in the end he compounds mistake after mistake" (舌頭落地. 將錯就錯. 果然), and of Yunmen, "Where's he running to? All the patch-robed monks in the world can't extricate themselves, so he loses" (走在什麼處去. 天下衲僧跳不出. 敗也).

Tianqi comments on Cuiyan's query, "Fishing in deep waters with a pole in his hands" (探竿在手), and on Baofu's response, "He sets things back for ages" (就身打劫). Tianqi's final note reads, "Fishing with a pole points clearly to a hidden blade" (垂釣. 旨明藏鋒); and his wrapping phrase says, "Adepts sing together in harmony" (作家唱和).

Verse: Cuiyan's teaching for thousands of years receives no response,
(T: This doesn't reveal the sharpness in his beautiful phrase, 美他句中不露鋒骨)
[Yunmen's] "Checkpoint": He expects to get paid, but he loses money.
That old fool Baofu: It's difficult to say if he should be scorned or praised.
Chattering Cuiyan: It's clear he's a thief!
Precious jade looks immaculate, but who can tell whether it's real or fake?
(T: This wording has no edges or corners, so it's hard to decipher 句無稜角. 誠然難辨)
Only Changqing is attuned by saying, "His eyebrows have grown!"
(Y: What does this mean? From head above to feet below there's nothing whatsoever that grows, 在什麼處. 從頂門上. 至脚跟下. 一莖草也無)

(T: He's the only one with enough intimate knowledge to make the right point, 獨許知音. 善拈善點)

翠巖示徒. 千古無對 / 關字相酬. 失錢遭罪 / 潦倒保福. 抑揚難得 / 嘮嘮翠巖. 分明是賊 / 白圭無玷. 誰辨真假 / 長慶相諳. 眉毛生也.

Comments: Yuanwu's prose comments suggest that "Xuedou uses great literary skill to string together the whole case from beginning to end on a single thread with this intriguing verse. He also says, 'Changqing, who knows Cuiyan best, suggests his eyebrows have grown'" (雪竇有大才. 所以從頭至尾. 一串穿却. 末後却方道. 長慶相諳. 眉毛生). "But tell me," Yuanwu adds mockingly, "where are they growing? Quickly take a very careful look!" (且道. 生也在什麼處. 急著眼看). It seems that Yunmen, usually praised lavishly by Xuedou and Yuanwu, is no better off than one who has lost his brows because he resorts to a cliché.

In capping phrases, Tianqi adopts a positive stance toward Cuiyan's outlook when he mentions hidden sharpness and supports Xuedou's view that this master is as bright as a fine jewel. Tianqi further agrees with Xuedou's assessment that, of the three Chan figures, only Changqing truly appreciates Cuiyan's teaching, although Yuanwu remains skeptical when he submits, no doubt in whimsical fashion, that there are no eyebrows left.

Ode 9

Zhaozhou's "East, South, West, and North Gates" 趙州東南西北門

Case: Yuanwu's introduction praises Zhaozhou indirectly by suggesting of the Chan master, "A bright mirror on its stand enables beauty and ugliness to reveal themselves. The sharpest sword held in his hand can either kill or give life, according to circumstances. [In the mirror], natives go while foreigners come, or foreigners come while natives go. [With the sword], living is attained in the midst of dying, and dying is attained in the midst of living" (明鏡當臺. 妍醜自辨. 鏌鎁在手. 殺活臨時. 漢去胡來. 胡來漢去. 死中得活. 活中得死). Yuanwu further says that this requires having "the eye that penetrates all barriers" (透關底眼) in order to find "the right place for making a complete turnaround" (轉身處), or radical change from folly to insight.

In the dialogue an anonymous monk asks, "What's Zhaozhou?" (如何是趙州) and the teacher says without explanation, "There're east, south, west, and north gates" (東門南門西門北門). As also implied in case 52, since the inquiry is about "what" (何) rather than "who" (誰), the question may refer to the famous town in northern China near a monumental stone bridge, which was a major feat of premodern engineering, where Zhaozhou led an eponymous temple. The master responds by evoking the imagery of place, since nearly all towns in that era were encompassed by a rectangular wall with each side having a gateway as the only entry or exit point; thus, the reply symbolically suggests the open-ended yet constricted quality of self.

According to a Chan verse Yuanwu cites about the teacher's approach, "The head priest knows how to welcome a guest, / Who doesn't realize he dwells in the capital city [or is one with buddha-nature]. / Zhaozhou enters the weeds to help people, / Oblivious to muddy waters all around" (侍者只知報客 / 不知身在帝鄉 / 趙州入草求人 / 不覺渾身泥水). Also, in a capping phrase Yuanwu remarks of Zhaozhou's response, "It's an open-and-shut case, but do you see this clearly? I'll strike!" (見成公案. 還見麼. 便打).

Tianqi says of the questioner, who seems to be intentionally downgrading Zhaozhou's dignity, "He borrows a hidden blade" (借事藏鋒), and of the master, "He turns a deficit into an advantage [or, uses another's knack to demonstrate his own]" (以機遣機). Tianqi's final note reads, "The hidden blade points clearly to the absolute" (藏鋒. 旨明絕待); and the wrapping phrase says, "He splits the arrow and seizes the nest" (劈筈奪窩).

Verse: Their respective abilities challenge one another with contesting phrasings,

(T: Two barriers are embedded in the question, which doesn't let go of the main point, 問中雙關. 當頭不讓)

But [Zhaozhou's] diamond eye of wisdom stays spotless.

(T: The pivot is disclosed in his answer, as people and environment are both removed, 答處就機. 人境雙奪)

Facing the eastern, southern, western, and northern gates,

The heaviest blows from countless hammers can't open them.

(Y: Using yourself as a hammer won't work since the gates are already open, 自是爾輪鎚不到. 開也)

(T: Ordinary reason is confounded when a divine sword has difficulty cutting through, 理事混然. 神劍難分)

句裏呈機劈面來 / 爍迦羅眼絕纖埃 / 東南西北門相對 / 無限輪鎚擊不開.

Comments: Xuedou's verse is thematically divided into two parts. The first couplet is a eulogy for the capabilities of Zhaozhou whose extraordinary, adamantine insight is highlighted by evoking an early Buddhist term (爍迦羅眼) that refers to seeing the perishability of all things coming and going such that these phenomena are grasped fully in the finest of detail because the mirror-like quality of the eye and its ultimately holistic vision remains inexorable. Tianqi, whose phrasing alludes to a passage about transcending both people and context appearing in the record of Linji (臨濟, d. 866), suggests that Zhaozhou's knack for sharpness resolves the relationship between self and place as posed by the monk's initial query.

In the final couplet, Xuedou reprimands his followers for failing to understand Zhaozhou's outlook. That occurs because, as both commentators point out, the gates of the city remain wide open for the wise to move through with ease, even as knocks fall short of hitting the mark for those lost in self-deceptions.

Ode 10

Muzhou's "What an Empty-Headed Fool!" 睦州這掠虛頭漢

Case: Yuanwu refers to this case, in contrast to dialogues that point either to a higher realm by challenging buddhas and bodhisattvas or to a lower realm by rescuing maggots and worms, as one that "faces neither up nor down" (儻或不上不). He further advises, "If there's a principle, follow the principle, but if there's no principle, follow precedent" (有條攀條. 無條攀例).

In the dialogue the master Muzhou (睦州, 780–877), a senior dharma brother to Linji, best known for unabashedly yelling at and striking disciples, asks a monk where he has come from and the novice responds with a shout (僧便喝). Muzhou says, "I've been shouted at by you" (老僧被汝一喝), and the monk hollers again. When Muzhou says, "What'll happen after the third and fourth shouts?" the monk does not reply, so Muzhou strikes him saying, "What an empty-headed fool you are!" (這掠虛頭漢).

Yuanwu remarks of Muzhou's reaction to the first shout, "He uses the opportunity to trap a tiger and turns a man into a monkey" (陷虎之機. 猱人作麼), and of the monk's second shout, "I'm afraid he has the head of a dragon, but the tail of a snake" (只恐龍頭蛇尾). But Yuanwu is characteristically skeptical in disingenuously praising Muzhou's punch, "If Muzhou were to keep up his decrees and actions, then the entire earth, grasses, and trees would be cut into pieces" (若使睦州盡令而行. 盡大地草木. 悉斬為三段). Of Muzhou's final insult Yuanwu says, "Here he lets go and falls back into secondary status" (放過一著. 落在第二).

Tianqi writes of the monk's question, "He's fishing in deep waters" (探竿), and of the failure to respond to Muzhou's challenge, "Hopeless!" (果失其照). Of the master's final actions Tianqi says, "He uses the great function to capture [the prey] alive" (大用生擒). Tianqi's final note reads, "Seizing the opportunity to trap a tiger points clearly to the great function fully expressed" (陷虎之機. 旨明大用全提); and his wrapping phrase comments, "Everything's balanced in his hands" (權衡在手).

Verse: Two shouts, and then a third shout,

> (Y: The sound of thunder booms, but there isn't even a drop of rain, 雷聲浩大. 雨點全無)

A Chan adept seizes the opportune moment for transformation.

> (T: Trying to solve the matter by shouting doesn't indicate a moment of transformation, since there're more powerful ways than beating the weeds to scare away snakes, 只解行喝. 不知機變. 打草驚蛇. 戒後強為)

But if he says he's "riding the head of a tiger,"
Then both turn out to be blind fools.

> (Y: A knowing phrase coming from the mouth of one who knows, 親言出親口)

Who's the real blind fool?

> (Y: The teacher decides, so he comes up with a final phrase, 教誰辨. 賴有末後句)

Bring him here so everyone can look him over!

> (T: Either the guest is blind, or the host is blind, or guest and host are both blind. Surely Xuedou finds clarity, but from the start he'd better not exclude himself! 或是賓瞎或是主瞎. 或是賓主一時瞎. 果然明得. 不可自專. 直須驗過始得)

兩喝與三喝 / 作者知機變 / 若謂騎虎頭 / 二俱成瞎漢 / 誰瞎漢 / 拈來天下與人看.

Comments: Xuedou begins with four lines of five characters each that comment on the exchange between Muzhou and an anonymous acolyte. The opening line refers to the monk's first two shouts as well as the master's rebuttal, both of which fall short, according to Yuanwu's capping phrase. The next line implies that the master's approach was successful in stimulating a spontaneous realization, but this evaluation is rebuffed by Tianqi's phrase as well as Xuedou's next couplet suggesting that both student and teacher are at fault.

In the final couplet consisting of three and seven characters, Xuedou interjects his own doubtful view by demanding facetiously that those who are blind disclose their identity. Yet Tianqi insists Xuedou's name is part of the list of fools. Also, Yuanwu's capping phrase on the fifth line is ambiguous because the first character of the second clause (賴) could imply that Xuedou makes "false accusations."

Ode 11

Huangbo's "Getting Drunk on Dregs" 黃蘗噇酒糟漢

Case: Yuanwu introduces Huangbo (黃蘗, d. 850?), Linji's mentor, as a teacher who uses "an impromptu word or phrase to startle the crowd and stir the masses; with just one device or in one situation he smashes chains and crushes shackles. When meeting an opportunity to transcend circumstances, he brings up matters suitable to transcendence" (等閑一句一言. 驚群動眾. 一機一境. 打鎖敲枷. 接向上機. 提向上事).

The dialogue cited by Xuedou is drawn from a longer version and involves a key Chan monastic practice that was common during the Tang dynasty and was established as a required training method in the annals of the Song dynasty; the practice then spread to Japan and Korea, where it was particularly emphasized. According to this approach, young monks were expected at certain times of the year, especially after the summer retreat, to travel widely around the countryside (行脚, C. *xingjiao*, J. *angya*) and to join new temples temporarily so they could learn from those teachers. Without such a practice, the novices' preparation was considered incomplete and their chances for attaining enlightenment were limited. However, the aim of this story is to challenge that form of practice when it is carried out in mechanical fashion.

The transformational impact of the case revolves around Huangbo's rhetorical sleight of hand. One day, while giving a sermon, he says that everyone in the assembly is "a person who gobbles down dregs" (噇酒糟漢), or drinks only the sediment at the bottom of the barrel so that if "they make a pilgrimage, they won't find a place to stay for even one night" (與麼行脚何處有今日). Huangbo further claims that "throughout the country, there are no true teachers of Chan" (還知大唐國裏無禪師麼). When challenged by a monk he explains, "It's not that there's no Chan, just no true teachers" (不道無禪. 只是無師).

Of Huangbo's initial putdown Tianqi remarks, "Delusion and sluggishness are caused by drinking too much wine; how long will it take to awaken from such a stupor?" (迷名滯相如酒所困. 如此行持何年得醒). Of the case's final pronouncement he comments, "Since there are no true teachers, everything's done in a sloppy way" (既是無師. 盡是杜撰). Tianqi's final note says, "Searching for a short or long time points clearly to fishing that helps people" (搜短為長. 旨明垂釣為人); the wrapping phrase reads, "Everything's balanced in his hands" (權衡在手).

Verse: With a stern and solitary outlook [Huangbo] never boasts,
(T: Is this a balanced or exaggerated evaluation? 本有權衡豈是強勉)
Ruling grandly over the seas, he distinguishes dragons from snakes.
Even Emperor Xuanzong was touched intimately by him,
And was held firmly in his clutches on three occasions.
(Y: When great capacity and great function are fully manifest, the whole world in ten directions and the mountains and rivers of the great earth all come to life at Huangbo's place, 若是大機大用現前. 盡十方世界. 乃至山河大地. 盡在黃檗處乞命)
(T: This sage is beyond reproach, but what about his Chan trainees? 聖主不讓. 豈容禪客)
凜凜孤風不自誇 / 端居寰海定龍蛇 / 大中天子曾輕觸 / 三度親遭弄爪牙.

Comments: Yuanwu says in prose comments that, even though the poem by Xuedou may seem "like a eulogy written for a portrait of Huangbo" (黃檗真贊相), such an interpretation is misguided since Huangbo never looked for fame or glory but only expected that "right within his words, there's a way to extricate himself" (他底句下. 便有出身處) from delusion and deception. Tianqi's capping phrase on the first line, however, offers a playful critique of Xuedou, who suggests in line two that Huangbo effectively tests any newcomer as soon as the novice enters the temple gate.

The second couplet returns to the theme of highlighting the political significance of Chan in that Huangbo was mentor both for the prominent minister Pei Xiu (裴休, 791–864), who helped record his teacher's sayings, and earlier in his career, for Xuanzong (宣宗, r. 846–859, a.k.a. Dazhong, 大中). Xuanzong inherited the throne from his corrupt brother Wuzong (武宗, r. 840–846), who was responsible for the devastating proscription of institutional Buddhism in 845 that saw the loss of hundreds of thousands of clerics and the torching of dozens of monastic libraries. While the ruler-to-be, who was sympathetic to Chan, was hiding in various temples during that destructive period, he encountered Huangbo who, during their interactions, twice slapped and once reprimanded him. When Xuanzong succeeded to the throne, he accorded this Chan master an imperial title.

Ode 12

Dongshan's "Three Measures of Hemp" 洞山麻三斤

Case: Yuanwu introduces Dongshan Shouchu (洞山守初, 910–990), a prominent follower of Yunmen, by returning to the paradoxical image of the double-edged sword evoked in case 9 in addition to other symbolism involving blades in various cases. According to his comments, the master "wields the sword that kills people and the sword that brings people to life, which is the classical teaching that remains crucial today. If he discusses killing, he doesn't harm a single hair, and if he discusses giving life, he loses his own" (殺人刀活人劍. 乃上古之風規. 亦今時之樞要. 若論殺也. 不傷一毫. 若論活也. 喪身失命).

In the dialogue, also included as case 18 in *Wumen's Barrier*, a monk asks, "What is buddha?" (如何是佛) and Dongshan says cryptically, "Three pounds of hemp" (麻三斤). Yuanwu remarks, "Clearly his straw sandals are worn thin as he points to a locust tree yet scolds a willow tree while weighing them on scales [the last phrase can also refer to a rare tree species]" (灼然. 破草鞋. 指槐樹罵柳樹. 為秤鎚). He also suggests that the case should be understood in light of Dongshan's well-known distinction between "dead words" (死句), which may sound persuasive but are ineffective when it comes to attaining enlightenment, and "living words" (活句) that are tasteless yet useful in cutting off fetters and attachments.

Of the query Tianqi writes, "He probes further" (請益), and of the answer, "The plain truth" (平實). Tianqi's final note reads, "A turning word pointing clearly to no fixed path" (拈轉話頭. 旨明無有意路); and his wrapping phrase says, "The question emerges from abstraction, but the answer reflects the present moment" (問以劫外. 答以今時).

Verse: The golden crow speeds, and the jade rabbit leaps,
Has any beneficial response ever been carried out in a careless way?
(Y: Like a bell struck or a valley resounding from an echo, 如鐘在扣. 如谷受響)
(T: Dongshan and Xuedou are insightful in helping people, 洞山雪竇徹底為人)
Whoever sees Dongshan only in terms of his response to situations,
Is like a lame tortoise or a blind turtle entering an empty dale.
Abundant flowers adorn a luxuriant brocade,
(Y: This is a double case. The same indictment is imposed for all kinds of crimes, 兩重公案. 一狀領過. 依舊一般)
Bamboos in the south, and evergreens to the north.
(Y: It's a triple case, even a quadruple case, like a head placed above a head, 三重也有. 四重公案. 頭上安頭)
I recall that during the exchange between Changqing and Officer Lu,
It was explained that one should laugh rather than cry.
(T: When you're absorbed in this case, just clap along and laugh, 你若只在事上. 正好拍手大笑)
Ha!
(T: He's laughing. The reward's the punishment, and the phenomenon's the principle. Come see for yourself, 此之一笑. 是賞是罰. 是事是理. 請着眼看).
金烏急. 玉兔速 / 善應何曾有輕觸 / 展事投機見洞山 / 跛鼈盲龜入空谷 / 花簇簇. 錦簇簇 / 南地竹兮北地木 / 因思長慶陸大夫 / 解道合笑不合哭 / 咦.

Comments: Xuedou's poem consists of eight main lines with six of these featuring seven characters and the first and fifth containing six characters, in addition to a concluding exclamation in one character added as a ninth line. According to Yuanwu, the opening resembles Dongshan's mysterious answer by referring to the sun and moon, symbolized by legendary animals, and the second line suggests the appropriateness of responding to circumstances. Tianqi highlights that Chan adepts, despite variability and unpredictability in methods, correct errors.

The next couplet, which insists on overcoming facile interpretations that explain the dialogue's keyword in terms of logical reasoning, refers to an exchange in which Dongshan tells a follower, "I won't explain this just for you, but I'll explain it to the assembly." He then goes to the dharma hall and says, "Words don't express phenomena, speaking doesn't accord with situations" (我不為汝說. 我為大眾說. 遂上堂云. 言無展事. 語不投機).

Yuanwu playfully suggests that the rhetorical flourish in conjuring natural images in the third couplet multiplies the complications wrought by, as well as the illumination gained from, the core dialogue. The final lines allude to a Chan conversation involving a funeral at which a temple priest became concerned when he heard a civil official laughing instead of crying, although Changqing later approved of that unconventional behavior. This reference sets the stage for Xuedou's concluding exclamation suggesting that he cannot help but be amused at the ignorance of most followers who fail to grasp the significance of Dongshan's living words. This occurs, for Tianqi, because those monks lapse into misunderstanding based on dead words by failing to see the profound interconnections that link cause and effect, transcendence and immanence, or living and dying.

Ode 13

Baling's "Snow Piled High in a Silver Bowl" 巴陵銀椀裏盛雪

Case: Baling (巴陵, fl. tenth century), a disciple of Yunmen and a dharma brother of Dongshan Shouchu featured in case 12, is also the key interlocutor of case 100. Yuanwu remarks of his teachings, "Clouds hang over the great plains, but the whole world is never concealed. When snow covers white flowers, it's hard to distinguish their shapes. The coldness is as severe as snow and ice, and the fineness is as slight as rice powder. The depths are hard for a buddha's eye to discern, and the secrets can't be fathomed by demons or heretics" (雲凝大野. 遍界不藏. 雪覆蘆花. 難分朕迹. 冷處冷如氷雪. 細處細如米末. 深深處佛眼難窺. 密密處魔外莫測).

In the cryptic dialogue a monk asks Baling, "What's the school of Kanadeva" (提婆宗)?" and the teacher replies indirectly, "Snow piled high in a silver bowl" (銀椀裏盛雪). Kanedeva (迦那提婆, C. Jianatipo, J. Kanadaiba) is considered the fifteenth Chan patriarch in India who was numbered among the heretics until he met the fourteenth patriarch Nāgārjuna, who valued his successor's skill in debating non-Buddhists. Baling's response highlighting the variabilities embedded in nonduality recalls a line from the "Song of Jeweled Mirror Samādhi" (*Baojing sanmei ge*, 寶鏡三昧歌) by Dongshan Liangjie (洞山良价, 807–869), founder of the Caodong school: "A silver bowl is filled with snow, a heron is hidden by the bright moon, / Similar but not the same, they're known by distinctive features, / Meaning isn't in words, but arises at pivotal moments" (銀碗盛雪. 明月藏鷺 / 類而不斉. 混則知處 / 意不在言. 來機亦赴).

Of the monk's question Yuanwu writes, "A white horse entering an area with reeds, but what's his point?" (白馬入蘆花. 道什麼點), and of the response, "He stuffs it down your throat; seven flowers bloom but the eighth withers" (塞斷爾咽喉. 七花八裂).

Tianqi says of the query, "Probing further to discern the host" (請益辨主), and of Baling's answer, "He hits the mark" (當央直指). Thus, Yuanwu offers a tongue-in-cheek putdown of both interlocutors, whereas Tianqi views the question as a good way of investigating Baling and the master's retort as a beacon of light. Tianqi's final note reads, "The radiant source points clearly to the absolute" (明宗. 旨明絕待); and his wrapping phrase says, "A correct answer lies in a misguided question" (問偏答正).

Verse: Old Xinkai (Baling) is like no one else!

> (Y: A thousand soldiers are easy to recruit, but one general is hard to find, so the venerable teacher uses many words, 千兵易得. 一將難求. 多口阿師)

He explains by saying, "Snow piled high in a silver bowl."

> (T: His words aren't based on obfuscation, which is why Xuedou offers high praise, 句不立玄. 故乃讚歎)

The ninety-six schools must learn this for themselves,

> (Y: You do, too. O Worthy. Don't you realize that all are buried in the same pit? 兼身在內. 闍黎還知麼. 一坑埋却)

If you don't know, ask the moon in the sky above.

> (T: Everyone knows what they depend on, but don't know to ask an insightful person how to attain it, 諸人自知負墮則可. 如有不知更問明眼人始得)

That Kanadeva school!

Red flags waving amid the pure Chan teaching.

> (T: Xuedou tries his best to make the point, but if you don't understand, it can't be explained, 雪竇盡力提持. 若然會得. 便解返擲)

老新開. 端的別 / 解道銀椀裏盛雪 / 九十六箇應自知 / 不知却問天邊月 / 提婆宗. 提婆宗 / 赤旛之下起清風.

Comments: "Xinkai" is another moniker for Baling, about whom Xuedou evokes a simple colloquial expression (端的別) in line one as the highest form of praise because his saying that uses monochromatic imagery symbolically defeats the ninety-six heretical schools, which held formal philosophical debates with Buddhism in ancient India. Alluding to the arcane customs of an early period in religious history implies that red flags of victory can be hung high for all Chan followers to see. Meanwhile, those bested by Baling, who is equated in the penultimate line with the Kanadeva school, have no recourse but to evoke moonlight to gain release from subtle clinging to stubborn ignorance.

According to the commentary of Tenkei (天桂, 1648–1735), an early modern Japanese Sōtō Zen master, it is Xuedou himself who takes up the triumphant banner and acts with his whole being by vanquishing heretics who seek truth outside the one mind. He shows nonbelievers how to apologize for their conceptual mistakes and repent for errors of judgment. So long as defeated debaters genuinely acknowledge and overcome their delusions, the Kanadeva-cum-Chan approach continues to flourish since it is invariably expressed through dynamic activities rather than idle chatter.

Ode 14

Yunmen Says, "An Appropriate Teaching" 雲門云對一說

Case: This gong'an and the next represent back-to-back, interconnected cases featuring complementary dialogues that appeared separately in Yunmen's recorded sayings. Both recall case 6 by similarly highlighting the issue of whether Buddhist teachings should be preached by an adept in order to correspond to particular occasions or can instead be effectively instructed even if—or, rather, because—they are inappropriate (倒; literally, "upside down").

In the dialogue a monk asks, "What are the teachings of a lifetime?" (如何是一代時教), which indicates the Buddha gave instructions for forty-nine years in front of a total of 360 assemblies of monks, but further implies the timeless nature of his majestic voice that never wavers or varies. Yunmen responds, "An appropriate (or timely) teaching" (對一說), which suggests that each directive must be responsive and suitable to the circumstances of followers being addressed. There is only one basic Buddhist message, yet it is conveyed differently based on a trainee's level of understanding.

Yuanwu's capping phrase expresses typical Chan irony, "An iron hammerhead with no hole; seven flowers bloom but the eighth withers; an old rat gnaws on raw ginger" (無孔鐵鎚.七花八裂. 老鼠咬生薑), evoking three images of futility: a useless tool, faltering blossoms, and a rodent eating what it should reject. Perhaps the dialogue exemplifies the ineffectiveness of words, rather than an exalted vision of truth. However, the opening section of Yunmen's record is titled "Responding to Occasions" 對機 (*xuanji*), which is similar to the notion of 機宜 (*jiyi*) mentioned in *Blue Cliff Record* cases 6, 8, 9, 12, and 61, and implies knowing what to do in any situation or, to cite a Chan saying, "speaking in tune with the specific circumstances." Yuanwu also points out Yunmen's capacity in comments on case 47: "He doesn't turn his back to questions since, by responding at the time or adapting to the occasion with a word or phrase, a mark or statement, he invariably finds a way to extricate himself" (更不辜負爾問頭. 應時應節. 一言一句.一點一畫. 不妨有出身處).

Tianqi says of Yunmen, "He hits the mark" (當央直指). His final note reads, "The radiant source points clearly to the absolute" (明宗. 旨明絕待); and his wrapping phrase repeats, "He hits the mark" (當頭直指).

Verse: "An appropriate teaching," how exceptional!
(T: These words are beyond compare, 句絕其比)
Like fitting a handle into an iron hammer with no hole.
(T: The question has no holes or gaps, but the answer shows all corners of the room, 問無孔竅. 答絕方隅)
Laughter rings out under the Jambu tree: Ha ha!
Last night the black dragon had its horn ripped out,
How extraordinary!
(T: He appears different from every angle, so it's necessary for everyone to pay close attention, 不同諸方. 要人着眼)
Old man Shaoyang holds one.
(Y: Where is it? Who's got the other? Deshan and Linji fall back three thousand paces, 在什麼處. 更有一橛. 分付阿誰.德山臨濟也須退倒三千)
(T: There are waves only in calm waters; there are no waves following a downpour, 只有湛水之波. 而無滔天之浪)

對一說. 太孤絕 / 無也鐵椎重下楔 / 閻浮樹下笑呵呵 / 昨夜驪龍拗解折 / 別別 / 韶陽老人得一橛.

Comments: The first line celebrates the three-character saying uttered by Yunmen as a remarkable achievement, and this is followed by three seven-character lines, a two-character interjection, and a final line with seven syllables. Xuedou continues with praise by comparing Yunmen's feat to the paradox of attaching a handle to a hole-less hammerhead, which recalls the Chan image of an iron flute without openings played upside-down (鐵笛倒吹). He also evokes the laughter that rings out from under the mythical Jambu tree, which in Buddhist cosmology covers the entire realm below the sacred peak of Mount Sumeru.

Xuedou additionally compares Yunmen's insightful phrase to the act of wrenching a horn or horns from a dragon and in the final line, while using a term of endearment (韶陽老人) for the master, he refers to a single object (一橛), apparently indicating one horn. This image could also represent the stake of a hammer or a tally showing that Yunmen attains a victory through his use of deceptively simple wording. Furthermore, the final phrasing could suggest a multiperspectival standpoint implying that, as much as has been achieved by Yunmen, there is still a flip side of any given situation or an outlook that is missing or left unexpressed by his cryptic utterance, as further suggested by the following case.

Ode 15

Yunmen Says, "An Inappropriate Teaching" 雲門云倒一說

Case: Yuanwu introduces this case and its relation to the previous dialogue involving Yunmen by evoking the symbolism of the double-edged sword at once "killing people and giving them life" (殺人刀活人劍). In this exchange a monk, presumably the same as in case 14, reverses the question by asking, "What about when there's no perceptible activity and there're no perceptible phenomena?" (不是目前機. 亦非目前事時如何). The master offers a three-word comment in contrast to case 14: "An inappropriate teaching" (倒一說), which implies taking an untimely or "upside down" approach.

In Yunmen's recorded sayings, these two dialogues are separate rather than consecutive, and the nuance of the second exchange's inquiry is a bit different from the *Odes*' version: "What about when there's no realm of mystery and nothing catches the eye?" (問不是玄機. 亦非目擊時如何). Whereas case 15 emphasizes the phenomenal world while also implying a basic distinction between movement and stillness, the exchange in Yunmen's record highlights two different realms, one metaphysical or transcendent and the other physical or immanent. The main point of both versions is that polarities are negated, thus indicating the emptiness of all provisional conceptual categories.

Yuanwu says of the monk's query, "Taking a leap, he falls back three thousand paces" (跳作什麼. 倒退三千 里), and of Yunmen's response, "It's an even score based on what benevolently comes out of his mouth. But since he doesn't let go, he's covered in overgrown weeds" (平出. 款出囚人口. 也不得放過. 荒草裹横身).

According to Tianqi's comment on the monk, "Understanding non-worldly principles, he asks an unexpected question" (悟非世理. 特呈解問), and on the master, "This response seizes the opportunity to show the point" (就機一點). Tianqi says in his final note, "Discerning the opportunity to act points clearly to settling this matter for eons" (見機而作. 旨明就身打劫); and his wrapping phrase reads, "He pulls out a wedge by using a wedge" (以楔出楔).

Verse: "An inappropriate teaching" fits the moment!

(Y: Without letting go, seven flowers bloom but the eighth withers. In the Jambu realm there're five thousand and forty-eight volumes [of the canon]. Half lies south of the river and half lies north, but both are held in his hands, 放不下. 七花八裂. 須彌南畔. 卷盡五千四十八.半河南半河北. 把手共行)

(T: Clarifying and releasing are both evident in the same action, 分明放過. 把手同行)

He's committed to dying the same and living the same as all of you.
Eighty-four thousand disciples couldn't take flight like one phoenix,
Yet thirty-three [patriarchs] enter the tiger's cave.

(Y: I alone know that even one true leader is hard to find in a den of wild fox spirits, 唯我能知. 一將難求. 野狐精一隊)

How extraordinary!

(T: His goal is to get people to pay attention, 故意提起令人着眼)

The moon's reflected in turbulent rapids.

(Y: Under the clear sky and bright sun, don't go mistaking reflections for reality. Or are you too busy to notice? 青天白日. 迷頭認影. 著忙作什麼)

(T: Shadows glimmering like the moon reflected in water; disciplined students don't neglect this perception, 影影灼灼如水中月. 戒其學者情見未忘)

倒一說. 分一節 / 同死同生為君決 / 八萬四千非鳳毛 / 三十三人入虎穴 / 別別 / 擾擾匆匆水裏月.

Comments: Cases 14 and 15 represent two sides of the same coin, with each capturing its own portion of the whole truth: whereas case 14 speaks of hitting its target in a suitable manner, case 15 suggests upending the mark by turning it topsy-turvy and inside-out in contradictory fashion. The reply in case 14, which not only talks about but constitutes an appropriate teaching, is enhanced by the untimely reply of case 15 that, although seeming out of sorts with its occasion, is nevertheless fundamentally apropos. A musical simile based on section 33 of the *Sūtra in Forty-Two Sections* (四十二章經) further suggests, "A harp emits no sound if the strings are stretched too much, and it also makes no sound if they're stretched too little. Only when the strings are stretched just right is the music fully in tune."

Therefore, inversions and reversals invariably apply in Chan discourse by leading in a creative process of disentangling entanglements (葛藤, C. *geteng*, J. *kattō*) toward attaining an experience of realization since, no matter what an adept says or does not say, this is considered a form of expressing truth (often deliberately as "untruth"). However, it must be realized that the manifold disciples who attended the Buddha's assembly did not gain an understanding that was known only to Mahākāśyapa and the subsequent patriarchs. Adepts like Yunmen are well aware that genuine insight must continue to reckon with ongoing disturbances and perplexities reflected in choppy waters.

Ode 16

Jingqing's Simultaneous Tapping and Pecking 鏡清啐啄同時

Case: Yuanwu introduces the master Jingqing (鏡清, 868–937), a dharma brother of Yunmen under the tutelage of Xuefeng, who "practices all day without ever practicing and preaches all day without ever preaching; thus, with freedom and autonomy, he takes the opportunity to tap the eggshell when the chick is pecking inside and wield the sword that kills and gives life"

(終日行而未嘗行.終日說而未嘗說.便可以自由自在.展啐啄之機.用殺活之劍).

According to the dialogue a monk asks, "If I'm pecking from within, would you start tapping from outside?" (學人啐. 請師啄), and Jingqing replies, "Are you alive or not?" (還得活也無). When the monk says, "If I weren't alive, everyone would laugh out loud" (若不活遭人恠笑), Jingqing retorts, "You're one more person living in the weeds" (也是草裏漢).

Yuanwu says of the monk's initial question, "Isn't this stirring waves when there's no wind?" (無風起浪. 作什麼); and of Jingqing's counter-query, "It lands a punch but he's buying the hat to fit the head, thus adding error upon error" (劄. 買帽相頭. 將錯就錯).

Tianqi writes of the query, "He borrows a hidden blade" (借事藏鋒), and of the response, "He tests one action with another action" (以機驗機). Of the master's final comment Tianqi remarks, "Although we can't help but die, we also exist within life. Jingqing makes this clear by taking one step at a time" (雖不住死. 又在其活. 故乃鏡清一點一拈).Tianqi's final note reads, "Showing emotion points clearly to his claws and fangs" (拈情. 旨明爪牙); and the wrapping phrase, also used in case 11 and numerous other instances, says, "Everything's balanced in his hands" (權衡在手).

Verse: Ancient buddhas had various lineal teaching styles,
But [Jingqing's] responses are often denigrated.
Since chick and hen don't know each other,
(Y: Because they don't know, they naturally tap and peck in unison, 既不相知. 為什麼却有啐啄. 天然)
Why are they tapping and pecking at the same time?
(Y: Shattering delusions into a hundred fragments, Xuedou's verse has the kindness of an old granny but don't misunderstand his intention, 百雜碎. 老婆心切. 且莫錯認)
(T: Tapping and pecking aren't forgotten when action and environment interact and enhance one other, but chick and hen are both forgotten when they're responding to one another, 啐啄未忘. 機境交加. 子母雙忘. 對待何有)
The pecking chick awakens but remains in the shell until there's another tap,
(Y: Wrong, so I'll strike! This is a double case, nay, a triple or even a quadruple case, 錯. 便打. 兩重公案. 三重四重了也)

(T: By saying that life exists within death, the host chases but the guest remains, 主之追處. 賓之呈處. 云死存活)

Throughout the world, patch-robed monks try in vain to carry out this process.

(Y: From the deepest past the darkness is vast and boundless, but nobody knows how to fill ditches or clog gullies, 千古萬古黑漫漫. 填溝塞壑無人會)

古佛有家風 / 對揚遭貶剝 / 子母不相知 / 是誰同啐啄 / 啄覺猶在殼重遭撲 / 天下衲僧徒名邈.

Comments: This poem has an anomalous construction with the first four lines containing five characters each followed by an eight-character line that is sometimes broken up into two or three components in various commentaries, plus a final line with seven characters. Yuanwu remarks that the first couplet is sufficient to get the main point across, but Xuedou chose to continue his writing to clarify the sense of immediacy and intimacy that is required according to the frequently misunderstood training technique taught by Jingqing. That approach stands in contrast with other pedagogical devices that focus on the role of the master, who tempers the student as part of a gradual path of cultivation or uses shouting and slapping designed to elicit a sudden realization.

Tenkei's commentary suggests that instructional methods of various Chan/Zen lineages, such as the "five positions" (五位), "four shouts" (四喝), "three mysteries" (三玄), and "four alternatives" (四料簡), lead only to confusion and delusion. But Xuedou's verse, he maintains, is an effective means of transforming conventional levels of (mis)understanding into genuine realization.

Yuanwu also cites a similar poem by the master Xiangyan (香嚴, ?–898): "The chick pecks and the hen taps, / When the chick awakens, there's no shell. / Chick and hen are both forgotten, / The response to circumstances is faultless. / Treading the same path in harmony, / Yet walking alone through the realm of marvelous mystery" (子啐母啄 / 子覺無殼 / 子母俱忘 / 應緣不錯 / 同道唱和 / 妙玄獨脚). This verse probably influenced Tianqi's capping phrase on line four, although he uses the double-edged term "forgotten" (忘) to indicate either sublime awareness or stubborn ignorance. Commentators agree that the moment of liberating the chick by simultaneously knocking at the shell encompasses the interactivity of living and dying.

Ode 17

Xianglin's "Sitting for a Long Time Is Exhausting" 香林坐久成勞

Case: Yuanwu introduces Xianglin (香林, 908–987), one of Yunmen's four main disciples for whom Xuedou was a second-generation successor following Zhimen (智門, ?–1031), as someone who "cuts through nails and slices iron, thus proving an authentic master of the Chan school" (斬釘截鐵. 始可為本分宗師). He knows that "If you flee from arrows and dodge swords, you couldn't possibly be a genuine adept" (避箭隈刀. 焉能為通方作者). Furthermore, Xianglin "finds the place where even a needle can't enter, and understands what it's like when white waves crash as high as the sky" (針劄不入處. 白浪滔天時如何).

In the brief dialogue a monk asks Xianglin what is perhaps the most common of all Chan queries, "the meaning of Bodhidharma coming from the west" (祖師西來意). The master says, "Sitting for a long time is exhausting" (坐久成勞), which describes how unremitting seated meditation (坐禪, *zuochan*) can seem painful and tedious even as a dedicated practitioner is willing to endure the strain as part of their practice.

Yuanwu remarks of this saying, "A fish swims and the water gets muddied, a bird flies and feathers fall, you fetch a dog and it starts yapping, but the eye of an adept punctures a heavy mallet" (魚行水濁. 鳥飛落毛. 合取狗口好. 作家眼目. 鋸解稱鎚).

Tianqi says of Xianglin's response, "It's a straightforward teaching" (平實直指), which indicates that nothing mysterious is implied. Tianqi's final note reads, "A radiant source points clearly to truth" (明宗. 旨明絕待); and his wrapping phrase is, "Trust whatever is held in your fingertips" (信手拈來), which highlights that awakening is embedded in everyday activities.

Verse: Whether just one or two, or thousands or tens of thousands,
Lay down your load and unburden yourself.

> (Y: From now on you'll be sanctified, but is this enough to earn a rest? 從今日去應須灑灑落落. 還休得也未)
>
> (T: Among all the patch-robed monks in the world, Xianglin's mind doesn't depend on mystery. He's unattached and natural, so easy to understand, 天下衲僧皆如. 香林心不立玄. 偏不附物. 自然輕快)

Turning to the left, turning to the right, or following from behind,

Zihu had no choice but to strike Liu Tiemo (Iron Grindstone).
(Y: I would've broken his staff and not let him do this since it's like shooting an arrow after the thief has fled. I'll strike, so beware! 山僧拗折拄杖子. 更不行此令. 賊過後張弓. 便打. 嶮)
一箇兩箇千萬箇 / 脫却籠頭卸却馱 / 左轉左轉隨後來 / 紫胡要打劉鐵磨.

Comments: Tenkei's commentary suggests the first two lines show that, even though their bodies ache from head to toe during constant sitting and their minds are preoccupied after reviewing all thought processes so they feel weary and drained, true adepts know that "one's eyes are horizontal, and nose is vertical" (眼睛鼻. 孔可端直) when correctly performing meditation. Thus, as reinforced by Tianqi's capping phrase, a true teacher remains steady and unfazed by distractions or attachments through casting aside spontaneously all fears or fetters while remaining flexible and attuned to the ebb and flow of shifting circumstances.

The second half of the verse alludes to a well-known story about an unusual female practitioner of the ninth century named Liu Tiemo (劉鐵磨, 780–859, also called Iron Grindstone Liu), who is featured in case 24 in a dialogue with one of her mentors, Guishan (潙山, 771–853). Liu gained the nickname from demonstrating a forceful and unflinching demeanor during dharma battles when she often bested her male teachers or counterparts.

According to Yuanwu's prose commentary, "Living in a hermitage on the side of the mountain, people from all over couldn't deal with her" (山下卓庵. 諸方皆不柰何他). One day a disciple of Guishan, Zihu, comes to visit and asks about her name and she replies, "That's not for me to say" (不敢). He then quips, "You turn to the left, and turn to the right" (左轉右轉), and she responds, "Teacher, don't you flip over" (和尚莫顛倒). Then, "Zihu strikes Liu before she stops speaking" (胡和聲便打). Xuedou's verse indicates that Zihu could not help but hit her, although Yuanwu does not approve of that action because it reveals a limitation in the teacher's approach.

Ode 18

Huizhong's "One-Piece Pagoda" 慧忠無縫塔

Case: This dialogue involves a complicated exchange between Emperor Suzong (宗李, 711–762) and National Teacher Huizhong (慧忠國師,

675–755), the ruler's personal mentor who has another conversation with Suzong featured in case 99. Huizhong requests that a "one-piece pagoda" (無縫塔) or seamless monument be built as a memorial, but he refuses to explain what this would look like. Instead, the master has a poem recited for the emperor by his disciple, Danyuan (躭源, n.d.), who appears in case 17 of *Wumen's Barrier* as Huizhong's attendant and is recommended here as someone eminently qualified to address the topic: "South of Xiang, north of Tan, / Gold abounds in the nation. / The [buddha's] ferryboat waits under a shadowless tree, / But in the crystal palace, it isn't recognized" (相之南. 譚之北 / 中有黃金充一國 / 無影樹下合同船 / 琉璃殿上無知識); Xiang and Tan are two names indicating the same place.

Yuanwu says of Danyuan's verse, "The son takes up the father's work, but he falls into secondary and tertiary levels" (子承父業去也. 落在第二頭第三頭). Tianqi remarks that Huizhong's silence "reveals his whole body" (全身直示), and that summoning Danyuan means, "One request, two responses" (一囑二薦).

Another level of intricacy pertains to capping phrases for each line of Danyuan's verse provided by Xuedou and given comments by Yuanwu. Although Tianqi's streamlined text does not include Xuedou's phrases, he offers his own caps for three of the four lines. To summarize, Xuedou says of line one, "One hand doesn't make a sound" (獨掌不浪鳴), and Tianqi writes, "Without intention, both sides are mysteriously linked" (雖不存意. 暗拈二邊). Of line two Xuedou says, "A walking staff is found in the forest" (山形拄杖子), and Tianqi offers, "A full effort to carry on" (盡力傍通). Of line three Xuedou writes, "The sea is calm and rivers are clear" (海晏河清). Of the final line, "He's made the point" (拈了也), and Tianqi comments, "This remark has long been useful for not descending into the role of guest yet not remaining as host" (註上良久. 不墮偏方. 不居正位).

Tianqi's final note says, "Hitting the target points clearly to not falling into lower status" (當央直示. 旨明不落階級), and his wrapping phrase reads, "There's one point raised yet another comment made" (一呈一註).

Verse: A "one-piece pagoda," so difficult to discern,

(Y: Your eyes can't see it. Blind! 非眼可見. 瞎)

(T: No, it's not difficult. Can't you see it already? 實際不受. 何有其見)

A dragon's coils don't thrive in calm waters.

(T: Huizhong and Danyuan are stuck in stagnant waters. Don't be troubled by emotions, but instead hold them up, 國師躭源皆是死水. 不恐逐生情. 故乃拈之)

As layers cascade, shadows keep gathering,

(Y: Your entire body's an eye, yet you always fall seven or eight times. Two by two, three by three. walking the old road; turn left and then right, and you'll get there, 通身是眼. 落七落八. 兩兩三三舊路行. 左轉右轉隨後來)

As seen for hundreds of thousands of years.

(T: It's not only for this moment but is displayed forever, 非但此時. 今古榜樣)

無縫塔. 見還難 / 澄潭不許蒼龍蟠 / 層落落. 影團團 / 千古萬古與人看.

Comments: The main interpretative issue concerns the question of whether the one-piece pagoda should be considered real and visible, which is usually denied as a sign of ignorance, or represents a visionary mode, as Tianqi implies. Or is the seamless monument something purely symbolic without any intention of being taken seriously, as suggested by Yuanwu's comment that somehow seems ambiguous enough to also indicate the flip side?

Whereas Danyuan's verse celebrates the truth of buddha-nature that prevails whether anyone recognizes it or not, Xuedou emphasizes the importance of valuing engagement with true reality in terms of, rather than by escaping, the turmoil and turbulence of everyday life encompassing flowing levels of activity. This is symbolized by the notion that dragons symbolically function more productively in stormy seas than in calm waters, which are unchallenging and thus uninspiring. Tianqi says ironically that both the National Teacher and Danyuan seem trapped in inactive streams.

Ode 19

Gutei's "Just Raise One Finger" 俱胝只竪一指

Case: Yuanwu's introduction begins by asking how to understand reality "even before a speck of dust arises or a single flower blooms" (塵未舉花未開時), and he replies, "It's like cutting a fabric: cut one thread and the whole fabric is severed. Or it's like dyeing a fabric: dye one thread and the whole fabric becomes colored. Right now, you must eliminate all entanglements"

(如斬一緉絲. 一斬一切斬. 如染一緉絲. 一染一切染. 只如今便將葛藤截斷). Therefore, one element effects all, although clinging to the notion of unity becomes an obstacle.

According to the case, "No matter what master Gutei's asked" (俱胝和尚凡有所問), the answer is always the same: "Just raise one finger" (只竪一指). The brief dialogue presented by Xuedou represents a drastically abbreviated version of a much longer narrative about the master Gutei (俱胝, fl. eighth century), which is told in Yuanwu's prose commentary and in case 3 of *Wumen's Barrier*.

According to the complex backstory featuring mythical as well as performative elements, when Gutei first practices meditation as a mountain hermit, a mysterious woman approaches and confounds him with a series of questions and gestures. Since he is at a loss for words, she refuses to stay the night in his hut but tells him she foresees that he will soon find his true spiritual mentor, a bodhisattva in the flesh. A few days later, the teacher Tianlong (天龍) appears and teaches Gutei one-finger Chan as a technique from which he never wavered. One day long after he had established his own community of followers, Gutei's attendant is asked by a guest visiting the temple about the master's pedagogical method and, when the lad holds up a finger, Gutei is enraged and cuts it off. As the attendant runs away screaming in pain, he looks back and Gutei once again raises his digit. The disciple instantaneously attains a full experience of enlightenment.

Yuanwu says of Gutei's act of cutting, "This old fellow calmly rips out the tongues of everyone in the world. When it's hot, all heaven and earth are hot; and when it's cold, all heaven and earth are cold" (這老漢也要坐斷天下人舌頭. 熱則普天普地熱. 寒則普天普地寒). Tianqi's capping phrase says, "He hits the mark" (當央直示).

Tianqi's concluding note reads, "Facing one another points clearly to the great function manifest here and now" (覿面相呈. 旨明大用現前); and his wrapping phrase is, "All things are one thing" (一切即一).

Verse: I deeply appreciate old Gutei for his appropriate and accessible teaching,

(Y: Lepers leading one another on the pathway to knowledge can't avoid using a particular device in a specific situation, 癩兒牽伴. 同道方知. 不免是一機一境)

Who else is like him in this vast universe?

(T: He never faltered throughout his life, 一生不改)

Cast a piece of driftwood into the ocean,
And a blind turtle will find it amid the nighttime waves.

> (Y: I'd drive them towards a realm where there's no buddha, 趕向無佛世界)
>
> (T: After following the precepts there's no need to seek great enlightenment; when learning together, just raising one finger is enough. As for talking of blind turtles, some of our colleagues may find that image useless, 戒勉後來不求大悟. 若學俱胝只去竪指. 但接盲龜. 此點有體無用之輩)

對揚深愛老俱胝 / 宇宙空來更有誰 / 曾向滄溟下浮木 / 夜濤相共接盲龜.

Comments: Yuanwu opens his prose commentary by saying "Xuedou masters the rules of literary discourse in every possible way, which he routinely uses to construct verses on unusual and specially selected gong'an cases by combining criticism with admiration" (雪竇會四六文章. 七通八達. 凡是誵訛奇特公案. 當面提持). Xuedou greatly appreciates Gutei, an otherwise little-known Chan figure, for consistently using one teaching technique in all circumstances.

The second half of the verse evokes an analogy that derives from a *Lotus Sūtra* passage suggesting that the opportunity to hear the dharma being preached, and thereby to attain enlightenment, is as rare as the case of a sightless turtle that comes to the surface of the water just as a piece of driftwood with a small hole passes by, so the animal clings to the object and gets carried along to dry land. Despite Xuedou's apparently sardonic implication that this approach can save the masses, both Yuanwu and Tianqi contradict the need for an external power to provide a chance for salvation. Instead, they emphasize the typical Chan view that everyone has the capacity to heed the one-finger teaching and discover a spiritual realm where no distinction is made between the knowledge of a buddha and that of ordinary people.

Ode 20A and B

Longya's "Why Did Bodhidharma Come from the West?" 龍牙祖師西來意

Case: For this case that includes two Xuedou verses, Yuanwu introduces a Chan adept as one who "overturns the great ocean, kicks over Mount Sumeru, scatters the white clouds with one shout, and smashes through empty space. Using a single device for each situation, he cuts off the tongues of everyone in the world, so there's no particular place for him to be found" (或有箇漢出來掀翻大海. 踢倒須彌. 喝散白雲. 打破虛空. 直下向一機一境. 坐斷天下人舌頭. 無爾近傍處).

The dialogue explores whether Longya (龍牙, 835–923), a follower of Dongshan Liangjie who established the Caodong school, is capable of fulfilling the adept's role. Longya encounters both Cuiwei (翠微, fl. ninth century), an otherwise obscure disciple of Danxia (丹霞, 739–824), and Linji, the founder of the school named after him. This account is also included in section 22 of Linji's recorded sayings, where there is a reverse order for the sequence of meetings plus a concluding anecdote.

The two encounters follow the same pattern: Longya poses a question about Bodhidharma coming from the west and Cuiwei asks him "to pass the meditation board, and then hits Longya with it" (與我過禪板來. 微接得便打), whereas Linji asks for the cushion (蒲團) before striking him. In both instances, Longya receives the reprimand and responds, "This shows the first patriarch's arrival in China has no meaning" (要且. 無祖師西來意).

In prose commentary, Yuanwu, who cites a passage by Xuedou from a different text supporting his view, maintains that Longya's reaction was overly passive and that a genuine Linji-school follower or a disciple of Deshan would have, instead, revealed their own dynamism in preempting the two teachers by, for example, tossing the objects at those requesting them. Yuanwu's capping phrase on Longya's statement that there is no meaning reads, "This fellow's talk falls into the secondary level since he draws his bow after the thief has fled" (這漢話在第二頭. 賊過後張弓). On the same remark made to Linji he says, "He makes his living inside the ghost cave while in flames, but thinks he's gained the advantage" (灼然在鬼窟裏作活計. 將謂得便宜).

Tianqi says of Cuiwei striking Longya, "The great function is fully expressed" (大用全提), of Longya's statement, "He accepts the abuse, but doesn't get the point since the other teacher asserts his will without needing any words" (空受痛棒. 不領大旨. 強作主宰. 反言無意), and of the exchange with Linji, "It's the same move as before" (行德同前). Tianqi's concluding note reads, "A radiant source points clearly to the great function" (明宗. 旨明大用); and the wrapping phrase says, "The truth of living is fully expressed" (正令全提).

Ode A: On Dragon Tusk (Longya) Mountain, there's a dragon without an eye,

When has stagnant water ever been conducive to the ancient teachings?
If you can't make use of your meditation board and cushion,
Just hand these over to Mr. Lu (Xuedou)!

(Y: But they won't be given since a lacquer bucket wouldn't consider doing that, 也則分付不著. 漆桶莫作這般見解)

(T: Xuedou here is referring to himself. Whether or not there's any meaning to the first patriarch's arrival, for now the matter's swept away, 雪竇自言. 若道無有祖意. 當時直要打出祖意)

龍牙山裏龍無眼 / 死水何曾振古風 / 禪板蒲團不能用 / 只應分付與盧公.

Xuedou then says, "I haven't exhausted the topic, so here's another verse" 師拈云. 這老漢也未勦絕. 復成頌曰 (T: Worried about not making himself clear, he versifies again, 恐逐境奔. 故再呈頌).

Ode B: Why would I ever need these implements, anyway?
Everyday practice is effective without trying to succeed the patriarchal lamp.

(Y: He's a man in the weeds who goes to sit beneath a black mountain and has fallen into a ghost cave, 草裏漢. 打入黑山下坐. 落在鬼窟裏去也)

The evening clouds haven't yet gathered,
Distant mountains stretch endlessly with layer upon layer of azure.

(T: Fearful of loneliness, he points to everyday existence, 恐墮孤危. 故指平實)

盧公付了亦何憑 / 坐倚休將繼祖燈 / 堪對暮雲歸未合 / 遠山無限碧層層.

Comments: The first verse, as in Ode 18, stresses that a dragon must be active, not in still water, but amid vast swells or billows of frothy waves that reach up to overflow the skies. Since Longya seems docile, he was reprimanded by his counterparts for not knowing how to respond. Xuedou evokes his own nickname, Mr. Lu (盧公), which Tianqi references and Yuanwu documents in his prose commentary, in asking for these materials.

The reason Xuedou writes a second verse is to disclaim that the previous poem's final demand was self-centered; there should be no implication of ambition or attachment underlying his request. Rather, the final couplet shows he seeks to point beyond human perceptions or interactions, including those involving Chan patriarchs, to the simple yet profound beauty of the natural surroundings as a mirror and model for attaining an authentic level of realization.

Ode 21

Zhimen's "Lotus Flower" 智門蓮花

Case: According to Yuanwu's prefatory remarks concerning the master Zhimen, "Setting up the banner of the dharma and establishing an essential teaching is like adding flowers to brocade" (建法幢立宗旨. 錦上鋪花.). This image refers to an adept offering his assembly a unique style of instruction that may seem redundant but is a meaningful embellishment of standard fare. Yuanwu furthermore advises learners, "When you lay down your load there's a feeling of supreme peace. If you can discern the significance of words, when shown one corner of a room you'll find the other three" (脫籠頭卸角馱. 太平時節. 或若辨得格外句. 舉一明三).

Also featured in case 93 (90), Zhimen was Xuedou's teacher who hailed from Zhejiang province and traveled to western Sichuan province to attain enlightenment under Xianglin in the Yunmen lineage, before returning east and settling at a monastery in the town of Suzhou in Jiangsu province, later led by Xuedou for a time. Zhimen is the most recent Chan teacher cited in the *Odes*. In the dialogue a monk asks, "What's a lotus flower that hasn't emerged from the water?" (蓮花未出水時如何), and the master replies, "A lotus flower" (蓮花). The novice then asks, "What about after it's emerged?" (出水後如何), and Zhimen says, "Lotus leaves" (荷葉).

Yuanwu is skeptical of the inquirer, who "is washing a lump of dirt in the mud" (泥裏洗土塊) while "making his living in a demon's cave" (鬼窟裏作活計), whereas Zhimen's responses point to the basic distinction between source and manifestations, "like counting one, two, three, four, five, six, seven, and thus stumping everyone in the world" (一二三四五六七. 疑殺天下人). Also, Yuanwu says Zhimen "makes everyone die from laughter" (笑殺天下人).

Tianqi remarks of the queries, "These derive from the bright empty eon" (問是借事用明空劫), and of Zhimen's replies, "Directly revealing the radiant source" (直截明宗). Tianqi's final note reads, "Hitting the mark points clearly to there being no fixed path" (當央直指. 旨明無有意路); and his wrapping phrase says, "The question is just this, but the answer is not 'not that'" (問有彼此. 答無是非).

Verse: "A lotus flower" and "lotus leaf" are his responses,

(Y: Grandmotherly kindness! The gong'an is revealed clearly and its purpose is displayed plainly, 老婆心切. 見成公案. 文彩已彰)

Is there any difference between flowers emerging from water and those still submerged?

(T: What emerges and what's submerged? If you can discern this, then your knowledge won't be divided into two opposite parts, 出水何如. 未出何如. 若乃見得. 方知不在兩頭)

North or south of the river, you can question any venerable teacher,
Which leads only to one foxlike doubt after another.

(Y: Bury them all together in one hole, as you (Xuedou) are the one who doubts. Since you can't avoid endlessly feeling doubt, I'll strike saying, "Do you understand?" 一坑埋却. 自是爾疑. 不免疑情未息. 打云. 會麼)

(T: If you don't receive an effective teaching, just ask about the submerged flower emerging from water. When you get the point, all doubts will be transformed, 若不領旨. 只去出水未出上問. 轉生其疑. 何時得了)

蓮花荷葉報君知 / 出水何如未出時 / 江北江南問王老 / 一狐疑了一狐疑.

Comments: In the first couplet, Xuedou praises the results of the dialogue, as he does in numerous other instances. The exchange between Zhimen and an anonymous novice shows that, although there is no fundamental distinction between the immersed flower and its exposed leaves, the former can be considered to represent original truth and the latter its overt appearances. Yuanwu and Tianqi both suggest that the verse at this point is perfectly clear.

The final lines turn to the twofold theme of undergoing feelings of doubt which, if taken superficially, may seem like a sign of instability and indecisiveness in regard to finding an authentic mentor; the name, literally "Old Wang" (王老), serves as a placeholder for any random teacher consulted during a trainee's itinerant travels to countryside temples. However, if experienced on a deeper level, doubting reflects a profound encounter with the emptiness of all conceptualizations.

Yuanwu says in his prose commentary about taking risks, "It's like wild foxes full of doubt walking on an icy river by listening for the sound of rushing water and, if they don't hear anything, they think they can cross. But if students endure 'one foxlike doubt after another,' how will they ever be able to attain peace and tranquility?" (如野狐多疑. 氷凌上行. 以聽水聲. 若不鳴方可過河. 參學人若一狐疑了一狐疑. 幾時得平穩去).

Ode 22

Xuefeng's "Turtle-Nosed Snake" 雪峰鼈鼻蛇

Case: Yuanwu's preface notes, "Everyone faces a crossroad before trying to construct a thousand-foot tower" (人人坐斷要津. 箇箇壁立千仞). This passage highlights how the case involves the way three masters in Xuefeng's lineage, including Changqing and Yunmen (featured together in case 8) in addition to Xuansha (玄沙, 835–908), react to an announcement that Xuefeng makes while giving a lecture to his assembly in a hall of his secluded temple.

Xuefeng tells his followers, "South of the mountain, there's a turtle-nosed snake. All of you need to go and take a good look" (南山有條鼈鼻蛇. 汝等諸人切須好看). The multifaceted image of the venomous serpent represents temptations and attachments that detract from the quest for enlightenment, or the challenges experienced by a dedicated yet still deluded disciple who faces the demands of an unrelenting mentor. Or, more positively, it represents overcoming ego by enduring what is known in comparative mysticism as the "dark night of the soul" and is sometimes referred to in Chan as dealing with the great doubt-block through a spiritual death that is a prelude to symbolic rebirth.

Changqing says after the sermon, "Today in the dharma hall a great many people are losing their lives" (今日堂中大有人喪身失). Xuansha, another prominent disciple of Xuefeng who started as an illiterate fisherman before becoming a monk, remarks, "Why even refer to the south side of the mountain?" (用南山作麼). Also, "Yunmen tosses down his staff right in front of Xuefeng and acts like he's frightened" (雲門以拄杖攛向雪峰面前作怕勢).

Yuanwu comments ironically on Xuefeng's opening saying, "If you see something strange as not strange, its strangeness dissolves on its own. In any case, it's quite strange, thus causing people to doubt" (見怪不怪. 其怪自壞.

大小大怪事. 不妨令人疑着). Of Yunmen's gesture Tianqi writes, "With one call and one response, authority and authenticity become intertwined" (一呼一遣. 權實並行).

Tianqi's final note says, "A fishing pole that helps people points clearly to adepts recognizing one another" (垂釣為人. 旨明作家相見); and the wrapping phrase reads, "Father and son sing harmoniously together" (父子唱和).

Verse: Elephant Bone Cliff (Mount Xuefeng) is so high that no one reaches it,
But those that do get there must be able to handle snakes.
(Y: A spirit recognizes a spirit, like a thief knowing a thief, 是精識精是賊識賊)
(T: His method is unobstructed, so even if the peak were ten thousand fathoms high he wouldn't be thwarted, 機峻無敵. 若萬仞崖. 須是作者方無阻隔)
Master Leng (Changqing) and Master Bei (Xuansha) don't offer much insight,
(Y: Their crimes are listed on the same indictment, but you're letting them go? 一狀領過. 放過一著)
(T: It's good to toss sand, but it's not always appropriate, 慶放沙收. 總不當機)
While so many monks are losing their lives.
Shaoyang (Yunmen) knows how to get deep into the weeds,
(Y: Although there are some benefits, that old fellow has just one eye and can't help but seem a bit devious, 猶較些子. 這老漢只具一隻眼. 老漢不免作伎倆)
But there's no place to find [the snake] to the south, north, east, or west.
Suddenly, he throws down his staff,
Right at the feet of Xuefeng, the snake's mouth opens wide.
Its gaping aperture appears in a flash of lightning,
If you raise your eyebrows, you'll miss it.
(T: The great function is fully displayed without leaving any trace, 須然大用全彰. 箇裏了無蹤跡)
Today the snake abides right here on Ru Peak (Mount Xuedou),
(Y: Today, I, too, have been wounded by its mouth, 山僧今日. 也遭一口)
Those who come hither one after another should skillfully observe.
象骨巖高人不到 / 到者須是弄蛇手 / 稜師備師不奈何 / 喪身失命有多少 / 韶陽知. 重撥草 / 南北東西無處討 / 忽然突出拄杖頭 / 拋對雪峰大

張口 / 大張口兮同閃電 / 剔起眉毛還不見 / 如今藏一乳峰前 / 來者一一看方便.

Follow-up: Xuedou shouts and says, "Look, the snake is beneath your feet!" (師高聲喝云. 看脚下) (Y: His bow is drawn after the thief has fled, 賊過後張弓) (T: Pulling one's nose suddenly reveals the great function, 拽回鼻孔.大用急提).

Comments: Yuanwu says in prose remarks that Xuedou understandably applauds the response by Yunmen, the founding figure of his Chan lineage, but his capping phrases on the twelve-line verse express typical skepticism whereas Tianqi is more admiring of all the interlocutors.

Xuedou evokes several nicknames in referring to the main participants and places, but in the poem's third section written over a century after the dialogue took place, he seeks to relocate the powerful symbolism of the story in terms of the immediacy of his own assembly that was similarly situated on an imposing mountaintop. By supplementing the lengthy verse with a spontaneous interjection, Xuedou exclaims that the snake is present among his group at that very moment and must not be overlooked. This utterance is again appreciated by Tianqi, but playfully scorned by Yuanwu.

Ode 23

Baofu's "Summit of Golden Peak" 保福妙峰頂

Case: Yuanwu makes clear that the main topic is not so much concerned with one of the names for the mythical celestial peak of Mount Sumeru (須彌山), the central component of traditional Buddhist cosmology, as it is with the process of testing the merits of adepts and their followers. He writes, "Jewels are confirmed by fire, gold is tested against stone, a sword must cut through a hair, and water is measured with a pole. For patch-robed monks, just one word, phrase, action, situation, exit, entry, thrust or parry reveals whether a person is deep or shallow, facing forwards or gazing behind" (玉將火試. 金將石試. 劍將毛試. 水將杖試. 至於衲僧門下. 一言一句. 一機一境. 一出一入. 一挨一拶. 要見深淺. 要見向背).

The dialogue once again involves two prominent disciples of Xuefeng. Baofu tests Changqing one day as they wander aimlessly in the mountains (遊山) by proclaiming, "Right here is the summit of Golden (or Marvelous)

Peak!" (這裏便是妙峰頂). His dharma brother responds, "So it is. What a pity!" (是則是. 可惜許). Xuedou interpolates a capping phrase, "These days, who could match what those fellows achieved while roaming the mountains?" (今日共這漢遊山. 圖箇什麼), and he adds while recalling Huangbo's saying in case 11, "I don't say that there'll be no [teachers] hundreds of thousands of years from now, just that there'll be precious few" (百千年後不道無. 只是少). Later Jingqing, on hearing of the original exchange, declares, "If not for Mr. Sun (Baofu), there'd be skulls strewn across these fields" (若不是孫公. 便見髑髏遍野).

Yuanwu caps Changqing's response to Baofu, "If you don't have an iron eye or a brass eyeball, you won't understand how those suffering from the same disease sympathize with one another. These two fellows ought to be buried in the same pit" (若不是鐵眼銅睛幾被惑了. 同病相憐. 兩箇一坑埋却). Of Xuedou's capping phrase he writes, "Inevitably Xuedou cuts others down to size. Still, there're some positive points as he's an observer wielding a sword" (不妨減人斤兩. 猶較些子. 傍人按劍). In prose comments Yuanwu points out that Zhaozhou refused to answer queries about Golden Peak. Yuanwu also recites lines from a verse written by one of his former colleagues during his early days of training: "Where there's no gain and no loss, / No affirmation and no negation, / There it stands" (向無得無失. 無是無非. 處獨露).

Tianqi says of Changqing's remarks, "If you get attached [to the peak], that'll become a major problem" (若執於此. 盡困中途), and of Jingqing's comment on the effectiveness of Baofu's statement, "If you don't have eyes to see this, you'll be disdained" (若不具眼看破. 便被他裁). Tianqi's final note reads, "Displaying dynamic activity that gains followers points clearly to mutual understanding" (呈機探扳. 旨明遞相酬唱); and his wrapping phrase says, "All this brings happiness" (總是心倖).

Verse: The lone summit of Golden Peak is rife with weeds,

(T: The peak's been resplendent from past to present, but these two fellows create entanglements, 直饒妙絕今古. 二人總是葛藤)

This passage seems quite clear, but how many really get the point?

(Y: Or see how to make use of it. No one in the world knows that it's worth about as much as a dried turd, like when someone leads themselves by their nostrils but can't find their own mouth, 用作什麼. 大地沒人知. 乾屎橛堪作何用. 拈得鼻孔失却口)

(T: The instruction is clear, but who gets the point? 指示分明. 你却與誰)

"If not for Mr. Sun (Baofu)'s" insightful remark,
(Y: Don't pay attention to the flying arrow, since he's caught the thief without realizing it, 錯看箭. 著賊了也不知)
Who knows how many skulls there'd have been?
(Y: They won't be able to come back to life, O Worthy, but are as numerous as hemp or millet seeds, 更不再活. 如麻似粟闍黎)
(T: These lines reiterate the case, 拈前公案)
妙峰孤頂草離離 / 拈得分明付與誰 / 不是孫公辯端的 / 髑髏著地幾人知.

Comments: Xuedou purposefully does not stray from or try to embellish the core dialogue, as pointed out in Tianqi's last capping phrase. As with other examples, Xuedou's goal is to bring the significance of the original exchange into the realm of his current teaching. The opening line suggests that all the talk of an ideal cosmic location supposedly removed from any sign of strife causes the manifestations of spiritual deficiency to become so prominent that typical practitioners are not able to perceive the peak.

However, engagement with the so-called weeds of ordinary life is carried out precisely to inspire a realization of transcendence that is inseparable from the realm of conflicts. In the final couplet, Xuedou praises Baofu by evoking Jingqing's remark and implies ominously that his own followers must awaken from their spiritual slumber lest they suffer the grim fate of those failing to grasp the real meaning of Golden Peak as a state of mind attainable here and now.

Ode 24

Liu Tiemo's "Communal Feast at Mount Wutai" 劉鐵磨臺山大會齋

Case: Yuanwu previews the dharma battle between Liu Tiemo (Iron Grindstone Liu), an ordained yet unaffiliated woman practitioner also mentioned briefly by Xuedou in Ode 17, and the master Guishan, who is featured in an encounter with Deshan in case 4. According to Yuanwu, a Chan adept is able to "stand on the summit of the highest peak where demons and non-buddhas can't perceive him, and stride across the bottom of the deepest ocean where even buddha's eye won't catch sight of him" (高高峯頂立. 魔外莫能知. 深深海底行. 佛眼覷不見). However, deficiencies remain in that,

"Even if eyes are like a shooting star and activity is like a flash of lightning, he can't avoid dragging his tail like a spirit tortoise" (直饒眼似流星. 機如掣電. 未免靈龜曳尾). This image, also cited in capping phrases on cases 4 and 47, symbolizes that even after achieving a long life featuring great skills, telltale tracks from one's movements are nevertheless left on the ground.

The cryptic dialogue starts when Liu, an explosive religious figure known for her ability to crush the strongest opponents in a contest of will and figuratively grind them into fine powder, arrives from a nearby hut at the mountain monastery of Guishan in southern Hunan province. In jest he declares, "So you've come, Old Cow!" (老牸牛汝來也). This is an ironic form of praise because Guishan is known for telling followers that he expected to appear after he died in the home of a lay donor as a water buffalo whose flank would be "inscribed with the phrase, Monk Guishan" (潙山僧某甲).

Liu responds by asking, "Teacher, will you be going to a large vegetarian feast being held tomorrow on Mount Wutai?" (來日臺山大會齋. 和尚還去麼), which is a ludicrous inquiry referring to a sacred site located hundreds of miles away in northerly Shansi province where the bodhisattva Mañjuśrī (Wenshu, 文殊) is believed to reside, as highlighted in case 35. Then Guishan lays down on the ground (山放身臥) to show that he has no intention of going, and Liu takes off (磨便出).

Yuanwu caps Liu's question about going to Wutai, "The arrow is shot, but misses the target. When a drum is struck in China, there's dancing in Korea" (箭不虛發. 大唐打鼓新羅舞). He says of her departure, "She's gone, after seizing the opportunity to act" (過也. 見機而作), and further suggests in prose comments that Liu and Guishan "merge perspectives" (境致) so that "when letting go they both let go, and when holding firm they both hold firm" (放則雙放. 收則雙收).

Tianqi says of Guishan's first utterance, "That's when he takes a plunge" (點他動落今時), and of Liu's question, "She blocks with a paradox that stirs stagnant water" (隔身反點靜沉死水). Of her leaving he writes, "They have a mutual understanding without committing any offense" (回互不犯). Tianqi's final comment reads, "Seizing the opportunity to act points clearly to adepts recognizing one another" (見機而作. 旨明作家相見); and his wrapping phrase says, "Auspicious!" (心倖).

Verse: While riding an armored horse she enters his fortress,

(Y: An adept accustomed to battle, she heads right for the general, who's outside his lair and fortified with the seven traits [of an adept], 慣戰作家. 塞外將軍. 七事隨身)

An imperial edict proclaims all six realms are at peace.
(T: Guishan is like an emperor maintaining peace in his land, 山如帝令. 天下太平)
Holding a golden whip he questions the returning visitor,
(Y: There's nothing new about two people holding each other up with a single staff, or beckoning one another while going and coming at the same time, 是什麼消息一條拄杖兩人扶. 相招同往又同來)
In the depths of the night, who travels with him along the royal pathway?
(T: In the end, since neither is guest nor host, who can express what they share? 末後二人不坐正偏. 故曰誰共)
曾騎鐵馬入重城 / 勅下傳聞六國清 / 猶握金鞭問歸客 / 夜深誰共御街行.

Comments: The seven traits of a genuine teacher, according to Yuanwu's capping phrase on the first line, mirror qualities attributed to a talented warrior: great capacity and function; wit and eloquence; authentic speech; the sword that kills or brings life; extensive learning; clarity of awareness; and the freedom to come and go unobstructed.

Both Yuanwu and Tianqi agree these two representatives of the Gui-Yang (溈仰, or Guishan-Yangshan, 溈山仰山) school of Chan that flourished during the Tang dynasty are able to interact at the same level, so no one is considered to have bested or lost to their counterpart. This unifying approach, as indicated in line four, evokes a state of clamor-free quietude whereby the lines of battle are removed, so there are no longer rivals in conflict but a pure camaraderie in pursuit of solitary yet mutually reinforcing levels of awareness.

Ode 25

The Hermit of Lotus Flower Peak Holds Up His Staff 蓮花峰庵主拈拄杖

Case: Yuanwu introduces the Hermit of Lotus Flower Peak (蓮花峰庵主), an obscure, unnamed, and undated second-generation follower of Yunmen who taught a small assembly in the vicinity of Mount Wutai without ever leading a full-fledged monastery. He is depicted as someone who realizes, "If activity doesn't break free from convention, it falls into a toxic sea; and if words don't startle the crowd, they remain trapped in vulgarity. But if someone distinguishes black and white in the moment a spark flies from a stone that's struck or decides in a flash of lightning between killing and bringing to life, they'll command all realms and stand firm while facing the edge of a thousand-fathom peak" (機不離位. 墮在毒海. 語不驚群. 陷於流俗. 忽若擊石火裏別緇素. 閃電光中辨殺活. 可以坐斷十方. 壁立千仞).

In the dialogue, while giving a lecture to his followers the Hermit raises his staff (拈拄杖示眾) and asks, "In the old days, if people reached [enlightenment], why did they choose not to abide there?" (古人到這裏. 為甚不肯). When "the assembly remains silent, the Hermit offers a response on their behalf" (眾無語自代): "Because they didn't benefit in the course of their daily lives" (為他途路不得力). Then he asks, "What do you think?" (畢竟如何) and again provides the answer, "Holding a staff across my shoulder, I don't look back at others but head straightaway into myriad peaks" (楖栗橫擔不顧人. 直入千峰萬峰去).

Yuanwu caps the reference to the Hermit by saying, "See how he has an eye on his forehead, but these days people get lost in a nest of complications" (看. 頂門上具一隻眼. 也是時人窠窟). Of the Hermit's final proclamation Yuanwu writes, "Yet, he deserves thirty blows for carrying a board on his shoulder. When you can see the jowls on his cheeks from behind, don't follow after him" (也好與三十棒. 只為他擔板. 腦後見腮. 莫與往來).

Tianqi's capping phrase for the Hermit's initial question reads, "If you see into the original source, why wouldn't you stay there?" (透得本地. 因何不住), and for the second query, "First you summon them and then you judge them" (徵前審後). Tianqi's final note says, "Fishing with a pole to help people points clearly to unceasing great efforts" (垂釣為人. 旨明大功不宰); his wrapping phrase reads, "He transforms efforts reflected in activities" (轉功就位).

Verse: When dust or sand troubles his eyes and dirt blocks his ears,

(Y: Hindered by three hundred blots, is there any limit to the chaos and confusion this causes? There're others who act that way, 懞憧三百檐. 鶻鶻突突有什麼限. 更有恁麼漢)

The Hermit doesn't dwell among the myriad peaks.

(T: He transforms through functions reflected in activities, whereas Xuedou transforms through activities that reflect functions—that's why it's said that a sage doesn't stand still, 菴主轉功就位. 雪竇轉位就功. 故曰不住)

Falling flowers and flowing streams are vast,

(Y: What a beautiful setting! If you act in a lightning flash without vainly lingering in deliberations, you'll look left to see a thousand beings and right to see ten thousand, 好箇消息. 閃電之機. 徒勞佇思. 左顧千生右顧萬)

Just raise your eyebrows: Where's he gone?

(T: When it's disclosed that dust covers everything each moment, without past or present, where is there to go? 塵塵獨露. 剎剎全彰. 無古無今. 更向何去)

眼裏塵沙耳裏土 / 千峯萬峯不肯住 / 落花流水太茫茫 / 剔起眉毛何處去.

Comments: Xuedou highlights how the dialogue dwells on the conundrum involving the apparent need for an adept to flee from the dusty world in relation to the futility of becoming so reclusive that he seems escapist and, thereby, lacking genuine realization. As Yuanwu's capping phrase on the first line shows, this difficult choice leads to multiple misperceptions and mistakes symbolized by a term for disorder (literally, "flapping falcons" 鶻鶻突突) used frequently in Chinese lore. The solution is to remain free from static outlooks and flexible enough to understand there is fundamentally no difference between transcendence and immanence, as suggested by Tianqi's capping phrases.

In prose comments Yuanwu cites a remark by Xuedou from his recorded sayings on the meaning of the case: "Someone who confronts any situation without being deceived is hard to find. He shatters high peaks and dissolves dark mysteries, breaking open double barriers despite not following the same pattern of others" (誰當機舉不賺. 亦還希. 摧殘峭峻銷鑠玄微. 重關曾巨闢. 作者未同歸). Xuedou completes this passage by interjecting self-referential phrasing that resembles the final couplet of verse 20A, "Old Lu (Xuedou) doesn't know which way he's going when he follows white clouds and flowing streams" (盧老不知何處去. 白雲流水共依依).

Ode 26

Baizhang's "Most Extraordinary Matter"百丈奇特事

Case: The dialogue for this gong'an involves an anonymous monk questioning Baizhang Huaihai (百丈懷海, 749–814), one of numerous prominent followers of Mazu who is featured in five cases in Xuedou's *Odes*. Baizhang was in turn the teacher of Huangbo and Guishan and, thus, the progenitor of both the Linji and Gui-Yang schools, two of the five houses (五家宗派, *wujia zongpai*) of Chan that started to become prominent during the Tang dynasty and greatly impacted Song-dynasty literature.

The novice asks, "What's the most extraordinary matter?" (百丈奇特事), and Baizhang responds, "Sitting alone atop Daxiong Peak" (獨坐大雄峯), a steep mountain located outside his monastery in Jiangxi province where he apparently retreated for solitary periods of intensive meditation. Whereas Baizhang suggests that his special activity involves spending contemplative time removed from the temple as a common training technique for Chan abbots, some later teachers reversed this implication by referring to internal practices, such as imbibing tea and rice in the refectory, raising the staff in the meditation hall, or giving sermons in the dharma hall. To conclude, the monk bows (僧禮拜) on hearing the reply, but Baizhang strikes him (丈便打).

Yuanwu writes in prose commentary that Baizhang is one who "faces all situations with an eye that doesn't flinch from danger or death" (臨機具眼. 不顧危亡). Of the novice's query he caps, "There's a resonance in his words and dynamic activity in his phrases. He tries to confound people but, although this monk has eyes, he doesn't understand what he sees" (言中有響. 句裏呈機. 驚殺人. 有眼不曾見). Regarding Baizhang smacking the inquirer Yuanwu offers, "He's an adept of our school, so why doesn't he speak eloquently? But this verdict isn't enacted in vain" (作家宗師. 何故來言不豊. 令不虛行).

Tianqi says of the monk's query, "Master of discernment" (辨主), and of Baizhang's reply, "He bears the full load" (全身擔荷). Of the novice's prostration he writes, "The question is a sign of gratitude for Baizhang's eye, and the bow shows his respect" (一謝具眼. 二點獨尊), and of the teacher's final slap, "This cuts him off twice" (正令雙截). Tianqi's final note reads, "Dynamic activity points clearly to the great function" (呈機.旨明大用); and his wrapping phrase says, "Everything's balanced in his hands" (權衡在手).

Verse: A colt of the heavenly horse (Mazu) gallops into the realm of the patriarchs,

(Y: Someone like Baizhang is born once in five hundred years. He's one or a half among myriad people, a loyal son continuing the efforts of his father, 五百年一間生. 千人萬人中有一箇半箇. 子承父業)

(T: He practices his method like an unfettered steed, 法中自在. 如駒絕絆)

Yet [Baizhang's] approach to letting go and gathering up is distinct.

(T: To capture or let go, to kill or give life: how to determine which action is taken? 擒縱殺活. 豈定一機)

In a flash of lightning or shooting sparks, he adapts to shifting circumstances,

What a laughingstock it was for [the monk] to try to grab this tiger's whiskers!

(Y: He deserves thirty blows. To gain a great reward, one must be a fearless person who can't avoid losing his life. I leave it to you, O Worthy, to take action, 好與三十棒. 重賞之下必有勇夫. 不免喪身失命. 放過闍黎一著)

(T: The monk ought to see he's powerless when Baizhang acts quickly with the ability of a sharp blade, 僧須具見. 不料其力. 丈機迅速. 善敢當鋒)

祖域交馳天馬駒 / 化門舒卷不同途 / 電光石火存機變 / 堪笑人來捋虎鬚.

Comments: The verse opens with a wordplay that also appears in Ode 75 (73 in the *Blue Cliff Record*), based on Mazu's name literally meaning "horse" (馬, *ma*) to imply that Baizhang carries on his teacher's legacy. Xuedou endorses Baihzang's approach to teaching but notes it is different from his mentor's method in terms of the extent to which they either hold firm or release their students.

According to Yuanwu's prose comments, however, "Sometimes letting go isn't present in holding firm, sometimes holding firm isn't present in letting go, and sometimes both letting go and holding firm aren't present. Hence the saying, 'On the same path, but not in the same groove.' In this verse, Baizhang seems to be crawling along on his hands and feet" (有時舒不在卷處. 有時卷不在舒處. 有時卷舒俱不在. 所以道同塗不同轍. 此頌百丈有這般手脚).

Although the query posed by the novice to Baizhang is worthwhile, does it demonstrate his own level of realization? For both Yuanwu and Tianqi, the monk falls short of expressing himself as a genuine practitioner, but their capping phrases implicitly present a challenge to readers who must decide whether and how they themselves will be able to attain spiritual insight.

Ode 27

Yunmen's "Objects Reveal the Golden Breeze" 雲門體露金風

Case: Yuanwu explains the remarkable capacity of Yunmen, an authentic Chan adept who continually modifies and adapts his teaching method to specific situations so that "If asked one question, he gives ten answers. Show him one corner, and he finds the other three. Seeing a rabbit, he immediately releases the falcon. He starts a fire by relying on wind. He doesn't spare raising his eyebrows, even when entering a tiger's lair" (問一答十. 舉一明三. 見兔放鷹. 因風吹火. 不惜眉毛則且置. 只如入虎穴時). That is, each teaching opportunity is unique and demands that the teacher offers food for those who are hungry and drink for the thirsty, while acting appropriately either gentle or strict.

According to the dialogue a monk asks, "What about when trees wither and leaves fall" (樹凋葉落時如), and Yunmen responds, "Objects reveal the golden breeze" (體露金風).

Of the monk's question, Yuanwu writes, "What season are we in? When a home's wrecked people die, and when people die their home's wrecked" (是什麼時節. 家破人亡. 人亡家破). Of the teacher's reply he says, "He holds up the sky, leans on the earth, and cuts through iron nails and shears. Uncovered and unspoiled, he's free of contamination and walks peacefully below a clear sky" (撐天拄地. 斬釘截鐵. 淨裸裸赤灑灑. 平步青霄).

Tianqi comments on the query, as in cases 49 and 56, "He borrows from others to show the solution" (借事呈解), and on Yunmen's answer, "It takes him just a moment to make this great effort" (就機一點. 拈他大功). Tianqi's final note says, "Seizing the opportunity to act points clearly to settling the matter forever" (見機而作. 旨明就身打劫); and his wrapping phrase is, "He shows how to gain insight by seeing" (以見遣見).

Verse: The question stems from the source, and so does the answer.
(Y: How could these be distinct? Yunmen is like a bell waiting to be struck, but his efforts aren't wasted, 豈有兩般. 如鐘待扣. 功不浪施)
(T: Host and guest meet one another, 主賓相符)
Three phrases can be discerned in an arrowpoint flying in the air.
(Y: First, middle, and last. Which phrase does his answer use? You must start by understanding Yunmen's three phrases, 上中下. 如今是第幾句. 須是向三句外薦取始得)

(T: But just observing three phrases is like shooting without a target, 三句外看. 射空無敵)

Cold gusts of wind are howling over the great plain,
Misty rains fall gently from the open sky.
Haven't you heard? The master sat at Shaolin temple for so long that he never returned.

(Y: Not one to be detained by lifeless people, generals chased him to the Yellow River, 更有不唧留漢. 帶累殺人. 黃河頭上. 瀉將過來)

Staying calm among all those gathered on Bear Ears Peak.

(T: Concerned with truth, he points to wall-gazing meditation as a path strewn with withered trees and fallen leaves, all objects revealing the golden breeze, 恐落平實故指面壁. 且道是樹凋葉落. 是體露金風)

問既有宗. 答亦攸同 / 三句可辨. 一鏃遼空 / 大野兮凉飈颯颯 / 長天兮疎雨濛濛 / 君不見. 少林久坐未歸客 / 靜依熊耳一叢叢.

Comments: Although Xuedou praises Yunmen's teaching methods in the first couplet, he also indicates that the dialogue was not a matter whereby the anonymous inquirer made a fool of himself by disclosing deficiencies. Rather, both student and teacher, and question and answer, are aligned in terms of deriving from the same wellspring of truth that manifests in diverse ways. Therefore, each utterance by Yunmen is to be understood in terms of three phrases (三句) or discernible levels of meaning that include heaven and earth conjoining, or the unity of query and response; following the waves, or adjusting to the needs of the student; and cutting off complications through radical rhetorical devices, such as paradox, tautology, or silence.

In the second couplet Xuedou turns to natural imagery that evokes late autumn approaching wintertime, when all trees except evergreens have faded and shed leaves. This symbolizes spiritual death, such that the demise of ego and accompanying attachments gives birth to endless possibilities for renewal. As indicated by Tianqi's previous capping phrase, since query and response are fully entwined, that state stands beyond dichotomies of now and then, or living and dying.

According to Tenkei, "In the last couplet the poet refers to the eternally unchanging yet fully active existence of Bodhidharma, who neither comes nor goes. He's lain in his coffin on Shaolin's twin-peaked mountain, which resembles the ears of a large bear, even prior to the beginning of time, but Xuedou urges everyone to open their eyes now to see this."

Ode 28

Nanquan's "Not Mind, Not Buddha, Not Things" 南泉不是心不是佛不是物

Case: This dialogue involves two dharma brothers who trained under Mazu: Nanquan (南泉, 749–835), the mentor of Zhaozhou who is featured in six gong'an in the *Odes*; and his dharma brother Baizhang Weizheng (百丈惟政 or Baizhang Niepan, 百丈涅槃, d. 828), an obscure teacher distinct from his famous namesake, Baizhang Huihai, an illustrious successor to Mazu's lineage. The core of the exchange closely resembles case 27 in *Wumen's Barrier*, in which Nanquan is questioned by an anonymous monk.

Here, Nanquan goes to "study" (參) with "teacher Baizhang" (和尚百丈). Although they are peers, the use of the honorific term suggests that Nanquan considers Baizhang a senior colleague. Baizhang asks, "Is there any teaching that the great sages haven't preached?" (從上諸聖還有不為人說底法麼), and Nanquan says, "Yes" (有). When Baizhang requests an explanation, Nanquan proclaims, "Not mind, not buddha, not things" (不是心. 不是佛. 不是物).

This is followed by an intricate conversation highlighting the significance of the character for preaching (說), which can also mean speaking, discussing, and so on in a nonreligious sense. First, Baizhang says, "You've just preached" (說了也) and, when asked by Nanquan what he thinks, Baizhang says, "I'm not someone with great wisdom, so how can I tell whether I've preached or not?" (我又不是善知識. 爭知有說不說). Nanquan admits, "I don't understand" (某甲不會), and Baizhang concludes ironically, "I've preached enough for you" (太煞與汝說了).

Yuanwu's capping phrases are critical of Baizhang, whose questions "compound error upon error" (將錯就錯) and whose final remark "adds frost to snow, showing he has a dragon's head but a snake's tail" (雪上加霜. 龍頭蛇尾作什麼). Conversely, Nanquan "demonstrates an auspicious ability to turn things around. When there's long, his approach is long; when there's short, his approach is short—he fits whatever scope is manifested" (賴有轉身處. 與長即長. 與短即短. 現長則就).

Tianqi, however, supports Baizhang's response, "You've just preached," which he says "makes the point unhurriedly" (點不疾流), in addition to the teacher's last comment that indicates, "He's already exhausted the matter, so why is there any need for another question?" (先已盡情. 何必重問).

Of Nanquan's reply Tianqi writes, "He sees the opportunity is elusive, so he scrambles to find it" (見機嚴密. 更探其的).

Tianqi's concluding note reads, "Fishing in deep waters with a pole in his hands points clearly to settling oneself for eons" (深竿在手. 旨明就身打劫); and his wrapping phrase is, "He's all dried up!" (乾出其身). These remarks refer to Baizhang and Nanquan, respectively.

Verse: Buddhas and patriarchs never tried to rescue people,
(Y: Every one of them protects his turf. If there're standards, then live by the standards. But if you hold on to just a single word in your mind, you'll go to hell as fast as an arrow, 各自守疆界. 有條攀條. 記得箇元字脚在心. 入地獄如箭)
But patch-robed monks from present and past compete with one another.
A bright mirror sitting on its stand reflects a full range of images,
One by one, they face south toward the Big Dipper [in the north].
(Y: Do you see how I stride into the buddha hall but leave through the mountain gate? In Korea they've entered the dharma hall, but in China they haven't yet beaten the drum, 還見老僧騎佛殿出山門麼. 新羅國裏曾上堂. 大唐國裏未打鼓)
Its handle hangs down, but there's no place to grasp it,
(T: Since the meaning is right in front of you, why inquire further? 當面直註. 何又更尋)
You may grip your own nostrils but lose track of your mouth.
(T: If you examine these words, it means that when you attend to what's in front you, you lose sight of what's behind; when you attend to what's behind you, you lose sight of what's in front, 若逐其句. 顧前失後. 顧後失前)
祖佛從來不為人 / 衲僧今古競頭走 / 明鏡當臺列象殊 / 一一面南看北斗 / 斗(半)柄垂無處討 / 拈得鼻孔失却口.

Comments: Xuedou's verse enhances the sense of ambiguity concerning which of the two adepts prevails in their complex interaction. The first two lines, along with Yuanwu's capping phrase, suggest that some Chan adepts promote their own way of teaching even though, in the end, words are meaningless. The second couplet evokes a magnificent paradoxical image of mirrors facing south to reflect a northerly constellation, as Xuedou prods his audience not to assume that appropriate teachings are readily available. In Tianqi's version, the first character of the fifth line is "half" (半), but this does not alter the meaning and could highlight the poet's conclusion that, as in case 26 of *Women's Barrier*, one truth gained invariably results in another perspective lost. Or, when looking in front, you can't see behind, and vice-versa.

Ode 29

Dasui's "This, Too, Goes Along" 大隋隨他去

Case: Yuanwu introduces the master Dasui (大隋, 878–963), a second-generation disciple of Baizhang and a dharma cousin of both Linji (stemming from Huangbo) and Liu Tiemo (from Guishan), with whom he is said to have studied for a time. After attaining enlightenment Dasui lived in the hollow of a tree for ten years in a remote part of Sichuan province until a monastic assembly was eventually formed around him. For Yuanwu, Dasui is able "to distinguish clearly between host and guest and differentiate insightfully a monk from a lay follower. He acts like a bright mirror in its stand or a bright pearl held in the palm of one's hand, so that when natives or foreigners appear, their sound is apparent and form is revealed" (明辨主賓. 洞分緇素. 直似當臺明鏡. 掌內明珠. 漢現胡來. 聲彰色顯).

The dialogue turns from concrete current circumstances to imagining the cosmic fire that is prophesied in Buddhism to occur at the end of a kalpa that lasts for an incalculable period. An anonymous monk is preoccupied with this topic, which is discussed in the *Benevolent Kings Sūtra* (仁王経) and refers to the formation, abiding, destruction, and emptiness of the universe when true Buddhist practice is no longer obeyed. Mainly concerned with a doubt-block concerning the demise of his own ego, the novice asks Dasui, "When the epochal conflagration consumes everything in the universe, will this, too, be destroyed?" (劫火洞然. 大千俱壞. 未審這箇壞不壞). The master replies, "Destroyed" (壞). The monk inquires, "So this, too, goes along?" (與麼則隨他去), and Dasui responds, "This, too, goes along" (隨他去).

Yuanwu says of Dasui's first response, "An iron hammerhead with no hole is thrown down in front of the monk, who's lost his nostrils. Even before he opens his mouth, he's already thoroughly exposed" (無孔鐵鎚當面擲. 沒却鼻孔. 未開口已前勘破了也); and for the final answer he writes, "The first arrow pricks him, but the second goes deep" (前箭猶輕. 後箭深).

Tianqi writes of the monk's first question, "He probes further the Buddhist teachings" (引教請益), and of Dasui's reply, "Pointing to the radiant source" (直指明宗). Of the second question Tianqi remarks, "Delusion is thereby expressed" (迷宗逐句), and of Dasui's response, "Ditto" (同前).

Tianqi's concluding note says, "The radiant source points clearly to truth" (明宗. 旨明絕待); and his wrapping phrase reads, "Following the current is marvelous" (隨流得妙), which refers to a teaching technique attributed to Yunmen that uses the same character (隨) evoked at the end of the dialogue by Dasui.

Verse: From within the blazing epochal conflagration, a question is raised about the end of time,
(Y: What he's saying is already mistaken, 道什麼. 已是錯了也)
By a patch-robed monk who confronts a double-barreled checkpoint.
(Y: How can you save someone who's been ripped apart from head to toe into a hundred layers on thousands of levels, 坐斷此人. 如何救得. 百匝千重. 也有脚頭脚底)
(T: Destroyed or not destroyed? This question contains two checkpoints, 壞與不壞. 問處兩關)
What a pity that the phrase, "This, too, goes along,"
Causes the monk to wander alone for thousands of miles over countless regions.
(T: The monk has no idea from the outset, so Dasui exposes him. Later, he tried returning to see Touzi, but Xuedou views this as stumbling about in vain, 當時不識. 後過投子點破. 復往大隋. 雪竇點他兩處蹉過)
劫火光中立問端 / 衲僧猶滯兩重關 / 可憐一句隨他語 / 萬里區區獨往還.

Comments: Xuedou draws on two main sources: one is an apocryphal account of the monk during the aftermath of his encounter with Dasui, and the other involves a traditional poetic comment. First, it is reported in a chronology-defying story that the pilgrim left Dasui in bewilderment and eventually came to study with master Touzi Datong (投子大同, 819–914), who was located in southeastern Anhui province. When Touzi told him to return to Dasui, he wandered for years and finally arrived back west, but only after the master had passed away. The poem alluded to is by an obscure Tang-dynasty monk named Jingzun (景遵, n.d.), who wrote, "The phrase, 'This, too, goes along' / Leads the monk to wander across a thousand peaks" (一句隨他語. 千山走衲僧).

Additionally, subsequent commentators have pointed out that a monk named Longji (龍濟, fl. tenth century), a contemporary of Xuedou who was not aware of his remark, is cited in case 30 of the *Record of Serenity* (從容錄, *Congrong lu*), a gong'an collection commentary from 1224 that is similar in structure to the *Blue Cliff Record* but based on poetic comments by Hongzhi Zhengjue (宏智正覺, 1091–1157). Asked the same question by a monk, Longji takes the opposite approach by saying, "Not destroyed" (不壞). When pressed why not, Longji says, "Because it's not destroyed" (為甚不壞). Hongzhi's verse begins, "Destroyed or not destroyed, / This, too, goes along with the vast universe" (壞不壞 / 隨他去也大千界).

Ode 30

Zhaozhou's "Zhenzhou Produces Big Radishes" 趙州鎮州出大蘿蔔頭

Case: This is one of numerous examples of Chan gong'an in which the state of mind of an unnamed inquiring monk is revealed through the quality of his query, to which a true master responds obliquely. During the brief but highly charged dialogical process, the novice's apparent proximity to, or distance from, embodying enlightened behavior is instantly and intuitively judged and dealt with accordingly by the teacher's wisdom, while subsequent commentators assess in disparate ways the relative levels of understanding on the part of the interlocutors.

In the exchange a monk asks Zhaozhou, "Teacher, I've heard that you studied intimately with Nanquan, isn't that so?" (承聞和尚親見南泉是否), which represents a snub regarding the integrity of the master, who was a student of Nanquan for over forty years until the age of sixty. After that, he spent twenty years wandering to various temples before establishing his own assembly at age eighty. Known not for using shouts and sticks, unlike many other Chan mentors, Zhaozhou responds by referring to a nearby village, "Zhen County produces big radishes" (鎮州出大蘿蔔頭). This misdirection through evoking an unrelated concrete situation recalls case 37 of *Wumen's Barrier* in which, when asked about why Bodhidharma came from the west, Zhaozhou answers, "Cypress trees in the courtyard" (庭前栢樹子).

Yuanwu says of the monk's probing query, "Thousands of times of hearing about it are not as good as one time of seeing it for yourself. He comes close to trimming Zhaozhou's eyebrows" (千聞不如一見. 拶眉分八字). Of the response he writes, "He holds up the sky and supports the earth, cuts through iron nails and shears, and his arrow flies past Korea. The monk's jowls can be seen even from behind his head, so don't bother chasing him away or telling him to come for study" (撐天拄地. 斬釘截鐵. 箭過新羅. 腦後見腮. 莫與往來).

Tianqi says the monk is a "Master of testing" (驗主), and that Zhaozhou's reply "points to the radiant source" (直下明宗). His concluding note reads, "Directly revealing points clearly to truth" (直指. 旨明絕待); and his wrapping phrase is, "Eternity's unborn (平常無生).

Verse: "Zhen County produces big radishes,"
Patch-robed monks all over the world cling to this example.
(Y: But it isn't so. Why waste time on idle, long-winded words? 爭奈不恁麼. 誰用這閑言長語)
(T: Patch-robed monks everywhere take this to the extreme, 天下衲僧取此為極)
Since they know only their own past and present,
(Y: [Eyes] half open and half closed, 半開半合)
How can they distinguish between a white swan and a black crow?
(Y: Full capacity means that long is long, and short is short. Those who know this are highly esteemed, 全機穎脫. 長者自長. 短者自短. 識得者貴)
(T: It's obvious there's no difference between past and present, but it's hard to distinguish between black and white, 須然今古無差. 爭奈難分黑白)
[Zhaozhou's] such a thief!
(Y: Nah! It's none other than Xuedou himself who's wearing shackles, 咄.更不是別. 自是擔枷過狀)
Grabbing the nostrils of patch-robed monks.
(Y: He threads them on a ring so as to turn the situation around, 穿過了也. 裂轉)
(T: Let's just say this old thief gets people to use their eyes, 言這老賊善換人眼)
鎮州出大蘿蔔 / 天下衲僧取則 / 只知自古自今 / 爭辯鵠白烏黑 / 賊賊 / 衲僧鼻孔曾拈得.

Comments: In explicating the approach that came to be known as "Big-radish Chan" (蘿蔔頭禪), both commentators take pains to emphasize that Zhaozhou's utterance is only applicable to the particular question asked and is not intended to set up a fixed principle to be promoted in other pedagogical contexts. Yuanwu's prose remarks refer to the master as "a thief stealing in broad daylight" (白拈賊相), and his saying as "flavorless talk that blocks people from speaking further" (無味之談. 塞斷人口).

Moreover, Yuanwu says, "If you're someone who gets it, you'll chew each bite carefully, but if you're someone who doesn't get it, you'll end up swallowing a jujube whole" (若是知有底人. 細嚼來嚥. 若是不知有底人. 一似渾崙吞箇棗), that is, without removing the pit. The capping phrases for the final line show Yuanwu and Tianqi agreeing that Zhaozhou's saying is not necessarily intended to confound followers, since he apparently leads the monk to experience awakening and practice rigorous self-discipline, often symbolized by a nose-ring that necessarily accompanies enlightenment.

Ode 31

Magu "Carries His Staff" 麻谷持錫

Case: Yuanwu speaks warily of the implications of this "roundabout case regarding the ancients" (古人公案. 未免周遮) that features Magu (麻谷, n.d.), along with two of his more senior dharma brothers under the tutelage of Mazu: Changqing and Nanquan. Yuanwu remarks, "One who doesn't move flexibly and isn't cognizant can't avoid entering a wild-fox cave," an image that stands in contrast to how a "dragon abides in water or a tiger rests in a mountain lair" (龍得水似虎靠山). For a true adept, "Letting go causes tiles and rocks to shine, and holding firm makes pure gold lose its luster" (放行也瓦礫生光. 把定也真金失色).

In the dialogue, Magu visits Changqing while carrying his walking staff (錫杖, *xizhang*, Skr. *khakkhara*), a tall stick usually made of wood from a forest, sometimes with a metal head containing either six rings symbolic of the realms of karma or twelve loops indicating the links of dependent origination. The tinkling warns minute living beings that a person is walking by, helps ward off the presence of demons, and reminds the holder of the basic nature of human consciousness.

Magu circles the master's seat three times and shakes his staff on the ground before standing still in a setting that recalls a famous Chan exchange that took place between Yongjia (永嘉, 665–713) and sixth patriarch Huineng. When Changqing says, "That's so" (是是), Xuedou comments "Wrong!" (錯). The scene is repeated when Magu visits Nanquan who says, "That's not so" (是不是), and Xuedou reiterates, "Wrong!" The conversation concludes when Nanquan tells the troubled Magu, "Changqing is right, but it's you who's not right. Getting blown freely by the currents will lead to your destruction" (章敬是. 是汝不是. 此是風力所轉. 終成敗壞).

Yuanwu writes of Xuedou's comments, "You can't just let him go" (放過不可), and of the final remark, "After all, Magu's entrapped by Nanquan and can't fend for himself" (果然被他籠罩. 爭奈自己何).

Tianqi says of Magu's opening gesture, "He takes the opportunity to test [Changqing]" (呈機校勘), and of the latter's response, "Illumination and function unfold at once" (照用同時). Of the finale he comments, "The fault lies with you (Nanquan) for not being a good teacher. Feelings are too high, so reality is no longer seen" (過在於汝. 非干師事. 情逐於境. 豈不喪真). Tianqi's concluding note reads, "Distinctions point clearly to raising emotions" (辨驗. 旨明拈情); and his wrapping phrase says, "Everything's balanced in his hands" (權衡在手).

Verse: There's this "wrong," and that "wrong,"
Don't try to avoid the contrast.

> (Y: A pair of hammerheads without holes; even Guanyin with her thousand hands can't lift them up. If you try, O Worthy, you'll get thirty blows from my cane, 兩箇無孔鐵鎚. 直饒千手大悲也提不起. 或若拈去闍黎喫三十棒)

Then waves will stay calm in the four seas,
Even as hundreds of rivers are receding.

> (T: There're two mistakes, but this and that are both valid, 便得兩錯. 是非皆絕)

An ancient rod jingles its twelve rings,

> (Y: How does it compare with mine? There's no eye on that staff, so don't make your living by holding it, 何似這箇. 杖頭無眼. 切忌向拄杖頭上作活計)

Each one is a gate leading to a road that's empty and forsaken.

> (T: A pure breeze, transcending all things, circulates freely around the staff, 杖上清風. 高超一切)

But not really forsaken!

(Y: After all, Xuedou fortuitously finds a place to turn around, but since he's still blind, I'll strike! 果然. 賴有轉身處. 已瞎了也. 便打)

A true adept seeks medicine even when there's no illness.

(T: Whether there was great merit before or no merit now, it's up to the poet to determine whether there's a remedy, 前拈大功. 今拈無功. 任是作者亦當治無)

此錯彼錯 / 切忌拈却 / 四海浪平 / 百川潮落 / 古策風高十二門 / 門門有路空蕭索 / 非蕭索 / 作者好求無病藥.

Comments: The theme of the first half of the verse is Xuedou's own capping phrases inserted into the dialogue suggesting that the opposite responses to Magu proffered by Changqing and Nanquan, with one positive and the other negative, are equally mistaken. For Tianqi, understanding how Xuedou's comment reflects the dynamics of these exchanges is key to resolving the case.

The second half focuses on the walking staff and how each of its rings, symbolizing basic Buddhist principles, offers a gateway to the path of awakening. The route may seem desolate because it involves ingesting bitter medicine, but it is important to reverse such an impression by recognizing that even the most advanced adept must continue to cultivate his insight and self-reliance after realization, or else he'll be the recipient of blows from a colleague's staff.

Ode 32

Senior Monk Ding Stands Still 定上座佇立

Case: In introducing this gong'an about the awakening of the determined, yet perplexed senior monk Ding (定上座, *ding* is literally samādhi, or supreme concentration), Yuanwu highlights the merits of master Linji's teaching: "When all delusions are cut off, a thousand eyes suddenly open, and when one phrase blocks all streams of thought, myriad obstacles stop. Is there anyone who will die the same and live the same [as Linji]?" (十方坐斷千眼頓開. 一句截流萬機寢削. 還有同死同生底麼).

In the dialogue Ding asks Linji, "What's the essential meaning of the buddha dharma?" (如何是佛法大意), and the teacher responds by "getting up from his meditation seat to grab Ding, and then slapping him and showing him the door" (濟下禪床擒住一掌便托開). When "Ding stands still" (定佇立), a monk who observed the episode recommends that he "bow" (禮拜), and while doing so, "he suddenly has a great awakening" (忽然大悟).

Yuanwu's capping phrases refer to Linji "grabbing Ding like a kind old granny would" (今日捉敗. 老婆心切), and to Ding standing motionless as "someone falling into a ghost cave" (已落鬼窟裏). Yuanwu also praises the bystander for "objectively seeing through the situation and empowering Ding" (冷地裏有人覷破. 全得他力), yet the senior monk's bow "substitutes diligence for incompetence" (將勤補拙). The apparent breakthrough is "like finding a lamp in darkness or a poor man discovering a jewel, yet he makes mistake after mistake" (如暗得燈. 如貧得寶. 將錯就錯).

Tianqi calls Linji's act toward Ding a "complete disclosure of the great function" (全提大用) and refers to the observer's injunction as "seeing what's missing" (見失傍提). On the experience of enlightenment Tianqi writes, "[Bowing] causes him to reach the goal" (因此達彼). Tianqi's final note says, "Directly revealing points clearly to the great function" (直指. 旨明大用); and his wrapping phrase reads, "The decree's fully expressed" (正令全提).

Verse: Following in the footsteps of Duanji (Huangbo)'s total dynamic activity,
(Y: The Yellow River's muddy from its source, and the son continues the efforts of his father, 黃河從源頭濁了也. 子承父業)
(T: Linji inherits Huangbo's total dynamism, 黃蘗全機. 臨濟紹之)
Why expect Linji to be calm and serene?
(T: He does what he must, why's there any doubt? 當央分付. 何必又疑)
He's like the deity Juling effortlessly lifting his hand,
(Y: He scares people to death with little boasting; once his flywhisk strikes, there's no need to test him again, 嚇殺人. 少賣弄. 打一拂子. 更不再勘)
To split asunder Mount Huashan into innumerable tiny pieces.
(T: When Ding's in doubt, Linji, tall as a mountain, crushes him in the palm of his hand, 定公疑. 高如山. 臨濟一掌粉碎)
斷際全機繼後踪 / 持來何必在從容 / 巨靈擡手無多子 / 分破華山千萬重.

Comments: Xuedou's verse celebrates the training techniques of Linji that rely on harshness accompanied by physical force, including shouting and slapping, and can be referred to by the East Asian expression, "You have to be cruel to be kind" (你必須殘忍才能善良). Xuedou refers to the nickname (斷際; literally, "cutting through") of Linji's teacher Huangbo, who slapped his student repeatedly until he attained awakening. Yuanwu's initial capping phrase makes a pun linking the first character in Huangbo's name (黃蘗) with the Yellow River (黃河) that is alluded to indirectly in Xuedou's second couplet. Both Yuanwu and Tianqi highlight the "like father, like son" quality of this example of Chan pedagogy.

The final lines praise Linji's approach by evoking the ancient legend of how the gigantic god Juling split one of the five great peaks of China located in Shaanxi province, east of Chang'an, so that the Yellow River could continue to flow. This brought countless benefits to that area of the country, but good fortune was accompanied by the constant threat of flooding. As Yuanwu notes in regard to line one, the Yellow River has always been known as the "muddy stream" (濁流); thus, the Chinese idiom "When the Yellow River flows clear" refers to an event that is hoped for but will likely never occur. Finally, Yuanwu and Tianqi compare Linji smacking disciples with his ceremonial flywhisk to Juling's monumental act of smashing a huge obstacle.

Ode 33

Zifu Draws a Circle 資福畫一圓相

Case: The master Zifu (n.d.), both here and in case 91, expresses himself by drawing a circle, which was the hallmark of his Gui-Yang lineal tradition that relied heavily on using figures or symbols as teaching tools. Yuanwu inquires, Zifu is one "who all day long doesn't distinguish east from west or south from north, but does this mean he's fast asleep? Sometimes his eyes are like shooting stars, but does that mean he's wide awake? Sometimes he calls the south the north, but does it mean he's mindful or mindless, a person of the Way or an ordinary person?" (東西不辨南北不分. 從朝至暮從暮至朝. 還道伊瞌睡麼. 有時眼似流星. 還道伊惺惺麼有時呼南作北. 且道是有心是無心. 是道人是常人).

In the dialogue, which Yuanwu refers to as an example of "discerning the trail within words while hiding one's capacity in a phrase" (這言中辨的句裏藏機), Zifu is confronted by Chencao (陳操), a mid-ninth-century government minister known for seeking out teachers from different Chan schools, including Muzhou and Yunmen, although some of those accounts defy chronology. As soon as Zifu sees Chencao, "he draws a circle" (畫一圓相). The official replies, "I know I made a mistake coming here like I was your disciple, but why did you draw a circle?" (操云弟子恁麼來. 早是不著便. 何更畫一圓相). Then, "Zifu slams the door of his room" (福便掩却門), and Xuedou adds, "Chencao has only one eye" (陳操只具一隻眼), an ambiguous epithet implying either partial sightlessness or lofty insight.

Yuanwu says of Zifu's symbol, "A spirit recognizing a spirit, a thief catching a thief . . . but do you see his diamond cage?" (是精識精. 是賊識賊 . . . 還見金剛圈麼), and of Xuedou's final remark, "Xuedou has an eye on his forehead, but what does he intend to say? He should use another circle because Chencao has the head of a dragon but the tail of a snake. However, at the key moment, Chencao should have pushed Zifu so hard there'd be no opening to advance through and no road to retreat upon" (雪竇頂門具眼. 且道他意在什麼處. 也好與一圓相. 灼然龍頭蛇尾. 當時好與一拶. 教伊進亦無門退亦無路).

Tianqi says of Zifu's circle, "He acts mischievously to test (暗機為驗), of Chencao's response, "He advances to show he got the point" (退己點人), and of Xuedou's last phrase, "The point is that Chencao can see in front but not behind" (點他見前失後). Tianqi's concluding note reads, "Investigation points clearly to the great function" (探干. 旨明大用); and his wrapping phrase says, "Everything's balanced in his hands" (權衡在手).

Verse: This circle rolls like a pearl and resounds like jade.

(Y: He stirs the Yellow River with a three-foot pole, 三尺杖子攪黃河)

(T: Zifu's circle is as effective as blade-like words, 福之圓相, 操之言鋒)

Horses and mules transport it, then it's loaded onto iron ships,

To be shared by all undisturbed voyagers, whether at sea or in the mountains.

(Y: If you're an undisturbed traveler, then you have no need for it. But you must be a voyager without concerns before you can get this point, 若是無事客也不消得. 須是無事始得)

(T: Loading ships with horses is routine, 船裝馬載. 只當尋常)

While fishing for a large sea turtle, he lets down a round cage.

(T: Don't try using too many styles, one teaching device suffices, 不用多端. 一機足矣)

團團珠繞玉珊珊 / 馬載驢馱上鐵船 / 分付海山無事客 / 釣鰲時下一圈攣.

Follow-up: Xuedou adds, "No patch-robed monk in the whole world can escape" (師復云. 天下衲僧跳不出) (Y: You, too, are stuck inside. Everyone's buried in the same hole, O Worthy, but can you manage to escape? 兼身在內. 一坑埋却. 闍黎還跳得出麼) (T: There's nothing left to say. How many practitioners among the various Chan streams stay trapped in a she\ll? 須言無事. 天下禪流幾人能出有無之殼).

Comments: Xuedou begins by lavishly praising Zifu's circle. In the second and third lines he suggests ironically that this pearl-like gem must be given to all pilgrims who venture forth and yet, as the capping phrases indicate, a genuinely unperturbed traveler has no real need for possessing this implement.

The final line compares Zifu's teaching method to someone fishing for a giant turtle that seems difficult to trap, unless the image refers to a blind or lame creature in desperate need of assistance and therefore eager for the cage. Xuedou's interjection indicates that the cage, like the turtle's shell, is a double-edged sword at once entrapping and enabling freedom. Yuanwu turns the tables and, with feigned civility, accuses the poet of being deficient, whereas Tianqi's remark acknowledges that Xuedou's last word is sufficient.

Ode 34

Yangshan's "Where Have You Just Been?" 仰山近離甚處

Case: According to Yuanwu's prose comments, "The point of testing a practitioner with gong'an is to get to know him intimately as soon as he opens his mouth. An ancient once said, 'Truly great people create transformations within the flow of everyday speech.' If you have an eye on your forehead, as soon as any matter is raised you immediately know where the chips fall and realize that for each question there's an answer that's altogether clear" (驗人端的處. 下口便知音. 古人道. 沒量大人. 向語脈裏轉却. 若是頂門具眼. 舉著便知落處. 看他一問一答. 歷歷分明).

In the dialogue the master Yangshan (仰山, 807–883) asks a traveling monk, "Where've you been?" (近離甚處), and the novice replies, "Mount Lu" (廬山), an impressive area with various magnificent peaks and beautiful including waterfalls that was often visited by Buddhist and Daoist intellectuals. Lu is located in northeastern Jiangxi province, some distance from Yangshan's temple in the southwestern part of the province. When the master inquires, "Did you reach Five Elders Peak?" (到五老峰麼), a set of cliffs that looks like a group of old men chatting, the monk says, "I didn't" (不曾), and the teacher retorts, "Then, O Worthy, you've never really been to Mount Lu!" (闍黎不曾遊山). Xuedou cites Yunmen's subsequent comment, "For the sake of being compassionate, this was a conversation held in the weeds" (皆為慈悲之故. 有落草之談).

Of Yangshan's second question Yuanwu remarks, "He shakes things up without any fuss. How could [the monk] have stumbled by?" (因行不妨掉臂. 何曾蹉過), and of the monk's reply, "Move over, as bearing a face red with shame isn't as good as speaking forthrightly. He's like someone who forgets what's happened yet also doesn't see what's coming" (移一步. 面赤不如語直. 也似忘前失後). Of Yunmen's comment Yuanwu writes, "The sword that kills is also the sword that gives life two or three times over. To get to know the road to the mountains, you must take it" (殺人刀活人劍. 兩箇三箇. 要知山上路. 須是去來人).

Tianqi says of Yangshan's opening query, "He's reaching for a hidden blade" (探拔藏鋒), and of the monk's answer, "He sticks to the facts" (實供). Regarding the master's putdown, Tianqi writes, "it's clear the monk didn't arrive" (點他不達), and of Yunmen's remark, "Words don't accomplish much, they only express entanglements" (言不行捧. 只打葛藤). Tianqi's final note reads, "Investigation points clearly to calmness" (探干. 旨明平懷), and his wrapping phrase is, "Settling the matter with a hidden blade" (就事藏鋒).

Verse: Who can tell whether it suggests getting out of or entering into the weeds?
(Y: Although there's an eye on your forehead, O Worthy, you can't discern, 頂門具一隻眼. 闍黎不解尋討)
White clouds gather, yet the fiery sun shines clear.
(T: It sounds peaceful, but life isn't like that, 平懷拈出. 免生異見)
Looking to the left, nothing's lost; glancing to the right, everything's ripened.
Don't you know that the revered recluse Hanshan (Cold Mountain),
Traveled to places so far away, it took him ten years to return?
(Y: It's not a matter of speed. Want to know where he is now? It's obvious. 也不早. 即今在什麼處. 灼然)
He said that he'd forgotten his way home.

(Y: This evokes Hanshan's freedom, but Xuedou misses the chance to follow up, so I'll strike, 渠儂得自由. 放過一著. 便打)

(T: He's missed the point and should've picked a different example, 迷名失旨. 舉例故點)

出草入草. 誰解尋討 / 白雲重重. 紅日杲杲 / 左顧無暇. 右盼已老 / 君不見. 寒山子 / 行太早. 十年歸不得 / 忘却來時道.

Comments: This irregular verse starts with three eight-character lines and then adds lines with six, eight, and five characters that reference passages culled from a famous verse by the mysterious Tang-dynasty hermit-poet known by the name of his usual dwelling place on Cold Mountain (寒山, fl. ninth century) in Zhejiang province near Mount Tiantai. Xuedou contrasts the novice's meager efforts in traveling around the celebrated peaks of Mount Lu, where many thinkers congregated, with the revered humility coupled with a sense of majesty embodied by Hanshsan.

A Hanshan poem discovered on Mount Lu reads, "If you want to find peace / Follow the way of Cold Mountain. / As a mild breeze blows through the deep pines, / Sounding more refreshing the closer you listen, / Here I sit, white haired, under a tree, / Carefully reading Daoist lore" (欲得安身處 / 寒山可長保 / 微風吹幽松 / 近聽聲愈好/ 下有班白人 / 嘮嘮讀黃老). However, the capping phrases by Yuanwu and Tianqi challenge any reliance on evoking this exquisite example of Chan literature by suggesting that Xuedou could have done a better job of explicating the deficiencies of the bewildered novice.

Ode 35

Mañjuśrī Questions Wuzhuo 殊問無著

Case: According to Yuanwu's introduction, a true adept is one who "distinguishes dragons from snakes, jewels from stones, monks from laymen, or resolution from uncertainty. But without an eye on your forehead or an amulet tucked under your arm, over and over you'll stumble and fall" (定龍蛇分玉石. 別緇素決猶豫. 若不是頂門上有眼. 肘臂下有符. 往往當頭蹉過). This ability is tested in the dialogue involving an encounter between the bodhisattva Mañjuśrī (文殊, Wenshu) and Wuzhuo (無著, literally, "No Attachment," 821–900), the posthumous name of a monk who was a follower of Yangshan known for traveling throughout China (and perhaps to India) in pursuit of authentic Buddhist teachings.

Wuzhuo visits Mount Wutai (遊五臺), a remarkable group of five major peaks in northern Shanxi province that was considered the earthly abode of Mañjuśrī, who appears there in forms both regal (as multicolored clouds) and unassuming (a beggar) in order to engage with and awaken dedicated pilgrims. In response to a query, Wuzhuo tells the bodhisattva he's come from "the south," which implies the typical Chan teaching style based on striving for sudden enlightenment through sitting meditation. He says the assemblies of monks there number "three or five hundred," but do not necessarily "follow the precepts" (少奉戒律).

Then, Mañjuśrī proclaims that in northern-style practice, renowned for visualizations of supernal events as well as strict adherence to regulations, "Ordinary people and sages dwell together, and dragons and snakes intermingle" (凡聖同居龍蛇混). Answering Wuzhuo's question, Mañjuśrī says that the congregations at Qinqliang temple on Wutai are "in front three by three, behind three by three" (前三三後三三), which either implies a numberless quality or means, "much the same."

Both Yuanwu and Tianqi criticize Wuzhuo for being too literal in his responses. Of his answer about followers in the south Yuanwu writes, "They're all wild-fox spirits, anyway" (盡是野狐精), and of the bodhisattva's final statement, "These are outrageous words, upside-down talk. But tell me, how many are there? Even the goddess of great compassion (Guanyin) with her thousands of hands couldn't count them all" (顛言倒語. 且道是多少. 千手大悲數不足).

Tianqi says of Wuzhuo's reply, "He relies too much on words" (依舊逐句), and of Mañjuśrī's last comment, "Illumination and function take place at the same time" (照用同時). Tianqi's concluding note reads, "Seeking followers points clearly to direct teaching" (探拔. 旨明直指); and his wrapping phrase says, "Grandmotherly kindness!" (老婆心切).

Verse: Thousands of peaks entwined together looking like indigo monasteries,

(Y: Can you see Mañjuśrī everywhere? 還見文殊麼)

Who says Mañjuśrī was involved in this dialogue?

(T: Everywhere he's completely apparent, but who can explain his words? 遍界全彰. 誰說對談)

I can only laugh at Wuzhuo's, "How many are in the assembly at Qingliang?"—
"In front three by three, behind three by three."

(Y: Please find it right under your feet, but there are thorns in the mud. A porcelain tea bowl falls to the ground, a lacquer plate breaks into seven pieces, 試請脚下辨看, 爛泥裹有刺. 碗子落地楪子成七片)

(T: Do you want to know about twos or threes? I've laughed enough already, 欲識二三. 盡在此笑)

千峰盤屈色如藍 / 誰謂文殊是對談 / 堪笑清凉多少衆 / 前三三與後三三.

Comments: Xuedou's verse evokes the powerful story that is said to have occurred after the dialogue, when Mañjuśrī shows Wuzhuo a brilliant crystal cup for drinking tea that is not available in the south. Then a young acolyte appears and points the monk toward the Diamond Cave, where he has a remarkable vision of countless monasteries with celestial attendants. However, "as soon as Wuzhuo turns his head, the vision of illusory temples and the boy immediately vanish, and there's just an empty valley" (著回首. 化寺童子. 悉隱不見. 只是空谷).

The poem transforms the supernatural occurrences so that they are interpreted as reinforcing the fundamental message that Wuzhuo is awakened by Mañjuśrī as part of a Chan encounter dialogue. Tenkei maintains that the bodhisattva can appear anywhere but that means nowhere at all. The first line of the verse makes a pun on the bluish color of the mountaintops, which is the second character in the Sinitic transliteration of *samghārāma* or Buddhist monastery (伽藍, C. *qielan*, J. *garan*). The final line, in unusual fashion, cites the keyword of the dialogue that is typically evoked in the opening line.

Yuanwu notes in prose comments that "there's a sword embedded in Xuedou's laughter, and if you can understand why he's laughing" (雪竇笑中有刀. 若會得這笑處), you'll see the meaning of "three by three." He also cites a verse by the so-called One-eyed Dragon of Mingzhao (明招獨眼龍, 890?–960?): "Throughout the world there're magnificent monasteries, / Mañjuśrī who fills the eyes is indeed the one speaking. / But not knowing how to open the buddha eye on hearing these words, / [Wuzhuo] turns his head and sees only indigo mountains and cliffs" (廓周沙界勝伽藍 / 滿目文殊是對談 / 言下不知開佛眼 / 回頭只見翠山巖). Mingzhao thus reinforces the priority of the natural landscape over and above a vision of infinite sacred buildings.

Ode 36

Changsha One Day Roams the Mountains 長沙一日遊山

Case: This dialogue is similar to cases 23 and 34 that deal with the aftermath of wandering in the wilderness outside temple grounds. The master Changsha (長沙, 788–868), a prominent disciple of Nanquan, returns from a walk one day and is asked by the head monk where he is coming from. The teacher replies, "I've been roaming the mountains" (遊山來), and the cleric presses him, "Where did you go?" (到什麼處來). Changsha says, "I began following the scent of fragrant meadows, and returned on the trail of falling flowers" (始隨芳草去. 又逐落花回). When the head monk comments, "That sounds like springtime" (大似春意), Changsha responds, "It's better than talking about how autumn dew drips from lotus leaves" (也勝秋露滴芙蕖). Xuedou adds, "Thanks for this reply!" (謝答話).

Of the monk's second question Yuanwu writes, "A thrust. If [Changsha] had gone somewhere, he couldn't avoid falling in the weeds. The two drag each other into a firepit" (掺.若有所至未免落草. 相牽入火坑). Of the monk's comment about the seasons Yuanwu says, "He follows after [Changsha], adding error to error: one hand is raised up, and one's tied down" (相隨來也. 將錯就錯. 一手擡一手搦), and of Xuedou's final quip, "A group of fellows playing with fire while floundering in the muck, these three should have their crimes listed on the same indictment" (一火弄泥團漢. 三箇一狀領過).

Tianqi says of the monk's second query, "He's asking for details about why Changsha wandered" (細辯來源), and of the response, "His words are truly beautiful" (句甚英美). Of the springtime comment Tianqi writes, "This points to the present moment" (點逐今時), and of Changsha's comeback referring to poignant autumnal imagery, "He talks about the flip side where water is stagnant" (拈他死水). Of Xuedou's quip Tianqi says, "Whether instantaneous or eternal, both are interconnected and entwined" (一个今時. 一个劫外. 雙點雙拈). Tianqi's concluding note says, "Fishing in deep waters points clearly to truth" (探竿. 旨明絕待); and his wrapping phrase reads, "Adepts recognizing one another" (作家相見).

Verse: The great earth is free of any speck of dust,

(Y: Who tries to break through open doorways? How many will miss the point that the world's peaceful, 豁開戶牖當軒者誰. 盡少這箇不得. 天下太平)

Whose eyes are not able to see this?
"I began by following the scent of fragrant meadows,
And returned in pursuit of falling flowers."
(T: He's simply reciting the case, 拈前公案)
A gaunt crane perches on a leafless tree,
A crazed monkey shrieks from a desolate cliff.
(T: Here Xuedou expresses his creativity, 雪竇呈機)
Changsha's meaning is limitless. Nah!
(Y: I'll strike. What's the point of the final phrase? Bury them all in the same pit since they've fallen into a ghost cave. A man in the weeds [Xuedou] draws the bow after the thief has fled but can't let go, 便打. 末後一句道什麼. 一坑埋却. 墮在鬼窟裏. 草裏漢. 賊過後張弓. 更不可放過)
(T: A pronouncement is made. Wary of falling into the ordinary, he cuts off all rules, 拈起令看. 恐落平實. 舉令一截)
大地絕纖埃 / 何人眼不開 / 始隨芳草去 / 又逐落花回 / 羸鶴翹寒木 / 狂猿嘯古臺 / 長沙無限意. 咄.

Comments: Both Yuanwu and Tianqi agree that the ode's main message suggests that a genuine Chan adept must find the proper balance between the wandering monk's seasonal imagery that harmonizes life and death and Changsha's emphasis on the desolation of autumn. These passages from the dialogue are buttressed by the poem's evocation of a frail fowl and a disorderly simian. Yet Yuanwu's comments dismiss the idea that Changsha bested the head monk or that Xuedou's observations are superior to the interlocutors since all three teachers can be criticized, whereas Tianqi's assessment is more supportive of the master's responses and the poet's versification.

As Tenkei comments, even though fundamentally there is no dust so that all people are free and independent, they are still unable to come and go without self-imposed obstacles based on rationalizations and calculations involving the oppositions of delusion versus enlightenment, or the ordinary versus the sacred. According to Yuanwu's prose remark, unless "one forgets conceptual barriers and volitional obstructions" (機關盡意識忘) and achieves "a state without allowing any leakage from external sensations" (無些子滲漏), the result is a misguided state of mind that "ancients referred to as 'remaining stuck in the realm of splendor' " (古人謂之猶在勝妙境界).

Ode 37

Panshan's "Triple World without Things" 盤山三界無法

Case: In the introduction Yuanwu draws a sharp contrast between the few Chan adepts who react spontaneously to a bolt of lightning or a clap of thunder without needing to hide their eyes or cover their ears and the deluded majority of practitioners who, instead, "lower their heads and linger in delusive thoughts without realizing that countless ghosts are haunting empty skulls right in front of them" (有般底. 低頭佇思. 意根下卜度. 殊不知髑髏前見鬼無數). He challenges the audience, "Tell me, without falling into deliberations or thinking merely in terms of gain versus loss, how will you respond to the words of a true teacher trying to awaken you?" (且道不落意根. 不抱得失忽有箇恁麼舉覺. 作麼生祇對).

In the terse gong'an the master Panshan (盤山, 720–814), one of numerous prominent disciples of Mazu, instructs his assembly (垂語) with a cryptic query, "Since the triple world is without things, where can you find the mind?" (三界無法. 何處求心). Yuanwu says with irony that "the ancients called such a case 'expressing liberation from a deep pit' because it starts out in a beneficial way but ends up with deleterious effects" (古人謂之解脫深坑. 本是善因而招惡果) by exposing and excoriating the roots of ignorance.

Of Panshan's initial phrase Yuanwu writes, "An arrow that's been shot will never come back to the bowstring. Like moonlight that enables people walking at night to see the path, this arrow hits the mark. Those who fully understand strike up a joyful, harmonious tune" (箭既離弦無返回勢. 月明照見夜行人. 中也. 識法者懼. 好和聲便打). Of the teacher's query he says, "Don't deceive people by bringing up this question again. You should examine it for yourself or I'll strike saying, 'How's that?'" (莫瞞人好. 不勞重舉. 自點檢看. 便打云. 是什麼).

Whereas Yuanwu seems to equivocate regarding the value of Panshan's inquiry, Tianqi remarks, "The first phrase grabs hold of the whole situation, and the second phrase grabs hold of each person. His meaning is straight and clear, so why even discuss it?" (上句奪境. 下句奪人. 意在直領. 豈可商量). Tianqi's final note says, "Directly revealing the radiant source points clearly to the nonduality of mind and things" (直下明宗. 旨明心法不二);

and his wrapping phrase reads, "He's fishing with a pole to save people" (垂釣為人).

Verse: "Since the triple world is without things, where can you find the mind?"

(Y: It's not worthwhile looking, just see for yourself or I'll strike saying, 'How's that?'" 不勞重舉. 自點檢看. 打云. 是什麼)

(T: So far he's just been reciting the case, but below he reveals his creativity, 上拈公案. 下呈其機)

White clouds create a canopy, streaming waters form a lute,
Playing one or more tunes no one gets.

(Y: Not falling into typical melodies yet borrowing from paths previously taken, the five sounds and six notes are thoroughly clear and don't need to be followed. But if you listen for it, you'll go deaf, 不落宮商非干角徵. 借路經過. 五音六律盡分明. 自領出去. 聽則聾)

After autumn evening rain passes, waters deepen in the pond.

(T: All emotions are distilled but no principle's proclaimed, like clear water in autumn. Ah, feel the water! 盡情吐露. 不領大旨. 如秋涼水. 豈水嘆也)

三界無法. 何處求心 / 白雲為蓋. 流泉作琴 / 一曲兩曲無人會 / 雨過夜塘秋水深.

Comments: Yuanwu's prose commentary is especially enthusiastic in praise of Xuedou's verse, which evokes the precious "flower garland realm" (華嚴境界, C. *huayan jingjie*, J. *kegon kyōkai*), indicating that one is all and all is one, thus forming a harmoniously interpenetrating universe. But Yuanwu rejects a misleading interpretation common at the time that Xuedou was "singing from within nothingness" (無中唱出), a notion also dismissed in commentary on case 87.

Yuanwu furthermore maintains that the verse has been judged as worthy of the skill (才) of the prestigious imperial Hanlin (翰林) Academy of poetry that flourished during the Tang dynasty. He compares Xuedou's ode to a stanza written a few decades later by the eminent lay poet Su Shi (蘇軾, 1037–1101), who often practiced Chan meditation and whose poem was famously interpreted by Dōgen (道元, 1200–1253), the founder of Sōtō Zen in medieval Japan: "Sounds of valley streams are the long broad tongue [of buddha] . . . / Singing 84,000 hymns during the night" (溪聲便是廣長舌 . . . 夜來八萬四千偈).

Xuedou's verse culminates in a deceptively simple yet exquisite final lyric that, according to Hakuin (白隱, 1686–1769), an early modern Japanese Rinzai Zen master, "sings the secret melody of 'the triple world without things.'" As Tianqi implies, this is a prominent example in the *Odes* for which all commentarial wording fails to capture the depths of meaning expressed by the poem.

Ode 38

Fengxue's "Patriarchal Mind Seal" 風穴祖師心印

Case: In the introduction Yuanwu contrasts the "path of gradual enlightenment, which isn't the typical approach but allows union with the Dao so that one enjoys unhindered movement while in the midst of a bustling marketplace" (論漸也. 返常合道. 鬧市裏七縱八橫), with the "path of sudden enlightenment, which doesn't leave any trace so a thousand sages can't track it" (論頓也. 不留朕迹. 千聖亦摸索不著). "How about," Yuanwu challenges, "when neither the sudden nor the gradual path are relied upon? To an attentive person one word is enough, just as an alert horse needs just a flick of the whip" (儻或不立頓漸. 又作麼生. 快人一言快馬一鞭).

The subtle relationship between a teacher's instructional method and its impact on those taught is captured in the dialogue involving the master Fengxue (風穴, 896–973), a great-grandson in Linji's lineage who first studied Confucianism and Tiantai Buddhism before becoming a Chan monk at the age of twenty-five. When invited to give a sermon in the dharma hall of a temple supported by the governor of Yingzhou in Henan province, where the Linji school was prevalent, Fengxue says, "The impression of the patriarchal mind seal functions like the Iron Ox. If the seal is removed, an impression is left, but if the seal is left, the impression is broken. If the seal is neither removed nor left, is there an impression made or not?" (祖師心印狀似鐵牛之機. 去即印住. 住即印破. 只如不去不住. 印即是不印即是). The Iron Ox refers to a huge icon supposedly built at the border of two provinces near the Yellow River to ward off flooding, with its head facing north to Hebei and its tail facing south to Henan province.

The senior monk Lubei (盧陂) is too hesitant to respond and is insulted four times in a row by Fengxue with a putdown, a shout, and two strikes from his flywhisk. Then the governor fares better when he says, "The buddha's law and the king's law are one and the same" (佛法與王法一般). When Fengxue asks, "On what basis do you say this?" (見箇什麼), the governor replies, "When what should be settled isn't settled, that leads to disorder" (當斷不斷反招其亂), and the master descends from his seat" (穴下座).

Yuanwu comments on Fengxue's query, "The heads of everyone in the world appear and disappear over and over. The truth's revealed, but I ask that you turn over meditation seats and disperse the great assembly by shouting" (天下人頭出頭沒有分. 文彩已彰. 但請掀倒禪床喝散大眾). Of the official's response he writes, "It seems like he's got it, but not really. Still, we must recognize that this observer has eyes. When someone of the eastern section of a temple dies, a person from the western side takes part in mourning" (似則似是則未是. 須知傍人有眼. 東家人死. 西家人助哀). Yuanwu says of Fengxue's silence, "He adds error to error, but seeing the situation he adjusts so that learning is attained" (將錯就錯. 見機而變. 且得參學事畢).

Tianqi says of Fengxue's question, "You can't have it both ways and expect to make your living in that fashion" (不住二邊. 正當恁麼. 又作麼生), and of the governor's remark about chaos, "Practicing to be in unison isn't really practicing, discontinuing to be in unison isn't really discontinuing" (合行不行. 合止不止). Of Fengxue stepping down he remarks, "Not only Lubei but Fengxue as well doesn't leave an impression" (非只盧陂. 亦有風穴. 故就拂迹). Tianqi's final note reads, "The great function is fully disclosed" (大用全提.旨明攙旗奪皷); and his wrapping phrase says, "Everything's balanced in his hands" (權衡在手).

Verse: [Fengxue] captures Lubei and has him sitting astride the Iron Ox,

> (Y: Among thousands of people he shows his unique skill, but the general of a defeated army needn't have his throat cut twice, 千人萬人中.也要呈巧藝.敗軍之將不再斬)

The shield provided by the three mysteries can't be swayed.
Mighty rivers rushing toward the king's castle—
One great shout causes their currents to flow backwards.

> (Y: One shout not only cuts the tongue out of your head, nay, it causes the Iron Ox of Shanzhou to run away and scares to death the Great Colossus (Maitreya) of Jiazhou, 不是這一喝截却爾舌頭. 咄. 驚走陝府鐵牛. 嚇殺嘉州大象)
>
> (T: The three mysteries and three essentials are embedded in this one shout. Silencing the words of Lubei causes the Yangzi River to reverse its course, 一喝中具三玄三要. 莫道盧陂. 任是長江一喝倒流)

擒得盧陂跨鐵牛 / 三玄戈甲未輕酬 / 楚王城畔朝宗水 / 喝下曾令却倒流.

Comments: Xuedou's verse and both commentators celebrate Fengxue's repeated criticisms of the senior monk that feature a shout. The master's symbolic lion's roar has the remarkable capacity to reverse the flow of the mighty river and, for Yuanwu, to frighten imposing icons. Yet Chan discourse often belittles the statues Yuanwu mentions, as in the saying, "The Great Colossus of Jiazhou eats grain, and the Iron Ox of Shanzhou gets sick to its stomach" (嘉州大象喫灸麩. 陜府鐵牛樗破肚).

It is also notable that Xuedou does not refer to the public official whose response apparently caused the master to say, in effect, *touché*. Some questions about this lacuna are as follows: Does Fengxue accept the governor's identification of Dharmic and royal law? If so, does this mean he defers Buddhism to the civil authority? Moreover, does the Chan teacher bow out of a reluctance to challenge his powerful lay supporter, or due to common courtesy?

Ode 39

Yunmen's "Peonies Ringed" 雲門花藥欄

Case: Yuanwu's introduction suggests that Yunmen "establishes the great function" (大用現前) by demonstrating to disciples that "If you want to realize the principle of buddha-nature, you should anticipate appropriate opportunities and circumstances; and if you want to refine pure gold that's been tempered hundreds of times, a true adept should use a forge and bellows" (欲知佛性義. 當觀時節因緣. 欲煅百鍊精金. 須是作家爐鞴).

In the dialogue a monk inquires of Yunmen, "What's the pure *dharmakāya*" (如何是清淨法身), or the Mahāyāna Buddhist notion of the fundamental unity of all things beyond the physical realm, and the master replies, "Peonies ringed" (花藥欄). This image refers to the support provided by gardeners growing exotic flowers that, having full and heavy blooms, tend to fall over without a device propping them up; therefore, it represents nature that seems more beautiful when tended and curated by human intervention. The monk asks, "When it's like this, then what happens?" (便與麼去時如何), and Yunmen says, "A golden-haired lion" (金毛獅子). Yunmen's initial response recalls cases that emphasize concrete existence, but his second remark is a sign of approval indicating the monk's query expresses a true understanding.

Yuanwu's capping phrases, however, tend to cast doubt on both the monk and the master. Of Yunmen's first answer he writes, "If the source of the question isn't authentic, the answer comes across as reckless . . . The slanted doesn't hold the upright" (問處不真. 答來鹵莽. . . 曲不藏直). Of the inquirer's reaction Yuanwu says, "He swallows the jujube whole. Let go of this folly" (渾崙吞箇棗. 放憨作麼), and of Yunmen's second reply, "Praising and belittling are two sides of a coin, but he makes mistake after mistake. What's going on in his mind?" (也褒也貶. 兩采一賽. 將錯就錯. 是什麼心行).

Tianqi's comments are less provocative when he says that Yunmen's first answer, "Points to everyday existence" (平實一指), and his second answer, "Hits the mark" (當央一點). Tianqi's final note reads, "Dragging one by the nose points clearly to no fixed path" (拽回鼻孔. 旨明無有意路), and the wrapping phrase says, "Everything's balanced in his hands" (權衡在手).

Verse: "Peonies ringed," but don't misunderstand,
> (T: Pay attention! 要人仔細)

Marks for weighing are put on the gauge, not the tray.
> (Y: How entangled! Everyone sees it their own way, so he can't avoid explaining it in terms of a known principle, 太葛藤. 各自向衣單下返觀. 不免說道理)
>
> (T: The meaning here is based on "peonies ringed," not the *dharmakāya*, 意在花藥闌上. 不在法身)

"When it's like this"? How pointless!
> (T: First know the truth, then apply it to the concrete realm. If it's not done that way, there's no point, 先執法智同後執平實. 總非本分故曰無端)

Everyone in the assembly, take a good look at this "golden-haired lion"!
> (Y: He reveals one point or a half, but it's like a puppy barking. Yunmen resembles someone from Puzhou [a place known for many thieves] shepherding a thief, 放出一箇半箇也是箇狗子. 雲門也是普州人送賊)
>
> (T: Everyone has two maladies, so even those with skill must take a closer look, 人人皆有此等二病. 便是英才也須着眼)

花藥欄. 莫瞞旰 / 星在秤兮不在盤 / 便與麼. 太無端 / 金毛獅子大家看.

Comments: Xuedou's verse supports Yunmen's responses but also suggests his expressions are vague enough that they need to be clarified for some followers to be able to unravel the apparent misconceptions of the monk, who probably suffers two inevitable and seemingly contradictory yet complementary deficiencies, as mentioned by Tianqi. Although it is not certain from the dialogue, these seem to refer to how the inquiring novice mistakes Yunmen's reference to flowers for an emphasis on specific objects or phenomena perceived, while also misjudging from the opposite direction the evocation of the lion's mane as a philosophical principle or noumena that remains independent of human sensations.

Therefore, the main aim of Xuedou's poem is to balance the scales, as in the image evoked in line two, which uses a typical measuring device as a metaphor for teaching disciples. Whatever rhetoric a master offers must be apropos to the complicated pedagogical situations of practitioners, who are plagued by defective conceptual tendencies.

Ode 40

Nanquan's "Flower in the Garden" 南泉指花庭前

Case: In the introduction Yuanwu maintains, "When the function of the mind ceases and is swept clean, an iron tree blossoms with flowers. Is there anyone who can demonstrate this point, or will all fail? Even those who seem free in every possible way can't avoid needing a teacher to pierce their nostrils" (休去歇去. 鐵樹開花. 有麼有麼黠兒落. 節. 直饒七縱八橫. 不免穿他鼻孔). Yuanwu also suggests in prose commentary the difference between an ideal and a false practitioner: "If his eyes move attentively and he hears alertly, he enjoys the superb flavor of ghee; but if he stays inert and his hearing is faulty, it tastes like poison" (若是眼目定動. 活底聞得. 如醍醐上味. 若是死底聞得翻成毒藥).

In the dialogue a high government official named Luxuan (陸亘, 764–834) says to Nanquan that, based on the teachings of Sengzhao (僧肇, 384–417?), a prominent Mahāyāna scholar who accompanied Kumarajiva's trip from India to China but was executed at a young age for disobeying civil authorities, "Heaven and earth have the same root and the ten thousand things are one substance, isn't this marvelous?" (天地同根. 萬物一體. 也甚奇恠). The master then "points to a flower in the garden" (指花庭前) and says, "Official, these days people look at blossoms as if in a dream" (時人見此一株花. 如夢相似).

Yuanwu remarks that Luxuan "makes his living in a ghost cave and, since the picture of a cake cannot satisfy hunger, he's haggling in the weeds" (鬼窟裏作活計. 畫餅不可充飢. 也是草裏商量). Of Nanquan's pointing to the flower he writes, "What's he talking about? Nah! The sūtras have teachers of scriptures and the śāstras have teachers of treatises, but none of it has anything to do with a genuinely reclusive monk. Nah! A capable teacher would've expressed a turning word that not only cuts off Nanquan but also brings to life all the world's patch-robed monks" (道恁麼. 咄. 經有經師論有論師. 不干山僧事. 咄. 大丈夫當時下得一轉語. 不唯截斷南泉. 亦乃與天下衲僧出氣). But he praises Nanquan's final remark, "You've lured the golden oriole down from the willow branch" (引得黃鶯下柳條).

According to Tianqi's comment on the official, "He only knows there's a special expression, but doesn't realize he can't understand it" (只見句奇. 不知自昧). Of Nanquan's response he says, "He cuts off the monk by showing he's wrong" (當央直截. 點他錯認). Tianqi's concluding note reads, "Raising a turning word points clearly and directly to the radiant source" (拈轉話頭. 旨明直下明宗), and the wrapping phrase says, "His dharma cave's filled with claws and fangs" (法窟爪牙).

Verse: Hearing, seeing, sensing, and knowing don't occur one by one,
(Y: Seven flowers bloom but the eighth withers. Eyes, ears, nose, tongue, body, and mind are all at once a hammerhead without a hole, 七花八裂. 眼耳鼻舌身意. 一時是箇無孔鐵鎚)
Mountains and rivers aren't viewed in a mirror.
(T: Sense organs and sensations are part of the same realm, which takes place within the world of awareness. However, fear of merging with sensations is the reason this state doesn't seem to exist, 根塵境對偶/ 識生其中. 恐成心境. 故曰不在)
When the moon sets in the frosty sky at midnight,
Whose silhouette is cast on the clear, cold pond?
(Y: Someone troubled should never try to explain their troubles to someone else who's troubled—explaining troubles to a troubled person ends up troubling them to death, 愁人莫向愁人說. 說向愁人愁殺人)
(T: Since things and self are intertwined, what about heaven and earth? Someone without a single thought is the one [silhouetted], 物我雙絕. 天地何有. 杳無一念. 故曰誰共)

聞見覺知非一一 / 山河不在鏡中觀 / 霜天月落夜將半 / 誰共澄潭照影寒.

Comments: Xuedou's verse is a meditation on perceiving phenomena in a way that avoids the abstractions preoccupying Lugen yet captures the ambiguity of Nanquan's reference to dreaming, which indicates neither a deficient state of delusion and unreality nor an ideal realm beyond dualistic misconceptions that falsely separate self and other, or things and perceptions. The sublime image of the moon going down in the sky implies the lunar body is reflected in the evening waters, thereby creating an experience of multiplicities that is valid from an everyday perspective but may seem misleading from a transcendental standpoint.

Xuedou's concluding rhetorical question about participating in this phantasm highlights the fragmentation of perceptions that never appear in the same way to different people. Yuanwu's capping phrase indicates ironically the difficulty of communicating such a vision of truth mixed with untruth, whereas Tianqi suggests the possibility of reciprocal understanding based on how the emptiness of the realm beyond thinking underlies all sensations.

Ode 41

Zhaozhou's "Person Undergoing the Great Death" 趙州大死底人

Case: Yuanwu introduces the exchange between two venerable masters: Zhaozhou, during the career phase after he attained enlightenment but before establishing his own temple; and Touzi Datong, who was Zhaozhou's junior colleague yet spiritual equal. Yuanwu points out the rarity of an encounter in which one adept tests a comparable master: "When positive and negative are merged, even sages can't tell them apart. When moving forward, backward, or sideways are entwined, even buddhas can't discern it (是非交結處. 聖亦不能知. 逆順縱橫時. 佛亦不能辨). Moreover, "One who's removed from the world transcends the ordinary but is called upon to reveal his ability as an accomplished teacher by walking on the edge of a sheet of ice and treading a sharp blade; he's unique like the horn of a unicorn or a lotus blossom encompassed by fire. On meeting another teacher who's also beyond this world, he recognizes they trek the same path" (為絕世超倫之

士. 顯逸群大士之能. 向氷凌上行. 劍刃上走. 直下如麒麟頭角. 似火裏蓮花. 宛見超方. 始知同道).

In the dialogue Zhaozhou asks Touzi, "What happens when someone who's undergone the great death comes back to life?" (大死底人却活時如何) and his colleague responds, "He doesn't go by night, he must get there in broad daylight" (不許夜行. 投明須到). The reply indicates that being reborn is a transparent rather than concealed event. In another version of the story, Zhaozhou disingenuously admits he's a thief, but Touzi is even more of a bandit.

Yuanwu comments on Zhaozhou's inquiry, "It's true that a thief doesn't usually rob from a poor household. Since he's used to being a guest, he has sympathy for visitors" (有恁麼事賊不打貧兒家. 慣曾作客方憐客). On Touzi's reply he remarks, "Seeing a cage, he smashes the cage, like a thief recognizing a thief. If he wasn't lying in the same bed, how would he know the covers were torn?" (看樓打樓. 是賊識賊. 若不同床臥. 焉知被底穿).

Tianqi's comment on Zhaozhou's question says, "He uses his capacity to test the host" (呈機驗主). Of Touzi's response he writes, "Since [Zhaozhou] already knows, [Touzi] explains it this way" (已見來情. 故乃拈之). Tianqi's final note is, "Fishing in deep waters points clearly to true emotion" (探竿. 旨明拈情); and his wrapping phrase reads, "A spirit recognizing a kindred spirit" (是精識精).

Verse: There's an eye while being alive that's the same eye when dying,
What's the use of trying to give an adept a dose of his own medicine?

> (Y: But if you don't test him, how can you discern the truth, so it's good to confront and investigate. Thus, it's necessary [for Zhaozhou] to question Touzi, 若不驗過. 爭辨端的. 遇著試與一鑒. 又且何妨. 也要問過)
>
> (T: Being reborn is a state of transcendence one knows only for himself, so why test others? 甦後同絕只可自知. 何必驗人)

Even ancient buddhas couldn't express their understanding.

> (Y: They had to rely on companions. A thousand sages haven't transmitted it and I also don't know how, 賴是有伴. 千聖也不傳. 山僧亦不知)

I'm not sure who can elucidate truth without scattering dust and sand.

> (T: Since a person arrives at truth even though his words don't convey it, who's able to provide a distinctive explanation of these strange circumstances? 已到之人又言未到. 誰能過此別說奇特)

活中有眼還同死 / 藥忌何須鑑作家 / 古佛尚言曾未到 / 不知誰解撒塵沙.

Comments: Xuedou's first couplet deals with the idea that the two interlocutors are of comparable status in terms of the quality of their respective enlightenment experiences, yet they engage in a dharma battle by testing one another's prowess and ability to react spontaneously to probing inquiries or comments, while conceding the aptitude embodied by their counterpart. However, the second couplet suggests that the most advanced level of proficiency in mustering the Chan knack for adapting to shifting situations through evocative utterances may seem futile, yet this remains a necessary stage since no genuine learning or elucidation can transpire without such an effort.

As Yuanwu notes in prose commentary of the basic conundrum about speaking embedded in the Chan teaching mission, "Honored old teachers throughout the land sit comfortably on carved wood seats, dishing out blows or shouting, raising their flywhisk or knocking this on their seat, and exhibiting spiritual powers or acting authoritatively, yet all of this is nothing more than scattering sand. But tell me, can this effort be avoided?" (天下老和尚據曲彔木床上. 行棒行喝竪拂敲床. 現神通作主宰. 盡是撒沙. 且道如何免得).

Ode 42

Layman Pang's "Wonderful Snowflakes" 龐居士好雪

Case: Yuanwu's introduction highlights the dilemmas faced by Chan adepts when instructing followers in that if their approach sounds distinctive (獨弄), it ends up "dragging around in the mud" (拕泥), but if they try "to harmonize with other teachings" (唱俱行), this leads to an obstructed state of facing a "silver mountain or iron cliff" (銀山鐵壁). Also, "if they discuss and debate, it's like seeing ghosts on top of one's skull, but if they get lost in thought, it's like sitting below a black mountain. Nevertheless, the radiant sun lights up the heavens and the gentle rustling of a pure breeze encircles the earth" (擬議則髑髏前見鬼. 尋思則黑山下打坐. 明明杲日麗天. 颯颯清風匝地).

In the dialogue Layman Pang (龐居士, 740–808), known for living and acting in a way that appears equal or superior to most monastic leaders, is accompanied to the front gate of a temple by an assigned group of itinerant monks as he is about to leave a meeting with the master Yaoshan (藥山, 745–828), a disciple of Shitou (石頭, 700–790). While walking, Pang "points to snow in the sky and says, 'Wonderful snow, one flake at a time doesn't fall any other place'" (士指空中雪云. 好雪片片. 不落別處). A monk asks, "Where does it fall?" (落在甚處). Pang strikes him once and reprimands two times ending with, "You see like a blind person and speak like a mute person" (眼見如盲. 口說如啞). 師別初問處. 握雪便打). Then, "Xuedou adds, 'As soon as the monk asked about where, I would've hit him with a snowball!'" (師別初問處. 握雪便打).

Of Pang's initial remark about snow falling Yuanwu writes, "He stirs up waves where there's no wind since his fingertips have eyes. There's a resonance in this old fellow's words" (無風起浪指頭. 有眼. 這老漢言中有響), and of the monk's query, "Good point, but although he seems to follow Pang's remark, he actually took the bait" (中也. 相隨來也.果然上鈎來). Also, Yuanwu says, "Xuedou's right, but he draws the bow after the thief has fled . . . he, too, has fallen into a ghost cave" (是則是. 賊過後張弓. 爭奈落在鬼窟裏了也).

Tianqi writes of Pang, "He uses his full capacity to construct a test since nothing moves" (全機為驗. 一切無過), of the monk, "He only knows about testing someone but doesn't know how to lose his ego" (只知驗人. 不知失己), and of Xuedou's remark, "Raising a point to cut off [ignorance] can't help but create entanglements" (一起便截. 免得葛藤). Tianqi's final note reads, "Fishing in deep waters points clearly to the great function" (探竿. 旨明大用); and the wrapping phrase says, "Everything's balanced in his hands" (權衡在手).

Verse: My snowball hits!
(Y: Watch him fall into secondary status, 爭奈落在第二機)
Even the honorable Pang couldn't have stopped it,
(T: Pang should've struck as soon as the monk opened his mouth. Otherwise, it gets too late to intervene, 開口便打. 他縱機峻不能插手)
Gods and humans wouldn't know how.
My eyes and ears are thoroughly pure,
(Y: Arrowpoints meeting in midair, but they see like a blind person and speak like a mute person, 箭鋒相拄. 眼見如盲. 口說如啞)
(T: The inner mind and the outer realm form one truth, 內心外境. 通是一真)

So pure through and through,
Even the blue-eyed barbarian (Bodhidharma) can't decipher.
(Y: They should all be buried in the same pit, 一坑理却)
(T: If truth is empty, then speaking and thinking have no path, 一真若空. 言思無路)
雪團打. 雪團打 / 龐老機關沒可把 / 天上人間不自知 / 眼裏耳裏絕瀟洒 / 瀟洒絕 / 碧眼胡僧難辨別.

Comments: Xuedou begins and seems to conclude by playfully applauding his own capping phrase, which highlights the limitation of Pang's approach to teaching that he considers too cerebral in failing to demonstrate responsive activity spontaneously. While Tianqi agrees with Xuedou's criticism of the layman, Yuanwu characteristically reprimands Xuedou's standpoint. After all, it takes a moment to grab the snow and form a snowball, so the opportunity would already have vanished.

According to Yuanwu's prose commentary, "many interpreters misunderstand the image of snow as illustrating a notion of uniformity" (古人以雪明一色邊事), thus involving all phenomena in a grand unity. He argues that Xuedou deliberately undermines this view in the final three lines by saying, ironically, that even the first patriarch could not discriminate eyes from ears or sensations from objects. Thus, the aim of Chan teaching is to refrain from any attachment to either abstractions cut off from concrete existence or material manifestations distanced from knowledge of underlying principles.

Ode 43

Dongshan's "No Cold or Heat" 洞山無寒暑

Case: According to Yuanwu's introduction to the proficiencies of Dongshan Liangjie, the founder of the Caodong school, "His commanding words prevail in heaven and on earth and are followed for eons. Even a thousand sages can't gauge his ability to subdue wild tigers and rhinos. His direct approach to teaching is unhindered, and his complete dynamism is displayed everywhere and anywhere" (定乾坤句. 萬世共遵. 擒虎兕機. 千聖莫辨. 直下更無纖翳. 全機隨處齊彰).

In the brief yet intricate dialogue a monk asks Dongshan, "How can we avoid the onset of cold and heat?" (寒暑到來如何迴避), and the master replies, "Why not go to a place where there's neither cold nor heat?" (何不向無寒暑處去). When the inquirer wants to know such a place, Dongshan responds, "When it's cold, O Worthy, you'll freeze to death, and when it's hot, O Worthy, you'll be scorched to death" (寒時寒殺闍黎. 熱時熱殺闍黎).

Yuanwu's capping phrase for the monk's initial query is, "It's not a matter of finding a particular time of year. Where's the place that [cold and heat] don't rip off one's head and tear apart one's face?" (不是這箇時節. 劈頭劈面在什麼處), and for the second question, "He tricks a boatload of people into abandoning ship. Trying to follow [Dongshan's] pivot, they take the bait as soon as it's offered" (賺殺一船人. 隨他轉. 也一釣便上). Of Dongshan's final retort Yuanwu writes, "The real doesn't conceal the false, and the slanted doesn't hide the upright. Looking out from a cliff to see wild tigers and rhinos offers a special opportunity for him to overturn the great ocean and kick over Mt. Sumeru. But tell me, where's this place?" (真不掩偽. 曲不藏直. 臨崖看虎兕. 特地一場愁. 掀翻大海踢倒須彌. 且道洞山在什麼處).

Tianqi says of the monk's first question, "This is the slanted asking the upright" (就偏問正); and of Dongshan's reply, "This is the slanted pointing to the upright" (就偏指正). Of the second question he writes, "This is the upright asking the upright" (就正問正), and of the second response, "[Dongshan] sees him chasing after the upright, so he points to the slanted" (見逐其正. 復指其偏). Tianqi's concluding note reads, "The interchangeability of upright and slanted points clearly to surpassing divisions between left and right" (正偏互換. 旨明左右無拘); and his wrapping phrase says, "No abiding in duality" (不住二邊).

Verse: An outstretched hand while standing on the edge of a thousand-foot cliff,

(T: An outstretched hand isn't an upright position, and a ten thousand-foot cliff isn't a slanted position, 垂手不居正位. 萬仞不住偏方)

Why refer to connections between the upright and slanted?

(Y: If there's a connection, what does it mean right now without being bound to dualistic thinking? When the wind blows, grasses bend, and when waters flow, conduits form, 若是安排. 何處有今日. 作麼生兩頭不涉. 風行草偃. 水到渠成)

(T: Following causality responds to circumstances, but leaving things alone can be just as valuable, 隨緣應用. 自然恰好)

The jade pavilion sparkles under the bright light of the moon,

A hunting hound bounding up the stairs comes up empty.

(Y: It wasn't just this one time it faltered. Why chase after a clump of dirt? I'll strike saying, "You're all followers of that monk," 不是這回. 蹉過了也. 逐塊作什麼. 打云. 爾與這僧同參)

(T: There's no principle to follow, so just heed examples of those who did or didn't get the point, 不領大旨. 只逐其句. 舉例點罰)

垂手還同萬仞崖 / 正偏何必在安排 / 琉璃古殿照明月 / 忍俊韓獹空上堦.

Comments: Xuedou deals with overcoming several levels of duality implied by the dialogue. The most obvious level is the distinction between hot and cold. The second level, as suggested by Dongshan, is between the outer realm involving the temperature at any given time and location and one's inner ability to cultivate an outlook that remains unaffected by extremes, even when there is no way to prevent the physical suffering external circumstances may inflict.

A third and crucial level, which is evoked by all three interpreters as a heuristic device for examining the case, is the theory of "five positions" (五位), a notion of the interactions of the opposite levels of upright and slanted, or straight and crooked. This doctrine is attributed to Dongshan Liangjie and the Caodong school, although numerous other Chan lineages made use of the concept in explicating the pathway toward enlightenment. However, it is not clear from his records that Dongshan necessarily would have understood the current exchange in this way.

While the second line and several of Yuanwu's remarks reflect some skepticism regarding the utility of five-positions theory, Tianqi's capping phrases on the case show an interesting way of applying the notion, even though his comments on the verse also seem critical. In addition, Xuedou's final couplet indicates that, while the theory may provide an attractive option symbolized by the glittering pavilion, in the final analysis the issue is whether the trainee represented by a useless hunting dog is or is not capable of getting the point.

Ode 44

Heshan's "Genuinely Beat the Drum" 禾山解打鼓

Case: In this dialogue the master Heshan (禾山, 884–960), who studied early in his career with Xuefeng but was not affiliated with one of the main branches of Chan, "gives his assembly an instruction" (垂語), "Learning through reason is called listening and learning by cutting off reason is called immediacy, but going beyond both options is considered true surpassing" (習學謂之聞. 絕學謂之鄰. 過此二者是為真過). A monk probes Heshan with four questions: what is true surpassing, what is truth, what is the meaning of "no-mind, no-buddha" (非心非佛), and "how to welcome an enlightened person" (向上人來時如何接)? Each time the teacher answers the same way: "Genuinely beat the drum" (解打鼓); the first character in this phrase can imply untying a knot or unraveling a problem.

Yuanwu says of Heshan's declaration about transcendence, "See how he has an eye on his forehead?" (頂門上具一隻眼作什麼). Then Yuanwu takes the unusual step of giving the same capping phrase for all four references to drumming: "An iron stake in iron shrubs, so unbreakable!" (鐵橛. 鐵蒺藜. 確確). For Heshan's final response he adds, "But, tell me, what status has he fallen into? He went all the way to India in the morning and came back to China the same night" (且道落在什麼處. 朝到西天暮歸東土).

Tianqi says of Heshan's comment on learning through reason, "It comes out of his mouth and into the monk's ears" (出口入耳), and of the notion of immediacy, "It's a lonely task trying to plug a hole in the sky" (沉空滯寂). Of the comment on nonduality by resisting either option Tianqi writes, "He doesn't fall into positive versus negative, but points clearly to fundamental reality" (不落有無. 方明本分). Of the first mention of drumming he says, "Since the monk is troubled, Heshan shows concrete existence" (恐滯一見故指平實), and of the monk's last query, "What can be shown to a venerated person?" (尊貴中人如何提携).

Tianqi's concluding note reads, "Bringing up a transformative saying points clearly to no fixed path" (拈轉話頭. 旨明無有意路); and his wrapping phrase says, "Directly revealing the radiant source" (直下明宗).

Verse: One teacher lifts a heavy rock, and another one hauls clumps of earth,

(Y: Generals often give commands outside channels. Both have their crimes listed on one indictment, since those suffering the same ailment understand one another, 塞外將軍令. 兩箇一狀領過. 同病相憐)

These examples have the impact of pulling a thousand-foot bow.

(Y: Even if there's a thousand-foot bow, it's still not effective. It's not meant for hitting an easy target, so why use it on a dead toad? 若是千鈞. 也透不得. 不可輕酬. 豈為死蝦蟆)

The venerable teacher on Elephant Cliff (Xuefeng) rolls out wooden balls,

(T: Three masters show the great function in their own way, so learn from those examples, 三處須是太用皆在孤危. 舉例令看)

But nobody compares with Heshan's, "Genuinely beat the drum!"

(T: They don't resemble the way Heshan discloses concrete reality,不似禾山用得平實)

Let me remind you, don't be confused:
Sweet tastes sweet, and bitter tastes bitter.

(Y: I appreciate the comment but since Xuedou wrongly appends this remark, he should receive thirty blows of my staff. Has he ever felt the rod? I'll strike at his vast obscurity! 謝答話. 錯下注脚. 好與三十棒. 喫棒得也未. 便打. 依舊黑漫漫)

(T: Those who offer warnings mustn't deceive. Solitary understanding requires seeing that both sides of the coin are perfectly clear, 告報諸方不得瞞盰. 孤危平實須要兩段. 分明則可)

一拽石. 二搬土 / 撥機須是千鈞弩 / 象骨老師曾輥毬 / 爭似禾山解打鼓 / 報君知. 莫莽鹵 / 甜者甜兮苦者苦.

Comments: The first three lines allude to several instances of Chan adepts using similar examples of everyday existence as teaching devices, including lifting stones and dirt attributed to two unnamed monks and handling a set of balls that was used by Heshan's teacher, Xuefeng, featured in five cases in the *Odes*. In a playful way, Xuedou finds all three teachings lacking when contrasted with Heshan's pedagogical approach.

However, Yuanwu's prose commentary lists additional occurrences of the method of repeating the same responses, thus indicating that Heshan's outlook is not unique. Yuanwu's capping phrases on the opening lines of the verse also disarm the apparent merits of Xuedou and the stories to which he refers. The capping phrases of Yuanwu and Tianqi on the final line continue skepticism by questioning the value of Xuedou's deliberately commonplace saying about the significance of tasting flavors, which in turn evokes case 43 on Dongshan's view of hot and cold.

Ode 45

Zhaozhou's "Seven-Pound Shirt" 趙州衫重七斤

Case: Yuanwu's introduction depicts Zhaozhou's prowess as a Chan teacher: "When he needs to speak, he speaks, and there's no rival to him in the whole world. When it's time for action, he acts, and his total dynamism can't be matched. He's like shooting sparks, flashing lightning, a sizzling flame fanned by breezes, or a sharp sword gleaming" (要道便道. 舉世無雙. 當行即行. 全機不讓. 如擊石火. 似閃電光. 疾焰過風. 奔流度刃). Furthermore, "When he uses a hammer and tongs to lift them up, his disciples can't evade losing their edge or having their tongues tied" (拈起向上鉗鎚. 未免亡鋒結舌).

In the dialogue a monk alludes to one of Zhaozhou's famous catchphrases used as an instructional device, "All things return to oneness; to what does oneness return?" (萬法歸一. 一歸何處). The master replies, as in other instances, with an example of material existence that seems incongruous, "When I lived in Qingzhou [his hometown], they made linen shirts weighing seven pounds" (我在青州. 作一領布衫. 重七斤).

Yuanwu says of the query, "He provokes the old fellow from lofty peaks, but he better not forget to stop making his living in a ghost cave" (拶著這老漢. 堆山積嶽. 切忌向鬼窟裏作活計). Of Zhaozhou's response he writes, "He spontaneously moves anywhere and everywhere with twists and turns that fill the skies, but can you see how Zhaozhou pulls on the nostrils of patch-robed monks?" (果然七縱八橫. 拽却漫天網. 還見趙州麼. 衲僧鼻孔曾拈得).

Tianqi says of the monk, "There's a challenge" (編僻), and of Zhaozhou, "He hits the mark" (當央直指). Tianqi's concluding note says, "The radiant source points clearly to truth" (明宗. 旨明絕待); and his wrapping phrase reads, "Trust what's held in your fingertips" (信手拈來).

Verse: The ancient awl (Zhaozhou) is challenged in his understanding,
But how many people know the "seven-pound shirt"?
(T: The question challenges but the answer is beyond emotion, 問是編僻, 答處絕情)
Right now, I'll toss it into West Lake,
(Y: Xuedou's dexterity enables him to do this, but I don't think it's necessary, 還雪竇手脚始得, 山僧也不要)
Thrown down amid the untainted breeze of Chan teaching, who will fetch it?
(Y: Tell me, from past to present, is Xuedou in tune with Zhaozhou or just jotting down notes? Does the follower know the teacher? 自古自今. 且道雪竇與他酬唱. 與他下注脚. 一子親得)
(T: The concrete reply of the adept completely overturns the monk's probing query, but this famous response can also be cast aside, 編僻之問. 平實之家答. 徹底掀翻. 名曰下載).

編辟曾挨老古錐 / 七斤衫重幾人知 / 如今拋擲西湖裏 / 下載清風付與誰.

Comments: The case is considered to fit one of the groups of eighteen types of dialogues categorized by Fenyang Shanzhao (942–1024, 汾陽善昭), in which a disciple attempts to challenge by striking directly at a teacher's supposed strength with the intention of exposing a fatal fallacy, so that the adept must reply with agility and finesse to win the battle. The verse quickly makes an intriguing thematic leap from the first couplet, which clearly approves of Zhaozhou's reply because it reflects neutrality and balance by betraying no emotion, as Tianqi's capping phrase indicates.

In line three Xuedou provides a scathing remark suggesting that Zhaozhou unwittingly creates new conceptual baggage in conjuring an obviously impractical image. The reference to the shirt may defeat his questioner's challenge, but it can also cause subtle attachments if misunderstood. West Lake may refer to the waterway located in the center of Hangzhou, about which dozens of Song-dynasty poems were written from the hillside above to celebrate the scenery at different times of the day and year. Or it may indicate the large pond beneath the magnificent waterfalls situated close to the temple buildings at Mount Xuedou.

The commentary by Tenkei maintains, "The final lines of this verse have no rival in quality in any era, ancient or modern." The pure breeze is something an adept would like to impart to his disciples, but it is not an object that can be given away to someone who does not already possess it or taken from a person who has attained it based on their words and deeds. What is required for authentic realization, according to Tenkei, is the true dharma eye that allows one to see the situation from both sides without being attached to either perspective.

Ode 46

Jingqing and the Sound of Raindrops 鏡清雨滴聲

Case: The introduction by Yuanwu suggests that the master Jingqing, also featured in case 16 on the simultaneous pecking of chick and hen at the shell (啐啄同時), thus indicating the harmonious interplay of teacher and disciple, meets his match in this gong'an record. As an adept, Jingqing's "slightest word can overcome ignorance by untying knots, as if he walks on thin ice or runs over sharp blades" (片言可折. 去縛解粘. 如氷凌上行. 劍刃上走). But Yuanwu cautions, "leaving aside his marvelous function in every direction, tell me, how does he perform at any given moment? (縱橫妙用則且置. 剎那便去時如何).

The intricate dialogue with an anonymous monk concerns the issue of self-awareness. When asked by the teacher what he hears outside the temple gates (門外), the novice says, "The sound of raindrops" (雨滴聲), and Jingqing proclaims critically, "Sentient beings are topsy-turvy by losing themselves while pursuing external things" (眾生顛倒. 迷己逐物). The monk then asks about the standpoint of Jingqing who says, "Almost, but I don't lose myself like that" (洎不迷己意旨如何). When the monk presses him again, Jingqing offers an analogy, "Transcending is easy, but expressing it is difficult" (出身猶可易. 脫體道應難), which reverses the typical examination-hell maxim, "Studying is easy, but passing is hard." The *Blue Cliff Record* version of the case ends by annotating the word "almost," which can also mean "soaked," as "His greatness is cut to size" (巨至切及也).

Yuanwu's comments give credit to the monk just as much or more than the master. Of Jingqing's first response he says, "A concern arises but Jingqing usually gets his way when he pulls in an interlocutor by depending on his own abilities" (事生也. 慣得其便. 鐃鈎搭索. 還他本分手脚), and of the monk pressing the teacher, "It seems like he suffers a defeat but he grabs the spear and turns it around" (果然納敗缺. 轉槍來也). Of Jingqing's final comment Yuanwu writes, "Nah! He just can't explain" (咄直得分疎不下).

Tianqi is more positive regarding Jingqing's topsy-turvy remark, "The point is evident in his words" (點逐其句). However, he notes that "the monk's suspicions are raised" (展轉生疑) when he asks for clarification. Of Jingqing's final comment he writes, "It's easy to express in words, but difficult to grab hold with your hands" (逐句則易. 撒手則難). Tianqi's concluding note reads, "Encountering things is a radiant source pointing clearly to dynamism revealed in words" (遇物明宗. 旨明句裏呈機); and his wrapping phrase says, "Everything's balanced in his hands" (權衡在手).

Verse: "Sound of raindrops," in the desolate hall,

(Y: Uninterrupted as everyone in the assembly listens, 從來無間斷. 大家在這裏)

Even an adept has a hard time responding.
If he says his understanding is one with the flux,
(Y: He's put his head in a pot of glue. If it's not called the sound of raindrops, then what's it called? 剌頭入膠盆. 不喚作 雨滴聲. 喚作什麼聲)
That's not really an understanding.
(T: If he's one with the flux, he forgets the place, and if he loses himself, he becomes preoccupied with things, 若作入流忘所. 依舊迷己逐物)
Whether there's an understanding or not,
Southern and northern mountains are drenched by driving rain.
(T: Looking all around to view mountains the south and north, we can say the sound of raindrops is one with the flux, 雙舉令看. . . 且道是雨聲是入流)
虚堂雨滴聲 / 作者難酬對 / 若謂曾入流 / 依前還不會 / 會不會 / 南山北山轉霶霈.

Comments: The poem has an irregular structure with 5-5-5-5-3-7 characters that features rhyming in the final five lines: Xū táng yǔdī sheng / Zuòzhě nán chóu duì / Ruò wèi céng rùliú / Yī qián hái bù huì / Huì bù huì / Nánshān běishān zhuǎn pāng pèi. Xuedou begins by gently chiding Jingqing while highlighting the dilemma faced by both interlocutors as well as those studying the case since no solution is proposed. The master dodges giving a direct answer to the monk's probe, but this does not seem satisfactory, so Xuedou offers an elegant lyrical image evoking how, in a robust rainstorm, the entire environment encompassing peaks at both ends of the range is overwhelmed by the sensation of falling water.

This setting surpassing the matter of individual awareness conjures a scene of pure objectivity as the only possible yet paradoxical way of clarifying the matter of perceptivity. Jingqing's criticism of those who are guided by externality is at once correct, in that such a preoccupation leads to delusion, and incorrect, because a holistic experience of nonduality transpires only through embracing what is within and without. Who hears the driving rain? The answer must reflect an understanding that one's essential, egoless nature requires full immersion in the surroundings without sacrificing subjectivity to the deception of chasing idly after objects.

Ode 47

Yunmen's "Six Don't Encompass It" 雲門六不收

Case: Yuanwu writes that an adept like Yunmen is able "to see the essence and function of the four seasons revolving in the sky and the myriad things arising on the ground" (天何言哉. 四時行焉). "But," he continues, "tell me where can you find a patch-robed monk detached from words and speech or movement and activity whether walking, standing, sitting, or lying down? With your mouth, throat, and lips shut tight, can this be discerned?" (且道向什麼處見得衲僧. 離却言語動用行住坐臥. 併却咽喉唇吻. 還辨得麼).

In the dialogue, which recalls case 39, a monk asks Yunmen, "What's the *dharmakāya*?" (如何是法身), which refers to the fundamental level of reality that is infinite, unmanifested pure illumination not represented by any category of classification or enumeration yet forming the basis for what is apparent throughout the universe, including the darkened and opaque. Yunmen responds, "Six don't encompass it" (六不收), probably indicating the basic Buddhist notion regarding how the six sense organs and sense objects give rise to six levels of consciousness (六根六塵六識), although Yuanwu's prose comments dismiss such a literal interpretation.

Yuanwu writes of the monk's query, "So many people have doubts and even a thousand sages couldn't express it, but this novice exposes Yunmen's flaws" (多少人疑著. 千聖跳不出. 漏逗不少). Of the reply he says, "He slices through iron nails and shears, like an octagonal millstone flying through the air, yet is like a spirit tortoise dragging its tail" (斬釘截鐵. 八角磨盤空裏走. 靈龜曳尾). The paradoxical remark about the hoisted millstone greatly inspired the teachings of numerous Japanese teachers who established the Zen movement.

Tianqi's comments repeat capping phrases he uses elsewhere: of the question he writes, "Probing further" (請益), and of the response, "He hits the mark" (當央直指). Tianqi's final note reads, "The radiant source points clearly to truth" (明宗. 旨明絕待); and his wrapping phrase says, "Trust whatever's held in your fingertips" (信手拈來).

Verse: One, two, three, four, five, six,

(Y: Keep counting and then start all over again until a drip of water turns into a drop of ice—so, why bother making the effort? 周而復始. 滴水滴凍. 費許多工夫作什麼)

Even the blue-eyed barbarian (Bodhidharma) can't add it up.
(T: Don't even try, as buddhas and patriarchs have difficulty expressing it, 蓋無意路. 佛祖難言)
Yet the master of Shaolin claimed he was succeeded by Shenguang (Huike),
And then, wrapped in his robe, he returned to India.
(Y: He deceived everyone! 賺殺一船人)
(T: It's not necessary to talk about his return, 不必言歸)
India's so vast, there's no way to find him there,
But every night he comes to stay with us right here on Ru Peak!
(Y: Tell me, is this the body of dharma (*dharmakāya*) or the body of buddha (*buddhakāya*)? Either way, I'll deliver thirty blows! 且道是法身是佛身. 放爾三十棒)
(T: Don't talk about finding him elsewhere, just look at who's staying on Ru Peak, 且道不在諸方. 你看乳峰誰宿)
一二三. 四五六 / 碧眼胡僧數不足 / 少林謾道付神光 / 卷衣又說歸天竺 / 天竺茫茫無處尋 / 夜來却對乳峰宿.

Comments: Xuedou's verse accomplishes two main goals evident throughout the collection, including (a) dislodging his followers from an attachment to a literal interpretation of the dialogue, however intriguing it seems; and (b) relocating traditional Chan lore in terms of the immediacy of his own current teaching environment. Therefore, Hakuin says this poem is the most effective one in the whole collection because of how it mocks an abacus-based approach to interpreting authentic awakening. Yuanwu remarks, "Xuedou excels at using his eyes to read between the lines of obscure passages and create an original verse that teaches others how to see" (雪竇善能於無縫罅處. 出眼目頌出教人見).

According to Yuanwu, "only a descendent of Yunmen's school would be capable of doing it this way" (須是還他屋裏兒孫始得), which shows that he regards lineal affiliation as key to understanding the case. As is often the case, Yuanwu's phrases cast a somewhat skeptical glance at both Yunmen's standpoint and Xuedou's imagery, and at the end of his prose comments it is recorded, "Yuanwu strikes while saying, 'Blind!'" (師便打云. 瞎). However, Tianqi supports situating the presence of Bodhidharma not in India or anywhere other than the assembly convened at Xuedou's temple.

Ode 48

Senior Monk Lang Throwing over the Tea Kettle 朗上座翻却茶銚

Case: In this complicated narrative featuring multiple levels of symbolism, including the relationship between local deities and the role of Chan rites developed in China, especially the tea ceremony, a government minister named Wang visits Zhaoqing (招慶) temple, even though the master is absent. When he arrives, senior monk Lang (朗上座) holds the tea kettle for his colleague Mingzhao (明昭), mentioned in comments on verse 35, but it suddenly turns over (翻却茶銚) in his hands. The minister asks what happened and Lang suggests the accident was caused by the stove god that props the kettle (捧爐神). The minister says, "If the kettle's propped by the stove god, then why did you turn it over?" (既是捧爐神. 為什麼翻却茶銚). The monk answers with a sarcastic remark, "Serve as an official for a thousand days, but lose your status in one morning" (仕官千日失在一朝).

Then, "the minister shakes his sleeves [as a sign of disdain] and leaves" (傅拂袖便去). Mingzhao reprimands Lang by saying, "You've taken your rice at Zhaoqing, but you wander off in the countryside, cutting down withered camellia trees [used for harvesting tea]" (朗上座喫却招慶飯了. 却去江外. 打野榸). Lang says, "What about you, teacher?" (和尚作麼生) and Mingzhao replies, "The spirit [literally, "non-human"] got the best of us" (非人得其便). Xuedou interjects, "If I'd been there, I would've kicked over that kettle!" (當時但踏倒茶爐).

Yuanwu says, "Lang doesn't know how to make tea, so he drags others into it" (不會煎茶. 帶累別人). Of Mingzhao's remark he writes, "After all, he only has one eye so was able to speak only half a truth, with one side lifting up and the other pushing down" 果然只具一隻眼. 道得一半. 一手擡一手搦). Concerning Xuedou's capping phrase, "He draws his bow after the thief has fled, so he can't be referred to as a member of Deshan's lineage [known for striking with staffs]. Since the whole bunch (Wang, Lang, and Mingzhao) are mischievous fools, Xuedou stands out" (爭奈賊過後張弓. 雖然如是. 也未稱德山門下客. 一等是潑郎潑賴. 就中奇特).

Tianqi says of Lang, "He only knows how to act, but doesn't realize he lacks knowledge" (只知呈機. 不知失智), of Mingzhao's second comment,

"It's a capping phrase that goes against the grain of expectations" (如此下語. 反惹人恠), and of Xuedou, "His decree's like a daredevil's sword" (如此行令. 誰敢當鋒). Tianqi's concluding note says, "A distinct standpoint missing the mark points clearly to a scorching blaze" (違宗失旨. 旨明惹火燒身); and his wrapping phrase reads, "Not living up to his duties" (不守本分).

Verse: The minister's question tries to stir the wind,
But Lang's response fails to deliver.
(Y: They're both cowards throwing mudballs to no avail or trying, unlike adepts, to put a round peg in a square hole, 弄泥團漢有什麼限. 方木逗圓孔. 不妨撞著作家)
(T: Lang's hopelessly deluded, 朗之迷宗)
Too bad this dragon (Mingzhao),
Doesn't show his fangs and claws.
(T: His roar can't be heard, 満瓶不響)
My fangs and claws produce lightning and thunder—
How many times have I been tossed about by the currents of billowing waves?
(Y: Seventy-two blows become a hundred-fifty, 七十二棒翻成一百五十)
(T: Old Xuedou boasts that trampling the stove is bold and daring, 雪老自誇. 踏爐之機無敢當堵)
來問若成風 / 應機非善巧 / 可悲獨眼龍 / 曾未呈牙爪 / 牙爪開. 生雲雷 / 逆水之波經幾迴.

Comments: Xuedou highlights the lack of insight demonstrated by the three interlocutors—minister Wang fails to entrap Lang while departing in a huff, the senior monk is chided by his elder, and Mingzhao is overly blunt in critiquing Lang. Xuedou's interjection in the dialogue seeks to salvage authentic Chan insight from this messy situation by emphasizing spontaneous disruptive action, like a mythical dragon stirring the cosmos, over and above the style of dead words.

However, Xuedou is no doubt aware that his ploy was disingenuously proposed long after the fact. Thus, it could be seen as one more example of empty speech, although that is still preferable to the deficiencies of the three rascals involved in the case.

Ode 49

Sansheng's "Golden Carp Passes through the Net" 三聖透網金鱗

Case: Yuanwu introduces this dialogue in which two Chan masters challenge one another by highlighting the difficulties involved in proclaiming genuine realization, which must always be tested and demonstrated in a dharma battle: "Probing seven times but breaking through the eighth, snatching drums and capturing flags through a hundred turns and a thousand measures, watching the front side while guarding the back, crouching on a tiger's head to capture its tail—none of this can prove someone is truly an adept" (七穿八穴. 攙鼓奪旗. 百匝千重. 瞻前顧後. 踞虎頭收虎尾. 未是作家).

In the case Sansheng (fl. ninth century), a disciple of Linji who compiled his mentor's recorded sayings and was known for having visited various teachers after attaining enlightenment, confronts Xuefeng with a question that recalls imagery in Ode 7. He refers to a Chinese legend indicating that proficient fish swim upstream through a powerful waterfall to transform into dragons, which symbolizes Chan awakening (like passing civil exams). According to Sansheng's inquiry challenging a rival in his temple, "When this golden carp passes through the net, what'll it eat?" (透網金鱗未審以何為食). Xuefeng retorts, "Once you've passed through, I'll let you know" (待汝出網來. 向汝道). Sansheng's comeback is, "A renowned teacher of fifteen hundred followers can't express it!" (一千五百人善知識. 話頭也不識). Xuefeng concludes the exchange by remarking, "This old monk has too many duties that he must attend" (老僧住持事繁).

In prose comments Yuanwu suggests the dialogue between "Xuefeng and Sansheng includes one exit and one entry, one thrust and one parry, without distinguishing between victory and defeat" (雪峯三聖. 雖然一出一入一挨一拶. 未分勝負在), since "both adepts hold their own by standing as tall as a ten thousand-foot pavilion" (兩家. 把定封疆. 壁立萬仞), which recalls the dynamic of case 41. Yuanwu says of Xuefeng's jibe, "He knocks down his rival's value but a skilled teacher stands on his merit" (減人多少聲價. 作家宗師天然自在), and of Sansheng's response, "His thunderbolt startles the crowd to death" (迅雷霹靂可殺驚群). Also, Yuanwu says that, although the Linji and Caodong schools have their respective interpretations, neither fully captures the flavor of this exchange.

Tianqi writes of Sansheng's initial question, "He shows how to unravel a knot; can you say this about an ordinary person?" (借事呈解. 出過凡聖以何為道), and of Xuefeng's final comment, "He doesn't distinguish between victory and defeat, but falls back a level" (不辨賢愚. 退已一陷). Tianqi's final comment reads, "This interaction is clear and auspicious" (互換. 旨明心倖); and his capping phrase says, "Adepts recognizing one other" (作家相見).

Verse: "The golden carp passes through the net," don't say it stays in stagnant water,
Shaking heaven and moving earth, swinging its fins, and flipping its tail.
(Y: An adept among adepts, but this isn't so extraordinary. Let him emerge, there's nothing to stop him, 作家作家. 未是他奇特處. 放出又何妨)
Spouting like a huge whale stirring manifold waves,
With one thunderclap, pure breezes blow.
(T: Sansheng's transformed into a whale, and Xuefeng resembles the sound of thunder, 三聖如鯨變化. 雪峰如雷相送)
The pure breeze of Chan teaching flows everywhere,
But how many people can feel it?
(Y: Xuefeng guards the front and Sansheng watches the back, but isn't this scattering dust and sand? I'll strike saying, "Where are you?" 雪峰牢把陣頭. 三聖牢把陣脚. 撒土撒沙作什麼. 打云爾在什麼處)
(T: Nothing else in the world compares to these marvelous masters, 二人之妙. 世非有比)
透網金鱗. 休云滯水 / 搖乾蕩坤. 振鬣擺尾 / 千尺鯨噴洪浪飛 / 一聲雷震清飈起 / 清飈起天上 / 人間知幾幾.

Comments: According to Yuanwu's prose remarks, his teacher Wuzu (五祖, 1024–1104) maintained that "the first couplet alone completes the verse" (此一句頌了也). Since line one restates from the dialogue that the golden fish passes through the net, the second line may seem unnecessary because Sansheng could not stay in unmoving water since a dragon "must be where the vast swelling floods of white foamy waves reach the skies" (必在洪波浩渺白浪滔天處).

The rest of Xuedou's poem praises interactions between Sansheng and Xuefeng, who do not try to best one another, although it may appear that the latter's final remark sounds either deferential and defeated or impatient and superior to the former's apparent putdown. Tenkei comments that such an open-ended query is typical of the Yunmen lineage but is unfathomable to other Chan schools. In the final line Xuedou questions whether and to what extent the exchange is genuinely understood.

Ode 50

Yunmen's "Rice and Water" 雲門飯飯

Case: Yuanwu's introduction highlights challenges faced by a teacher training disciples to attain the status of an adept who must "go beyond stages and surpass skillful means, so that every action is mutually responsive, and each phrase corresponds to those of another teacher. But if someone hasn't entered the gate of great liberation and attained a great function, how can they measure up to buddhas and patriarchs, or fully reflect our school's teachings?" (度越階級超絕方便. 機機相應. 句句相投. 儻非入大解脫門. 得大解脫用. 何以權衡佛祖. 龜鑑宗乘.). Furthermore, "Tell me, when taking control of a situation, whether going backward or forward, up-and-down or sideways, can you utter a phrase expressing your true self?" (且道當機直截. 逆順縱橫. 如何道得出身句).

In the dialogue a monk asks Yunmen, "What is sensation-by-sensation samādhi?" (如何是塵塵三昧), which refers to attaining a supreme state of concentration such that each and every aspect of perception encompasses the interplay between sense organs and sense objects that no longer disturb or disrupt genuine self-awareness. Yunmen responds, "Rice in the bowl, water in the pitcher" (鉢裏飯桶裏水), which represents another example of answering an abstract question by pointing to concrete everyday existence, thus recalling Layman Pang's famous saying that "carrying water and chopping wood" (運水及搬柴) constitutes enlightenment.

Yuanwu writes of the novice's query, "Monks all over the world build their nests in caves. His mouth's filled with frost, but isn't he scattering sand and dirt? (天下衲僧盡在這裏作窠窟. 滿口含霜. 撒沙撒土作什麼). Of Yunmen's comment he says, "His satchel carries awls and lets gold and sand intermingle but this adds error upon error since, within palace gates, no one asks the way to the capital" (布袋著盛錐. 金沙混雜. 將錯就錯. 含元殿裏不問長安).

Tianqi writes of the monk's question, "Probing further" (請益), and of Yunmen's response, "The lid fits the box perfectly" (函蓋相應). His final note says, "Directly revealing the radiant source points clearly to no fixed path" (直下明宗. 旨明無有意路); and his wrapping phrase reads, "Trust what's held in your fingertips" (信手拈來).

Verse: "Rice in the bowl, water in the pitcher,"

(Y: You must rinse your mouth out for three years before you'll get it, 漱口三年始得)

Even the most talkative teacher is at a loss for words.

(T: What a strange comment; body and mouth are never severed, 註上之奇. 通身是口不能分訴)

The North Dipper and the Southern Star don't stand apart,

(Y: Why refer to east as west? Sitting and standing are clear; a tall person is a tall *dharmakāya* and a short person is a short *dharmakāya*, 喚東作西作什麼. 坐立儼然. 長者長法身. 短者短法身)

(T: Everything's what it is, nothing moves or turns, 一一當然. 悉無動轉)

White breakers touching the sky arise from flat land.

(Y: They emerge from several fathoms beneath your feet as guest and host interact, but suddenly they're over your head. What'll you do? I'll strike, 脚下深數丈. 賓主互換. 驀然在爾頭上. 爾又作麼生. 打)

(T: Everything standing still gets ripped asunder. It's flipped around and turned upside down, so you must learn to live accordingly, 悉滯定量. 所以又破. 忽乃顛拈倒用. 你却又作麼生)

Whether following or not, holding firm or not,

Everyone's a rich man's son caught without his pants.

(Y: Pathetic, according to this scornful observer, 郎當不少. 傍觀者哂)

(T: When you try doing something, you can't, but when you don't try, you can, 欲行不能行. 欲止不能止)

鉢裏飯. 桶裏水 / 多口阿師難下嘴 / 北斗南星位不殊 / 白浪滔天平地起 / 擬不擬. 止不止 / 箇箇無裩長者子.

Comments: Yuanwu compares this verse to Odes 14 and 75 (73) because in the opening couplet Xuedou reiterates the keyword but in the next lines delves into paradoxes or parables. The passage about the waves is especially appreciated by commentators as key to understanding the multiperspectival worldview of Chan adepts. The final line alludes to a parable in the *Lotus Sūtra* about the prodigal son of a wealthy man who loses even his trousers before his status is recovered and his fortune returned.

Xuedou is influenced by a Hanshan poem that universalizes the moral deficiencies featured in this case: "Suffering on every level, / But vainly discussing their own ideas. / Even if skillful, they're lost in a swamp, / Lacking ability, they stay behind closed doors. / The sun rises over the cliff, but it stays dark, / The mist vanishes, but the valley remains hidden. / All these rich men's sons / Getting caught with their pants down" (六極常嬰苦. 九維徒自論. 有才遺草澤. 無勢閉蓬門. 日上巖猶暗. 煙消谷尚昏. 其中長者子. 箇箇總無裩).

Ode 51

Yantou's "Last Word" 巖頭末後句

Case: Yuanwu introduces this complicated gong'an involving Xuefeng and Yantou (巖頭, 828–887), his senior colleague under the mentorship of Deshan, through highlighting some of the challenges faced by an aspiring adept: "Tell me, is it better to let go or hold firm? When you get to that stage, if there's the slightest trace of an explanation you'll remain obstructed by verbal discussions, but if you make use of instructional devices related to circumstances it'll be like a ghost clinging to weeds in the forest" (且道放行即是. 把住即是. 到這裏. 若有一絲毫解路. 猶滯言詮. 尚拘機境. 盡是依草附木). Moreover, "If you unswervingly realize genuine liberation, you won't avoid hoping to return home ten thousand miles away, but will you ever get there?" 直饒便到獨脫處. 未免萬里望鄉關. 還搆得麼. 若未搆得).

The story can be divided into three segments. First, Xuefeng lives in a hermitage (住庵), probably during the Chinese government's persecution of Buddhism, when many temples were shuttered. A couple of monks come by to pay respect and in greeting them he asks, 'What is it?' " (二僧來拜. 峰見. 兩手托門放身出云. 是什麼). The monks repeat, "What is it?" and Xuefeng abruptly goes inside. Next, the monks travel to stay at the temple of Xuefeng's dharma brother, Yantou. After hearing what happened he says, "Alas, I regret not telling Xuefeng long ago about the last word. If only I'd told him, then no one in the world would question the old teacher" (噫我當初悔不向他道末後句. 若向伊道. 天下人不奈雪老何). Finally, "at the end of the summer retreat, the monks bring up this topic again to request further instruction" (至夏末再舉前話請益), and Yantou says, "Xuefeng and I were born together, but we won't die together. Do you want to know the last word? Just this!" (雪峰與我同條生. 不與我同條死. 要識末後句. 只這是).

Yuanwu says of Xuefeng returning to his hut in disappointment, "Muddy grounds have thorns, but he's like a dragon without feet or a snake with horns. That's exactly why he's so hard to deal with" (爛泥裏有刺. 如龍無足. 似蛇有角. 就中難為措置). Of Yantou's final remark he writes, "Even though he tricks a boatload of people into abandoning ship, I don't believe him. He almost expresses the meaning, but in the end not quite" (賺殺一船人. 我也不信. 洎乎分疎不下).

Tianqi says of the monks repeating Xuefeng's query, "They lose sight of his question" (失見悞問), and of his return to the hut, "He clearly shows a way beyond" (全提向上). Of Yantou's final comment he writes, "He's too exhausted to explain" (竭力提持). Tianqi's concluding note reads, "Hitting the mark points clearly to a blade hidden in words" (當央直示. 旨明句裏藏機); and his wrapping phrase says, "No one really knows" (不遇知音).

Verse: "The last word" can be explained,
It occurs when brightness and darkness are interwoven.

> (Y: It already exists prior to speech, but if you look right at it, you'll go blind. Try explaining, but it can't be expressed. It has a head but no tail, or a tail but no head, 已在言前. 覷著則瞎. 舌頭落也. 說不著. 有頭無尾有尾無頭)

Born together, [Xuefeng and Yantou] intimately share knowledge,
By not dying together, they go separate ways.
Separate ways!
Even gold-headed Buddha and blue-eyed Bodhidharma are at a loss.

> (T: There are many edges in the darkness, so being very careful is the responsibility of buddhas and patriarchs who know how to make distinctions, 暗中既異. 不得粗心. 任是佛祖. 也要辨別)

Let's return home from south, north, east, or west,
In the deep night, together we'll watch snow falling on high peaks.

> (Y: Still half a month away from getting there . . . Blind people, do they know the last word? I'll strike! 猶較半月程 . . . 箇瞎漢. 還識得末後句麼. 便打)
>
> (T: Dark at night but bright with snow. At this moment, throughout the entire realm you can see who's in darkness and who's in brightness, 夜是暗. 雪是明. 正當此時. 四海咸來. 你看誰明誰暗)

末後句. 為君說 / 明暗雙雙底時節 / 同條生也共相知 / 不同條死還殊絕 / 還殊絕 / 黃頭碧眼須甄別 / 南北東西歸去來 / 夜深同看千巖雪.

Comments: The opening lines suggest the last word represents a universal solution which is at once everywhere and nowhere. The next two couplets highlight discrepancies between masters going in different directions, as per Yantou's assessment mentioned to the perplexed monks but not fully understood even by the Buddha or Bodhidharma.

In the final lines Xuedou moves in another thematic direction to conjure an integration of incomparable unity and the endless multiplicity of perspectives by depicting a homecoming to no particular place. This enables everyone to experience the brightness of the snowfall from the standpoint of seeing the interplay of light and dark, as well as high and low, here and there, and other apparent polarities. According to Tenkei, who prefers that Yantou would say, "Not this," the lyrical imagery at the end of the poem constitutes Xuedou's own "last word."

Ode 52

Zhaozhou's Stone Bridge 趙州石橋

Case: This gong'an resembles several examples, especially cases 12, 39, and 45, in which there is an emphasis on concrete existence rather than abstraction. Here, the main topic is an impressive and well-used bridge near the site of Zhaozhou's temple. A visiting monk says, "For a long time I heard about the stone bridge, but now that I'm here, I only see an ordinary bridge [made of logs]" (久響石橋. 到來只見略彴).

The actual bridge was designed and constructed of limestone in the early seventh century by the craftsman Li Chun to stand over the Xiaohe River about 280 kilometers southwest of Beijing and facilitate trade between north and south China in an area threatened by summer and autumn flooding. Also known as the Anjiqiao (安濟橋, "Safe-crossing Bridge") or Dashiqiao (大石橋, "Great Stone Bridge"), this is the oldest standing viaduct in China and the world's largest and longest lasting open-spandril segmental stone arch bridge that is used today only by pedestrians.

The teacher replies to the monk's query, "You only see an ordinary bridge, but you don't see the stone bridge" (汝只見略彴. 不見石橋). When the monk asks, "What's the stone bridge?," Zhaozhou says, "Donkeys cross and horses cross" (度驢度馬). The viaduct symbolizes the pathway to overcoming severe challenges while pursuing enlightenment and it also serves as an epithet for the master whose character is called into question by an upstart's wordplay.

Yuanwu writes of the monk's opening rebuff, "Here's someone who tries to grab the tiger by its whiskers, which is what patch-robed monks are supposed to do" (也有人來捋虎鬚. 也是衲僧本分事). Of the teacher's response he says, "Once again, Zhaozhou gains the advantage by acting like an old man selling his teachings at a marketplace" (慣得其便. 這老漢賣身去也), and of the monk's simple query, "He climbs right onto Zhaozhou's hook" (上釣來也. 果然).

Tianqi writes of the monk's initial comment, "He uses something tangible to challenge an adept" (借事驗主. 眇視趙州), and of Zhaozhou's response, "He contradicts the monk to show a deeper meaning" (就見反追. 深識來風). Of the monk's next question Tianqi says, "He takes the opportunity to test the teaching device" (就機驗機), and of Zhaozhou's comeback, "He hits the mark" (當央直指). Tianqi's concluding note reads, "Host and guest interacting points clearly to no fixed path" (主賓互換. 旨明無有意路); and his wrapping phrase is, "Auspicious!" (心倖).

Verse: His approach is lofty without becoming haughty,

(T: Everyone else seems haughty, but this old adept stays even-handed, 諸方孤危. 此老平實)

When he sets out in the ocean to catch a giant turtle.

(Y: He cuts off distinctions between sacred and profane; shrimp, clams, snails, or oysters aren't worth asking about. Skillful people don't come in groups of two or three, 坐斷要津不通凡聖. 蝦蜆螺蚌不足問. 大丈夫漢. 不可兩兩三三)

(T: Don't fish just for shrimp in the great sea. Profound wisdom isn't a matter of small virtue, 大海不釣其蝦. 大智不為小德)

It's laughable to compare this to Zhaozhou's contemporary, Guanxi,
Who once made a futile effort by saying, "Quick as an arrow."

(T: This refers to a generic topic, so where's the fresh insight? 用處一般. 爭奈尖新)

孤危不立道方高 / 入海還須釣巨鰲 / 堪笑同時灌溪老 / 解云劈箭也徒勞.

Comments: The first couplet suggests that Zhaozhou's instructional approach serves the bodhisattva teaching mission without lapsing into the inaccessibility and incomprehensibility of arrogance or the counterproductive posturing of some leaders who make a point that, in the end, is more about expressing their selfhood than breaking through the spiritual obstacles plaguing the interlocutor. Capping phrases on line two by Yuanwu and Tianqi suggest that effective discursive devices designed deliberately to perplex followers must never be petty or vindictive.

In the final couplet Xuedou highlights the deficiencies of a similar exchange once undertaken by a lesser-known colleague of Zhaozhou named Guanxi (灌溪, ?–895), who was enlightened under Linji. That dialogue focuses on a wordplay regarding Guanxi's name, which literally means "roaring stream." A monk says, "I've long heard of the roaring stream but now that I'm here I only see a retting-hemp pool" (久響灌溪. 及乎到來. 只見箇漚麻池).

The master says, "You only see a retting-hemp pool but you don't see the roaring stream" (汝只見漚麻池. 且不見灌溪). When the monk asks, "What's the roaring stream?" Guanxi replies, "Quick as an arrow" (劈箭急). Although the Chan tradition generally praises this repartee, Xuedou's evaluation is that it merely toys with a pun but does not reveal the genuine character of the teacher in the way accomplished by Zhaozhou's rhetorical skills.

Ode 53

Mazu's Wild Ducks 馬祖野鴨

Case: Yuanwu introduces Mazu as an adept who realizes that "nothing's hidden in the universe, so his complete dynamism is always revealed. He confronts situations without being obstructed and fully expresses himself in every move. In speaking there's no bias, yet he has the capacity to devastate people" (遍界不藏. 全機獨露. 觸途無滯. 著著有出身之機. 句下無私. 頭頭有殺人之意).

In the dialogue, often compared to case 46 that is similarly concerned with perceiving external phenomena, Mazu walks along with his follower Baizhang when they "see a flock of wild ducks flying by" (野鴨飛過). Using this ordinary moment as an opportunity for extraordinary instruction, Mazu asks, "What's that?" (是什麼), and Baizhang says, "Wild ducks." Mazu next asks, "Where've they gone?" (什麼處去也), and Baizhang says, "They've flown away" (飛過去也). Mazu then twists the nostrils of Baizhang so hard he cries, "Ouch," and demands, "Where've they flown?" (何曾飛去).

This exchange involving both verbal sleight of hand and physical punishment is based on the notion that at the very moment the teacher raises the question the ducks have already vanished from their spot. Mazu shows that Baizhang's sensation is partial since, from the standpoint of the birds, it is people below who seem to have moved. In a sequel to the main story cited in Yuanwu's prose commentary, right before Mazu's lecture the following day Baizhang leaves his seat. Later in the abbot's quarters Mazu asks him to explain, and Baizhang claims his nose no longer hurts. The teacher says, "You deeply know current affairs!" (爾深知今日事), thus leading the disciple to a great awakening. Yuanwu remarks that Baizhang "is seamlessly transformed and remains unfettered like a glowing jewel" (阿轆轆地. 羅籠不住. 自然玲瓏).

Yuanwu says of the opening, "Two fellows down in the weeds are rolling around, so what made them notice the ducks?" (兩箇落草漢草裏輥. 驀顧作什麼), and of Baizhang's first reply, "His nostrils are already in the hands of another person since he only speaks the obvious. The next ladleful of foul water will be even more poisonous" (鼻孔已在別人手裏. 只管供欵. 第二杓惡水更毒). Of Mazu's final question he writes, "Don't deceive people. This old fellow from the beginning has been making his living in a ghost cave" (莫瞞人好. 這老漢元來只在鬼窟裏作活計).

Tianqi says of Mazu's second question, "He was stuck before but now he's back on track" (前之已蹉. 後之復提), of Baizhang's reply, "They'll never get there" (依舊不達), and of Mazu's final query, "This shows the great function" (大用急提). Tianqi's concluding note reads, "Following the conditions of people points clearly to revealing the radiant source" (隨緣令人. 旨明就事明宗); and his wrapping phrase is, "Grandmotherly kindness!" (老婆心切).

Verse: "Wild ducks," but who knows where?
(T: Checking them out from down below, 審其下落)
Seeing them coming, Mazu encounters Baizhang.
By describing clouds covering mountains and the moon reflected by the sea.
(Y: The ladle's handle on the east side of the temple is long, and the ladle's handle on the west side is short. Do you realize how many entanglements are created? 東家杓柄長. 西家杓柄短. 知他打葛藤多少)

Baizhang didn't understand when Mazu said, "They've flown away,"
He, too, wanted to fly, but instead got caught in Mazu's grip.
(T: Perplexed by external things his nose is grabbed, 恐逐外物. 故扭其鼻)
Speak up!
(Y: What's there to say? Don't make me speak, too. Don't make a wild duck cry. Good heavens! You deserve thirty blows of the stick right where you sit, since nobody knows where they've gone, 什麼道. 不可也教山僧道. 不可作野鴨子叫. 蒼天蒼天. 脚跟下好與三十棒. 不知向什麼處去)
(T: This is a spontaneous example of casting a pole to teach followers, 活處垂釣)
野鴨子. 知何許 / 馬祖見來相共語 / 話盡山雲海月情 / 依前不會還飛去 / 欲飛去. 却把住 / 道道.

Comments: The verse, consisting of three lines with seven characters each surrounded by two six-character interjections and a final reduplicative injunction, makes it clear that Xuedou holds Baizhang accountable for his delusion and praises Mazu's way of handling the disciple. Whereas Tianqi concurs with this assessment, as does the Chan tradition generally, Yuanwu's capping phrase and prose comments suggest that both teacher and disciple are at fault because the account concludes with Mazu's vague rhetorical question that leaves the matter unresolved (despite the follow-up anecdote indicating otherwise).

Finally, Xuedou's command to his followers to offer a spontaneous remark by expressing a high level of insight that would be contrary to Baizhang's reticence is considered by Tenkei to epitomize the teaching method of the Yunmen school that is distinct from that of other Chan lineages.

Ode 54

Yunmen Extends Both Hands 雲門門展兩手

Case: Yuanwu introduces Yunmen, the founder of Xuedou's lineage featured in eighteen cases, as a genuine Chan adept "who's transcended the dichotomy of birth and death, and thus uses transformative activities to smash all barriers. Effortlessly, he cuts through iron and severs nails. Wherever he goes embraces heaven and earth" (透出生死. 撥轉機關. 等閑截鐵斬釘. 隨處蓋天蓋地).

In the dialogue Yunmen asks a visiting monk, "Where've you come from?" (近離甚處) and the answer is, "Xichan" (西禪, n.d.), which apparently refers to his having studied at the temple of a descendant many generations later in the lineage of Nanquan, the mentor of Zhaozhou. When the teacher asks, "What words and phrases are used by Xichan?" (西禪有何言句), "the monk extends both hands" (僧展兩手) and "Yunmen gives him a slap" (門打一掌). The monk says, "Let me explain" (某有話在), but this time Yunmen extends both of his hands and "the monk is speechless" (僧無語), so Yunmen hits him again.

Yuanwu comments on Yunmen's question about Xichan's teaching, "I'd like to discuss it but fear it would startle you, O Teacher" (欲舉恐驚和尚); also he says, "Xichan profoundly distinguished various styles" (深辨來風) and "Xichan was just like you, O Teacher, someone talking in his sleep" (也似和尚相似寐語). Of the monk extending his hands Yuanwu says, "He's lost, like someone allowing a thief to plunder his home. From now on people will doubt him" (敗闕了也. 勾賊破家. 不妨令人疑著), and of the teacher's final action, "Let the monk go, since it's Yunmen who should get the beating. Why? When what should be settled isn't settled, that leads to disorder" (可放過. 此棒合是雲門喫何故. 當斷不斷返招其亂).

Tianqi remarks that the start of the dialogue is commonsensical (常理), but with Yunmen's slap the opportunity for mutual testing has been taken in that "One remark, two points investigated" (一截二驗). Of the monk protesting Tianqi says, "One thought, two points distinguished" (一拈二辨), and of the monk's reticence, "His tricks are used up" (伎倆已盡). Tianqi's concluding note reads, "Settling the matter by striking the monk points clearly to fully revealing rectitude" (就身打劫. 旨明全提正令); and his wrapping phrase says, "Everything's balanced in his hands" (權衡在手).

Verse: In one action he grabs the tiger's head and tail,
(Y: A thousand soldiers are easy to recruit, but one superb general is hard to find, 千兵易得一將難求)
[Yunmen]'s awe-inspiring dignity spreads throughout four hundred domains.
Didn't the monk sense how much danger he was in?
Xuedou says, "I would've let him go."

(Y: If he doesn't let go and act in such a fashion, then everyone in the world would suffer at least once. Just sit down on the meditation mat, 若不放過又作麼生. 盡天下人一時落節. 擊禪床一下)

(T: Xuedou isn't satisfied, since both men have ignored each other from beginning to end, 雪竇不怡. 點他二人不顧前後)

虎頭虎尾一時收 / 凜凜威風四百州 / 卻問不知何太嶮 / 師云. 放過一著.

Comments: The verse begins with exceptional praise for Yunmen. However, the third line is ambiguous: Xuedou seems to criticize the monk's failure to keep up with the master, yet the passage is sometimes interpreted as highlighting the shortcomings of the teacher's style. The two parties either do not take each other seriously enough or, conversely, communicate from a standpoint of mutual concern and support.

The typical pattern of four lines with seven characters is disrupted by the appended line that reflects Xuedou's personal view. One implication is that he feels it is time for the monk to be released rather than reprimanded but is disappointed with both interlocutors. Another interpretation is that Xuedou declines to comment conclusively, thus leaving it up to readers to decide the judgment for themselves. Among the Five Houses of Chan, each lineage had its special way of teaching that was acceptable, but not necessarily accessible, to the other branches. Hakuin remarks, "The secret of the Yunmen school inherited by Xuedou is that there's no need for any explanation."

Xuedou's final utterance, which according to Tianqi's phrase lets the monk off the hook, recalls the ode to case 20 in *Wumen's Barrier* that refers to master Songyuan's (松源, 1132–1202) comment on the great strength yet cryptic utterances of a typical adept: "Raising a leg, he kicks up the fragrant ocean, / Lowering his head, he peers down from the fourth realm of meditation. / There's no space vast enough for his body— / Let someone else write a phrase . . . (擡脚踏翻香水海 / 低頭俯視四禪天 / 一箇渾身無處著請 / 續一句)." The last line uses just three characters that are open-ended, much like Xuedou's four-character ending.

Ode 55

Daowu's "I Won't Say" 道吾不道

Case: Yuanwu introduces this gong'an by highlighting an adept's remarkable degree of flexibility in that "self-confident intimacy with all of reality attains realization immediately, and following the currents in their twists and turns accomplishes direct transmission" (穩密全真. 當頭取證. 涉流轉物. 直下承當). Moreover, "this enables cutting off deceit and deception in an instantaneous spark or flash, mounting the head of a tiger to grab its tail, or climbing atop a thousand-foot wall, as there's not just one way to help people" (向擊石火閃電光中. 坐斷誵訛. 於據虎頭收虎尾處. 壁立千仞. 則且置. 放一線道. 還有為人處也無).

The dialogue is complicated because it involves several interlocutors over a couple of generations, with comments interjected by Xuedou and another observer. Also, the last section shifts the thematic focus of the narrative from the philosophical relationship between life and death to the role of commemorating a master's relics (先師靈骨, literally "spiritual bones"), which is the primary focus of the verse. There are several different versions in various collections, and Tianqi's account is a bit different at the end from the *Blue Cliff Record.*

To summarize the story, the master Daowu (道吾, 769–833) and his disciple Jianyuan (漸源, n.d.) make a condolence call at the home of a congregant. When "Jianyuan taps the coffin and asks if the corpse is alive or dead" (源拍棺云. 生耶死耶), Daowu replies, "I won't say it's alive, and I won't say it's dead" (生耶不道. 死耶不道). Daowu persists in this approach until Jianyuan hits him. After Daowu eventually dies, Jianyuan questions the teacher's disciple, Shishuang (石霜, 807–888), now the current master, who repeats Daowu's words, but this time Jianyuan attains an awakening.

A day later, Jianyuan picks up a small shovel (鍬子) and starts scraping across the floor of the dharma hall (法堂) in search of Daowu's relics. Shishuang says, "Vast waves are boundless, and swells of breakers flood the sky—where will you find our late teacher's remains? (洪波浩渺. 白浪滔天, 覓什麼先師靈骨). Xuedou interjects, "Good heavens, good heavens!" (蒼天蒼天), and Jianyuan says, "I'll try to find them right here" (正好著力). Tianqi's version has Shishuang adding, "This is surely no place to try" (一物也無. 著什麼力), "but Jianyuan keeps moving the shovel" (源持鍬便行). Both versions conclude with the monk Taiyuan Fu (太原孚, n.d.) remarking, "The teacher's relics are still here" (先師靈骨猶在).

Yuanwu says of Xuedou's comment, "It's already too late, like shooting the arrow after the thief has fled—bury them all in the same pit" (太遲生. 賊過後張弓. 好與一坑埋却), and of Taiyuan's remark, "Does everyone see the relics in a flash of lightning? By wearing worn-out sandals, he creates quite a contrast" (大眾見麼. 閃電相似. 是什麼破草鞋. 猶較些子).

Of Shishuang saying not to use the shovel Tianqi writes, "Afraid of falling into the ordinary, he highlights death by holding up life" (恐執平實. 以死拈活), and when Jianyuan keeps digging he suggests, "Cutting off life and death raises the bright side" (截斷二邊. 獨明向上). Tianqi's final note reads, "Using one teaching device after another points clearly to smashing nests of errors" (以機呈機. 旨明就窩打免); and his wrapping phrase says, "There's no falling into lower status" (不落堦級).

Verse: Hares and horses have horns, but oxen and goats don't,

(T: Ancient threats impact the present, and the present impacts ancient threats, 劫外徹於今時. 今時徹於劫外)

Like a wisp of hair as high as mountain peaks.

(T: Nothing's there, yet complete dynamism is revealed in a few words as the radiance of Daowu's answer prevails, 不容一法. 全機獨露四句. 只明道吾答處)

The golden relics are still here,
But, since foaming waves flood the sky, where can you find them?

(Y: Xuedou lets Shishuang go. The relics are right under your feet, but you'll miss them as they can't be seen or heard, 放過一著. 脚跟下蹉過. 眼裏耳裏著不得)

Nowhere at all!
Even he who returned to the west on one sandal loses track.

(Y: If the ancestral shrine isn't completed, this will affect the remains of lineal descendants. I'll strike saying, "Why are they right here?" 祖禰不了. 累及兒孫. 打云. 為什麼却在這裏)

兔馬有角. 牛羊無角 / 絕毫絕氂. 如山如嶽 / 黃金靈骨今猶在 / 白浪滔天何處著 / 無處著 / 隻履西歸曾失却.

Comments: The first couplet consisting of eight-character lines establishes several paradoxes to showcase the meritorious responses by Daowu and Shishuang that enlighten Jianyuan. The next two lines referring to Daowu's relics as "golden" (黃金) repeat Shishuang's lyrical evocation of towering waves to dismiss a literal emphasis on trying to discover the master's remains that preoccupies Jianyuan. Like the futility of trying to make a distinction between life and death, which are interwoven and interdependent, the relics are at once existent and nonexistent. Therefore, Bodhidharma's apparent inability to locate them while traveling back to India ironically indicates that he knows just where they are, which is nowhere at all.

Ode 56

Qinshan's Single Arrowhead 欽山一鏃破

Case: In the introduction Yuanwu suggests that the teaching dilemma confronting the master Qinshan (欽山, n.d.), a lesser-known disciple of Dongshan Liangjie, derives because "all buddhas never appeared in the world" (諸佛不曾出世) and "the first patriarch never came from the west" (祖師不曾西來), so "there's no teaching for people" (亦無一法與人) and "no transmission of the mind" (未嘗以心傳授). Therefore, "since people today don't realize this, they desperately seek truth outside themselves, but aren't aware the one great matter that can't be apprehended by a thousand sages is right under their feet" (自是時人不了. 向外馳求. 殊不知自己脚跟下. 一段大事因緣. 千聖亦摸索不著. 只如今見不見聞不聞). In order to "understand just now that seeing isn't seeing and hearing isn't hearing, or that explaining isn't explaining and knowing isn't knowing, they need to come to terms with this cave of complications" (只如今見不見聞不聞. 說不說知不知. 從什麼處得來. 且向葛藤窟裏會取).

In the dialogue an itinerant Chan acolyte named Liang (良禪客) asks Qinshan, "What's a single arrowhead that smashes three barriers?" (一鏃破三關時如何), and the teacher replies, "Let's have a look at this 'Lord of Barriers'" (放出關中主看). Liang says, "Given that you're asking, I'll give it a try" (與麼則知過必改), and Qinshan demands, "What're you waiting for?" (更待何時). Liang retorts, "A well-shot arrow doesn't go anywhere" (好箭放不著所在) and he starts to leave (便出), but the teacher grabs him and remarks, "Let's put aside the arrowhead that smashes three barriers, just try shooting me with an arrow" (一鏃破三關且止. 試與欽山發箭看). When "Liang hesitates, Qinshan hits him seven times saying, 'This stubborn fellow will be puzzled for over thirty years'" (良擬議. 山打七棒云. 且聽這漢疑三十年).

Yuanwu writes of Liang's question, "His threat can't be avoided, so Qinshan can't escape facing down a savvy commander" (嶮不妨奇特. 不妨是箇猛將), and of Liang's statement about the arrow, "After all, he tries to shift course but his second blow doesn't inflict any pain" (果然. 擬待翻欵那. 第二棒打人不痛). Regarding Qinshan's final comment Yuanwu says, "It's correct from beginning to end and head to toe but he should receive blows of the staff" (令合恁麼. 有始有終. 頭正尾正. 這箇棒合是欽山喫).

Tianqi says of Liang trying to walk away, "He loses his lordly status" (失其主張) and of Qinshan's final assessment, "His dharma cave's filled with claws and fangs" (法窟爪牙). Tianqi's concluding note says, "Seizing the opportunity to act points clearly to capturing flags and snatching drums" (見機而作. 旨明攙旗奪鼓); and his wrapping phrase reads, "Everything's balanced in his hands" (權衡在手).

Verse: Let me show you the "Lord of Barriers,"

(Y: That's alright, but once you stumble upon him, you'd better make a hasty retreat! 中也. 當頭蹉過. 退後退後)

When you shoot an arrow, don't be careless!

(Y: A dead person can't be brought back to life. What a mess! 一死不再活. 大誵訛過了)

Remove an eye, and the ears are deafened,
Lose an ear, and both eyes are blinded.
I appreciate how one arrowhead pierces three barriers,

(T: This can't be named, 空擔虛名)

The arrow's path is perfectly clear.

(T: Vanished, it's not seen by the naked eye, 現成空缺. 嘆其無眼)

Don't you know that Xuansha once said:

(Y: A leper leading his companions to create entanglements—but note that this isn't actually a saying by Xuansha, 癩兒牽伴. 打葛藤去也. 那箇不是玄沙)

"A skillful person is intrinsically the forefather of mind."

(T: To know the lord of lords requires clarifying the eternal eon with a mirror-like mind, at once reflecting sages and ordinary people, 要識主中之主. 須明空劫已前. 方能不落. 心鏡聖凡)

與君放出關中主 / 放箭之徒莫莽鹵 / 取箇眼兮耳必聾 / 捨個耳兮目雙瞽 / 可憐一鏃破三關 / 的的分明箭後路 / 君不見. 玄沙有言兮 / 大丈夫. 先天為心祖.

Comments: The verse focuses on Qinshan's first rebuttal when he demands that Liang demonstrate why he is a so-called Lord of Barriers since, as Yuanwu's prose comments indicate, the traveler came charging ahead like a courageous general "but, alas, in the end his bow's broken and his arrows don't hit" (末後可惜許. 弓折箭盡).

For Xuedou, shooting an arrow fosters a negative synesthesia in that ears becomes useless without eyes, and vice-versa, but this paradoxically represents a quality only embodied by an authentic adept. Therefore, mind is an abstraction that is less relevant to understanding the Chan pivot than the dynamic activities of teachers. However, Yuanwu points out that the true source for the quote attributed to Xuansha is the master Guizong (歸宗, fl. ninth century), a disciple of Mazu also featured in case 71 (69), who ironically precedes the saying with, "It's a shame . . ." (可憐).

Ode 57

Zhaozhou's "I Alone Am the Honored One" 趙州唯我獨尊

Case: According to Yuanwu's introduction, "Before attaining enlightenment everything's impenetrable like a silver mountain or an iron wall, but after enlightenment you realize that from the beginning you are the silver mountain or iron wall" (未透得已前. 一似銀山鐵壁. 及乎透得了. 自己元來是鐵壁銀山). Should someone ask what this means, Yuanwu says, "If you can realize right now a single activity and observe a single situation, you'll be able to cut off distinctions between the ordinary and sagely from a standpoint beyond conceptualization" (或有人問且作麼生. 但向他道. 若尚箇裏. 露得一機. 看得一境. 坐斷要津不通凡聖. 未為分外).

This case and the next two dialogues revisit the main saying used in case 2 by providing different resolutions for Zhaozhou's exchanges with inquiring monks who challenge his understanding. Here a novice says to Zhaozhou, "Attaining the way isn't difficult, just avoid picking and choosing. But what does it mean to not pick and choose?" (至道無難. 唯嫌揀擇. 如何是不揀擇). Zhaozhou responds, "I alone am the Honored One in heaven and on earth" (天上天下唯我獨尊), and the monk says, "That's still picking and choosing" (此猶是揀擇). When Zhaozhou reprimands, "You're a mumbling fool, where's there any picking and choosing?" (田厙奴. 什麼處是揀擇), "the monk's speechless" (僧無語).

Yuanwu says of the monk's first question, "So many people can't swallow or doubt the existence of iron shrubs, but his whole mouth is filled with frost" (鐵蒺藜. 多少人吞不得. 大有人疑著在. 滿口含霜), and of Zhaozhou's reply, "Bones are piled high on the ground, and the nostrils of patch-robed monks are pierced all at once with a diamond stud" (平地上起骨堆. 衲僧鼻孔一時穿却. 金剛鑄鐵券). Of the monk's second query Yuanwu remarks, "Mountains crumble and rocks shatter" (山高石裂), and of the final silence, "Zhaozhou refrains from dishing out thirty blows since the monk's stunned" (放爾三十棒. 直得目瞪口呿).

Tianqi says of the novice's question, "A fortunate concern" (心倖辯主), and of Zhaozhou's reply, "His whole self's clearly expressed" (全身指註). Of the next query he writes, "He goes after the teacher one sentence at a time" (逐句反追), and of Zhaozhou's insult, "He hits the mark" (當央一點). Tianqi writes of the master's probe, "He quickly makes an evaluation" (急處一提); and of the monk's silence, "His emotion got the best of him" (情封於物). Tianqi's concluding note reads, "Showing true dynamism through words points clearly to demonstrating absolute power" (句裏呈機. 旨明盡力提持); and his wrapping phrase says, "Everything's balanced in his hands" (權衡在手).

Verse: As deep as the ocean, as firm as mountains!

(Y: Can anyone shake him? But that's just half the story, 什麼人撼得. 猶在半途)

Like a mosquito flying in a raging storm.

Or an ant hoping to push over an iron wall.

(T: Zhaozhou's the mosquito flying around, and the monk's the ant pushing the wall, 州如猛風鐵柱. 僧如蚊蝱螻蟻)

What's picking and choosing?

(Y: This is like carrying water to sell by a river, but what does it teach us about Zhaozhou? 擔水河頭賣. 道什麼趙州來也)

A cloth drum stretched to the roof!

(T: Xuedou's final remark hits the drum dead center, 末後急提. 如鼓當央).

似海之深. 如山之固 / 蚊蝱弄空裏猛風 / 螻蟻撼於鐵柱 / 揀兮擇兮 / 當軒布鼓.

Comments: The first line celebrates Zhaozhou's prowess and the next two, as Tianqi points out, contrast without ambiguity the freedom of the master with the self-deception of the novice, although Hakuin identifies both the mosquito and the ant with the monk's uncertainty. The fourth line refers to the process of selecting one option or the other during activities, thus making all decisions double-edged because they lead either to the deficiencies of the monk or the post-enlightenment wisdom of the teacher.

Acolytes are endlessly frustrated by the unpredictability of Zhaozhou's responses. The final image suggests either an inability to make sounds productively, due to the turmoil caused by mishandled discernments, or the extensive capacity of an adept's wisdom. Yuanwu comments in prose, "Haven't you heard it said that if you want to attain an intimate understanding, you shouldn't start by asking a question" (何故不見道. 欲得親切. 莫將問來問).

Ode 58

Zhaozhou's "There's No Explanation" 趙州分訴不下

Case: This dialogue is the second in a series of three cases that provide a sequel to Zhaozhou's exchange in case 2 regarding a passage from the opening of the *Inscription of the Faithful Mind* by third Chan patriarch Sengcan. It begins with a monk asking, "Attaining the way isn't difficult, just avoid picking and choosing, but for people these days, isn't that just a bunch of platitudes?" (至道無難. 唯嫌揀擇. 是時人窠窟否). Zhaozhou replies, "I was once asked this question by somebody, but it's now five years later and I still don't have an explanation" (曾有人問我. 直得五年分訴不下). Is this a refreshingly frank though likely duplicitous response, or a way of dodging the query?

Yuanwu says of the monk's question, "It's a double case. Zhaozhou doubts the monk, who acts like someone treading on a scale that's hard as iron. However, once the encounter's taken place, the master wants to teach the novice how to become less arrogant" (兩重公案. 也是疑人處. 踏著秤鎚硬似鐵. 猶有這箇在. 莫以己妨人). Of Zhaozhou's response Yuanwu writes, "Speaking honestly is better than bearing a face red with shame or being like a monkey eating a caterpillar, or a mosquito biting an iron ox" (面赤不如語直. 胡孫喫毛蟲. 蚊子咬鐵牛).

Tianqi says of the monk, "He auspiciously tests the master" (心倖驗主), and of Zhaohou indicating he cannot explain the meaning of the core saying, "That's another punishment" (隔身點罰). Tianqi's concluding note reads, "Displaying emotion points clearly to his claws and fangs" (拈情. 旨明爪牙); and his wrapping phrase says, "His speech and thought are traceless" (言思無路).

Verse: An elephant king trumpets, and a lion cub roars.
(T: Free and boundless, 自在無畏)
Flavorless words shut people's mouths.
(Y: When insulting one another, they go jaw to jaw with an iron spike, but where's there to bite into? . . . While spitting on each other, both get sprayed with the other's slobber. Ha! O Worthy, what're you

saying? (相罵饒爾接嘴. 鐵橛子相似. 有什麼咬嚼處... 相唾饒爾潑水. 咦闍黎道甚麼)

(T: How true this is, 註十絕待)

All over south, north, east, and west, crows are flying and rabbits are running.

(T: Xuedou shows us his insight, 雪竇呈機)

象王嚬呻. 獅子哮吼 / 無味之談. 塞斷人口 / 南北東西. 烏飛兔走.

Comments: The verse anomalously consists of just three lines with eight characters each (two sets of four characters). The first line highlights the ability of Zhaozhou's use of everyday language, rather than resorting to sticks and shouts, to illumine his perplexed followers. The next line reinforces the notion that coarse talk, when evoked in the right circumstances, is equal to the powerful cries of majestic animals because it compels the ignorant to abandon false assumptions. Yuanwu is characteristically skeptical of both Xuedou and the novice, whereas Tianqi's brief capping phrase supports the poet's approach.

Like the opening of Ode 12, the final line refers to images of the blackbird that appear on the surface of the sun and the hare on the moon to show that the incessant flux of ordinary reality, manifested in every direction above and below, demonstrates the futility of clinging to false perceptions. Therefore, the aim of Xudou's verse is to redirect the novice's questioning mind toward a self-reliant yet humble and self-deprecating awareness of the fundamental conditions of everyday reality without pretext or pretense.

Ode 59

Zhaozhou's "Quote It in Full" (盡此語)

Case: Yuanwu introduces Zhaozhou as a Chan adept who "contains the heavens and covers the earth by transcending the sagely and surpassing the ordinary" (該天括地. 越聖超凡). Furthermore, he discloses the wondrous mind of nirvāṇa right on the tips of myriad weeds and turns weapons into ploughshares to establish decisively the lifeline of patch-robed monks" (百草頭上指出涅槃妙心. 干戈叢裏點定衲僧命脈).

In the dialogue a monk probes Zhaozhou, "Attaining the way isn't difficult, just avoid picking and choosing, but as soon as you speak words, that's picking and choosing. O Teacher, how do you help people?" (至道無難. 唯嫌揀擇. 纔有語言是揀擇. 和尚如何為人). The master counters, "Why don't you quote the passage in full?" (何不引盡此語). The monk replies, "I only remember so much" (某只念到這裏), and Zhaozhou says, "It's just this: attaining the way isn't difficult, just avoid picking and choosing" (只這至道無難. 唯嫌揀擇).

Yuanwu says of Zhaozhou's challenge to the monk, "This thief seems like an ordinary person, but he can outsmart any ruler. A thief steals in broad daylight by riding another thief's horse to chase that thief" (賊是小人智過君. 白拈賊. 騎賊馬趁賊), and of the monk's forgetfulness, "These two fellows are playing with a mudball, but the monk has encountered a thief too difficult to match" (兩箇弄泥團漢. 逢著箇賊. 垛根難敵手). Of Zhaozhou's final remark Yuanwu writes, "In the end, the old teacher prevails since the monk's eyes are snatched away and he's buried in defeat" (畢竟由這老漢. 被他換却眼睛. 捉敗了也).

Tianqi says of Zhaozhou's first retort, "That settles the matter" (就身套他), of the monk's incapacity to recall, "He's fallen into a dark cave" (輸己陷人), and of master's final saying, "He shows how to gain insight by seeing" (以見遣見). Tianqi's concluding note reads, "Pulling in with his lasso points clearly to a dharma cave filled with claws and fangs" (紅綿套索. 旨明法窟爪牙); and his wrapping phrase is, "Everything's balanced in his hands" (權衡在手).

Verse: If soaked by water, he doesn't get wet,
If chilly winds blow, he doesn't shiver.
(T: Nothing affects him, 一切不到)
He walks like a tiger and moves like a dragon,
(T: Zhaozhou's completely dignified, 州之全威)
Spirits groan and gods shriek,
(Y: Everyone covers their ears. When wind blows, the grass bends but, O Worthy, don't become like your students, 大眾掩耳. 草偃風行. 闍黎莫是與他同參)
(T: Such an embarrassment for the monk! 僧之悲愁)
Who's the one with a head three feet high?
He confronts you without using words while standing on one foot.
(Y: Nah! With head back, he lets go of the monk, but this mountain goblin shouldn't be released, so I'll strike, 咄. 縮頭去. 放過一著. 山魈. 放過即不可. 便打)

(T: By applying this ancient example to the present situation, the bystander (Xuedou) accomplishes the great function, 舉古例今. 傍通大用)

水洒不著 / 風吹不入 / 虎步龍行 / 鬼號神泣 / 頭長三尺知是誰 / 相對無言獨足立.

Comments: In the first four lines Xuedou highly commends the benefits of Zhaozhou's personality expressed in his approach to teaching the inquiring monk by combining natural and supernatural imagery. Yuanwu's prose comments suggest that the poem could have ended at that point. His capping phrase on the fourth line evokes a Confucian aphorism about how a strong leader impacts his followers, although it along with Tianqi's phrase also chides Xuedou for seeming unoriginal.

The last two lines recall a saying by Dongshan Liangjie who replied when asked what a buddha is, "His head's three-feet high but his neck's only two inches" (頭長三尺頸長二寸). According to Yuanwu's prose remark, there should not be a literal focus on such exaggerated depictions because "The true person has always been within; everyone should investigate this thoroughly so they can see it for themselves" (真箇在裏了也. 諸人須子細著眼看).

Ode 60

Yunmen's "This Staff Transforms into a Dragon" 雲門拄杖子化為龍

Case: In the introduction Yuanwu depicts the pedagogical dilemma faced by a teacher such as Yunmen who knows, "Buddhas and sentient beings are fundamentally without any difference, and mountains and rivers are indistinguishable from oneself" (諸佛眾生本來無異. 山河自己寧有等差). The question is then raised, "Why is all this divided into polarized sides? If the teacher evokes transformative words or keywords that cut off rules, that's not letting go. But if there's no letting go, the great earth can't be apprehended" (為什麼却渾成兩邊去也. 若能撥轉話頭. 坐斷要津. 放過即不可. 若不放過. 盡大地不消一捏).

According to the case, "Yunmen holds up his staff before the assembly and says, 'This staff transforms into a dragon that swallows the whole universe.

Where will you get hold of mountains, rivers, and the great earth?' " (雲門以拄杖示眾云. 拄杖子化為龍. 吞却乾坤去了. 山河大地什麼處得來).

Yuanwu says of Yunmen raising the staff, "His point is appropriate to the occasion. By wielding a sword that kills people and gives life, he snatches away everyone's eyeballs" (點化在臨時. 殺人刀活人劍. 換却爾眼睛了也). Of the staff engulfing the world he says, "All patch-robed monks everywhere lose their lives once Yunmen has stuffed their throats. O Worthy, where will you settle down?" (天下衲僧性命不存. 還礙著咽喉麼. 闍黎向什麼處安身立命), and of Yunmen's final challenge, "In ten directions there're no walls, and on four sides there're no gates for east, west, south, or north anywhere in the world. So, where is it?" (十方無壁落. 四面亦無門. 東西南北四維上下. 爭奈這箇何).

Tianqi writes of Yunmen's challenge to his followers, "Truth's in the mind, what's outside?" (契理於心. 外相何有). His final note reads, "Truth that isn't outside things points clearly to casting a pole to instruct people" (理非外物. 旨明垂釣為人); and his wrapping phrase says, "Mind and environment aren't separate" (心境不二).

Verse: "This staff swallows the whole universe!"

(Y: What's he saying? That staff's used only to beat dogs, 道什麼. 只用打狗)

Don't waste your time speaking about peach blossoms floating on the water.

(Y: Create an opening above and a thousand sages will stand downwind, 撥開向上一竅. 千聖齊立下風)

A fish that singes its tail doesn't grasp clouds or seize the mist,
But those with gills exposed need not lose heart.
I've spoken, but do you understand me?

(T: He's addressed both sides, but is he clear or unclear? 拈了二邊. 知不知也)

You should let your spirit soar freely,

(T: This doesn't change the universe, 不住化點自然乾淨)

And stay apart from turbulence and turmoil.

(T: If you try to change, it's you who'll suffer, 若逐化點便遭困苦)

If seventy-two blows aren't enough,
Even a hundred-fifty wouldn't be sufficient.

(Y: A just decree, but how could it only be this many? How about three thousand blows in the morning and eight hundred in the evening? Would that do any good? (正令當行. 豈可只恁麼了. 直饒朝打三千暮打八百堪作什麼)

拄杖子. 呑乾坤 / 徒說桃. 花浪奔 / 燒尾者不在拏雲攫霧 / 曝腮者何必喪膽忘魂 / 拈了也. 聞不聞 / 直須洒洒落落 / 休更紛紛紜紜 / 七十二棒且輕恕 / 一百五十難放君.

Follow-up: Xuedou, wielding his staff, steps down from his seat and the whole assembly all at once runs away in fright (師驀拈拄杖下座. 大眾一時走散) (T: Xuedou displays the whole function and congregants must bear the brunt of their shortcomings, 雪竇全提大用. 大眾當機辜負).

Comments: According to Yuanwu's prose comments on line one, "Yunmen helps people by taking an indirect path, but Xuedou helps people through a direct course. That's why Xuedou doesn't refer to the staff shapeshifting into a dragon. Without resorting to such talk he recites, 'The staff swallows the universe,' but he doesn't indulge in explanations" (雲門委曲為人. 雪竇截徑為人. 所以撥却化為龍. 不消恁麼道. 只是拄杖子呑乾坤. 雪竇大意免人情解).

Yuanwu suggests that Xuedou in effect completes the verse two times: once at the end of line four, after deconstructing the analogy used in case 7 and elsewhere of fish swimming upstream to turn into dragons; and second, after five additional lines in which Xuedou has both encouraged and disparaged the pursuits of his followers. Still not satisfied with the reaction from his followers, however, as Yuanwu remarks ironically, "After finishing the poem Xuedou picks up his staff once again to help them overcome their difficulties. Nevertheless, there wasn't a single drop of blood dripping from anyone's skin" (一時頌了也. 却更拈拄杖. 重重相為雖然恁麼. 也無一箇皮下有血).

Ode 61

Fengxue's "Speck of Dust" 風穴一塵

Case: Yuanwu introduces Fengxue, also featured in case 38 that similarly treats Chan's intricate relationship with the government, as someone involved "in setting up the dharma flag and its basic instructional message as the primary concern of a genuine teacher" (建法幢立宗旨. 還他本分宗師). But, Yuanwu also demands, "Tell me, can he by himself set the religious order right by speaking just one useful phrase?" (且道獨據寰中事一句作麼生商量).

The case offers a paradoxical tale regarding the management of civic and religious institutions at a crucial turning point in Chinese history, when a disunified and unstable country in the mid-tenth century was soon to embark on the establishment of the Song dynasty that strongly supported Chan communities, though perhaps at the sacrifice of the traditional emphasis on the solitude of creative recluses, like Hanshan, unbound by conventional restrictions. While giving a talk to his assembly Fengxue says, "If there's a speck of dust, the whole nation flourishes, but if there's no speck of dust, the whole nation perishes" (若立一塵. 家國興盛. 家國興盛. 家國喪亡). After reciting this, "Xuedou raises his staff and asks, 'Are there any patch-robed monks around here who'll live and die together?'" (雪竇拈拄杖云. 還有同生同死底衲僧麼).

The irony of rulership is further indicated in a longer version included in some Chan records, in which Fengxue also says that "villagers scowl" (野老嚬蹙) when the nation is strong, but "feel peaceful" (野老安貼) when it's weak. Moreover, "When this is understood, there's nothing else to learn since everything becomes your teacher. But if this isn't understood, then you must rely on a cleric to be your teacher" (於此明得去. 闍梨無分. 全是老僧. 於此明不得. 老僧即是闍梨. 闍梨與老僧). Furthermore, teachers and clerics "can either enlighten or deceive the entire world. Do you want to know who the cleric is?" (亦能悟却天下人. 亦能瞎却天下人. 要知老僧與闍梨麼). Fengxue "then pats himself and says, 'He's right here'" (這箇却是闍梨).

Yuanwu says of Fengxue standing in front of his assembly, "He stirs clouds and causes rain, trying to be both host and guest" (興雲致雨. 也要為主為賓). Of the nation doing well he writes, "That's not the affair of his lineage" (不是他屋裏事), and of the nation perishing, "All things are radiant, so what use is a nation? That's the affair of his lineage" (一切處光明. 用家國作什麼. 全是他家屋裏事). Also, of Xuedou's final pronouncement Yuanwu says, "Return those words to me. Although he's correct, it's like making even what's uneven. You need to know what Xuedou meant from the beginning. If you know, then you're free and independent, but if you don't know, you'll get three thousand blows in the morning and eight hundred in the evening" (還我話頭來. 雖然如是. 要平不平之事. 須於雪竇商量始得還知麼. 若知許爾自由自在. 若不知朝打三千暮打八百).

Tianqi writes of Fengxue's first comment, "A speck of dust isn't singular and perfectly clear" (纖塵不立一性圓明), of the second comment, "When activity is exhausted, one forgets there's nothing in particular to rely on" (機盡情忘杳無依倚), and of Xuedou's capping phrase, "No one gets it but you and me" (未有得者. 我與你立). Tianqi's final note reads, "Fishing in deep waters points clearly to non-abiding" (垂釣. 旨明無住); and his wrapping phrase says, "Great effort isn't a matter of supervision" (大功不宰).

Verse: Peasants of old hearing about this wouldn't unknit their brows,

(Y: There's nobody for three thousand paces. Delicious food won't be eaten by someone who's already full, 三千里外有箇人. 美食不中飽人喫)

For now, the whole nation is established on a firm foundation.

(T: Delusions are gone and truth prevails, 去妄明真)

But, today, do we have savvy strategists and brave generals?

(Y: Are there any at all? The land is vast and there are precious few, but don't go beating your own chest, 有麼有麼. 土曠人稀相逢者少. 且莫點胸)

I alone feel the pure breeze of Chan teaching that blows for miles and miles.

(Y: If there's nobody with you, who will sweep the grounds? Xuedou's another sage living in the clouds, 旁若無人. 教誰掃地. 也是雲居羅漢)

(T: Truth's attained in solitude, not as part of a group, 獨得無共)

野老從教不展眉 / 且圖家國立雄基 / 謀臣猛將今何在 / 萬里清風只自知.

Comments: The verse comments on the conundrum of Chan Buddhism as a religious organization overseen by governmental regulation while needing to establish a thriving communal foundation through the vehicles of monastic hierarchy and behavioral rules, which may in the end supplant the role of reclusive contemplation as the authentic basis of the tradition.

Although Yuanwu's capping phrase on line three playfully asks him not to boast, Xuedou indicates disingenuously that he alone as the resident adept is able to comprehend and perpetuate the genuine style of teaching symbolized by wafting breezes. Tenkei's remarks suggest that Xuedou laments a lack of leadership, yet he uses this lapse as an opportunity to enjoin his followers to realize for themselves how the impact of an iota of dust reverberates throughout all local and national institutions.

Ode 62

Yunmen's "Lantern" 雲門燈籠

Case: Yuanwu introduces Yunmen as an adept who makes use of "knowledge that needs no teacher yet produces the marvelous function of non-doing, or compassion that's unconditioned but allows one to become a close friend without needing to be asked. In just one phrase there's killing and giving life, and in just one action there's releasing and holding firm" (以無師智. 發無作妙用. 以無緣慈. 作不請勝友. 向一句下. 有殺有活. 於一機中. 有縱有擒).

The dialogue, not included in Yunmen's recorded sayings although it appears in several gong'an collections, is based on the master's citation of a prominent passage from the *Treatise on the Hidden Treasure* (*Baozang lun*, 寶藏論) attributed to Sengzhao, also cited in case 40, which Yuanwu notes "was widely accepted as authoritative in Chan circles" (皆與宗門說話相符合). During a lecture to his assembly Yunmen says, "In heaven and earth and throughout the universe, there's a treasure hidden in this rugged body (literally, mountain-form)" (乾坤之內. 宇宙之間. 中有一寶. 秘在形山). According to the next sentence in Sengzhao's text, the jewel is "utterly empty, still, difficult to perceive within or without, and is known as the 'so mysterious' (玄玄)." This citation evokes the notion of universal buddha-nature.

What is particularly intriguing about the case is how Yunmen follows with a deliberately perplexing instruction that addresses the matter of attaining unity with absolute truth while living amid the conflictive circumstances of concrete existence: "Pick up a lantern from the buddha hall and place it on the main monastery gate" (拈燈籠向佛殿裏. 將三門來燈籠上). This injunction emphasizes the priority of an inner radiance concealed within the flesh and bones of corporeal existence yet shining brightly to overcome any preoccupation with material objects, including the passageway that facilitates both entering and leaving the monastery.

Yuanwu writes of the final part of Sengzhao's saying, "This hits hard" (拶點), and of the first phrase by Yunmen, "The point's still up for grabs" (猶可商量). Of his second instruction Yuanwu says, "Great teacher Yunmen is correct, but he creates confusion. If you consider what he says carefully, you won't be able avoid smelling his feces" (雲門大師是即是不妨誵訛. 猶較些子. 若子細撿點將來. 未免屎臭氣).

Tianqi says of Sengzhao's notion of the cosmos, "This makes it clear" (明其依報), and of his reference to hiddenness, "The treasure is concealed in one's body" (寶隱在身). For Yunmen's full instruction he writes, "Afraid of giving an explanation based on emotion, he focuses on the present moment" (恐乃情解. 今故直指). Tianqi's final note reads, "The radiant source points clearly to displaying emotion" (明宗. 旨明拈情); and his wrapping phrase says, "Smashing barriers reveals the truth" (破權顯實).

Verse: Look and see,
(Y: A black dragon plays with a pearl, 驪龍玩珠)
Who's casting a fishing pole from the ancient shore?
(Y: Xuedou draws his bow after the thief's fled; you can see his jowls from the back of his head, 賊過後張弓. 腦後見腮)
(T: Who notices this? 急看是誰)
Clouds rolling by and water overflowing,
(T: First he points to someone concerned with becoming attached to the essence, and now he shows us everyday reality, 先指其人恐執本體. 今示平實)
See for yourself the bright moonlight shining on white reed flowers.
(Y: Look and you'll go blind. If you understand Yunmen's saying, you'll see that Xuedou got the last word, 看著則瞎. 若識得雲門語. 便見雪竇末後句)
(T: Moonlight isn't flowers and the rugged body isn't six sensations, so use your eyes to see for yourself, 明月非蘆花. 形山非六寶. 應須着眼自看)
看看 / 古岸何人把釣竿 / 雲冉冉. 水漫漫 / 明月蘆花君自看.

Comments: According to a prose comment by Xuedou as cited by Yuanwu from another text, "The treasure was hung on a wall, but for nine years Bodhidharma didn't dare look straight on. If any patch-robed monk wants to see it now, I'll strike with my staff" (掛在壁上. 達磨九年. 不敢正眼覷著. 而今衲僧要見. 劈脊便棒). However, the verse bypasses a consideration of the Sengzhao citation and instead deals with the meaning of Yunmen's saying about the lantern, a directive that deliberately perplexes as part of his bodhisattva mission to save followers from ignorance based on an attachment to symbols.

Xuedou depicts the master overlooking a calm and boundless realm that may also seem desolate and at risk of being overwhelmed by tides. Line three replaces the ominous comment in the saying included in Yunmen's recorded sayings, "Thunder roars and clouds gather" (雷起雲興), with a bucolic flavor. The final line presents an enchanting monochromatic image recalling case 13, although Tianqi's capping phrase indicates that the key to Chan realization lies in pure awareness of spiritual radiance instead of connections with objects.

Ode 63

Nanquan Cuts a Cat in Half 南泉斬猫為兩段

Case: Yuanwu introduces Nanquan as a Chan master, who "pays attention to the realm beyond thinking and takes seriously whatever confounds speaking. When thunder resounds and shooting stars soar, he drains swamps and topples high peaks" (意路不到. 正好提撕. 言詮不及. 宜急著眼. 若也電轉星飛. 便可傾湫倒嶽).

In the dialogue, which is divided into two cases in Xuedou's *Odes*, although other collections join these into a single narrative, we find: "One day Nanquan sees the monks of the eastern and western halls quarreling over a cat" (南泉一日東西兩堂爭猫兒). Traditional Chan monasteries organized officers appointed by the abbot into two camps: the eastern side for administrative functions like managing temple affairs such as funding and planning, and the western side for ritual activities like regulating meditation and devotion, but the west usually had more senior clerics.

Here, the groups of supervisory monks engage in a heated conflict over ownership of a kitty; felines often were pets that provided companionship for weary recluses and protection of temple grounds from rodent infestations, and they also symbolize the quiet suppleness to which Chan adepts aspired. On seeing the problem, "Nanquan grabs the cat and says, 'If you speak up, I won't kill it.' The assembly remains silent, so he cuts the cat in half" (南泉見遂提起云. 道得即不斬. 眾無對. 斬猫兒為兩段).

Yuanwu writes of the opening scene, "It's not just today they're squabbling, how pathetic!" (不是今日合鬧. 也一場漏逗), and of the final action, "How quickly it happens! If he hadn't killed the cat, they'd all be playing with a mudball. However, Nanquan shoots the arrow after the thief's fled. Falling into secondary status, he should've been struck before lifting the kitty" (快哉快哉. 若不如此. 盡是弄泥團漢. 賊過後張弓. 已是第二頭未舉起時好打).

Tianqi writes of Nanquan admonishing the assembly, "His complete dynamism saves others" (全機垂鈞), of the group's silence, "This doesn't prevent the killing" (不妨截斷), and of the cut, "Neither ordinary people nor sages are present" (凡聖不存). Tianqi's concluding note reads, "Directly revealing the radiant source points clearly to the expression of his decree" (直下明宗. 旨明正令全提); and his wrapping phrase says, "Killing is hardly the point" (截斷是非).

Verse: Both halls are filled with insincere Chan monks,
Kicking up smoke and dust in hopeless fashion.

(Y: Do you see what they've done? This is an open-and-shut case, but there's still something to think over, 看爾作什麼折合. 現成公案. 也有些子)

(T: Monks in name only, 有名無實)

Fortunately, Nanquan carries out his ruling—
With one slash of a knife, the cat's cut without regard for which side was right.

(Y: Shattered into hundreds of pieces. But if someone gets hold of his knife, let's see what he'd do. He can't just let go, so I'll strike! 百雜碎. 忽有人按住刀. 看他作什麼. 不可放過也. 便打)

(T: It was correct to sever the cat, 正令一截)

兩堂俱是杜禪和 / 撥動烟塵不奈何 / 賴得南泉能舉令 / 一刀兩段任偏頗.

Comments: The verse praises Nanquan's extreme act. Many interpretations bring up ethical questions regarding the sacrifice of an innocent living being to awaken people from attachments. Those comments are often critical of the apparent instance of antinomianism or violating conventional morality for the sake of a higher truth justifying the reprehensible deed. However, according to Yuanwu's prose comments, "There's no killing; the point of this story is not a matter of killing or not killing. The meaning's clear, but it can't be found in opinions based on emotions or sensations" (其實當時元不斬. 此話亦不在斬與不斬處. 此事軒知. 如此分明. 不在情塵意見上討).

Xuedou emphasizes that the value of cutting lies in Nanquan's unwavering impartiality toward the two groups, as well as his rejection of all distinctions between life and death, right and wrong, or human and non-human beings in the intense moment of decision-making. As Tenkei points out, "One instantaneous blow of the blade cuts through delusions, without regard for whether the head or tail of the cat might be longer or shorter." Therefore, the ending phrase of the verse could be interpreted as, ". . . the cat's severed without concern for the proportionality of the pieces" (任偏頗). Although Yuanwu characteristically challenges Nanquan and duplicitously proposes hitting him, Tianqi agrees with Xuedou's assessment that the master's decree was necessary to end the conflict.

Ode 64

Zhaozhou Takes Off His Sandals 趙州脫鞋

Case: According to this sequel to case 63 (in many collections the two dialogues are combined), "Nanquan tells the story of the cat and questions Zhaozhou" (南泉舉問趙州), who at the time was head monk in Nanquan's temple long before he became an abbot of his own monastery. Then, "Zhaozhou abruptly takes off his straw sandals, places them on his head, and walks away" (州便脫草鞋. 於頭上戴出), and Nanquan says, "If you'd been there, the cat would've been saved" (子若在. 恰救得猫兒).

As an unusual textual discrepancy, the Tianqi version does not include the phrase about Zhaozhou putting the shoes on his head. Moreover, in another version included as case 14 in *Wumen's Barrier*, the opening phrase reads, "That night, after Zhaozhou returned from outside the temple" (晚趙州外歸), which suggests that he was away completing errands and managed to stay aloof from the quarrels.

Yuanwu writes of Zhaozhou's removing his sandals, "He can't avoid leaving a trail of muddy water" (不免拖泥帶水), and of Nanquan's final comment, "Singing and clapping they harmonize together, but those who know this tune are rare in making the right mistake" (唱拍相隨. 知音者少. 將錯就錯). In prose comments Yuanwu says, "Zhaozhou makes use of living words, not dead words. Every day he's renewed and each moment he's refreshed. Even a thousand sages couldn't stir up a hair's breadth of leakage. You must display your own lineal style to see the great function of complete dynamism so it's said by him, 'I'm the king of dharma who lives freely'" (他參活句. 不參死句. 日日新時時新. 千聖移易一絲毫不得. 須是運出自己家珍. 方見他全機大用. 他道. 我為法王於法自在). The last phrase references a famous passage in the *Lotus Sūtra* regarding the Buddha's expedient teachings.

Tianqi says of Nanquan recounting the cat story, "He sums things up" (疏通前旨), of Zhaozhou's sandals, "His intimacy [with Nanquan] demonstrates the great function" (親呈大用), and of the teacher's final remark, "Born with virtue" (出身賞德). Tianqi's concluding note says, "Fishing in deep waters points clearly to the great function" (垂釣. 旨明大用); and his wrapping phrase reads, "Father and son singing harmoniously" (父子唱和).

Verse: After the case is completed, Nanquan questions Zhaozhou,
(Y: This is hanging a medicine bag on the back of a hearse, 喪車背後懸藥袋)
Who rambles freely amid the streets of Chang'an.
(T: Outstanding virtue can't be contained, 美德無拘)
No one understands why he put sandals on his head,
But on returning to his mountain home, he finds repose.
(Y: He should be given thirty blows right where he stands. But tell me, where does the blame lie? He stirs waves where there's no wind. He lets others go, but I wonder if those who aren't like him will be so special, 脚跟下好與三十棒. 且道過在什麼處. 只為爾無風起浪. 彼此放下只恐不恁麼. 恁麼也太奇)
(T: His mind's in accord with the situation, 合心便罷)
公案圓來問趙州 / 長安城裏任閒遊 / 草鞋頭戴無人會 / 歸到家山即便休.

Comments: Line one represents the only instance in the collection where Xuedou refers to an encounter dialogue as "gong'an" (公案), but this term was commonly used by the time of Yuanwu's commentary a century later. The poem praises yet acknowledges the puzzling quality of Zhaozhou's absurd gesture showing his indifference or disdain for conflict. Some commentators point out that, since the matter of arguing about the cat was settled in the previous case, Zhaozhou had nothing more to add than an intriguing confirmation of what Nanquan accomplished.

The second and fourth lines set up a deceptively simple contrast between two symbolic spaces highlighting Zhaozhou's level of proficiency. One place is the Tang-dynasty capital of Chang'an (長安), which literally means "eternal peace" and often symbolizes the pinnacle of Chan realization. Tenkei argues, however, that Xuedou evokes this urban image as a congested and disorderly location, so Zhaozhou's ability to roam freely is that much more significant. The second space is Zhaozhou's home village, where he returns to enjoy true calmness no longer interrupted by feuding colleagues. Yuanwu maintains that when someone feels, " 'Only I myself know and experience it,' they are able to understand the spiritual locale where Nanquan, Zhaozhou, and Xuedou all function in unison" (唯我能知. 唯我能證. 方見得南泉趙州雪竇同得同用處).

Ode 65

A Non-Buddhist Questions the Buddha 外道問佛

Case: Yuanwu poses a challenge to Chan adepts when compared to the virtues of buddha, who "appears without form but fills the ten directions of space while extending everywhere, and responds without thinking yet cover lands and seas effortlessly" (無相而形. 充十虛而方廣. 無心而應). Therefore, "even if a teacher understands three corners when one is raised or sizes up quantities with a quick glimpse, or if the blows of his staff fall like rain and his shouts resemble roaring thunder, that doesn't mean he walks in the footsteps of the truly supreme person" (遍刹海而不煩. 舉一明三目機銖兩. 直得棒如雨點喝似雷奔. 也未當得向上人行履在).

In this dialogue a non-Buddhist (外道, implying "heretic," that is, a Hindu philosopher) questions the Buddha, "I don't ask about words or no-words" (不問有言. 不問無言). Then, "The World Honored One waits calmly for a while and the non-Buddhist says appreciatively, 'Your kindness and mercy have dispersed clouds of delusion and allowed me to gain entry'" (世尊良久. 外道讚歎云. 世尊大慈大悲. 開我迷雲. 令我得入). Later, "after the non-Buddhist leaves, Ānanda asks, 'What did he do to say that he gained entry?' and the Buddha replies, 'He's like an exceptional horse running off as soon as he sees the shadow of the whip'" (外道去後阿難問佛. 外道有何所證. 而言得入. 佛云. 如世良馬見鞭影而行).

Yuanwu writes of the non-Buddhist's awakening, "A clever fellow—after just one pushback he's turned into a bright pearl rolling in a bowl" (伶俐漢一撥便轉. 盤裏明珠), and of Ānanda's question, "He causes others to doubt. He wants the whole assembly to understand, but it's like trying to use a pot made of pig iron" (不妨令入疑著. 也要大家知. 錮鑄著生鐵).

Tianqi says of the non-Buddhist's query, "This is the guest investigating the host" (雙截驗主), and of his breakthrough, "Yes versus no is lost in the clouds, but the Buddha's patience is the sun fostering enlightenment" (有無如雲. 良久如日. 故呈其悟). Tianqi's final note reads, "Resolving the matter through the dynamism of a single act points clearly to hitting the mark" (就

機一指. 旨明當央直示); and his wrapping phrase says, "Watch the rabbit release the eagle" (見兔放鷹).

Verse: The wheel of Chan activities isn't turning,
But when it does, it goes in two ways.
(Y: The left eye is half a pound, the right eye is eight ounces, 左眼半斤右眼八兩)
Like a bright mirror placed on a stand,
(Y: But do you see old Śākyamuni? One push and it turns, but it breaks by shattering into pieces! 還見釋迦老子麼. 一撥便轉破也破也. 敗也敗也)
Showing the difference between beauty and ugliness.
(T: If, like a mirror, you wait a while, there're no distinctions, 良久如鏡. 有無自分).
With beauty and ugliness distinguished, clouds of delusion are dispersed,
Does any dust linger within the gates of compassion?
Think of an exceptional horse, anticipating the shadow of the whip,
Every time, it gallops like the wind for thousands of miles.
(Y: It rides out of the buddha hall through the main gate. Turning around would be wrong but if it can't be let go, so I'll strike, 騎佛殿出三門去也. 轉身即錯. 放過即不可. 便打)
(T: Thinking of the wisdom of the non-Buddhist, this shows the compassion of Ānanda, 因思外道之俊. 故示阿難之慈)
Yet it can be called back! I'll just snap my fingers three times.
(Y: The sound of Xuedou's thunder is impressive, but there's no rain at all, 雪竇雷聲甚大. 雨點全無)
(T: Blame comes first and then punishment, but at least he makes an effort, 責前戒後. 免隋大功)
機輪曾未轉 / 轉必兩頭走 / 明鏡忽當臺 / 當下分妍醜 / 妍醜分兮迷雲開 / 慈門何處生塵埃 / 因思良馬窺鞭影 / 千里追風喚得回 / 喚得回. 鳴指三下.

Comments: The first couplet refers to the possibilities of speech and silence, and the next four lines evoke the capacity of Śākyamuni's empty mirror-like response to the Hindu philosopher that does nothing more or less than reflect the true facts appearing right in front of him without excess or lack, judgment, or indifference. Thus far, Xuedou's focus is on the Buddha's method of instructing a non-Buddhist.

The next couplet highlights how a horse's sprint symbolizes the outsider becoming a worthy disciple. Although there are Zen admonitions suggesting that such a steed should not be expected or required to turn back, Xuedou's final interjection indicates that its course can be reversed by an expert handler. According to Tenkei, however, the poet's proclamation sounds more wistful than daring.

[Here begins a sequence of twenty-eight verses in different order than the *Blue Cliff Record*; Ode 94 resumes the regular sequence.]

Ode 66 (82 in BCR)

Dalong on the Indestructible *Dharmakāya* 大龍堅固法身

Case: According to Yuanwu's introduction, Dalong (n.d.), a lesser-known third-generation descendant of Deshan's lineage, understands that "a fishing pole with its line cast is known only by someone with the true eye, and dynamic Chan activity beyond ordinary teaching methods is practiced effectively only by a genuine adept" (竿頭絲線具眼方知. 格外之機作家方辨).

In the dialogue featuring a question about ultimate reality that recalls case 39 and a response that resembles case 21 and verse 12, a monk asks, "Our bodies ultimately decompose, so what's the indestructible *dharmakāya*?," which refers to the highest level of realization identified in Mahāyāna teachings with the supreme buddha beyond historical manifestations or visualization. Dalong responds, "Flowers blooming in the hills resemble brocade, valley streams flowing assume a deep shade of indigo" (山花開似錦. 澗水湛如藍).

According to many traditional interpretations, trying to scrutinize the aloof and seemingly irrelevant saying of Dalong is "like using a club to strike the moon, or doing something that's invariably useless" (如揮棒打月. 永遠撲空) because, as Yuanwu indicates, "The question lies in the answer, and the answer lies in the question" (問在答處. 答在問處). Nevertheless, the first phrase can be taken to symbolize the moment of arising that quickly turns into withering, and the second phrase suggests that phenomena appearing static to the naked eye move constantly, thus cojoining the fleeting and timeless. Hillside flowers and streams are fundamentally impermanent and so is the supposedly everlasting dharma-body, which is basically no different than a flesh-and-bones corpus.

Yuanwu says of the monk's question, "His remark makes two sides seem like opposites, but this distinction is correct" (話作兩橛. 分開也好), and of Dalong's answer, "A hammerhead without holes strikes a cloth board that can't be torn apart. When someone arrives from a faraway province, I'll head off for a distant locale" (無孔笛子撞著氈拍板. 渾崙擘不破. 人從陳州來. 却往許州去).

Tianqi says of the query, "He moves from delusion to truth" (去妄明真), and of Dalong's reply, "He hits the mark" (當央直指). The final note reads, "Holding up a turning phrase points directly to the unity of everyday and absolute reality" (拈轉話頭. 旨明平實絕待); and the wrapping phrase says, "The question's upright, but the answer's slanted" (問正答偏).

Verse: He asks without knowing and gets an answer without understanding.

(T: Question and ignorance are both timeless, but answer and misunderstanding occur right now, 問以劫外. 不知劫外. 答以今時. 不會今時)

The cold moon and severe breeze fall on junipers standing on ancient peaks.

I chuckle to think of the saying, "When, on the road, you encounter a person of the Way,

(Y: You need to experience this intimately before getting the point. Give me back my staff since here they come, and it's turning into a crowd, 也須是親到這裏始得. 還我拄杖子來. 成群作隊恁麼來).

Don't resort to either speech or silence."

[Dalong] holds a pale jade whip,

And smashes a black dragon's jewel.

If he didn't smash it, any number of flaws would proliferate.

(T: If it's not smashed, attachments get more stubborn, 若不打破, 便執為奇)

This country's laws list three thousand transgressions.

(Y: That's not even half the story, as there are eighty-four thousand laws. In this instance, countless eons of uninterrupted hell wouldn't cover even a portion of the crimes. 只道得一半在. 八萬四千無量劫來墮無間業. 也未還得一半在)

(T: Any variation from obeying the law will damage one's reputation and lead precipitously to a loss of status, 違法損身. 執功失位)

問曾不知. 答還不會 / 月冷風高. 古巖寒檜 / 堪笑路逢達道人 / 不將語默對 / 手把白玉鞭 / 驪珠盡擊碎 / 不擊碎. 增瑕纇 / 國有憲章. 三千條罪.

Comments: The first line shows that the monk defies the Chan principle of seeing the question and answer interwoven due to persistent attachments, and the second line evokes a harsh yet serene natural setting of endurance that complements the sumptuous imagery mentioned by Dalong. The next two lines, recalling the saying that forms case 36 of *Wumen's Barrier*, support the image expressed in the final couplets of the master obliterating a highly prized jewel to prevent further sedimentation of the monk's ignorance.

According to Yuanwu's prose remark, the monk "breaks three thousand laws all at once when he commits a single crime" (三千條罪. 一時犯了也). This occurs because of his insistence on putting forth an inquiry that fails to reveal any degree of genuine self-awareness and is disdained by the master.

Ode 67 (83)

Yunmen's "Ancient Buddhas and Visible Columns" 雲門古佛與露柱

Case: In this dialogue Yunmen identifies the pure realm of authentic Chan awareness with an example of concrete existence, while ending his brief soliloquy with an expression of obscure yet elegant lyrical imagery. During a lecture he asks, "Ancient buddhas and visible columns are merged. What level of spiritual activity does this represent?" (古佛與露柱相交. 是第幾機). Instead of waiting for a response, "on behalf [of those remaining silent] he says" (自代云), "On southern mountains clouds gather, and on northern mountains rains fall" (南山起雲. 北山下雨).

The term "visible columns" (露柱) refers to free-standing pillars constructed on temple grounds that, along with commonly used materials like lanterns (燈籠), a master's staff (拄杖), or a ceremonial flywhisk (拂子), are considered emblematic of genuine realization since objects are sanctified by embodying the universality of buddha-nature. In some instances, columns are said to be animated with eyes for studying the dharma, wombs for giving birth to buddhas, or wings for flying to the sky. In addition, the term can refer to the dragon-shaped part at the end of the first pillar of the imperial bench, which symbolizes strength and power. A demythological standpoint is reflected, however, in a Chan admonition: "People without sincere intentions expect to collect food in empty fields and suppose that flowers will bloom on columns, but what're they thinking?" (既沒有發大心的人. 卻期望於空田中收取糧食. 要求露柱上開出花朵. 哪有這個道理呢).

Yuanwu writes of Yunmen's opening, "These examples are three thousand paces apart, so connecting them causes seven flowers to bloom but the eighth withers" (三千里外沒交涉. 七花八裂), and of his lyrical comment, "since no one understood, he had to speak up" (既無人會. 後來自代云). Regarding the image of clouds Yuanwu says, "They can't be seen in heaven or earth, and a knife can't cut through them" (乾坤莫覩. 刀斫不入), and of the rain, "Not a drop falls; half the river lies to the south, and half to the north" (點滴不施. 半河南半河北).

Tianqi notes of Yunmen's first remark, "Buddhas represent one's innermost nature, and columns represent the physical realm. Nature and form intersect, but who can explain how?" (佛喻性. 柱喻形. 性形相交. 且道是誰). Of the final images he writes, "He hits the mark" (當央直指). Tianqi's concluding note reads, "Fishing with a pole points clearly to truth" (垂釣. 旨明絕待); and the wrapping phrase says, "There's no mystery to unravel" (不存玄解).

Verse: "Southern mountains are cloudy, northern mountains are rainy,"
Thirty-three patriarchs see each other face to face.

> (Y: Wherever I look, I don't see. Xuedou gets bystanders involved, like hanging a lantern on a column, 幾處覓不見. 帶累傍人. 露柱掛燈籠)

In Korea, they assemble in the dharma hall,
But in China, they haven't beaten the drum.

> (Y: It comes a few moments too late so take back this saying, which at first doesn't get the point but then goes too far, 遲一刻. 還我話頭來先行不到. 末後太過)
>
> (T: Korea's a foreign land and China's our native land, but these are provisional rather than fixed ideas, 新羅明格外. 大唐明本地. 只要活潑. 不可定椿)

Joy occurs amid suffering, suffering occurs amid joy,
But who'd ever say that pure gold is the same as a dung heap?

> (Y: Using both eyes will determine, so just look. Alas, it's a pity this doesn't help! Tell me, which phrase refers to ancient buddhas and

which to visible columns? 具眼者辨. 試拂試看. 阿剌剌. 可惜許. 且道是古佛是露柱)

(T: Suffering and joy are mixed, but gold and dung are distinct, so stop talking about ancient buddhas and visible columns, 苦樂須混. 金糞兩辨. 休把古佛而為露柱)

南山雲. 北山雨 / 四七二三面相覩 / 新羅國裏曾上堂 / 大唐國裏未打鼓 / 苦中樂. 樂中苦 / 誰道黃金如糞土.

Comments: According to Yuanwu's prose comments, "Xuedou's first line [evokes Yunmen's teaching style] that knows how to buy a hat to fit the head, and to watch the wind before setting the sails, so he jots down various annotations with the edge of a blade" (雪竇買帽相頭. 看風使帆. 向劍刃上與爾下箇注脚). The second line equates nature with the transmission of Chan ancestry (literally, "four times seven, plus two times three" 四七二三, with Bodhidharma playing a double role of last Indian and first Chinese patriarch). "After that," Yuanwu continues, "Xuedou moves in a different direction by opening a path that creates entanglements enabling one to grasp Yunmen's meaning" (後面劈開路, 打葛藤要見他意).

Yuanwu also points out that Xuedou borrows the notion of distinguishing gold from dung, which Tianqi playfully suggests is an irrelevant analogy, from a poem by Chanyue, a Tang-dynasty monk also alluded to in odes 3 and 100. The original verse reads in part, "The height of mountains and depth of oceans is unfathomable . . . Practicing the path is difficult, causing so many hardships. See for yourself!" 山高海深人不測 . . . 行路難行路難. 君自看).

Ode 68 (66)

Yantou's Hearty Laugh 岩頭大笑

Case: Yuanwu introduces the master Yantou, who "undertakes activities appropriate to circumstances with the ability to capture a tiger. Attacking from the front or the flank, he uses strategies for seizing a thief. Adapting to light or darkness, he knows when to let go or hold firm. Understanding how to handle a deadly snake is the everyday fare of an adept" (當機覿面. 提陷虎之機. 正按傍提. 布擒賊之略. 明合暗合. 雙放雙收解弄死蛇. 還他作者).

In the dialogue the master asks a monk who "comes from [the western capital of] Chang'an (西京來)," "After the Huangchao incursion was suppressed, did you get his sword?" (巢過後收得劍麼), thus referring to the prized weapon of a defeated rebel leader. When the monk says, "I got it" (收得), Yantou sticks out his neck and gives a shout, and the monk says, "Your head's fallen" (師頭落也). Then Yantou "lets out a hearty laugh" (頭大笑). Later the monk tells the story to Xuefeng, Yantou's erstwhile dharma brother who had his own large assembly of followers, but "Xuefeng delivers thirty blows to drive him away" (峰打三十趂出).

Yuanwu says of the impact of Yantou's query on the monk, "He's defeated before he even opens his mouth as Yantou punctures his skull" (未開口時納敗缺了也. 穿過髑髏), and of the monk commenting that the teacher's head is cut off, "He only sees that the tip of an awl is sharp, but he doesn't see the tip of a chisel is blunt" (只見錐頭利. 不見鑿頭方). Of Xuefeng striking the monk Yuanwu writes, "Although it's true that he cuts through iron nails and shears, why does he only give thirty blows without continuing to strike until he breaks the staff? What he does misses the point" (雖然斬釘截鐵. 因甚只打三十棒. 拄杖子也未到折在. 且未是本分).

Tianqi says of the monk's duplicitous claim that he holds the sword, "He's answering one step at a time" (逐句妄答), of Yantou's laughter, "The point's reflected in his style, but this seems obscure to many" (點他昧己. 反責他人), and of Xuefeng striking the monk, "First there's brightness, but that's eliminated" (光前絕後). Tianqi's concluding note reads, "Settling things based on the radiant source points clearly to manifesting the great function" (就事明宗. 旨明大用現前); and his wrapping phrase is, "A blade hidden in the cave of a tiger" (藏鋒陷虎).

Verse: The monk says he picked up the sword after Huangchao's rebellion was suppressed,

(Y: What's the point of this reckless fellow wielding a tin knife? 孟八郎漢有什麼用處. 只是錫刀子一口)

Yantou's hearty laughter is an appropriate response from a knowing adept.

(T: An adept understands the sword is ludicrous, 此劍此笑. 作者方知)

Thirty blows from Xuefeng's cane are too light a punishment,

(T: Xuefeng strikes but he could have forgiven the monk, 峰處喫打. 又且可恕)

To take advantage means to lose the advantage.

(Y: The case is settled, but it's a shame there wasn't more careful attention from the start; only a few are aware of this, 據欵結案. 悔不慎當初. 也有些子)

(T: By holding out his neck with a hearty laugh, Yantou gains an advantage, but he doesn't realize this also means he gives up an advantage, 引頸大笑. 只道得了便宜. 不知全失便宜)

黃巢過後曾收劍 / 大笑還應作者知 / 三十山藤且輕恕 / 得便宜是落便宜.

Comments: The opening lines praise Yantou's mocking reaction to the monk's false bravado in pretending the nonexistent blade has felled the teacher. Yantou's aloof posture became renowned when he was tragically killed by a burglar's dagger in 887, just three years after the defeat of Huangchao, and he let out a great shout that was too difficult even for Hakuin to comprehend centuries later. According to Yuanwu's prose comment, "I always teach people to observe this way to pivot in a way that transforms any barrier; being hesitant leaves you far removed from understanding this model" (山僧尋常教人覷這機關轉處. 若擬議則遠之遠矣).

In the third line Xuedou playfully chides Xuefeng for being overly lenient, and the final saying represents a succinct yet evocative expression of the paradoxical implications of the relationship between the monk and two eminent teachers. This recalls case 26 in *Wumen's Barrier*: "When two monks roll up bamboo blinds at the same time, Fayan says, 'One gain, one loss'" (時有二僧. 同去卷簾. 眼曰. 一得一失). According to Wumen's prose remark, "Who's gained and who's lost? Let's not discuss the matter of gaining advantage or suffering disadvantage" (是誰得誰失. 然雖如是. 切忌向得失裏商量).

Here, the monk feels that he's taken the upper hand in his initial dealings with Yantou, but it becomes clear he has lost when confronted by both masters. However, for the teachers who have gained through severely admonishing the deficient follower, by going to all this trouble that does not result in a positive outcome, the situation turns into a detriment they too must face.

Ode 69 (67)

Mahāsattva Fu Expounds the Sūtra 傅大士講經

Case: This dialogue features a couple of personae who also are prominent in case 1, Emperor Wu of Liang and his attendant, the Buddhist master

Zhigong, in addition to Mahāsattva Fu (497–569), even though the chronology connecting them seems questionable. Fu was the author of *Verse Comments on the Diamond Prajñā Sūtra* (金剛般若經來頌, *Jingang borejing laisong*) and was also known for the influential Chan-like paradoxical verse, "Empty-handed I hold a hoe, / Riding on a water buffalo. / I pass across a bridge, / The bridge flows, but the water does not" (空手把鉏頭 / 步行騎水牛 / 人在橋上過 / 橋流水不流).

Fu is also said to have developed the revolving sūtra-repository device used in Buddhist monasteries, as well as the ritual practice of turning this storehouse three times to accrue spiritual value that is equal to a full reading of the scriptures. At the time this case would have taken place, Fu was believed to have lived as a recluse in a secluded mountain retreat outside the local capital of Nanjing, where he occasionally visited the town's marketplaces. It was there that a government official learned of his reputation as a teacher and reported that to Emperor Wu.

In the story the emperor invites Fu to give a lecture expounding the *Diamond Sūtra*. Then, "Fu ascends the altar and shakes the dais one time before stepping down" (士於座上揮案一下下座). When "the emperor appears startled" (帝愕然), Zhigong says, "Your majesty, do you understand?" (陛下還會麼). Wu admits that he does not and the master declares, "The Mahāsattva has concluded his lecture on the sūtra" (大士講經竟).

Yuanwu says of the emperor's request, "Bodhidharma's brother has arrived! His presence is not unusual in fish markets and wine shops, but is it appropriate for the world of patch-robed monks?" (達磨兄弟來也魚行酒肆即不無. 衲僧門下即不可). Of Fu's behavior Yuanwu says, "He's just like a shooting star gushing forth, then vanishing. His approach is not really correct but at least he doesn't trouble anyone with complications" (直得火星迸散. 似則似是則未是. 不煩打葛藤), and of Zhigong's question, "He deserves thirty blows" (也好與三十棒). Of Zhigong's final pronouncement Yuanwu writes, "If Emperor Wu had driven both Fu and Zhigong out of the country, he would've become an adept. Those two should be buried in the same pit!" (當時和誌公. 一時與趕出國. 始是作家. 兩箇漢同坑無異土).

Tianqi says of Fu's silence, "He shows fully the great function" (大用全提), and of Wu being stunned, "The horror!" (驚怖). Of Zhigong's question and statement he writes, "Seeing that Wu falters, he can't help but provide annotations [on Fu's lecture]" (見蹉急提. 不免註上). Tianqi's concluding note reads, "Hitting the mark points clearly to demonstrating the great function" (當央直指. 旨明大用全彰); and his wrapping phrase says, "The correct decree reveals truth" (正令絕待).

Verse: Instead of staying in his hut at the Twin Trees,
(Y: How can you conceal a sharp awl in a small purse? 囊裏豈可藏錐)
Fu went to the land of Liang, where he stirred up dust.
(T: Don't speak about yourself, just expound the sūtra, 言不守分却來講經)
At that time, if it weren't for old Zhigong,
(Y: A thief shouldn't need to be dragged along by a leper, 作賊不須本. 有牽伴底癩兒).
He, too, would've had to flee the country.
(Y: His crime is exactly the same, so I'll strike, 正好一狀領過. 便打)
(T: If it weren't for Zhigong's support, his escape would've been just like Bodhidharma's, 不是志公扶持. 亦同達摩出國)
不向雙林寄此身 / 却來梁土惹埃塵 / 當時不得志公老 / 也是悽悽去國人.

Comments: The first line refers to the fact that Fu planted two saplings near his retreat and implies that the Mahāsattva would have been just as productive had he stayed aloof since his unorthodox actions confounded people in the capital. He could have remained serene and solitary but instead chose to preach. As Yuanwu mentions in prose commentary, "Fu held up the supreme view and displayed his sword point . . . but it was like fine wine diluted by water from Zhigong, or a nutritious bowl of soup contaminated by Zhigong's rat shit" (傅大士只拈向上關捩子. 略露鋒鋩 . . . 如美酒一盞. 却被誌公以水攙過. 如一釜羹. 被誌公將一顆鼠糞污了).

The second line of Xuedou's verse is double-edged since the reference to causing dust to fly around suggests that Fu's teaching method perplexes Wu and others, but this forces them to work through their bafflement and develop a deeper lever of understanding. The final couplet compares the cases of Bodhidharma and Fu as two monumental masters who, before the highest secular authority in the land, established the necessity of using skillful means to instruct the significance of the dharma for those too ignorant to understand it on their own.

Ode 70 (68)

Yangshan Questions Sansheng 仰山問三聖

Case: In the introduction to this gong'an featuring two unrivalled masters interacting with one another efficaciously, Yuanwu depicts their ability to "shatter the heavens and reverse the earth's course, or to capture tigers and rhinos while distinguishing dragons from snakes. They must be exceptionally active fellows capable of matching each other word for word, and pivot for pivot" (掀天關翻地軸. 擒虎兕辨龍蛇. 須是箇活鱍鱍漢. 始得句句相投機機相應).

The dialogue recalls yet differs in outcome from case 7 in that both stories revolve around a simple query concerning a monk's name. Yangshan and Sansheng meet as equals from different lineages (Gui-Yang and Linji, respectively), but both are traced back to the greatness of Baizhang, the teacher of Guishan and grand-teacher of Linji. Yangshan asks, "What's your name?" (汝名什麼), and Sansheng says, "Huiji" (慧寂). When Yangshan replies, "Huiji is my name" (慧寂是我), Sansheng says, "My name is Huiran" (我名慧然). Then Yangshan "lets out a hearty laugh" (仰山大笑).

Yuanwu writes of Yangshan's query, "His name is about to be stolen because he lets a thief ransack his home" (名實相奪. 勾賊破家), and of Sansheng's first reply, "He cuts off Yangshan's tongue, takes his flag, and steals his drum" (坐斷舌頭. 攙旗奪鼓). Of Sansheng's correct name Yuanwu says, "He steals in the noisy marketplace by revealing his true identity" (鬧市裏奪. 去彼此却守本分), and of Yangshan's laugh, "We can say that on this occasion he buys flowers to embellish brocade" (可謂是箇時節. 錦上鋪花).

According to Yuanwu's prose comments, Yangshan roaring with laughter demonstrates both the real and provisional, illumination and function. Since he's crystal clear from every angle, his true self finds a place to function freely. His chuckle, however, isn't the same as Yantou's laugh [in case 68], which reflects the bitter taste of medicine but rings out for all eternity with the impact of a pure breeze freely flowing" (仰山呵呵大笑. 也有權有實. 也有照有用. 為他八面玲瓏. 所以用處得大自在. 這箇笑與巖頭笑不同. 巖頭笑有毒藥. 這箇笑. 千古萬古. 清風凜凜地).

Tianqi says of Yangshan asking his peer's name, "Probing further" (探竿), and of Sansheng's duplicitous reply, "Breaking an arrow to rob the nest" (劈筈奪窩). Of Yangshan correcting him Tianqi writes, "Cross-checking" (收機反驗), of Sansheng's real name, "One shown, two gained" (一呈二收), and of the laugh, "One shown, two rewarded" (一呈二賞). Tianqi's concluding note reads, "Holding and releasing interactively points clearly to settling the matter for all time" (收放交互. 旨明就身打劫); and his wrapping phrase says, "Adepts seeing one another" (作家相見).

Verse: This teaching shows both holding firm and letting go,

> (T: Capturing and killing grants life when it occurs between two adepts, 擒縱殺活. 二俱作家)

Riding a tiger requires superlative skill.

> (Y: If you don't have an eye on your forehead or a talisman under your arm, how could you get there? Riding is one thing, but I worry whether he can dismount, 若不是頂門上有眼肘臂下有符. 爭得到這裏. 騎則不妨. 只恐爾下不得)
>
> (T: It's quite a feat to ride a tiger without ever getting hurt, 善如騎虎. 各各無傷)

Once the laughter subsides, no one knows where it drifts off,

> (T: There's no trace when its sound dims, 杳無踪跡)

Leaving us only with the sadness of loss for time immemorial.

> (Y: Right now, where is it? Nah! Since it's a great laughter, why does this stir a wind of lament? The whole earth is flooded with dark shadows, 如今在什麼處. 咄. 既是大笑. 為什麼却動悲風. 大地黑漫漫)
>
> (T: Such skill will continue to inspire, 如此之才. 可為榜樣)

雙收雙放若為宗 / 騎虎由來要絕功 / 笑罷不知何處去 / 只應千古動悲風.

Comments: The first couplet indicates tremendous admiration for the superb abilities of Yangshan and Sansheng, whose testing of one another over a deceptively simple matter brings out the best qualities in both, even though Yuanwu typically expresses some cynicism while Tianqi lavishes additional praise.

The final lines suggest an atmosphere of longing and regret as Xuedou suggests that he and his followers, less than two centuries but over a couple of major dynastic changes later, cannot hope to recreate the marvelous atmosphere of Yangshan laughing aloud that evokes a recognition of Sansheng's knack for expressing his magnanimity. Tenkei maintains that the phrase in line three, "no one knows" (不知), captures the true flavor of the entire poem.

Ode 71 (69)

Nanquan Draws a Circle 南泉畫一圓相

Case: According to Yuanwu's characterization of the spiritual quandary faced by the three participants in this gong'an, "When there's no place to find an entry, the mind seal of patriarchal teachers has the capacity of an iron ox to pass through a thicket of thorns. A patch-robed monk is like a snowflake falling on a red-hot fireplace. Set aside probing seven times and breaking through the eighth to reach level ground, what will he do to avoid getting lost in the realm of myriad distractions?" (無啗啄處. 祖師心印. 狀似鐵牛之機. 透荊棘林. 衲僧家. 如紅爐上一點雪. 平地上七穿八穴則且止. 不落寅緣. 又作麼生).

In the brief yet intricate narrative that includes a couple of minor but important variations between the *Blue Cliff Record* and Tianqi versions, "Nanquan, Guizong, and Magu are traveling to pay their respects to National Teacher Zhong (d. 775)" (南泉歸宗麻谷谷去拜忠國師), whose pedigree in studying with sixth patriarch Huineng was recognized by the imperium. The *Blue Cliff Record*'s version adds the character 同 to highlight the travelers form a group. According to that version, "they pause midway" (至中路), but this detail is also left out of the Tianqi edition.

Then, "Nanquan draws a circle on the ground and says, 'If you can speak, we'll go on'" (泉於地上畫一圓相云. 道得即去). Guizong "sits inside the circle" (於圓相中坐; Tianqi leaves out 中). Magu "genuflects in a woman's style of worship" (便作女人拜) by curtsying the knees, rather than setting them on the ground, and placing two hands in front of the chest with the slightly bent body representing a salute. Nanquan declares, "So, we shouldn't go on" (恁麼則不去也), and Guizong replies, "What're you thinking?" (是什麼心行), but the Tianqi version reads, "What a good thought!" (是何心倖).

Yuanwu says of Nanquan's circle, "He stirs up waves where there's no wind so others will understand. He's abandoned a ship that's wrecked on a mass of land, but if there were no testing, how else would he determine what's true?" (無風起浪. 也要人知. 擲却陸沈船. 若不驗過. 爭辨端的). Of Magu's reaction he says, "When one person beats the drum, all three play along" (一人打鼓. 三箇也得), and of Nanquan's final instruction, "Someone who extricates halfway is a fine person singing a harmonious song, a true adept indeed!" (半路抽身是好人. 好一場曲調作家作家).

Tianqi writes of Nanquan's demand, "An obscure pivot creates a test" (暗機為驗), of Guizong, "Sitting down as a response hits the mark" (坐皆報化. 當央直示), and of Magu, "Bending intimately shows the great function" (曲為今時. 大用親呈). Of Guizong's final remark he comments, "He keeps contradicting Nanquan one point at a time" (一點一拈. 前後相違). Tianqi's concluding note says, "Fishing in deep waters points clearly to the great function" (探竿.旨明大用); and his wrapping phrase reads, "Adepts recognizing one another" (作家相見).

Verse: Youji's arrow shoots the monkey,
How straight it flies, circling the tree!
(T: Nanquan's question represents the monkey, his response is the arrow, and the two (Guizong and Magu) are the targets, 問如猿. 答如箭. 二人並中其的)
Out of thousands or even tens of thousands,
(Y: As many as grains of hemp and millet or a pack of wild fox spirits, but what about Nanquan himself? 如麻似粟. 野狐精一隊. 爭奈得南泉何)
Who else could hit the mark?
(T: Adepts are many, but there's nobody in second place, 作者須多. 不如二老)
[Nanquan] calls out, "Come, let's go home,"
(Y: Since they're a bunch of fellows playing with a lump of mud, it's better to go back, even if only partway, 一隊弄泥團漢. 不如歸去好. 却較些子)
So they stop climbing the path to Caoxi.
(T: From past to present, they aren't going, 盡古盡今. 不過如此)
由基箭射猿 / 遶樹何太直 / 千箇與萬箇 / 是誰曾中的 / 相呼相喚歸去來 / 曹溪路上休登陟.

Follow-up: Xuedou adds, "The path to Caoxi is flat and level, so why stop climbing?" (復云. 曹溪路坦平. 為甚休登陟) (Y: Not only Nanquan extricates himself halfway, but Xuedou does, too. However, a good thing is not as good as nothing. Xuedou's also afflicted by an ailment, 不唯南泉半路抽身. 雪竇亦乃半路抽身. 好事不如無. 雪竇也患這般病痛) (T: Venerable Xuedou offers instructions to his assembly, 雪老垂釣).

Comments: The first four lines with five characters praise Nanquan by comparing his actions to a legendary hunter who snared a white monkey that was so swift it toyed with arrows shot by others. When Youji pulled the bow, the monkey tried to escape, but the seemingly supernatural arrow circled the tree and killed it. One wonders, could either Youji or Nanquan hit their mark a hundred times out of a hundred tries?

The final couplet with seven characters suggests that traveling to Caoxi, the symbolic home of the sixth patriarch, is necessary and essential. According to Yuanwu reinforcing Xuedou's appended admonition, "The path to Caoxi is dust-free, traceless, exposed, clear, level, and smooth, so why stop climbing? Each person must be aware of their own footsteps" (曹溪路絕塵絕迹. 露裸裸赤灑灑. 平坦坦倫然地. 為什麼却休登陟. 各自看脚下).

Ode 72 (70)

Baizhang Asks Guishan 百丈問潙山

Case: Yuanwu introduces this gong'an with an important injunction for all potential followers of the Chan path: "A wise person listens to a single word, and a quick horse heeds a single lash of the whip. Ten thousand years are contained in one thought, and one thought lasts ten thousand years. You must know this intuitively even before any topic is raised" (快人一言快馬一鞭. 萬年一念一念萬年. 要知直截. 未舉已前).

The dialogue, as the first in a series of three cases that use the same core element, starts with the following note that is not included in the Tianqi version: "Guishan, Wufeng, and Yunyan (雲巘, 780–841) were all standing together as assistants in the presence of Baizhang" (潙山五峯雲巖. 同侍立百丈), an unlikely notion according to conventional chronology. Then, Baizhang asks Guishan, "With your voice stifled and lips shut, what'll you say?'" (併却咽喉唇吻作麼生道). When Guishan responds, "Please, O Teacher, you speak" (却請和尚道), Baizhang says, "It's not that I couldn't speak but fear that if I did, it wouldn't lead to worthy successors" (我不辭向汝道. 恐已後喪我兒孫).

Yuanwu says of the three attendants, "Ha ha ha! From first to last this is a confused bunch. If they're going east, then I'll head west" (阿呵呵. 終始誵訛. 君向西秦我之東魯). Of Baizhang's challenge he writes, "It's hard to find even one general" (一將難求), of Guishan's reply, "He follows the teacher's path" (借路經過), and of the final remark, "He can't avoid using grandmotherly kindness, but his face reveals shame" (不免老婆心切. 面皮厚三寸).

Tianqi writes of Baizhang's query, "He's asking a mouth that's been shackled" (鎖口探扳), of Guishan's reply, "He sees by looking" (以見撈見), and of Baizhang's final remark, "One conjecture, two conclusions" (一推二拈). Tianqi's final note reads, "Seeking and testing points clearly to receiving pushback" (探扳. 旨明返擲); and his wrapping phrase says, "Guishan turned a deficit into an advantage" (以機遣機).

Verse: "Please, O Teacher, you speak,"

(Y: These words cover the whole universe, but Baizhang's already cut his hand with a sharp blade, 函蓋乾坤. 已是傷鋒犯手)

A tiger sprouts a horn as it leaps out of the jungle.

(T: Not relying on words and phrases, he's like a tiger jumping from the underbrush, 不逐言句. 如虎出草)

Over the ten continents, springtime ends as flowers fade and wither,

(Y: Every place is pure and cool, but no amount of praise can capture it, 觸處清涼讚歎也不及)

(T: A spring that lasts one hundred years is incomparable, 百年一春. 須奇非比)

Yet coral reefs are lit up by dazzling sunlight.

(T: Guishan robbing his teacher's vigor by tossing back the question is like a coral reef illumining the sun! 山奪師機. 還問於師. 如珊瑚樹奪日之光. 返照於日)

却請和尚道 / 虎頭生角出荒草 / 十洲春盡花凋殘 / 珊瑚樹林日杲杲.

Comments: Yuanwu suggests in prose comments that "the three attendants give very different answers" (此三人答處. 各各不同) in this and the next two cases, but Guishan's reply "stands as tall as a thousand-foot wall" (也有壁立千仞). Tianqi agrees that the key to the case is not Baizhang's lament but, rather, the disciple's apparently brash response that offers resistance instead of deference to the challenge presented by the teacher.

Yuanwu then comments, "Xuedou's first line [quoting Guishan] already displays his distinctive poetic ability, but he presses the matter further to make it easy for people to understand" (雪竇便向此一句中. 呈機了也. 更就中輕輕撈. 令人易見). Moreover, "Xuedou completes the verse in the first couplet but has the skill to turn things around and alter the meaning . . . his words evoke a graceful elegance that twists and turns productively" (雪竇只一句頌了也. 他有轉變餘才... 語帶風措. 宛轉盤礴).

Xuedou then evokes an ancient Chinese legend about a seemingly eternal spring that eventually wanes after many cycles. This image, Yuanwu points out, is complemented by the marvelous notion highlighting the singular brilliance of Guishan, "Only the coral reef doesn't fade and wither, as it receives light and reflects it back to the sun" (獨有珊瑚樹林不解凋落. 與大陽相奪. 其光交映).

Ode 73 (71)

Baizhang Asks Wufeng 百丈問五峰

Case: This is the second in a series of three gong'an featuring Baizhang's abrupt challenge to leading disciples regarding the complex relationship between speech and silence. Just as Guishan receives praise in case 72 (70) for offering a vigorous comeback to his teacher, in this dialogue when Wufeng (五峰, n.d.) is asked the same question, he is admired by Xuedou and Yuanwu for "utilizing illumination and function at the same time" (也有照用同時).

The question posed by Baizhang is again, "With your voice stifled and lips shut, what'll you say?" (併却咽喉唇吻作麼生道). Wufeng replies, "O Teacher, you shut up!" (和尚也須併却), and Baizhang gives a verbal salute to this self-confident albeit disingenuously rude disciple, "In a land without people, I'll take my hat off only to you" (無人處斫額望汝).

Yuanwu writes of Baizhang's query, "Ha ha ha! His arrow is shot all the way past Korea" (阿呵呵. 箭過新羅國), and of Wufeng's reaction, "He captures the flag and steals the drum. With a single phrase he cuts off the currents and puts to rest myriad complications" (攙旗奪鼓. 一句截流. 萬機寢削). Of Baizhang's final comment Yuanwu suggests, "Even in expansive territory, it's exceedingly rare to meet someone like this" (土曠人稀相逢者少此).

Tianqi writes of Wufeng, "He sees by not looking" (以見截見), and of Baizhang's last remark, "One reward, one penalty" (一賞一罰). Tianqi's concluding note says, "Seeking and testing points clearly to direct realization" (探扳. 旨明直截); and his wrapping phrase reads, "He splits an arrow to rob the nest" (劈筈奪窩).

Verse: "O Teacher, shut up!"

> (Y: This is so, prior to any words, and cuts off everyone's misunderstandings, 已在言前了. 截斷眾流)

Observe Wufeng's countermove that fights off dragons and snakes.

(T: It's like facing down a large army by killing its chief commander, 如臨大陣. 以將殺將)

Let's recall the great General Li,

Who once shot an eagle soaring thousands of miles in the sky.

(Y: Do all of you know this? Now tell me, where does the arrow land? Right on target, but I'll hit saying, "It's flown by," 大眾見麼. 且道落在什麼處. 中也. 打云. 飛過去也)

(T: The question is the eagle flying and the answer is the divine arrow, so there's no need to utter another word, 問如飛鶚. 答如神箭. 言不放空)

和尚也併却 / 龍蛇陣上看謀略 / 令人長憶李將軍 / 萬里天邊飛一鶚.

Comments: Xuedou again repeats the main expression of the dialogue. In prose comments Yuanwu maintains that, while "Guishan seals off his boundaries, Wufeng instead charges ahead like a horse leading the pack on the front lines without the slightest hesitation. His function is direct and swift yet perilous and steep, unlike Guishan stretching out in a carefree manner" (潙山把定封疆. 五峯截斷眾流. 這些子. 要是箇漢當面提掇. 如馬前相撲. 不容擬議. 直下便用緊迅危峭. 不似潙山盤礴滔滔地).

Xuedou then evokes a military metaphor to highlight a Chan adept's prowess in besting his interlocutor by referring to a legendary commander and famous archer. Li is best known for battling Hun invaders on the northern frontier of the Han dynasty and is also said to have unleashed shots with a remarkable efficiency that resembles Wufeng's spontaneous response. As Yuanwu further explains, "Wufeng demonstrates a twofold strategy of projecting outward and stabbing inward, so he's free to move in any direction. There are generals who rely on their own two hands and feet, whereas others concoct a grand scheme to mobilize hordes of soldiers and horses that charge ahead to face down ranks filled with dragons and snakes" (如排兩陣突出突入. 七縱八橫. 有鬪將底手脚. 有大謀略底人. 匹馬單鎗. 向龍蛇陣上).

Ode 74 (72)

Baizhang Asks Yunyan 百丈問雲巖

Case: The last in the series of three gong'an involving a challenge delivered by Baizhang to prominent followers, this dialogue features Yunyan at a time when he was studying with Baizhang for two decades before eventually attaining enlightenment under Yaoshan and then becoming the teacher of Dongshan Liangjie. This case leads to a very different evaluation than the previous two, however. As Yuanwu says in prose comments on Ode 72, in sharp contrast to the meritorious Guishan and Wufeng, who both effortlessly get the best of their teacher, Yunyan unfortunately reveals "he can't save himself" (也有自救不了).

The conversation begins with the identical question, "With your voice stifled and lips shut, what'll you say?" (併却咽喉唇吻作麼生道). When Yunyan replies, "O Teacher, can you speak or not?" (和尚有也未), Baizhang remarks, "I won't have worthy successors" (喪我兒孫). Thus, a cycle is completed following the dialogue with Guishan, during which the teacher expresses concern about fostering genuine descendants.

Yuanwu says of Baizhang's query, "A toad comes out of its nest. Say something!" (蝦蟆窟裏出來. 道什麼), and of his last comment, "Obviously, the answer he received got only halfway there before veering off track" (灼然有此答得半前落後). In prose comments Yuanwu refers to a traditional Chan verse that counsels, "When words don't go beyond old clichés, / How can you overcome fetters? / White clouds cover the valley / So many people are deluded about the source" (語不離窠臼. 焉能出蓋纏. 白雲橫谷口. 迷却幾人源).

Yuanwu also points out, "In the Caodong tradition Yunyan's approach is known as 'breaking through' (觸破), so it's said, 'A hermit throws open the Phoenix Tower but dares not utter the current emperor's name.' That's why, to attain truth, it's first necessary to pass over a thicket of thorns. If you can't make it, then from beginning to end you'll get stuck in irrelevant details without ever being able to cut them off" (洞下謂之觸破. 故云. 躍開仙仗鳳凰樓. 時人嫌觸當今號. 所以道. 荊棘林須是透過始得. 若不透過. 終始涉廉纖. 斬不斷).

Tianqi says of Yunyan, "He uses words in a way that's at odds with the challenge" (逐句違令), and of Baizhang's last declaration, "He hits the mark" (當頭一點). His final note says, "Probing further points clearly to mutual misunderstanding" (探拔. 旨明失互); and his capping phrase reads, "Observing isn't necessarily being detached" (見不離位).

Verse: "O Teacher, can you speak or not?"

(Y: Truth's right in front of Yunyan, but instead he chases waves, pursues ripples, and gets mired in muddy waters, 公案現成. 隨波逐浪. 和泥合水)

Golden-haired lions don't crouch on the ground.

(Y: No kidding, but what's his function? What a shame! 灼然. 有什麼用處. 可惜許)

(T: He only knows to use words, which give no pushback, 只知逐句. 不能返擲)

Two or three at a time, they tread an oft-trodden path,

(Y: He needs to transform himself and show his spirit, but he stumbles over his own two feet, 轉身吐氣. 脚跟下蹉過了也)

The master of Daxiong Peak (Baizhang) fruitlessly snaps his fingers.

(Y: A dead man can't come back to life. It's sad and pitiful, expressing Baizhang's lament, 一死更不再活. 可悲可痛. 蒼天中更添怨苦)

(T: Since Yunyan doesn't see what's transcendent, Baizhang sighs in disappointment, 見不超羣. 彈指空嘆)

和尚也有未 / 金毛獅子不踞地 / 兩兩三三舊路行 / 大雄山下空彈指.

Comments: The third and final poem in the series again opens by quoting the keyword of the dialogue. In prose commentary Yuanwu says of the second line, "Xuedou wraps up the case by indicating that Yunyan seems to be a golden-haired lion, but when a lion captures its prey it conceals its teeth, hides its claws, and crouches on the ground to leap forth. Whether the prey is large or small, the lion always summons its full majesty in making a total effort" (雪竇據欵結案. 是則是. 只是金毛獅子. 爭柰不踞地. 獅子捉物. 藏牙伏爪. 踞地返擲. 物無大小. 皆以全威. 要全其功). However, Yunyan does not live up to this level of achievement.

Furthermore, Tenkei suggests that Yunyan tries to turn the tables to test Baizhang but falls short because he lacks a lion's fierce sense of courage and cunning. According to Hakuin, the absence of claws and fangs leaves Yunyan trekking the spiritual path in routine fashion, accompanied by other similarly uninspired trainees, so even Baizhang cannot help him.

Ode 75 (73)

Mazu's "Zang's Head's White, Hai's Head's Black" 馬祖藏頭白海頭黑

Case: Yuanwu introduces Mazu as a Chan adept who understands, "Explaining the dharma is not explaining and not teaching, and hearing the dharma is not hearing and not attaining. Since explaining is already not explaining and not teaching, how's it preferable to not explaining? Since hearing is already not hearing and not attaining, how's it preferable to not hearing?" (夫說法者. 無說無示. 其聽法者. 無聞無得. 說既無說無示. 爭如不說. 聽既無聞無得. 爭如不聽). However, "not explaining and not hearing still have some value. Since all of you are now listening to me explain, is there a way to avoid this conundrum?" (而無說又無聽. 却較些子. 只如今諸人. 聽山僧在這裏說. 作麼生免得此過).

In the dialogue a monk asks Mazu, "Going beyond the four propositions and hundred negations, O Teacher, please point to the meaning of Bodhidharma coming from the west" (離四句絕百非. 請師直指某甲西來意). The master says, "Today I'm tired and can't explain it to you, so go ask Zhizang (智藏, n.d.)" (我今日勞倦. 不能為汝說. 問取智藏去). Zhizang tells the monk, "Today I've a headache and can't explain it to you, so go ask my dharma brother Hai (Baizhang)" (我今日頭痛. 不能為汝說. 問取海兄去). Baizhang says, "Even now I still don't understand" (我到這裏却不會). When the monk tells him about these meetings, Mazu declares, "Zang's head's white, Hai's head's black" (藏頭白海頭黑). These references to opposite colors allude to two clever thieves in Chinese lore, with the so-called black bandit being more devious.

Yuanwu writes of Mazu's initial response, "He retreats three paces and the monk stumbles past him without realizing it" (退身三步蹉過也不知), of the novice going to Baizhang, "Again the monk turns to someone else. Clutching to hope, he cries out" (轉與別人. 抱贓叫屈), and of Mazu's last remark, "Within the imperium the emperor makes decrees, but outside its boundaries generals give the orders" (寰中天子勅. 塞外將軍令).

Tianqi says in a atypically verbose style of the first part of the monk's question, "There're words and there're no words, there're no words and there're no no-words, there're not any no-words and there're not 'not' any no-words: that's going beyond the propositions and negations" (有句. 無句. 非有非無句. 非非有非非無句. 四句一離. 百非自絕). Of Zhizang's response he says, "Illumination and function occur at the same time" (照用同時), and of Baizhang's reaction, "Don't stress since for thousands of years the teaching's been immeasurably obscure" (不用忉忉. 從教千古萬古黑漫漫). Tianqi's final note reads, "Direct revealing points clearly to truth" (直指. 旨明絕待); and his wrapping phrase says, "Everything's balanced in his hands" (權衡在手).

Verse: "Zang's head is white, Hai's head is black."

(Y: Half closed and half open; one hand lifts up and the other presses down; gold resounds and jewels chime, 半合半開. 一手擡一手搦. 金聲玉振)

But even insightful patch-robed monks don't understand.

(Y: You need to travel around to temples for thirty years; this ends only when your nostrils are pierced by a teacher. That's why you feel my scowl, 更行脚三十年. 終是被人穿却爾鼻孔 山僧故是口似匾檐)

(T: There's no flavor to these words, 句中無味)

A colt (Mazu) tramples to death everyone in the world,
But Linji isn't someone who steals in broad daylight.

(Y: Although Mazu and Linji are abundantly talented, both are snared by Xuedou, 直饒好手. 也被人捉了也)

(T: Even if there're no tracks left by his footsteps, Linji does not make enough of an effort, 不留踪跡. 臨濟未及)

The four propositions and hundred negations—
Among all the people in the world, I alone know this!

(Y: Why do you refer to "I"? Give back your staff! If there're no people there's no self, no gain and no loss, so what's there to know? 用我作什麼. 奪却拄杖子. 或若無人無我無得無失. 將什麼知)

(T: Once words are eliminated and negations cut off, is there anything to know? 離句絕非. 何有共知)

藏頭白. 海頭黑 / 明眼衲僧會不得 / 馬駒踏殺天下人 / 臨濟未是白拈賊 / 離四句. 絕百非 / 天上人間只我知.

Comments: The poem begins by quoting the main expression from the dialogue, with Xuedou praising Mazu's final saying as an example of why he seems like a stampeding steed (*ma* 馬 means "horse"; see Ode 26). Yuanwu also notes that his teacher Wuzu once called Mazu the "master of roadblocks" (封后先生).

Yet the poet critiques Mazu's prominent descendant, Linji, founder of a lineage that rivaled Xuedou's own Yunmen school in the early eleventh century, for not being so swift or cunning. Tianqi suggests that a typical monk can't understand the significance of Mazu because his words are flavorless, which indicates not a weak or dry manner of speaking but an approach that reflects the neutral taste of impartiality and nondiscrimination. Xuedou concludes by claiming his superior status, but Yuanwu and Tianqi agree that this bold claim is intended in tongue-in-cheek fashion.

Ode 76 (74)

Jinnui's Rice Pail 金牛飯桶

Case: In the introduction Yuanwu says of Jinnui (金牛, n.d.), a Mazu disciple who was once bested in an exchange by then-junior Linji, "Wielding a sharp sword horizontally, he cuts off a nest of entanglements with its point. Hanging a clear mirror high up, he expresses Vairocana's seal in one phrase. When feeling calm and confident, he puts on clothes and eats meals, but when it's time for spiritual powers to be enacted, what'll he do? (鏌鎁橫按. 鋒前剪斷葛藤窠. 明鏡高懸. 句中引出毘盧印. 田地穩密處. 著衣喫飯. 神通遊戲處. 如何湊泊).

The dialogue indicates, "At every midday meal Jinnui carries a rice pail and, laughing aloud, does a jig in front of the monks' hall while calling out, 'Bodhisattvas, come eat!'" (金牛和尚每至齋時. 自將飯桶. 於僧堂前作舞. 呵呵大笑云. 菩薩子喫飯來). It was commonplace for Chan assemblies to assume the presence of beneficent spiritual beings at their ceremonies. Xuedou interjects, "Although he does this, Jinnui isn't sincere" (雖然如此. 金牛不是好心). Sometime later a monk asks Changqing, "As for the ancient wayfarer saying, 'Bodhisattvas, come eat,' what's the point?" (古人道. 菩薩子喫飯來. 意旨如何慶云). Chanqqing replies, "I suppose it's his way of giving thanks" (大似因齋慶讚).

Yuanwu says of Jinnui's actions, "He makes use of pure ghee and poison at the same time, perfectly displaying gems and jewels, but what can he do when there're so few who understand?" (醍醐毒藥一時行. 是則是七珍八寶一時羅列. 爭奈相逢者少). Of Xuedou's remark he writes, "A thief catching a thief, a spirit finding a spirit. Whoever tries to explain right from wrong must be someone who understands right and wrong" (是賊識賊. 是精識精. 來說是非者. 便是是非人). Of the question posed to Changqing he says, "From the start he doesn't realize he's lost" (元來不知落處), and of Changqing's reply, "He wraps up the case in a way that's relevant to the person he's talking to" (相席打令. 據欵結案).

Tianqi writes of Jinnui, "Displaying the great function" (大用全提), and of Xuedou's remark, "The reason for pointing out the offense is fear that Jinnui fails to adapt activity to circumstances" (恐落機境辜負金牛. 故乃拈之). Of the monk's question he says, "He doubts" (疑問), and of Changqing's answer, "Illumination and function occur at the same time" (照用同時). Tianqi's final note reads, "Fishing with a pole points clearly to a great river flowing" (垂釣. 旨明大川); and his wrapping phrase says, "Adepts singing in harmony" (作家唱和).

Verse: Laughing aloud in the shadows cast by the steamy haze,
(Y: In his laugh there's a blade, so why all the enthusiasm? The world's patch-robed monks don't know he fails, 笑中有刀. 熱發作什麼. 天下衲僧不知落處)
He uses both hands to offer rice.
(T: Directly showing the main point, 當央分付)
Those who are cubs of the golden-haired lion,
(Y: They must from the outset be unbound by habits. Maybe they have eyes, but I fear their eyes don't see, 須是他格外始得. 許他具眼. 只恐眼不正)
Would spot this deception three thousand paces away.
(Y: This hopeless scene isn't worth half a penny. Wonder where the deception lies, you blind fool! (不直半文錢. 一場漏逗. 誵訛在什麼處. 瞎漢)
(T: He's no seer, 未舉先知)
白雲影裏笑呵呵 / 兩手持來分付他 / 若是金毛獅子子 / 三千里外見誵訛.

Comments: The first line refers literally to "white (or puffy) clouds" (白雲), but here the phrase indicates the steam rising from the pail of boiled rice held every day by Jinnui. In the last couplet Xuedou enhances the element of cynicism by evoking the notion that the teacher's activity is false or deceitful (誵訛), although this term is often used with a double-edged quality since Chan masters are compared to thieves tricking their followers with skillful means.

Should Jinnui's private ceremony for the bodhisattvas' benefit meet approval or skepticism? A skeptical outlook is reinforced by Yuanwu's capping phrases on the case, whereas Tianqi adopts a more respectful tone toward the teacher. The implication is that, while genuine bodhisattvas easily recognize purposeful duplicity, Jinnui's routine rite remains a viable and valuable way to inspire monks to embrace performing austerities with great gusto.

Ode 77 (93)

Daguang Performs a Dance 大光作舞

Case: It is understandable that in the original version of Xuedou's *Odes* this case follows the previous one in which Jinnui dances while making an offering to bodhisattvas, and Changqing responds to a monk's question about his purpose. Here a monk asks the master Daguang (大光, 837–903), a disciple of Yaoshan, "Why did Changqing say, 'I suppose it's [Jinnui]'s way of giving thanks?'" (長慶道. 因齋慶讚. 是如何). Then, "the teacher performs a dance" (光作舞), and the "monk bows" (僧拜). Daguang inquires, "What did you see to make you bow?" (見箇什麼便拜), and the "monk performs a dance" (僧作舞) while Daguang proclaims, "A wild fox spirit!" (這野狐精).

Yuanwu says of Daguang's jig, "Don't mislead people by acting the same way Jinnui did" (莫賺殺人. 依舊從前恁麼來), and of the master's challenge to the monk's prostration, "A good idea is to pressure him to determine if he's gotten the point" (也好一拶. 須辨過始得). Of the monk's dance Yuanwu writes, "He draws a cat by sticking to a pattern so, after all, he's misunderstood like someone playing with his own shadow" (依樣畫猫兒. 果然錯會. 弄光影漢), and of Daguang's last comment, "It's difficult to repay his kindness, which expresses what all the patriarchs have transmitted" (此恩難報. 三十二祖只傳這箇).

Tianqi says of the monk's query, "He asks to settle any doubts" (請决其疑), and of Daguang's dance, "He personally shows the great function" (大用親呈). Of the monk's bowing he writes, "He should forget others and see for himself" (投他知見), and of the master's challenge to the monk, "He judges others based on true seeing" (審他見處). Also, of the monk's jig, "He's trying to connect activity and circumstance" (果逐機境), and of Daguang's final remark, "One point, two conclusions" (一點二拈). Tianqi's final note reads, "Displaying emotion points clearly to the great function" (拈情. 旨明大用); and his wrapping phrase says, "Everything's balanced in his hands" (權衡在手).

Verse: The first arrow hits lightly, but the second penetrates deeply,

(Y: A hundred shots and a hundred hits, there's no way around it, 百發百中. 向什麼處迴避)

(T: Daguang's dance is the first arrow, and his saying about the wild fox is the second, 作舞是前箭. 野狐是後箭)

Who says yellow leaves are the same color as gold?

(T: An attachment to leaves loses sight of gold, and an attachment to gain leads to a loss of status, 執葉失金. 執功失位)

If the waves of Caoxi were all the same,

(Y: Is there a limit to those playing with mudballs? If you draw a cat by sticking to a pattern, you must let it go, 弄泥團漢有什麼限. 依様畫猫兒. 放行一路)

Innumerable people would drown on dry land.

(Y: Meeting someone who's truly alive, O Worthy, makes you tired of patch-robed monks who can't figure things out and don't break free, 遇着活底人. 帶累天下衲僧. 摸索不着. 帶累闍黎. 出頭不得)

(T: When there's emotion, sincerity gets trapped by innocence, 若在情識. 誠陷天真)

前箭猶輕後箭深 / 誰云黃葉是黃金 / 曹溪波浪如相似 / 無限平人被陸沉.

Comments: The first couplet praises Daguang's two very different responses to the monk: one reaction is performative and leads the novice toward imitation that seems unworthy of an adept; and the other is rhetorical by accusing the monk, perhaps disingenuously, of being a phony pretending to have wisdom. Line two alludes to a sūtra passage in which parents offer their son yellow leaves not as a matter of fraud, but an expedient device to stop temporarily the child's suffering until his level of understanding matures.

The last couplet refers to sixth patriarch Huineng, who is often evoked by the location of his temple. Huineng's teachings gave rise to multiple streams and branches transmitting in their respective ways the creativity of novel approaches seeking to overcome the delusions of diverse followers, although later commentators sometimes regretted that the proliferation of competing Chan philosophies caused confusion among trainees.

Ode 78 (91)

Yanguan's "Rhinoceros-Horn Fan" 鹽官犀牛扇子

Case: According to Yuanwu's introduction, the master Yanguan (鹽官, 750–842), a successor of Mazu, "transcends emotion and detaches from views, removes bonds and unravels sticking points, while upholding the supreme teaching and propagating the treasury of the true dharma eye, yet he also responds equally in all directions and is forthright in every respect" (超情離見. 去縛解粘. 提起向上宗乘. 扶豎正法眼藏. 也須十方齊應八面玲瓏. 直到恁麼田地).

In the dialogue Yanguan asks for his "rhinoceros-horn fan" (犀牛扇子), but the assistant says, "It's broken" (扇子既破). The rhinoceros's horn was considered a precious item in traditional China often used for ornamental in addition to medicinal or magical purposes. Here it indicates an object that seems valuable yet is an impractical luxury that nevertheless symbolizes the transmission of the dharma. When Yanguan demands, "If the fan's broken, bring me the rhinoceros" (扇子既破, 還我犀牛兒來), the "attendant doesn't respond" (者無對).

Xuedou adds capping phrases to comments proposed by four predecessors: Touzi refers to flaws and Xuedou says, "I'd take an imperfect horn" (我要不全底頭角); Shishuang complains he wouldn't have the fan for himself and Xuedou says, "The rhinoceros is still here" (犀牛兒猶在); Zifu draws a circle and writes the word "rhino" inside and Xuedou comments, "Why didn't you show us this before?" (適來為甚不將出); and Baofu says the master should ask someone else while Xuedou remarks, "A pity all his efforts are in vain" (可惜勞而無功).

Yuanwu says of Xuedou's view of Touzi, "What does he accomplish, adding error to error" (堪作何用. 將錯就錯), of Shishuang, "Look out, he almost fell into error but pulled back" (嶮. 洎乎錯認. 收頭去), of Zifu, "He can't tell the difference between gold and brass, he's down in the weeds" (金鍮不辨. 也是草裏漢), and of Baofu, "Also part of the problem, he should get thirty blows" (兼身在內. 也好與三十棒. 灼然).

Tianqi writes of Yanguan's first request, "There's a resonance in his words" (言中有響), of his next demand, "The truth of emptiness drives the person away' (法空追人), and of the monk's silence, "He's busy losing out" (忙然失所). Tianqi says of Xuedou's remark on Baofu, "His unkindness seems spiteful" (反恩為讐). Tianqi's final note reads, "Settling the matter based on the radiant source points clearly to activity expressed in words" (就事明宗. 旨明句裏呈機); and his wrapping phrase says, "Adepts singing in harmony" (作家唱和).

Verse: The rhinoceros-horn fan has been used for a long time,

(Y: In summer when it's cool, and in winter when it's warm; everyone has a fan, is there anyone who doesn't know how to use it? 遇夏則涼遇冬則暖. 人人具足. 為甚不知. 阿誰不曾用)

But when asked, nobody has any idea.

(T: Fools and sages alike are lost in ignorance, 凡聖皆具. 自昧絕知)

A boundless pure breeze touches the horn on the rhino's head,

(T: 'Boundless' refers to ancient ancestors 諸老, 'breeze' indicates the fan 扇子, and 'horn' symbolizes the rhinoceros 犀牛)

Just like clouds and rain that, once passed, can't be grasped.

(Y: Heavens! This is like losing all your money as punishment for a crime, 蒼天蒼天. 也是失錢遭罪)

犀牛扇子用多時 / 問著元來總不知 / 無限清風與頭角 / 盡同雲雨去難追.

Follow-up: Xuedou adds, "If you want the pure breeze to return and the horn to grow back, I invite you Chan practitioners to each give a turning word for, 'If the fan's broken, bring me the rhinoceros.' " A monk says, "Let's all go practice in the meditation hall." Xuedou exclaims, "I cast my pole to fish a whale, but caught a frog," and gets down from his seat (復云, 若要清風再復頭角重生. 今請禪客各下一語. 問云. 扇子既破. 還我犀牛兒來. 僧出云. 大眾參堂去. 師喝云. 拋鉤釣鯤鯨. 釣得箇蝦蟆. 便下座).

Comments: The opening lines show the fan is used as an implement for temple rites that are taken for granted and thus poorly understood. In the final line Xuedou suggests that trying to interpret the comments of four predecessors, which were originally relevant to a particular pedagogical situation, is like trying to clutch the mist, thus playfully undermining the role of his own capping phrases.

Most scholars agree the supplemental narrative was added to the second edition of the collection but, assuming it is valid, this passage reveals a great deal about how Xuedou presented the odes orally and at least sometimes followed up with repartee through expressing here how unhappy he is with his disciples' lack of insight.

When a monk tries to usurp the teacher's authority by instructing the assembly to meditate, Tianqi remarks, "The case is raised, but then it's dropped" (拈前截後). Yuanwu, however, blames any apparent misconception on Xuedou, who he says, "brought this situation on himself and now draws his bow after the thief's fled" (招得他恁麼地. 賊過後張弓). Tianqi adds skeptically regarding all parties, "Dwelling in caves they don't show any sign of attaining buddha's path" (法窟爪牙. 末後拂迹).

Ode 79 (92)

The World-Honored One Takes His Seat 世尊一日陞座

Case: Yuanwu introduces the Buddha as "discerning the tune as soon as lute strings are plucked, which is hard to find in thousands of years. Like a hawk pursuing a hare as soon as it comes into view, he seizes every moment. Embodying each teaching in a single phrase, he encompasses all sand in a single grain" (動絃別曲. 千載難逢. 見兔放鷹. 一時取俊. 總一切語言為一句. 攝大千沙界為一塵).

According to the dialogue, "One day the World Honored One ascends his seat" (世尊一日陞座) to give a sermon. Then "Mañjuśrī sounds the gavel saying, 'Clearly behold the teaching of the king of dharma, the teaching of the king of dharma is thus'" (文殊白槌云. 諦觀法王法. 法王法如是); the latter phrase represents the refrain typically uttered at the conclusion of the sermons. The bodhisattva then says, "The World Honored One steps down from his seat" (世尊下座).

Yuanwu writes of the Buddha sitting, "Guest and host both fail; not the only instance of delusion" (賓主俱失. 不是一回漏逗), and of Mañjuśrī's proclamation, "A son intimately gets the point" (一子親得). Of the Buddha departing he writes, "Someone who's troubled should never try to explain their troubles to someone else who's troubled—explaining troubles to a troubled person ends up troubling them to death. Beating the drum and playing the lute, the two masters mutually engage one another" (愁人莫向愁人說. 說向愁人愁殺人. 打鼓弄琵琶. 相逢兩會家). Yuanwu also points out in prose commentary that some people claim, "The meaning lies in silence or the pause; speech illumines the unsayable and speechlessness illumines the sayable" (意在默然處在良久處. 有言明無言底事. 無言明有言底事). However, Yuanwu prefers the saying, "Speaking when silent, silent when speaking" (默時說說時默).

Tianqi comments on Mañjuśrī striking the gavel, "His great function startles the crowd" (大用驚眾), and on the bodhisattva's remark, "He comments freely" (盡情註解). Of the Buddha stepping down he writes, "Seeing delusions, he can't avoid trying to clear them up" (見殊漏泄. 不免拂迹). Tianqi's concluding note reads, "Direct showing points clearly to the great function" (直示. 旨明大用); and his wrapping phrase says, "Teachers singing in harmony" (師資唱和).

Verse: Among the multitude of sages lined up, only an adept knows,

(Y: Don't slander old Śākyamuni, leave the task up to Linji or Deshan. Amid many thousands it's hard to find one or even half, 莫謗釋迦老子好. 還他臨濟德山. 千箇萬箇中難得一箇半箇)

(T: Only between a buddha and a buddha can it be known, 唯佛與佛乃能知之)

The decree of the king of dharma shouldn't have been like this.

(T: He's an adept, but he's no seer, 若是作者. 未舉先知)

Had the assembly included "a person of Saindhava,"

Mañjuśrī wouldn't have needed to sound the gavel.

(Y: Why not sound the gavel once? Second or third strikes are altogether unnecessary, so try speaking a phrase appropriate to the situation. Watch out! 更下一槌. 又何妨. 第二第三槌總不要. 當機一句作麼生道. 嶮)

(T: If at the time those genuinely spiritual were present, why was there a need for a white gavel or composing an ode? 於今若有英靈. 何用白槌頌古)

列聖叢中作者知 / 法王法令不如斯 / 會中若有仙陀客 / 何必文殊下一槌.

Comments: The verse suggests that, instead of listening to a brief comment followed by striking a gavel, a genuine Chan master standing among the eighty thousand bodhisattvas, arhats, and solitary enlightened beings who heard the Buddha's sermons, according to traditional lore, would not have required any words or sounds to gain an understanding of the dharma king's message. The meaning and significance of his teachings would already be abundantly clear prior to any verbalization or action.

The phrase "a person of Saindhava" in line three alludes to an ancient Indian legend cited in various Buddhist scriptures about a loyal and prescient attendant serving their lord, who might at any time need one of four items: when ready to wash, the attendant would bring the Saindhava of water without having to be asked; when eating, they would immediately serve salt; when the meal was done, they offered a bowl to drink a beverage; and when the lord desired to leave the palace, the attendant brought a horse. The assistant anticipates and acts according to the lord's wishes without hesitation, just as a Chan adept knows how to deal with unpredictable pedagogical situations spontaneously and with aplomb.

Ode 80 (75)

Wujiu's "Unfair Blows!" 烏臼屈棒

Case: Yuanwu says of the master Wujiu (烏臼, n.d.), a disciple of Mazu known for wielding his stick, "The sacred point of his bejeweled sword always revealed right before us kills people and brings them to life. It moves here or there and gains or loses all at once. If he wants to pick it up, he's free to; and if he wants to put it down, he's also free" (靈鋒寶劍. 常露現前. 亦能殺人亦能活人. 在彼在此. 同得同失. 若要提持. 一任提持. 若要平展. 一任平展).

In the dialogue a monk visiting Wujiu from a different assembly is asked "to compare the dharma paths" (定州法道何似這裏), and says, "they're no different" (不別). When Wujiu hits him, the monk says, "Since there're eyes on that staff, you shouldn't hit people recklessly" (棒頭有眼. 不得草草打人), but then "he's hit again three times" (又打三下), and leaves.

Wujiu calls out, "Someone's been receiving unfair blows" (屈棒元來有人喫在), so "the monk turns around" (僧轉身) and, when "offered the handle" (汝要山僧與汝) by Wujiu, "he grabs the stick and hits the master three times" (手中棒. 打臼三下). Wujiu cries, "Unfair blows! Unfair blows!" (屈棒屈棒) and says, "I was hit recklessly" (草草打著箇漢), so "the monk bows" (僧便禮拜). When Wujiu asks, "Teacher, is this how you act?" (和尚却恁麼去也), "the monk roars in laughter and goes away" (僧大笑而出), while Wujiu remarks, "Cut it out!" (消得恁麼. 消得恁麼).

Yuanwu says of the monk's initial response, "Among all the dead fellows this one is alive" (死漢中有活底), of Wujiu's hitting, "Of course his decree is carried out" (灼然. 正令當行), and of the monk's retort, "Here's an adept who gets the point since he's a lion's cub" (也是這作家始得. 却是獅子兒). Also, of Wujiu's penultimate comment Yuanwu writes, "Check!" (點), of the monk's laugh, "A skillful Chan itinerant spontaneously acts like a fierce tiger with a pure breeze at his back . . . Nobody gets the best of him" (作家禪客天然有在. 猛虎須得清風隨 . . . 天下人摸索不著), and of Wujiu's last utterance, "Too bad he let him off the hook instead of smacking him across the back. Where do you think the monk went?" (可惜放過. 何不劈脊便棒. 將謂走到什麼處去).

Tianqi says of Wujiu's final remark, "If the monk doesn't cut it out, it's still a fair exchange" (拈他不消如此賣弄). His concluding note reads, "The mutual interaction of host and guest points clearly to adepts recognizing one another" (主賓互換. 旨明作家相見); and his wrapping phrase reads, "All's in order" (皆有權衡).

Verse: Summoning is easy, but sending away is difficult,

(T: Even if you rob someone, you can let them go. When two adepts meet, they bring out the best in each other, 縱而能奪. 收而能放. 二俱作家. 所以深賞)

Carefully observe the interchange of swords crossing.

(Y: For both adepts, there's one exit and one entry, as there're two men holding a single staff. But tell me, which one's got the upper hand? 一出一入. 二俱作家. 一條拄杖兩人扶. 且道在阿誰邊)

The rocks of ages crumble quickly,

The dark depths of oceans dry up.

Old Wujiu! Is there anyone else like you?

(Y: What a shame that this old fellow knows right from wrong, but there's nobody else like him for hundreds of thousands of miles, 可惜許. 這老漢不識好惡. 也是箇無端漢. 百千萬重)

(T: He can release or hold firm, or be guest one moment and host the next, 能放能收. 忽賓忽主)

Offering your handle was extraordinary!

(Y: Even before anything was said by the visitor, Wujiu was about to dish out blows, but he himself deserves thirty strikes. Tell me what he's done, 已在言前. 洎合打破蔡州. 好與三十棒. 且道過在什麼處)

(T: Buddhas and patriarchs confronting one another are equally virtuous, 佛祖權衡. 善及平分)

呼則易. 遣則難 / 互換機鋒仔細看 / 劫石固來猶可壞 / 滄溟深處亦須乾 / 烏臼老. 烏臼老. 幾何般 / 與他杓柄太無端.

Comments: According to Xuedou's verse, the verdict is that the junior interlocutor more than adequately meets the challenge presented by Wujiu's "unfair blows." The monk turns things around, both literally and figuratively, when he takes command of the staff while walking away with an attitude of aloof indifference.

At the same time, the master lives up to his potential by reacting appropriately to an apparent opponent who he recognizes as a worthy Chan master, so he gives away his weapon and lets himself suffer from the monk's prowess. Therefore, there are no winners or losers in this exchange since mutual enhancement emerges as an auspicious result of two skilled adversaries making the most of one another's advantages and disadvantages.

Ode 81 (76)

Danxia's "Have You Eaten Yet or Not" 丹霞喫飯了也未

Case: Yuanwu introduces the master Danxia as one who realizes that enlightened awareness "is as tiny as a grain of rice yet encompasses the whole universe and is beyond light or darkness. Its depths are unfathomable, and its heights are unimaginable. Holding firm or letting go are both encompassed, but how does one find an exceptional place to experience the unrestricted realm?" (細如米末. 冷似氷霜. 畐塞乾坤. 離明絕暗. 低低處觀之有餘. 高高處平之不足. 把住放行. 總在這裏許還有出身處也無).

In the dialogue Danxia asks a visiting meditator, "Where've you come from?" (甚處來) and the novice says, "The foothills of the mountain" (山下來), which implies he is a hermit rather than an ordained priest. The master says, "Have you eaten yet or not?" (喫飯了也未). When the hermit says yes, Danxia queries, "Did the person who brought you food have eyes?" (將飯與汝喫底人. 還具眼麼), and "this leaves the monk speechless" (僧無語). Later, Changqing asks Baofu, "Giving food is an act of kindness, so why wouldn't the person have eyes?" (將飯與人喫. 報恩有分. 因甚不具眼), and Baofu says, "Giver and receiver are both blind" (施者受者. 二俱瞎漢). Changqing remarks, "If they use up all their energies, do they become blind?" (盡其機來. 還成瞎否) and Baofu queries, "Would you say I'm blind?" (道我瞎得麼).

Yuanwu writes of Danxia asking about eyes, "By making his utmost effort to ensnare the monk, this query wraps up the meaning of the case. At that time the monk deserved to have his meditation seat overturned" (雖然是倚勢欺人. 也是據欵結案. 當時好掀倒禪床. 無端作什麼). Of Baofu's last quip he caps, "Both of them are stuck in the weeds, with a dragon's head but a snake's tail . . . I would've said, 'You're blind!' or 'You got only half the point!' Since they're both adepts, why don't they first reach the village and, after that, go to the shop"? (兩箇俱是草裏漢. 龍頭蛇尾 . . . 只向他道瞎. 也只道得一半. 一等是作家. 為什麼前不搆村後不迭店).

Tianqi writes of the monk's silence, "He's busy losing his place" (忙然絕所), and of Changqing asking Baofu, "Making a pivot to test a pivot" (借機

驗機). Of Baofu's first reply he says, "Both're cut off, both're held up" (雙截雙拈), and of Baofu's final remark, "To keep talking about whether 'I'm blind or not' sadly fails to see this as an open-and-shut case" (盡情說了我還瞎否. 現成公案可惜錯認). Tianqi's concluding note says, "Fishing in deep waters with a pole in one's hands points clearly to snatching away delusions" (探竿在手. 旨明欺瞞做賊); and his wrapping phrase reads, "Two victories, two defeats" (二勝二負).

Verse: Whether "using up all one's energies" or "going blind,"
It's like holding down the head of an ox to make it eat grass.
    (T: Forcing others how to see and feel is one way of fostering successors, 責他情見. 有陷後人)
All twenty-eight Indian and six Chinese patriarchs,
    (Y: If there's a rule, follow it. Xuedou implicates numerous former sages; he doesn't just blame one person, 有條攀條. 帶累先聖. 不唯只帶累一人)
Lose sight of the precious contents of the dharma.
    (Y: Everyone in the world's showing off. Give back my staff! They've dragged me down, so I'm lost, too, 盡大地人換手搥胸. 還我拄杖來. 帶累山僧也出頭不得)
    (T: Buddhas and patriarchs show what happens when there's no understanding or following the precepts, 一切佛祖皆是直指. 不以本分豈不壞法)
Once missing, it can't be retrieved,
    (Y: Although it's right beneath your feet, it's never found, 在爾脚跟下. 摸索不著)
Causing gods and humans to drown on dry land.
    (T: Already in the depths of darkness, there's nothing left but to fall into a cave, 既昧大旨. 無不遭陷)
盡機不成瞎 / 按牛頭喫草 / 四七二三諸祖師 / 寶器持來成過咎 / 過咎深. 無處尋 / 天上人間被陸沉.

Comments: The verdict seems clear-cut in that Danxia delivers a powerful putdown of an irregular practitioner, who does not know how to eat literally, in terms of not taking his meals according to behavioral guidelines since he's not a member of the assembly, and figuratively, in that he hasn't ingested genuine Chan teachings so is incapable of recognizing the dharma eye.

Furthermore, according to all three commentators, there is a negative evaluation of Changqing and Baofu, who lead each other astray during their repartee. Tenkei argues that the root of the problems reflected in the misguided approaches of the anonymous hermit and the otherwise respected teachers "is not knowing how to eat because they're utilizing the chopsticks of discriminatory thinking, which leads only to spiritual oblivion." Tenkei suggests facetiously that Xuedou should instruct his followers to avoid eating grass through their nose.

Ode 82 (77)

Yunmen's "Rice Cake" 雲門餬餅

Case: In the introduction Yuanwu explains the pedagogical dilemma faced by Yunmen in that "When turning to the superior he pierces the nostrils of everyone in the world like a hawk capturing a dove, but when turning to the inferior he leaves his own nostrils in the hands of others like a tortoise hiding in its shell" (向上轉去. 可以穿天下人鼻孔. 似鶻捉鳩. 向下轉去. 自己鼻孔在別人手裏. 如龜藏殼). After a pause Yuanwu maintains, "If there's a rule to obey, follow the rule, but if there's no rule, follow an example" (有條攀條無條攀例).

In the case Yunmen asks, "What teaching surpasses that of buddhas and transcends the patriarchs?" (如何是超佛越祖之談), and he himself replies, "A rice cake" (餬餅). In prose comments Yuanwu says this dialogue "is similar to Dongshan's 'three measures of flax' [case 12] and Heshan's 'genuinely beat the drum' [case 44] because just saying 'a rice cake' is hard to fathom" (與麻三斤解打鼓一般. 雖然只道餬餅. 其實難見). However, Yuanwu criticizes "subsequent interpreters who've tried to create logical explanations . . . or clutch at interpretations by current Chan lecturers" (後人多作道理若恁麼會... 得多知多解. 如今禪和子道).

Moreover, Yuanwu says of Yunmen's question, "He breaks through and suddenly there's thunder resounding over the scorched land as he presses ahead" (開. 旱地忽雷. 拶), and of the master's answer, "His tongue rests on the roof of his mouth, then he's done" (舌拄上齶. 過也).

Tianqi writes of the query, "Probing further" (請益), and of the reply, "He hits the mark" (當央直指). Tianqi's concluding note says, "Holding up this turning word points clearly to a realm beyond meaning" (拈轉話頭. 旨明無有意路); and his wrapping phrase reads, "Directly revealing the radiant source" (直下明宗).

Verse: There are so many Chan itinerants who talk about going beyond talk,
Don't you see the gaps and excesses their approaches create?
(Y: It's obvious even before words are spoken, but Xuedou doesn't realize his own shit stinks, 已在言前. 開也. 自屎不覺臭)
(T: They only know about transcending buddhas and patriarchs, but don't know about cutting off the roots of ignorance, 只知要超佛祖. 不知打作兩截)
Even Yunmen's "rice cake" can't put a stop to such misapprehensions,
(Y: He's taken out your eyes and put in wooden beads, 將木槵子換却爾眼睛了也)
Still today, these delusions and deceptions pervade the world.
(Y: I'll draw a circle and say, "Don't you know what this means?" Why be concerned with the words of others? The great earth is so desolate it kills people with sadness, so I'll strike, 畫箇圓相云. 莫是恁麼會麼. 咬人言語. 有甚了期. 大地茫茫愁殺人. 便打)
(T: Trying to stitch up those gaps doesn't work because of the extent of delusions they reflect, 當縫一[祝/土]. 又不渾淪. 故曰誵訛)
超談禪客問偏多 / 縫罅披離見也麼 / 餬餅[祝/土]來猶不住 / 至今天下有誵訛.

Comments: The main aim of Xuedou's verse is to reprimand deficient Chan trainees who fail to comprehend the significance of Yunmen's cryptic utterance and cast about for false views that compound rather than alleviate fabrications. In the end, these approaches reflect abundant self-deceptions. Yuanwu and Tianqi concur with Xuedou regarding the futility of such an uninformed outlook.

The third character in line three is an irregular configuration [祝/土] that is broken down in both versions of the text. Cited also in Tianqi's final capping phrase, it is defined in the *Blue Cliff Record* as "referring to the six sensations" (仄六切塞也), which are delineated in early Buddhist texts as the source of human attachments that lead to suffering. In the final line Xuedou laments the ongoing impact of self-generated deficiencies that cannot be overcome.

Ode 83 (78)

Sixteen Bodhisattvas Taking a Bath 十六開士浴

Case: This gong'an is based on a parable from chapter five of the *Heroic March Sūtra*, about how twenty-five bodhisattvas attain enlightenment by using one of the five senses: a group of five bodhisattvas gain insight through seeing and one does through smelling, two through tasting, and another through hearing. In addition, sixteen bodhisattvas gain wisdom through touching water while bathing, which is not a matter of washing to remove filth or refresh the body but gaining peace of mind based on the sensation of water.

First, Xuedou cites the sūtra passage, "In ancient days there were sixteen bodhisattvas who, at the time for monks to wash, filed in to bathe" (古有十六開士隨僧沐浴), and "suddenly they were awakened based on water" (忽悟水因). Then the master demands of his followers, "All you eminent Chan virtuosos, do you understand their saying, 'Wondrous subtlety discloses clarity so we've become descendants of buddhas.' Realization is attained after probing seven times and piercing through the eighth" (諸禪德. 作麼生會. 他妙觸宣明. 成佛子住. 也須七穿八穴始得).

Yuanwu writes of the gathering of sixteen sages, "What's the use of forming a crowd? Among this whole bunch there's nobody who can speak up!" (成群作隊. 有什麼用處. 這一隊不喞𠺕漢). Of the saying cited by Xuedou, Yuanwu says, "Patch-robed monks throughout the world only seek but can't find its meaning. What happens when you have two heads but three faces? (天下衲僧到這裏摸索不著. 兩頭三面作什麼). Of the final admonition he comments, "Each blow of the staff leaves a bruise, but you can't avoid my jolting and beating you. Have you heard about what Deshan and Linji used to do?" (一棒一條痕. 莫辜負山僧好. 撞著磕著. 還曾見德山臨濟麼).

Tianqi writes of the bodhisattvas' awakening, "How impressive to see that they surpass conventional boundaries so that each one resides in the buddha realm" (令人着眼. 身境俱絕. 一道清孤. 各住佛地), and of Xuedou's admonition, "To dwell as a solitary seeker who makes a great effort, you must from the outset let go of all attachments" (若住清孤墮於大功. 直須撒手始無拘繫). Tianqi's concluding note reads, "Citing a scripture about breaking through emotion points clearly to resolving the matter for our entire lineage" (引教破情. 旨明就路還家); and his wrapping phrase says, "Great effort isn't enough" (大功不宰).

Verse: Monks complete the path to attain enlightenment,

(Y: The story's right here, but I'll dish out three thousand blows in the morning and eight hundred at night. Leaping out of an adamantine trap can't be achieved from one story, 現有一箇. 朝打三千暮打八百. 跳出金剛圈. 一箇也不消得)

And lie down in bed with legs stretched out,

(T: There's only one person who understands, but we don't need more than that, 大了底人只消一个. 何必用多)

Talking of attaining perfect realization as in a dream.

(Y: Fast asleep, explaining a dream. Since this is seen only in a dream, why listen to sleep talking? 早是瞌睡更說夢. 却許爾夢見. 寐語作什麼)

Although bathed in fragrant water, I'll spit in their face.

(Y: Nah! This adds another layer of mud on top of dirt. Don't shit on clean ground! 咄. 土上加泥又一重. 莫來淨地上屙)

(T: If you cling to the idea of realization attained in a dream, then you deserve to be spit at, 若執我悟圓通. 依舊作夢. 似這般人只好驀臉唾)

了事衲僧消一箇 / 長連床上展脚卧 / 夢中曾說悟圓通 / 香水洗來驀面唾.

Comments: In telling the story Xuedou adopts a reverent tone toward the significance of the sūtra passage for explaining how enlightenment is based on sensations in a vivid and dramatic way that challenges his followers. But in the ode, he switches abruptly to a flippant and iconoclastic standpoint by mocking those attached to the mythical quality of this account. The capping phrases on the first couplet reinforce his intended meaning.

According to Yuanwu's prose commentary, "Xuedou holds up the significance of the scripture . . . but his verse goes beyond the usual interpretation by showing his followers how to avoid staying trapped in a nest of complications. Instead, his goal is to enable disciples to immediately become pure and unbound" (雪竇拈他教意. . . 出他教眼頌. 免得人去教網裏籠罩半醉半醒. 要令人直下灑灑落落). They thereby are free of all spiritual contaminations, rather than just physically clean from washing. However, because any attachment to the parable becomes, in effect, something filthy, Xuedou repudiates the story of the bodhisattvas in a way that resembles case 45 when he tosses Zhaozhou's heavy shirt into the lake.

Ode 84 (79)

Touzi's "All Sounds Are Buddha Sounds" 投子一切聲是佛聲

Case: According to Yuanwu's introduction of Touzi, "His great function manifests right before us without sticking to conventional models, and he captures someone alive without exerting any superfluous effort" (大用現前. 不存軌則. 活捉生擒. 不勞餘力). Furthermore, he's known for "being plain and truthful by using speech that stands out from the crowd; when he gets a question from an ordinary person, as soon as he opens his mouth, you can see how savvy he is" (朴實頭. 得逸群之辯. 凡有致問. 開口便見膽).

In the dialogue a monk asks Touzi, "All sounds are the sounds of buddha, isn't that so?" (一切聲是佛聲是否), thus evoking a notion expressed in numerous sūtras, and Touzi replies, "That's so" (是). The monk says, "O Teacher, don't let loose fart sounds!" (和尚莫屁沸碗鳴聲), and "Touzi hits him" (投子便打). Then the monk, alluding to another scriptural passage, asks, "Aren't both coarse words and subtle speech based on the same primary principle?" (粗言及細語. 皆歸第一義), and Touzi says, "That's so." When the monk retorts, "O Teacher, can I call you an ass?" (喚和尚作頭驢得), Touzi strikes again.

Yuanwu says of the monk's initial query, "He knows how to grab the tiger by the whiskers or cause thunderclaps to resound in a clear sky, but he doesn't notice that his own shit stinks" (也解捋虎鬚. 青天轟霹靂. 自屎不覺臭). Of the next question about speaking Yuanwu writes, "He grabs the tiger's whiskers a second time, but isn't this like clutching the loot while crying out that he's the one wronged? East, west, south, and north are all made of reflections and echoes" (第二回捋虎鬚. 抱贓叫屈作什麼. 東西南北. 猶有影響在). Of Touzi's final act, "It won't do to let this monk off the hook. He should be struck, but why stop hitting before the staff's been broken?" (著. 不可放過. 好打. 拄杖未到折. 因什麼便休去).

Tianqi says of Touzi's first reply, "The activity of a tiger in its cave" (陷虎之機), and of the first hit, "The correct decree is fully expressed" (正令全提). Of the monk's second question he writes, "He only knows how to test someone, but doesn't understand when someone's testing him" (只知驗人不知人驗), and of Touzi's second reply, "He sells himself to help this monk" (賣身套他). Tianqi's final note reads, "A deluded person transforming himself points clearly to fully express the great function" (輸己陷人. 旨明大用全

提); and his wrapping phrase says, "Everything's balanced in his hands" (權衡在手).

Verse: O Touzi! The wheels of your dynamism spin unobstructed,
(Y: What else could he do? It's something, 有什麼奈何他處. 也有些子)
(T: He responds by using all his vitality, 應用甚活)
Letting go one time and holding firm twice, it's the same either way.
(Y: Once he's gouged out your eyeballs, how will you be able to see Touzi? 換却爾眼睛. 什麼處見投子)
(T: He leaves no space before or after the disciple's words, 一个是字. 前後無空)
It's too bad that the number of people playing along the tides is limitless,
In the end, they'll die from falling in the current.
(Y: What a shame they can't escape the trap! A troubled person shouldn't try to explain their troubles to another troubled person, 可惜許. 爭奈出這圈繢不得. 愁人莫向愁人說)
(T: The monk allowing himself to be struck by Touzi is like people playing and dying in the tide, 僧陷投子反被子打. 如弄潮人還死潮中)
What if they suddenly come back to life,
(Y: My meditation seat shakes as I'm startled by this thought and I, too, step back three thousand paces, 禪床震動. 驚殺山僧. 也倒退三千里)
Like the roaring sounds of hundreds of rivers flowing backwards!
(T: Old Xuedou extricates himself by saying the monk lives again, but Touzi knows how risky this is, 雪老出脫這僧若然得活. 投子十分太險)
投子投子. 機輪無阻 / 放一得二. 同彼同此 / 可憐無限弄潮人 / 畢竟還落潮中死 / 忽然活 / 百川倒流鬧聒聒.

Comments: Xuedou begins by lavishly praising the ability of Touzi to bob and weave while escaping from ensnarement by the monk's pesky questions. Touzi remains forthright and direct yet resorts to using the staff as a stern reprimand. The second couplet chastises the monk for trying but failing to thrive near the strong current of Touzi's leadership that overwhelms his meager attempts to one-up the teacher and shows, as Hakuin's comments point out, the arrogance of misguided trainees who make light of superior combatants in a dharma battle.

However, the final couplet proposes that the monk may be able to resuscitate, as symbolized by the reverse surging of the waters of a multitude of streams. Xuedou evokes a remarkable image of reversing the waters that was previously used by Dongshan Liangjie and other teachers to illustrate what it takes for those who are deluded to attain awakening. According to Tenkei, these lines are not expressed out of hope, but instead offer a dirge for ordinary Chan assemblies in that living dragons rarely come flying out from among commonplace practitioners.

Ode 85 (80)

Zhaozhou's "Tossing a Ball into the Rapids" 趙州急水上打毬子

Case: Like the previous two cases—case 83 on sixteen bodhisattvas bathing, and case 84 on vulgar sounds—this gong'an deals with the basic Buddhist notion of sensations or levels of consciousness involving seeing, hearing, touching, smelling, and tasting, plus the sixth consciousness of self-awareness.

In the dialogue featuring two prominent teachers, a monk asks Zhaozhou, "Does a newborn baby encompass the six consciousnesses, or not?" (初生孩子. 還具六識也無), and the response is, "It's like tossing a ball into the rapids" (急水上打毬子). The monk later asks Touzi, "What's the meaning of tossing a ball into the rapids?" (急水上打毬子. 意旨如何), and he says, "Each and every instant of thought, the flow never stops" (念念不停流).

Yuanwu writes of the monk's question, "His dynamism is like a flash of lightning, but what newborn baby is he talking about?" (閃電之機. 說什麼初生孩兒子), and of Zhaozhou's reply, "It's rushed by, so even a savvy hawk can't keep up. You must investigate the flux" (過也. 俊鷂趁不及. 也要驗過). Of the question posed to Touzi he says, "This involves two adepts investigating each other; both get that it's rushed by!" (也是作家同驗過. 還會麼. 過也), and of Touzi's reaction, "He's creating entanglements" (打葛藤漢).

Tianqi says of Zhaozhou's response, "The rushing stream not standing still is a metaphor for all things" (水急不存. 一物喻上), of the monk's question for Touzi, "He doubts, so he tries again" (沉疑再决), and of Touzi's reply,

"This annotates Zhaozhou's saying" (雙註前法). Tianqi's final note reads, "Raising this case points clearly to displaying dynamism through words" (正案傍提. 旨明句裏呈機); and his wrapping phrase says, "Entering a place where there's a hidden blade" (入就藏鋒).

Verse: A question's been raised about whether the six consciousnesses are inactive,

(Y: Although the monk has eyes, he's blind, and although he has ears, he's deaf. Yet a bright mirror is in its stand and a bright pearl is held in the palm of his hand. Xuedou sums it up in just one line, 有眼如盲. 有耳如聾. 明鏡當臺. 明珠在掌. 一句道盡)

(T: The six consciousnesses are unremarkable, that's why they seem inactive, 六根渾然故曰無功)

Both adepts discern why this is being asked.

(T: Zhaozhou and Touzi are indeed true adepts, 趙州投子二俱作家)

A ball tossed on surging rapids—

(Y: From beginning to end it keeps rushing by, that's what he's saying, 始終一貫. 過也. 道什麼)

Does anyone see clearly that it never stays where it lands?

(Y: Try watching and you'll go blind as it rushes by, but you can pick it up along the shore, 看即瞎過也. 灘下接取)

(T: Who realizes that nothing ever stays where it is? 不存一物誰人解看)

六識無功伸一問 / 作家相共辯來端 / 茫茫急水打毬子 / 落處不停誰解看.

Comments: The first two lines highlight that, while the monk's question seems to be triggered by a logical investigation concerning whether the unformed mind of an infant is capable of self-awareness, the two skilled masters understand the underlying cause of the inquiry: the question reveals the monk is uncertain about his own ability to achieve an insight beyond ordinary apprehension that is compared by Laozi and other sages to the state of mind of an innocent child.

The second couplet focuses on the imagery used by Zhaozhou and Touzi showing that the impermanence of existence serves as the basis of all phenomena, including the newborn's consciousness. In the final analysis, this level of understanding must be attained to resolve the monk's initial question. As Tenkei points out, Xuedou highlights the boundlessness of authentic awareness seen as the transcendental living waters of Chan activity or the eye of a true master, so the ode's final rhetorical question exposes and reverses the foolishness of the monk's query.

Ode 86 (81)

Yaoshan's "Watch the Arrow" 藥山看箭

Case: In the introduction Yuanwu says of Yaoshan, "He captures the flag and beats the drum, but a thousand sages can't find him. He cuts off delusions, but ten thousand techniques don't get the best of him. This is due neither to the wondrous functioning of spiritual powers nor a fundamental essence. Tell me, what's the basis for attaining such marvelous achievements?" (攙旗奪鼓. 千聖莫窮. 坐斷誵訛. 萬機不到. 不是神通妙用. 亦非本體如然. 且道. 憑箇什麼. 得恁麼奇特).

In the dialogue a monk asks Yaoshan, "When elk are gathered on the grassy plain, how does one shoot the king of elks?" (平田淺草麈鹿成群. 如何射得麈中麈), which refers to a mythical animal known for horns as sharp as swords that defends its herd against tigers. [Note that 麈 sometimes appears as 麆 and implies, "Lord of Sounds" (音主)]. The teacher replies, "Watch the arrow!" (看箭). The monk throws himself down (僧放身便倒) and Yaoshan calls out, "Attendant, drag this dead man away" (侍者拕出這死漢), so the monk runs off (僧便走). Yaoshan concludes, "Is there no limit to those playing with mudballs?" (弄泥團漢有什麼限), and Xuedou adds, "Although he was alive after taking several steps, he was bound to die by the fifth" (三步雖活五步須死).

Yuanwu says of the monk's question, "He tries to enter his enemy's stronghold and show his horns, but he's got an arrow lodged in the back of his head" (把髻投衙. 擎頭帶角出來. 腦後拔箭), and of Yaoshan's answer, "He goes right ahead and overtakes him. Only by running downhill will you meet him" (就身打劫. 下坡不走. 快便難逢. 著). Of the monk falling down he writes, "You'll find him in a coffin, but see that he comes back to life in the midst of death and allows his spirit to carry on" (棺木裏瞠眼. 死中得活. 猶有氣息在), of Yaoshan's final comment, "Too bad he lets the monk go. He acts according to the rules, but that's adding frost to snow" (可惜許放過. 據令而行. 雪上加霜), and of Xuedou's remark, "One hand lifts up and one presses down. Even if the monk would run a hundred steps, he'd still lose his life" (一手擡一手搦. 直饒走百步. 也須喪身失命).

Tianqi writes of Yaoshan's arrow, "He sees by looking" (以見用見), of the monk falling down, "He seizes the opportunity to act" (見機而作), and of the teacher calling the attendant, "He shows how to gain insight by seeing" (以見遣見). Of Yaoshan's final saying he comments, "Claws and fangs in his dharma nest wrap up this case" (法窟爪牙. 據欵結案), and of Xuedou's remark, "At first there's a village, then there're no more shops, and in the end all is decimated" (前不構村. 後不迭店. 終不勦絕). The concluding note says, "Seizing an opportunity to act points clearly to raising the flag and beating the drum" (見機而作. 旨明攙旗奪鼓); and his wrapping phrase reads, "Everything's balanced in his hands" (權衡在手).

Verse: "The king of elks," watch out!

(T: People are told to see it with their own eyes, 令人着眼)

(Yaoshan) shoots an arrow, and the monk walks several steps.

(Y: He leaps with vitality but only for a few paces, as he's been dead for a long time, 活鱍鱍地. 只得三步. 死了多時)

(T: He doesn't break free from attachments, 未出綣績)

If he'd taken five steps, a crowd would be gathered to chase down a tiger.

(T: If not for him, who else would dare do it? 若解番身. 誰敢當鋒)

Hunters are born with the true eye.

(Y: This is so for Yaoshan, but what about Xuedou? It doesn't really concern either one, so it's not my business or anyone else's, 藥山則故是雪竇又作麼生. 也不干藥山事. 也不干雪竇事. 也不干山僧事. 也不干上座事)

(T: This refers to the great Chan teacher Yaoshan, 大手宗師須還藥山)

麈中麈. 君看取 / 下一箭. 走三步 / 五步若活. 成羣趂虎 / 正眼從來付獵人.

Follow-up: Xuedou adds by calling out, "Look there's an arrow!" (師高聲云. 看箭) (Y: One punishment for all their crimes . . . Stuff it down their throats, 一狀領過 . . . 已塞却爾咽喉了也) (T: This is his final fishing expedition, 末後垂釣).

Comments: The first two lines quote or echo four sayings from the case, as Xuedou seeks to establish the conceptual and rhetorical basis for evaluating the monk's actions, and whether he is resuscitated during his exchange by feigning death or merely appears so partway (after a few steps) but by the end (fifth step) is lost in frustration and futility.

The third line implies that the teacher will form a posse, like the king of elks gathering his herd, if needed to track down a tiger-like follower rather than a stumbling novice. Nevertheless, not only the huntsman but all beings have the potential for genuine insight. According to Tenkei, the key to interpreting the poem's relation to the dialogue lies in the interjection when Xuedou exclaims another passage drawn from the case, this time in tailored fashion to highlight that the flight of the arrow, instead of an individual, symbolizes the true meaning of dharma.

Ode 87 (84)

Vimalakīrti's "Dharma Gate to Nonduality" 維摩不二法門

Case: Yuanwu's introduction begins with a Mādhyamika-style double negation when he writes, "Although one says that 'it is,' there's nothing to which 'it' refers, and although one says, 'it's not,' there's no 'it' to be negated. When 'it is' and 'it's not' are left behind, and gain and loss are forgotten, then there's clarity and purity within complete freedom" (道是是無可是. 言非非無可非. 是非已去. 得失兩忘. 淨裸裸赤灑灑). Yuanwu further suggests that concrete expressions are deficient, such as the saying, "In front the buddha shrine and main gate, and in back the abbot's room and private quarters" (面前是佛殿三門. 背後是寢堂方丈.).

In the dialogue the bodhisattva-cum-exceptional lay practitioner Vimalakīrti, who, feigning illness, resides temporarily in a ten-foot square that is visited by Buddhist luminaries, asks Mañjuśrī, "What's a bodhisattva's entry into the dharma gate of nonduality?" (何等是菩薩入不二法門). The reply is, "According to my view, in all things there're no words and no speech, no pointing and no awareness, just cutting off all questions and answers" (如我意者. 於一切法. 無言無說. 無示無識. 離諸問答). Then Mañjuśrī asks the same question of Vimalakīrti, whose response is a total and disturbing silence. Xuedou asks, "What did Vimalakīrti say?" (維摩道什麼), and exclaims, "Thoroughly exposed!" (勘破了也), a capping remark also prominent in case 4.

Yuanwu writes of Mañjuśrī's question, "Not even the buddhas of the triple world, let alone the Golden Grain Buddha (Vimalakīrti), can open their mouths without failing. The bodhisattva turns the spear around and stabs him to death. The arrow hits Vimalakīrti just as he was shooting at others" (這一靠莫道金粟如來. 設使三世諸佛. 也開口不得. 倒轉鎗頭來也. 刺殺一人. 中箭還似射人時). Of Xuedou's query Yuanwu says, "Nah! He gathers ten thousand arrows to his chest and speaks truth" (咄. 萬箭攢心. 替他說道理), and of his last comment, "It's so not only the previous time, but now, too. Yet Xuedou draws his bow after the thief's fled. . . . There's danger, as even a golden-haired lion is confused" (非但當時. 即今也恁麼. 雪竇也是賊過後張弓. . . . 嶮. 金毛獅子也摸索不著).

Tianqi writes of Mañjuśrī's challenge, "He returns the invitation" (返請其佳), of Xuedou's first comment, "I'm afraid this has been going on for a long time, but all of sudden it happens now" (恐逐良久. 急處一提), and of the final remark, "He claims to penetrate the silence, but nothing is revealed" (點破默然. 拈其不露). Tianqi's concluding note reads, "Fishing in deep waters points clearly to what lies beyond" (探竿. 旨明向上); and his wrapping phrase says, "Demonstrating truth to one another" (遞相演揚).

Verse: Nah! Old Vimalakīrti,

(Y: Why scorn him? . . . this deserves thirty blows. 咄他作什麼 . . . 好與三十棒)

Pretending to be sick out of compassion for living beings.

(T: Old Xuedou feels bad for him but doesn't know what else to say, 雪老深嘆. 不遇知音)

Lying ill in Vaiśālī,
His whole body withered and frail.
The teacher of the seven primordial buddhas (Mañjuśrī) arrives,

(Y: When a guest comes, one must assist him, but when a thief comes, one must beat him. Mañjuśrī brings along a crowd, so he must be an adept, 客來須看. 賊來須打. 成群作隊. 也須是作家始得)

Entering the tiny room that's swept clean.

(T: All clutter is removed to receive Mañjuśrī, 除去所有. 接待文殊)

He asks about the gate of nonduality,
At that moment Vimalakīrti begins to fall.
But he doesn't fall!

(Y: He finds life in the midst of death, there's some breath left in him, 死中得活. 猶有氣息在)

The golden-haired lion is undeterred.

(T: He doesn't fall down since buddhas and patriarchs could express it in words, 非是靠倒. 佛祖到此亦不能言).

咄. 這維摩老 / 悲生空懊惱 / 臥疾毗耶離 / 全身太枯槁 / 七佛祖師來 / 一室且頻掃 / 請問不二門 / 當時便靠倒 / 不靠倒 / 金毛獅子無處討.

Comments: The verse begins with a playful disdain for the deliberately duplicitous methods of Vimalakīrti, who pretends to be sick to lure eminent emissaries of Buddha, including the second wisest being in the pantheon, Mañjuśrī, who arrives while others are reluctant. But in the last two couplets Xuedou offers the highest praise for the layman's feat in maintaining a lofty silence that defeats any attempt by so many revered companions to articulate the meaning of nonduality.

After eight lines of five characters each, the verse ends with a three-character interpolation followed by a seven-character endorsement and thereby repudiation of Vimalakīrti's adversaries. Although appearing vulnerable to Mañjuśrī's effort at turning things around, Vimalakīrti resuscitates through profound reticence that exposes all untruths that have been spoken.

Ode 88 (85)

Tongfeng's "Tiger's Roar" 桐峯虎聲

Case: Yuanwu introduces the adept Tongfeng (桐峯, n.d.), an obscure, reclusive follower of Linji, "Holding the world firmly without allowing any leakage is the true mission of a patch-robed monk; releasing light from one's forehead is the adamantine eyeball of a patch-robed monk; touching iron and turning it into gold or touching gold and turning it into iron is the staff of a patch-robed monk; and cutting off the tongues of everyone in the world is the bravado of a patch-robed monk" (把定世界不漏纖毫. 是衲僧正令. . . 頂門放光. 是衲僧金剛眼睛. . . 點金成鐵. 忽擒忽縱. 是衲僧拄杖子. . . 坐斷天下人舌頭. 是衲僧氣宇).

In the dialogue "a monk visits the hermitage of Tongfeng and asks, 'If you suddenly encountered a tiger, what would you do?'" (僧到桐峰庵主處便問. 者裏忽逢大虫. 又作麼生). Then, "the hermit roars like a tiger" (主作虎

聲), and "the monk acts afraid" (僧作怕勢), so "the hermit laughs aloud" (主大笑). The monk says, "You old thief!" (這老賊), and Tongfeng asks, "What can you do about it?" (爭奈老僧何), but the monk "stops short" (休去). Xuedou adds, "It's clear both are thieves who would cover their ears when stealing a bell" (是則是兩箇惡賊只解掩耳偷鈴).

Yuanwu says of the monk's question, "This fellow is only good at playing in the shadows" (作家弄影漢), and of the hermit's reply, "He adds error to error but has teeth and claws, so they live and die together" (將錯就錯. 却有牙爪. 同生同死). Of Xuedou's comment he says, "The words are still ringing in our ears. Both have been reproached by Xuedou, but tell me, at that time what could they have done to avoid his criticism? No patch-robed monk anywhere would succeed" (言猶在耳. 遭他雪竇點檢. 且道當時合作麼生免得點檢. 天下衲僧不到).

Tianqi writes of the monk's query, "He's borrowing a hidden blade" (借事藏鋒), and of the hermit's laughter, "There's some degree of praise in this sound" (賞其知音). Of the monk's comeback Tianqi says, "That's his view" (拈上之見), of Tongfeng's retort, "In his boast both are being tested" (一誇二驗), and of Xuedou's remark, "His point is at once to let go and hold firm" (點他解放不解收). Tianqi's concluding note says, "Seizing the opportunity to act points clearly to making the most of the radiant source" (見機而作. 旨明遇物明宗); and his wrapping phrase reads, "Following causality responds to circumstances" (隨緣應用).

Verse: If you see a chance but fail to seize it, this will bother you for a thousand miles.

(T: Not following a mission leads only to complications, 不行正令. 只打葛藤)

His stripes are fine, but he doesn't show he's got claws or fangs.

(Y: I only fear that using them would be wrongminded. Let's talk about him when his claws and fangs are ready, 只恐用處不明. 待爪牙備向爾道)

(T: Two youngsters squabbling, 二俱雛兒)

Don't you know, there was once a spontaneous encounter on Daxiong Peak?

(Y: If there's a rule, go by the rule, but if there's no rule, follow an example. 有條攀條. 無條攀例)

The peal of thunder and lightning shook the earth.

(T: Adepts creating an exemplary model, 師資作家. 舉例令看)

O Worthies, do you know it or not?

(Y: Grandmotherly kindness . . . yet Xuedou creates complications. 老婆心切. . . 雪竇打葛藤)

Grab the tiger's tail and hold onto its whiskers!

(Y: How will you react when a tiger suddenly appears? All the patch-robed monks in the world won't help . . . I'll strike asking, why didn't you say, "You old thief!"? 忽然突出如何收. 收天下衲僧在這裏 . . . 喝打云. 何不道這老賊)

(T: Applying this lesson to one's life leads to becoming an adept, 拈起令看. 如此擒縱始是作家)

見之不取. 思之千里 / 好箇斑斑. 爪牙未備 / 君不見. 大雄山下忽相逢 / 落落聲光皆振地 / 大丈夫. 見也無 / 收虎尾兮捋虎鬚.

Comments: The first two lines continue the approach of Xuedou's capping phrase for the case, in which he accuses both the monk and the hermit of being rascals unable to conceal their crimes because they lack genuine temerity and cunning. The next two couplets contrast the current encounter with a similar, albeit more celebrated instance involving the eminent teacher Baizhang and his main disciple, Huangbo.

According to this account, Huangbo lets out a tiger's roar when challenged and is then hit by his mentor. Later that night Baizhang tells the assembly, "At the base of Daxiong Peak there's a tiger, so all of you must watch out when you go there. Today, I was the one bitten!" (大雄山下有一虎. 汝等諸人出入切須好看. 老僧今日親遭一口).

Ode 89 (86)

Yunmen's "Radiant Light" 雲門光明

Case: Yuanwu says of Yunmen, "He holds the world firmly, without allowing the slightest leakage; he cuts off countless flows without leaving behind a drop. As soon as someone opens their mouth they're mistaken, but if one hesitates the chance is missed. Tell me, where does the eye come from that pierces all barriers? (把定世界不漏絲毫. 截斷眾流不存涓滴. 開口便錯擬議即差. 且道作麼生是透關底眼).

In the dialogue "Yunmen tells the assembly" (雲門垂語云), "Everyone has a radiant light, but when you look for it, it recedes in darkness. What's the radiant light all people possess?" (人人盡有光明在. 看時不見暗昏昏. 作麼生是諸人光明). Yunmen then "answers on behalf of the monks" (自代云) by saying, "The refectory and main gate" (厨庫三門). In some versions the response reads, "The monks' hall, buddha hall, refectory, and main gate" (僧堂佛殿厨庫三門). Yunmen also remarks, "A good thing can't be compared to nothing" (好事不如無).

Yuanwu says of Yunmen's opening pronouncement, "When black lacquer buckets look [for light], they're blinded. Mountains are mountains and rivers are rivers, but this is like washing black ink in a bucket of lacquer" (黑漆桶. 看時瞎. 山是山水是水. 漆桶裏洗黑汁). Of Yunmen's first answer Yuanwu writes, "That's grandmotherly kindness, but why does he create entanglements?" (老婆心切. 打葛藤作什麼), and of the second, "He knows he's only halfway there, but it still amounts to something" (自知較一半. 猶較些子).

In prose commentary Yuanwu compares the message of nondualism embedded in the dialogue to a passage from Shitou's *Merging of Sameness and Otherness* (參同契, *Cantongqi*): "Right within light there's darkness, but don't perceive it as darkness. Right within darkness there's light, but don't perceive it as light" (當明中有暗. 勿以暗相覩. 當暗中有明. 勿以明相遇). He also cites a verse by Panshan, "Light doesn't shine on objects, / Nor do objects exist. / When light and objects are both forgotten / What remains?" (光非照境. 境亦非存. 光境俱忘. 復是何物).

Tianqi says of Yuanwu's initial statement, "It's entirely spiritual light, that's why it can't be seen" (皆有靈光. 因何不見), of his answer, "Afraid of dropping his pole, he shows us momentary phenomena" (恐陷竿頭. 故示刹塵), and of the final remark, "Afraid that we'd become attached to the ordinary, he adds some contrast" (恐執平常. 復再拈之). Tianqi's concluding note reads, "Hitting the mark points clearly to not falling into duality" (當央直指. 旨明不落二邊); and his wrapping phrase says, "Grandmotherly kindness!" (老婆心切).

Verse: Each person is illumined by their own light,
Yunmen shows you that path.

(Y: Why does he stop with just one path? Ten suns are shining altogether, but he's only shown us a single path, 何止一線. 十日並照. 放一線道即得)

(T: The situation's obvious; I'd say it again, 是境皆顯. 我又重示)

Yet flowers fall and trees don't provide shade,

(Y: He's filling a black lacquer bucket with black ink, 黑漆桶裏盛黑汁)

When looking, who doesn't see this?

(T: To hold up something based on nothing leads to concern about making the right effort, 以無拈有. 恐執大功)

Whether you see it or not,

(Y: Both horns are cut off. Blind! 兩頭俱坐斷. 瞎)

Ride an ox while sitting backwards to enter the buddha hall.

(Y: Even Xuedou makes his living in a ghost cave. Don't you see that at midnight the sun comes out, and at noon the midnight watch is signaled, 雪竇也只向鬼窟裏作活計. 還會麼. 半夜日頭出. 日午打三更)

自照列孤明 / 為君通一線 / 花謝樹無影 / 看時誰不見 / 見不見 / 倒騎牛兮入佛殿.

Comments: The first couplet celebrates Yunmen's teaching method by paraphrasing its essential point and proclaiming this the true path, which is playfully challenged by Yuanwu and Tianqi. The next two lines reinforce the master's comment regarding temple buildings by offering examples of decay and desolation that are apparent to the naked eye yet must be considered to partake of genuine radiance.

The last couplet highlights the paradox of Yunmen's final remark by mentioning a technique carried out by Daoist and other reclusive practitioners who mount an ox without looking ahead toward the destination. This time the entrance leads to the buddha hall, perhaps the central edifice on Chan temple grounds, although monastic rules texts suggest it is not needed since, in principle, all beings are already buddha. In prose commentary Yuanwu cautions that Yunmen "doesn't intend an understanding of things based on nothingness" (又不得作無事會), since the virtue of radiant light continually abounds. But Tenkei suggests the poet's switches perspectives drastically to create an existential turnabout within the realm of uncertainty, which enables his followers to avoid taking a dead-end path of idle speculation.

Ode 90 (87)

Yunmen's "Medicine and Illness Quell Each Other" 雲門藥病相治

Case: Yuanwu says Yunmen is "an insightful fellow without a nest, sometimes standing on the summit of a solitary peak where weeds grow profusely and sometimes moving freely in the bustling marketplace" (明眼漢沒窠臼. 有時孤峯頂上草漫漫. 有時鬧市裏頭赤灑灑). Moreover, "Suddenly, he's a wrathful titan with three heads and six arms, or suddenly, he's the Sun-Face or Moon-Face buddha releasing the light of all-embracing compassion. In each mote he manifests all bodily forms, and to help people according to their needs he willingly slogs through the mire" (忽若忿怒那吒. 現三頭六臂. 忽若日面月面. 放普攝慈光. 於一塵現一切身. 為隨類人. 和泥合水).

In the brief case, "Yunmen instructs his assembly" (雲門示眾云), "Medicine and illness quell each other. Everything in the whole world is medicine. What is the self?" 藥病相治. 盡大地是藥那. 箇是自己).

Yunmen says of Yunmen's first assertion, "A combined form is ungraspable" (一合相不可得), of the second point, "A bitter gourd's bitter to the root, you'd better toss it" (苦瓠連根苦. 擺向一邊), and of his final query, "A sweet melon's sweet to the stem, you'd better grab it" (甜瓜徹蔕甜. 那裏得這消息來).

Tianqi writes, "If medicine is illness, that's the self" (若作藥病. 那是自己). His final note reads, "Causing confusion points clearly to a pole that instructs people" (破惑. 旨明垂釣); and his wrapping phrase says, "Displaying emotion" (拈情).

Verse: "Everything in the whole world is medicine,"
From ancient to current times, what a great mistake!
(Y: There's a resonance in these words set down with a brushstroke. Nah! 言中有響. 一筆句下. 咄)
(T: From ancient to current times medicine's prepared, and from ancient to current times there're great mistakes, 古今作藥. 古今大錯)
Don't build a carriage from behind closed doors,
The thoroughfare's empty and isolated.
(Y: Set foot outside and you enter the weeds, but by mounting a horse you can see the road. Xuedou holding this in his fingertips is truly exceptional, 脚下便入草. 上馬見路. 信手拈來. 不妨奇特)
(T: Piercing the nostrils of the deluded causes death; if there's no nose-piercing, the path's naturally open and clear, 妄生穿鑿終是死見. 若不穿鑿自然開豁)
So many mistakes!
(Y: One arrow fells two eagles, 一箭落雙雕)
(T: This holds up nothing, 此乃拈無)
Even if one's nose is stuck up in the air, still it must be pierced.

(Y: Your head's fallen. I'll hit saying, "Pierced!" 頭落也. 打云. 穿却了也)

(T: Not falling into something versus nothing doesn't mean you're an adept, 不落有無亦非作家)

盡大地是藥 / 古今何大錯 / 閉門不造車 / 通途自寥廓 / 錯錯 / 鼻孔遼天亦穿却.

Comments: Xuedou begins by citing a keyword from the case, but in this instance, instead of offering praise, he comments rather sarcastically in the second line on the apparent deficiency of Yunmen's standpoint that can easily be misunderstood by deluded practitioners who look for facile explanations.

The next couplet illustrates a typical misapprehension by alluding to a famous expression by the ancient Daoist philosopher Zhuangzi (莊子, n.d.). In his era, it was becoming common to build carriages so that the wheels were fit to the size of ruts constructed in the road, but Zhuangzi boldly claimed that through the power of intuition he could design a carriage from inside, without needing to measure the route. Xuedou, however, reverses this implication in order to highlight the significance of self-cultivation, while also supporting in the fourth line the Daoist view of unfettered spiritual wandering.

The final couplet emphasizes that all forms of articulating the experience of enlightenment are invariably unfounded and misconstrued, including Xuedou's approach. Therefore, it is imperative that adepts continue to have their nostrils pierced to ensure their teachings are appropriate to any circumstances that arise; that is, illness continues after a dose of medicine and this condition requires an additional remedy. The capping phrases reinforce the poet's ironic self-criticism regarding the arrogance of authority when it is not underscored by authentic realization.

Ode 91 (88)

Xuansha's "Man with Three Disabilities" 玄沙三種病人

Case: In the introduction Yuanwu says that adepts like Xuansha "take charge of any situation and hit the mark by smashing golden chains and hidden barriers. In accord with their Buddhist mission, they leave no tracks or traces. But tell me, why allow for so much delusion?" (當機敲點. 擊碎金鎖玄關. 據令而行. 直得掃蹤滅跡. 且道誵訛在什麼處).

According to the dialogue Xuansha presents this challenge: "Old adepts everywhere speak constantly of benefiting living beings. Suppose they meet someone with one of three kinds of disability. How would true teachers guide them? (諸方老宿盡道利生接物. 忽有三種病人來. 作麼生接). Then, "A blind person wouldn't see the teacher pick up a gavel or raise his flywhisk; a deaf person wouldn't hear him speak of contemplation; and a mute person wouldn't be able to explain the teachings" (患盲者. 拈槌豎拂他又不見. 患聾者. 語言三昧他又不聞. 患啞者. 教他說又說不得).

In the second part of the case a monk questions Yunmen about Xuansha's meaning. When Yunmen "asks the monk to bow" (汝禮拜著), the master also pretends "to poke him with the staff" (拄杖挃). As the monk backs away, Yunmen says, "You're not blind" (汝不患聾). Similar tests prove the novice is neither deaf nor mute and, at the conclusion it is said, "This monk gains insight" (其僧於此有).

Yuanwu writes of Xuansha's first statement, "Adepts set up shop according to whether their lineages are loquacious or taciturn" (隨分開箇鋪席. 隨家豐儉), and of the monk's realization, "He draws his bow after the thief's fled, his teacup's broken" (賊過後張弓.討什麼碗). In prose commentary Yuanwu suggests, "If the monk had been savvy when Yunmen told him to bow, he would've immediately turned over his meditation seat. Then how would so many complications have occurred?" (當時若是箇漢. 等他道禮拜著. 便與掀倒禪床. 豈見有許多葛藤).

Tianqi says of Xuansha's query, "Meeting a teacher face to face but coming up empty is blindness" (對面親呈. 空示如瞎), and of the monk's insight, "The goal's been fully attained, but explaining it isn't possible" (方達全機. 非說可及). Tianqi's final note reads, "Fishing with a pole to help people points clearly to hitting the mark" (垂釣為人. 旨明當央直示); and his wrapping phrase is, "Everything's balanced in his hands" (權衡在手).

Verse: The blind, the deaf, the mute,
In their dimness, cannot respond to circumstances.
Everywhere in the world,
This is sad and lamentable.

> (Y: What're you pitying and lamenting? It's half clear and half unclear, 笑箇什麼. 悲箇什麼. 半明半暗)
>
> (T: Pitying the blind is not blind; lamenting those who aren't mute is mute, 笑他盲者不盲. 悲他不啞却啞)

If Lizhu's sharp eye can't find a pearl,

How could Shiguang's keen ear recognize a subtle tune?
Compare those instances to sitting quietly by an open window,
(Y: You must do this to attain realization, but don't make your living in a ghost cave. All of a sudden Xuedou smashes the lacquer bucket, 須是恁麼始得. 莫向鬼窟裏作活計. 一時打破漆桶)
As leaves fall and flowers bloom, each at its appropriate occasion.
(T: How can one argue with the rationale of this natural setting? Old Xuedou boasts that he's the true inheritor of the Chan legacy, 理本自然豈消安排. 雪老自誇高超二子)

盲聾瘖啞 / 杳絕機宜 / 天上天下 / 堪笑堪悲 / 離朱不辯正色 / 師曠豈識玄絲 / 爭如獨坐虛窗下 / 葉落花開自有時.

Follow-up: Xuedou adds: Do you understand or not? It's an iron hammerhead without a hole (復云. 還會麼也無. 無孔鐵鎚) (Y: That's what Xuedou says, but it's regrettable he stopped there, so I'll strike, 自領出去. 可惜放過. 便打) (T: Don't you know what's special about an iron hammerhead? 你既不會. 何異鐵鎚).

Comments: The first two couplets reinforce the basic message of the case by highlighting the unfortunate qualities of disability that symbolize the deficiencies of typical practitioners, although the capping phrases modify this point. Then, Xuedou refers to Lizhu and Shiquang, two semi-mythical Chinese teachers well known for their acute perceptions who nevertheless let down their leaders at crucial moments by not being able to discern exactly what was asked of them.

Xuedou contrasts these problematic examples with the contemplative approach of sitting quietly while reflecting on reality by observing the invariable transformations of the cyclical rotations of the four seasons. However, his appended comment is challenged by both Yuanwu and Tianqi, who suggest the poet has unfortunately fallen back on the use of a stereotypical image that is evoked so many times by various commentators.

Ode 92 (89)

Yunyan's "Bodhisattva of Compassion" 雲岩大悲菩薩

Case: Yuanwu remarks of the Chan paradox of perception, "What if all over your body there were eyes you couldn't see, ears you couldn't hear, a mouth you couldn't explain, and mental functions you couldn't know?" (通身是眼見不到. 通身是耳聞不及. 通身是口說不著. 通身是心鑒不出).

In the dialogue Yunyan asks Daowu, his dharma brother under the mentorship of Yaoshan, "What does the Bodhisattva of Great Compassion (Guanyin) do with so many hands and eyes?" (大悲菩薩用許多手眼作麼), and the senior colleague replies, "It's like someone reaching back with their hands to grab a pillow in the middle of the night" (如人夜半背手摸枕子). When Daowu questions his understanding, Yunyan says, "Your whole body's hands and eyes" (徧身是手眼). Daowu comments, "This saying's worthwhile, but it gets only eighty percent" (道即太煞道. 只道得八成). Pressed by Yunyan to do better, Daowu says, "All over your body are hands and eyes" (通身是手眼), a phrase changing just the first character of the phrase from 徧 to 通.

Yuanwu writes of Daowu's reply, "Why didn't he say something of his own? He's a blind man leading other blind men" (何不用本分草料. 一盲引眾盲). In prose commentary Yuanwu says, "Right at the start Daowu should've given him a blow of the staff across his back to avoid so many later complications" (當初好與他劈脊便棒. 免見後有許多葛藤). Also, of Yunyan asking his elder brother again, Yuanwu suggests, "How can one get the point by accepting another's interpretation? Daowu must be challenged further" (取人處分爭得. 也好與一拶). Of Daowu's final remark, "A shrimp can't leap over the Big Dipper. He's clawed out your eyes and snatched your tongue, but has he gotten a hundred percent or not? He's calling his own father 'daddy'" (蝦跳不出斗. 換却爾眼睛. 移却舌頭. 還得十成也未. 喚爹作爺).

Tianqi writes of Daowu's first saying, "There're no eyes on his hands as he gropes for the pillow at night" (手上無眼. 深夜識枕), of Yunyan's next saying, "His insight has no root" (悟理非根), and of the junior brother asking Daowu again, "He's afraid he doesn't understand, so he probes further" (恐有不諦. 故求深進). Tianqi's final note reads, "Detaching oneself to be a bystander points clearly to overcoming confusion through nonduality" (隔身傍註. 旨明渾然不二); and his wrapping phrase is, "Grandmotherly kindness!" (老婆心切).

Verse: "Your whole (徧) body," or "all over (通) your body,"
Try to interpret this and you'll end up a million miles away.

(Y: It won't do to let anyone off the hook, so why say only a million miles? 放過則不可. 何止十萬里)

(T: All words reflect delusions and invariably express them, 此言諸方妄認. 及至臨時無蹤)

Spreading its wings, a great phoenix soars over multifarious clouds,
Causing the breeze to stir the waters of the four seas.
Is there a speck of dust that suddenly arises?

(Y: He's adding footnotes for Chan practitioners, why doesn't he cut this out? 重為禪人下注脚. 斬拈却著那裏)

What wisp of hair hasn't stopped stirring?

(Y: So exceptional, I'm blown away. Not! 别別. 吹散了也. 截)

Don't you see?
There's a net of jewels reflecting one another with shimmering patterns.

(T: Everything in the universe is unobstructed and the way of nature speaks for itself, 周遍含容一多無礙. 自然之道豈用造作)

Do hands and eyes appear on my staff?
Nah!

(Y: After three or four shouts, then what? 三喝四喝後作麼生)

(T: Right now he should beat and shout instead of observing how things are manifested, 即今棒喝. 你看却從何處發現)

徧身是. 通身是 / 拈來猶教十萬里 / 展翅鵬騰六合雲 / 摶風鼓蕩四溟水 / 是何埃壒兮忽生 / 那箇毫釐兮未止 / 君不見 / 網珠垂範影重重 / 棒頭手眼從何起 / 咄.

Comments: The opening lines suggest that the different sayings about the bodhisattva are essentially the same, despite the alteration of the first character, so this renders any conceptual debate about their relative merits extraneous and counterproductive. The next couplets offer a set of images capturing the magnificent magnanimity of Guanyin, who at once transcends and dramatically influences everything in the world by purifying all realms from dust or impurity, yet delusions and deceptions remain.

In the penultimate line Xuedou evokes the flavor of the Huayan school's holistic philosophy symbolized by Indra's "net of jewels," whereby each gem not only reveals all the others but also triggers reflections upon reflections without any limit or pause. Then the last line turns dramatically to the concrete image of the master's staff, which is often said to have the ability to see who it strikes beyond the adept's own sensation, but the poet does a quick turnabout to dismiss such an impractical rhetorical flourish typical of Chan.

Ode 93 (90)

Zhimen's "Swallowing the Full Moon" 智門含明月

Case: Yuanwu's introduction suggests that for Zhimen, Xuedou's teacher in the Yunmen lineage also featured in case 21, "even a thousand sages haven't transmitted a single phrase prior to sound, yet the single thread right before us remains long-standing and unbroken. He's pure and open, free and unbound, with hair sticking up and ears perked" (聲前一句千聖不傳. 面前一絲長時無間. 淨裸裸赤灑灑. 頭鬔鬆耳卓朔). The last image evokes the unkempt irreverence yet prescient attentiveness of wandering recluses such as Tang poet Hanshan and his eccentric companions.

In the dialogue a monk asks, "What's the essence of wisdom?" (如何是般若體), and Zhimen replies, "An oyster engulfing the bright moon" (蚌含明月). Then the monk asks, "What's the function of wisdom? (如何是般若用), and Zhimen says, "A hare getting pregnant" (兔子懷胎). Both images draw from folktales indicating that oysters produce pearls when they rise to the surface during a full moon, especially in mid-autumn, and rabbits conceive their young under the brightness of the lunar body, also in fall.

Yuanwu writes of Zhimen's first reply, "The slanted doesn't conceal the upright. He's adding a layer of frost to snow" (曲不藏直. 雪上加霜又一重), and of the monk's second query, "He falls back three thousand paces!" (倒退三千里). Of the teacher's response Yuanwu says, "It's dangerous to make your living in the shadows as you won't escape Zhimen's nest of entanglements . . . but is it the 'essence' or 'function' of wisdom? In fact, he's tossing mud on dirt" (嶮. 向光影中作活計. 不出智門窠窟. . . 般若體是般若用. 且要土上加泥).

Tianqi says of the monk's query, "Probing deeply" (請益), of Zhimen's reply, "He hits the mark" (當央直指), and of the second dialogue, "Ditto" (問答同前). His concluding note reads, "The radiant source points to truth" (明宗. 旨是絕待); and his wrapping phrase says, "He cuts off both heads" (坐斷兩頭).

Verse: A bit of emptiness beyond speech and emotion,

> (Y: A scattered mind is the difference between disruptive thoughts and detachment. The buddha eye observes without looking, 擬心即差動念即隔. 佛眼也覷不見)
>
> (T: Essence transcends words and thoughts, 體絕言思)

When humans and gods see Subhūti.

(T: This allusion means that one shouldn't be isolated or avoid attachments to deeds—that's the message, 舉例令看. 莫守孤危. 免執大功. 於此註破)

An oyster engulfing a mysterious rabbit has such a profound meaning,
That's long been causing troubles among Chan lineages.

(Y: When shields and spears are laid to rest, there's peace in the world, but do you understand? I'll strike saying, "O Worthy, how many blows can you take?" 干戈已息天下太平. 還會麼. 打云. 闍黎喫得多少)

(T: It's Subhūti who remains isolated, not knowing Zhimen's view of reality, 空生又困孤危. 不知智門平實)

片虛癡絕謂情 / 人天從此見空生 / 蚌含玄兔深深意 / 曾與禪家作戰爭.

Comments: The opening couplet refers to the Buddha's disciple Subhūti, whose name literally means "born from emptiness" (空生). As Xuedou points out in Ode 6, the Chan tradition criticizes Subhūti's usually valued experience, which is rewarded by the gods with a shower of blossoms, because it symbolizes lapsing into a false contemplative standpoint that must be overcome.

The enigmatic third line evokes the incongruity of an oyster absorbing an unseen hare. Tenkei maintains that the "mysterious rabbit" (玄兔) mentioned here refers to the image of the moon. Xuedou thus links the first and second responses offered by Zhimen as if they are interchangeable in that essence and function are mere labels for a unified vision of existence that consists of ongoingly interactive dynamic activities. Tenkei also cautions in reference to the final line that the proliferation of schools, factions, branches, and streams of Chan that came about even before, especially during, and long after the Song dynasty often ends in hopeless disputation that misses the essential point underlying this and, indeed, all cases.

Ode 94

The *Heroic March Sūtra*'s "Not Seeing" 楞嚴經不見

Case: In the first instance since case 66 to follow the same sequence of cases as in the *Blue Cliff Record*, Yuanwu's introduction recalls number 93 (90) but has a different ending that reads, ". . . a white ox stands in an uncluttered field" (聲前一句. 千聖不傳. 面前一絲. 長時無間. 淨裸裸赤灑灑. 露地白牛), an image referring to unobstructed concentration.

Citing the second chapter of the *Heroic March Sūtra*, Xuedou refers to a lengthy discussion with the then-deluded Ānanda when the Buddha paradoxically says of human perception, "If you say you see my seeing when we both look at the same thing [this clause is not cited by Xuedou], when I'm not seeing, why don't you see my not-seeing? If you see my not-seeing, it's clearly not seeing the form I'm not seeing. If you don't see my not-seeing, it's clearly not seeing a thing, so how can you be sure it's not you [who's seeing]?" (吾不見時. 何不見吾不見之處. 若見不見. 自然非彼不見之相. 若不見吾不見之地. 自然非物. 云何非汝).

Yuanwu writes of the opening passage, "That's good news! What's the use of seeing? Even old Śākyamuni had deficiencies" (好箇消息. 用見作什麼. 釋迦老子漏逗不少), and of the final query, "Talking of you or me misses the point. I'll strike saying, 'Do you see old Śākyamuni?' Why did the ancients not accept this? I'll strike saying, 'He's right under your feet, do you understand?'" (說爾說我總沒交涉. 打云. 還見釋迦老子麼. 爭奈古人不肯承當. 打云. 脚跟下自家看取. 還會麼).

Tianqi says of the opening, "I don't see, but why don't you see my not seeing something somewhere?" (我不見物. 何不見我不見物處), and of the next passage, "Seeing me is not seeing things; seeing no things is seeing nothing, as there's not something there to be seen" (見我不見物處. 此見非對物有. 見非物有. 離物存見). Of the finale he writes, "Seeing me not seeing anything is intrinsically non-seeing. Seeing that suggests tracelessness isn't you, then who? (見我不見之地. 自然無見. 見間無跡. 不汝而誰).

Tianqi's concluding note reads, "Directly seeing the transcendent light separates you from viewing things" (直明向上. 旨明雙離物見); and his wrapping phrase says, "Humans and the environment plunder one another" (人境俱奪).

Verse: A whole elephant and a whole ox are no different,

(Y: You're a half-blind man with half-open and half-shut eyes; why cling to fences and grope walls? One cut creates two parts, 半邊瞎漢. 半開半合. 扶籬摸壁作什麼. 一刀兩段)

(T: "Whole elephant" means wholly seeing an elephant; "whole ox" means wholly seeing no ox. Whether existent or not, these sights

(T: ... appear dim to our eyes, 全象全見象有. 全牛全見牛無. 有無之見皆是眼中之翳)

Adepts have long been trying to name and adhere to this.

(T: From past to present, people can't escape the duality of existence and nonexistence, 古今之人未出有無)

If you want to see the ancient gold-headed Buddha,

(Y: Nah! That old barbarian, you blind fellow, is right at your feet, 咄. 這老胡. 瞎漢. 在爾脚跟下)

Every speck of dust [or sensation] each moment is halfway there!

(Y: Standing there you've missed him, what more can I say? How long will it take you to see him in your dreams? 脚跟下蹉過了也. 更教山僧説什麼. 驢年還曾夢見麼)

(T: Not abiding in existence or nonexistence means seeing Buddha in every speck each moment right now; that's why it's said to be halfway there, 不住有無. 刹塵見佛亦是今時. 故曰半途)

全象全牛翳不殊 / 從來作者共名摸 / 如今要見黃頭老 / 刹刹塵塵在半途.

Comments: The first line draws on two traditional parables, with nearly opposite yet complementary implications that are evoked in Buddhism and other traditions: in one, several blind men try to perceive an elephant but think there are only trees (legs), a rope (tail), or two fans (ears), and so on, without being able to take in the entire being; and in the other analogy, first mentioned by Zhuangzi, a butcher with powerful intuition claims to carve an ox without looking.

The second couplet highlights the notion that the Buddha is ever-present in all aspects of ephemeral existence. Xuedou also cautions, with the final phrase as reinforced by the capping comments, that realizing this so-called truth is but one more conceptual fabrication needing to be revoked and reversed as an expedient teaching device.

Ode 95

Changqing's "Two Kinds of Speech" 長慶二種語

Case: According to Yuanwu's introduction, "Where there's buddha, don't linger; if you do, your head'll sprout horns. Where there's no buddha, quickly run past; if not, weeds'll grow high" (有佛處不得住. 住著頭角生. 無佛處急走過. 不走過. 草深一丈). Moreover, "Even if you're pure and open, free and unbound, without dynamic activities aside from things and without things aside from dynamic activities, you won't avoid standing by a stump waiting for a rabbit" (直饒淨裸裸赤灑灑. 事外無機機外無事. 未免守株待兔).

In the dialogue Changqing says, "Even if it's said that arhats have three poisons, you shouldn't maintain that the Tathāgata has two kinds of speech. The Tathāgata isn't speechless; it's just that he doesn't have two kinds of speech" (寧說阿羅漢有三毒. 不說如來有二種語. 不道如來無語. 只是如來無二種語). Baofu, Changqing's dharma brother, asks, "What's Tathāgata's speech? (作麼生是如來語), and Changqing replies, "How could a deaf man hear it?" (聾人爭得聞). Baofu then says, "I knew you were talking on the secondary level" (情知你向第二門頭道), and Changqing asks him, "What's Tathāgata's speech?" (作麼生是如來語). Baofu responds, "Go have tea" (喫茶去).

Yuanwu writes of Changqing's opening remarks, "He's all over the place, but what kind of third or fourth level is he talking about?" (周由者也. 說什麼第三第四種), of his last question, "It's a mistake, but he shows a bit of progress" (錯. 却較些子), and of Baofu's reply, "Good point but let me ask, does he really understand or is he stumbling around?" (領. 復云. 還會麼. 蹉過了也).

Tianqi writes of three poisons, "In the triple world, where life and death prevail, these refer to greed, anger, and folly" (出三界. 了分段之生死. 貪真嗔妄. 貪嗔不了曰痴), and of the lack of two kinds of speech, "Not speaking of nothing or something is direct pointing, and there're no distinctions involved in direct pointing" (不道無有指示. 只是無別指示). Of Baofu's tea remark he says, "He hits the mark by showing there are claws and fangs in his dharma nest" (當央一截. 法窟爪牙).

Tianqi's final note reads, "Fishing in deep waters with a pole in his hands points clearly to 'one gain, one loss'" (深竿在手. 旨明一遞一刮); and his wrapping phrase says, "Adepts recognizing one another" (作家相見).

Verse: Whether on the primary or secondary level,
(Y: In my royal storehouse, there's no such thing, 我王庫中無如是事)
A reclining dragon doesn't stay in still waters.
(Y: Only someone who travels the same path knows this, 同道方知)

(T: Primary and secondary levels are both stagnant water, 第一第二皆是死水)

When a place is covered by moonlight, the dragon settles the waves,

(T: Moonlight without a dragon is called stagnant water, 有月無龍名之死水)

When a place is without any breeze, it stirs the waters.

(T: If there's a dragon but no moonlight, this is called living water; if you want to bring someone to life, don't use dead words, 有龍無月名之活水. 若是活人不逐死句)

O Chan man Leng (Changqing)!

(Y: He allows a thief to ransack his house, so he can't go to the marketplace since he's lost all his money as punishment for his error, 勾賊破家. 閙市裏莫出頭. 失錢遭罪)

You've failed to pass through the Dragon Gate in the third month.

(Y: Not one in ten thousand is able to step back and respect others; he only holds his breath and withdraws his voice, 退己讓人. 萬中無一. 只得飲氣吞聲)

(T: Changqing takes seriously his responsibility as an adept, but Baofu's the one who's made the point, 長慶任是作家. 也遭保福一點)

頭兮第一第二 / 臥龍不鑑止水 / 無處有月波澄 / 有處無風浪起 / 稜禪客. 稜禪客 / 三月禹門遭點額.

Comments: The first four lines highlight the ways Changqing and, to a lesser extent, Baofu have missed the message during their dharma battle based on the former's explanation of the notion that, contrary to convention, the Buddha used two kinds of speech, whether primary or secondary, effusive or reticent, absolute or relative. A true adept, symbolized by the dragon that prefers a turbulent sea to motionless waters as a venue to flex its prowess, knows when to quiet its movement and the time for activity appropriate to current conditions.

In the final couplet Xuedou criticizes Changqing, who he refers to by a nickname for an itinerant practitioner, because he loses to Baofu, who is also deficient. As Tenkei explains, although Changqing was at times an active dragon, when it comes to this exchange, he falls short. Hakuin emphasizes that the teacher could not soar beyond the distinction of first and second levels of discourse. These lines also caution followers of Xuedou to avoid a similar sense of disillusionment.

Ode 96 A, B, and C

Zhaozhou's "Three Turning Words" 趙州三轉語

Case: This anomalous gong'an simply indicates, "Zhaozhou instructs his assembly about three turning words" (趙州示眾三轉語), which refers to how images of buddha are all destructible yet teach a timeless spiritual message. Yuanwu's lone capping phrase says, "What's he talking about? These three aren't the same" (道什麼. 三段不同).

In prose commentary Yuanwu explains that Zhaozhou remarks, "The real buddha exists within" (真佛屋裏坐), but Xuedou believed that citing this was overly generous and therefore deficient. To help others escape from their ignorance, he composed a verse for each of the sayings: "If a clay buddha passes through water, it dissolves" (泥佛若渡水. 則爛却了也); "If a gold buddha passes through a furnace, it melts" (金佛若渡鑪中. 則鎔却了也); and "If a wooden buddha passes through fire, it's burned" (木佛若渡火. 便燒却了也).

According to Yuanwu's evaluation, "Xuedou's one hundred odes are complicated with judgments and comparisons, but only the three verses cited here directly contain the vitality of a patch-robed monk, yet they're invariably difficult to understand. If you can penetrate the meaning of the three verses, I'd say you've completed your Chan studies" (雪竇一百則頌古. 計較葛藤. 唯此三頌直下有衲僧氣息. 只是這頌也不妨難會. 爾若透得此三頌. 便許爾罷參). Furthermore, Yuanwu mentions that his teacher Wuzu "always used to teach his followers to examine these three odes" (尋常教人看此三頌).

Tianqi's concluding note reads, "Clarifying reality by exposing delusions points clearly to one's true nature" (舉妄明真. 旨明了性非要); and his wrapping phrase says, "Not falling into the secondary" (不落二邊).

Ode A: "A clay buddha can't pass through water."
(Y: It's been soaked until the nose falls apart, yet it raises waves when there's no breeze, 浸爛鼻孔. 無風起浪)
Shenguang [literally, "Divine Light," or Huike] illumines heaven and earth,
(T: The highest post and the lowest pillar, 上標下柱)
Standing in the snow without taking a rest.
(Y: When one person utters a falsehood, ten thousand people transmit it as if it were true, adding errors upon errors, 一人傳虛萬人傳實. 將錯就錯)

Who wouldn't want to carve this image?

(T: Light doesn't shine on ancestors in vain; it shines on the enlightened mind that's ungraspable, 光未見祖妄生穿鑿. 見祖方悟心非外得)

泥經不度水 / 神光照天地 / 立雪如未休 / 何人不雕僞.

Ode B: "A gold buddha can't pass through a furnace."

Those coming to meet Zifu,

(Y: Xuedou, too, goes there, but I fear he'll lose his life, 又恁麼去也. 只恐喪身失命)

Find words of warning on his front door.

(Y: An illiterate would have no way of understanding this, even if it were about a cat, 不識字底猫兒也無話會處)

Is there any place without a pure breeze?

(T: The previous ode shows essence, and this one reveals function. To understand, practice anywhere, everywhere, 前示其體. 今示其用. 若然會得. 天下橫行)

金佛不度爐 / 人來訪紫胡 / 牌中數箇字 / 清風何處無.

Ode C: "A wooden buddha can't pass through fire,"

This makes me think of an oven,

Suddenly smashed apart by a monk's staff.

(Y: He holds the staff in his hands but can't use it to help people. Who doesn't hold it in their hands? 在山僧手裏. 山僧不用人. 阿誰手裏無)

[The deity dwelling there] realizes he'd betrayed his true self.

(Y: Alas! It takes thirty years to attain, but it's better to be lost forever than to depend on the interpretations of sages, 蒼天蒼天. 三十年後始得. 寧可永劫沈淪. 不求諸聖解脫)

(T: Essence and function occur right at this moment, spontaneously casting aside pretensions of nobility, 一體一用皆是今時. 忽然脫落本來尊貴)

木佛不度火 / 常思破竈墮 / 杖子忽擊著 / 方知辜負我.

Comments: Each poem revolves around a Chan legend featured in the last three lines. Ode A evokes the story of second patriarch Huike who waited in the deep snow for a chance to meet Bodhidharma sitting in his cave before cutting his arm. The second ode refers to a legend, also mentioned in Yuanwu's prose comments on case 22, in which master Zifu's sign says,

"Watch out for the dog!" (紫胡有一狗), to scare away inferior seekers. Ode C cites the legend of a sage who, when asked to prevent an oven from causing disasters, "hits the stove three times, so that it topples over and collapses of itself. Suddenly a man appears wearing a blue robe and high hat standing reverentially in front of the master" (擊三下. 竈乃自傾破墮落. 須臾有一人. 青衣峨冠忽然立師前設拜曰). The stove god then confesses his transgressions before attaining realization. A brief moral lesson at the end of each verse urges followers toward correct practice.

Ode 97

The *Diamond Sūtra*'s "Transgressions Are Extinguished" 金剛經罪業則為消滅

Case: Like case 94, this gong'an is entirely a citation from section 16 of the *Diamond Sūtra*, a scripture prized by the Chan tradition. In the introduction Yuanwu maintains, "If you take up one and let go another, you're not yet a true adept; and if you understand three corners when just one is shown, this still may be at odds with essential teaching. Even if you move heaven and earth or change the four corners, or through recitations make thunder crash or lightning flash, cause clouds to fly or rain to pour, push aside swampland or overturn peaks like emptying a pitcher or a bowl, you're still not even halfway there" (拈一放一. 未是作家. 舉一明三. 猶乖宗旨. 直得天地陡變四方絕唱. 雷奔電馳雲行雨驟. 傾湫倒嶽甕瀉盆傾. 也未提得一半在). Yuanwu concludes, "Is there anyone among you who can rotate the North Star or shift the axis of the earth?" (還有解轉天關能移地軸底麼).

The passage cited by Xuedou says, "If someone's scorned and reviled by others, it's because in previous lives they committed transgressions and now fall into the realm of evil. But, by virtue of undergoing scorn and vilification from others in this life, the transgressions of former lives are extinguished" (若為人輕賤. 是人先世罪業應墮惡道. 以今世人輕賤故. 先世罪業則為消滅).

Yuanwu writes of falling into evil, "Retribution isn't usually received with equanimity" (酬本及末. 只得忍受), and of extinction, "This is adding a layer of frost to snow, or melting ice with boiling water" (雪上加霜又一重. 如湯消氷).

Tianqi says of evil, "The deluded self is caused by all the contempt and revilement" (迷己從緣. 十界皆為輕賤), and of extinction, "Suddenly, when enlightenment's realized, what hasn't vanished?" (忽悟天真. 何事不畢). Tianqi's final note says, "Holding up the radiant truth points clearly to fully overcoming illusions" (舉權明實. 旨明幻盡覺圓); and his wrapping phrase reads, "Directly revealing the radiant source" (直下明宗).

Verse: Holding the bright jewel in one's hand,

(Y: Above, it reaches the sky; below, it penetrates the Yellow Springs of Hades, 上通霄漢. 下徹黃泉)

Whoever has merit is rewarded.

(T: Everyone attains this when, all of a sudden, enlightenment is realized, 人人具有. 忽悟名賞)

When neither foreigner nor native is reflected,

(Y: Inside and outside are absolutely void, but still something's there, 內外絕消息. 猶較些子)

The jewel is completely lacking in capacity.

Since it doesn't reflect anyone at all,

(T: The jewel's attained in itself since, in responding to circumstances, all situations are forgotten such that ordinary people and sages no longer appear, 達性得珠. 對緣應現. 機絕功忘. 凡聖不通)

The Demon King loses his way.

(Y: Non-Buddhists and the king of demons don't see any trace of themselves, 這外道魔王. 尋蹤跡不見)

O Gautama!

Do you recognize me or not?

(T: Don't say that for the demon king buddhas and patriarchs are invisible, 莫道波旬佛祖不見)

明珠在掌 / 有功者賞 / 胡漢不來 / 全無伎倆 / 伎倆既無 / 波旬失途 / 瞿曇瞿曇 / 識我也無.

Follow-up: Xuedou adds, "Thoroughly exposed!" (復云. 勘破了也) (Y: Each blow of my staff leaves its mark; it was already so before he said this, 一棒一條痕, 已在言前) (T: The main point to be valued is that meaning is held in one's own hands, 點執尊貴. 意在垂手)

Comments: The first couplet emphasizes a positive method for interpreting the scriptural passage by evoking the image of a bright jewel reflecting all phenomena as symbolic of the universality of buddha-nature beyond the distinction of good and evil. According to Yuanwu, "the first two lines complete the versification of the case" (此兩句頌公案畢). The next couplet reveals the fundamental role of emptiness underlying the image of illumination, so that the gem is now understood as basically unreflective. Therefore, in couplet three, demons and heretics are unable to find themselves, thus ironically pointing to the overcoming of evil karma.

Xuedou concludes by calling out to Gautama for assistance and release, while implying that even the Buddha could not acknowledge one who casts no reflection. Or perhaps this indicates that the poet himself receives scorn, but his final interjection may suggest that he goes beyond the need for transcendental aid. However, Yuanwu cautions, "Is this Xuedou exposing Gautama, or Gautama exposing Xuedou? Those with the true eye should try to confirm this through careful observation" (是雪竇勘破瞿曇. 瞿曇勘破雪竇. 具眼者試定當看).

Ode 98

Tianping's "Wrong!" 天平錯

Case: Toward the end of the collection—one theory holds that this introduction has been swapped with case 100 because it seems like a coda—Yuanwu comments with disingenuous humility on the limitations of his own interpretations that were first delivered as lectures during the ninety-day intensive summer practice periods held in 1111 and 1112: "All during the retreat, my talks have been creating complications that burdened and exhausted the monks who came here from all over the land. When the Diamond Treasure Sword cuts directly through all deceptions, I start to realize the manifold levels of my ineptitude" (一夏嘮嘮打葛藤. 幾乎絆倒五湖僧. 金剛寶劍當頭截. 始覺從來百不能).

In the two-part dialogue Tianping (n.d.), an heir of Xuefeng's lineage, visits the master Xiyuan (n.d.) from the Linji school and says, "Don't say you understand the buddha dharma, as I can't find anyone able to discuss an appropriate phrase" (莫道會佛法. 覔箇舉話頭人也無). One day Xiyuan calls the guest by his personal name and, as Tianping raises his head, the teacher says "Wrong!" (錯). When Tianping takes a couple of steps, Xiyuan says the same and then asks, "I just said 'wrong' twice. Am I wrong, or are you wrong?" (適來這兩錯. 是西院錯. 是上座錯). Tianping admits, "I'm wrong" (從漪錯) and Xiyuan replies, "Wrong!" Xiyuan then invites Tianping to stay for the summer retreat, but he departs. Some years later, when he has his own assembly after long periods of itinerancy, Tianping says, "At the time I didn't say I was wrong, but as soon as I started traveling south I knew I was wrong" (我不道恁麼時錯. 發足南方去時. 早錯了也).

Yuanwu writes of Xiyuan's second "wrong," "It splits Tianping's guts and wounds his heart. Everyone refers to this as a double case, but they don't know it's like pouring water into water, or trading gold for gold" (劈腹剜心. 人皆喚作兩重公案. 殊不知似水入水. 如金博金), and of the conclusion, "What can he do about the two 'wrongs'? It's a thousand or ten thousand wrongs, but it doesn't lead anywhere other than causing people much distress" (爭奈這兩錯何. 千錯萬錯. 爭奈沒交涉. 轉見郎當愁殺人).

Tianqi says of Tianping's initial remark, "Boasting to others of having Chan insight is like a horse galloping off" (誇他有禪. 所以馳騁), and of his final comment, "He gives short shrift to prior concerns but talks at length about his present prowess" (訴前之短. 呈今之長). Tianqi's final note reads, "Towing him by the nostrils points clearly to revealing directly the radiant source" (拽回鼻孔. 旨明直下明宗); and his wrapping phrase says, "Grandmotherly kindness!" (老婆心切).

Verse: Followers of the Chan school trying to act so carefree,
(T: Beating the grass to scare the snakes, 打草驚蛇)
Fill their bellies with learning, but what's the use?
Old Tianping is sad and pitiable,
For saying he regretted his itinerancy.
(Y: He was already wrong before he started traveling, so what was the purpose in wearing out his sandals? Then he tried to erase this with a simple brushstroke, 未行脚已前錯了也. 踏破草鞋堪作何用. 一筆句下)
(T: It's sad that he can't explain himself, and pitiable that his understanding's in vain, 悲他無言. 笑他空會)
So wrong!
Xiyuan's pure Chan teaching quickly disposes of him.
(Y: Don't speak only of Xiyuan; even buddhas of past, present, and future and old masters throughout the world end up falling back three thousand paces, 莫道西院. 三世諸佛天下老和尚. 亦須倒退三千始得)
(T: Do you understand these two wrongs? The old teacher's style blows away Tianping's delusions, 會得這兩錯. 二老家風一時氷消瓦解)

禪家流. 愛輕薄 / 滿肚参來用不著 / 堪悲堪笑天平老/ 却謂當初悔行脚 / 錯錯 / 西院清風頓銷鑠.

Follow-up: Xuedou adds, "Suppose a monk approaches and says, 'Wrong! How does my (Xuedou's) 'Wrong' compare with Tianping's 'Wrong'?" (復云. 忽有箇衲僧出云. 錯. 雪竇錯何似天平錯). (Y: Xiyuan appeared in this world to settle the matter, but I'll strike saying, "Wrong!" (西院又出世. 據欵結案. 打云. 錯) (T: He's fishing in the four seas, 鈎垂四海).

Comments: All three commentators here agree that Tianping seems hopeless from the outset because he misunderstands the meaning of the one-word barrier "Wrong," and in the aftermath of the main narrative admits to a deeper level of deficiency. Some interpreters explain this by distinguishing between the drawbacks of "crystal-bowl (or supposedly pure) Chan" and the merit of "leather-bag (or pragmatic) Chan."

In that vein Yuanwu notes that his teacher Wuzu once said, "There's a kind of person who practices meditation like a crystal pitcher filled with pastry: it can't be turned over or cleaned out, and if you bump it the bowl immediately breaks" (有一般人參禪. 如琉璃瓶裏搗糍糕相似更動轉不得. 抖擻不出. 觸著便破). In contrast, in carrying a leather bag, "even if it's thrown down from the highest mountain the carrier won't tear apart" (若要活潑潑地. 但参皮殼漏子禪. 直向高山上. 撲將下來. 亦不破亦不壞). Moreover, Tenkei suggests that Xuedou's final remarks about the meanings of mistakenness function as a wedge to remove a wedge, a rarely implemented but highly effective teaching device.

Ode 99

National Teacher Huizhong's "Crown of Vairocana" 慧忠國師毗盧頂

Case: Yuanwu says of National Teacher Huizhong, "When a dragon intones, mists appear, and when a tiger roars, winds blow" (龍吟霧起虎嘯風生. 出世宗猷金玉相振). Furthermore, "Going beyond worldly appearance to where gold and jade are mixed, and to intensive activity when arrowpoints meet in midair, nothing's concealed in the whole universe as far and near are proportionally displayed and past and present are clearly discerned" (通方作略箭鋒相拄. 遍界不藏遠近齊彰. 古今明辨).

In the dialogue that refers to interlocutors also included in case 18, Emperor Suzong asks Huizhong, "What's the Ten-Body Trainer?" (如何是十身調御), which refers to how the Buddha tames and brings under control many different levels of his being. The National Teacher replies, "O patron, walk all over the head of Vairocana" (檀越踏毘盧頂上行). When the emperor says, "I'm afraid I don't understand" (寡人不會), Huizhong responds, "Do not consider your own self the pure *dharmakāya*" (莫認自己清淨法身).

Yuanwu writes of the initial question, "The emperor of Tang China is a skilled ruler, who carries a crown on his head while wearing carefree shoes" (作家君王. 大唐天子. 也合知恁麼. 頭上捲輪冠脚下無憂履), and of Huizhong's reply, "He takes Suzong by the hand as they walk together on the slopes of Mount Sumeru. There they go!" (須彌那畔把手共行. 猶有這箇在). Of the final response Yuanwu says, "Although Huizhong creates complications he still finds a way to extricate himself, but when intoxicated he troubles others to death" (雖然葛藤. 却有出身處. 醉後郎當愁殺人).

Tianqi says of the first answer, "Vairocana itself is the *dharmakāya*" (梵語毗盧. 此云法身), and of the second response, "One point's raised, two notes are made" (一拈二註). Tianqi's concluding note reads, "Holding up emotion points clearly to transcendence" (拈情. 旨明向上); and his wrapping phrase says, "Grandmotherly kindness!" (老婆心切).

Verse: "Teacher of the Nation" is a powerful name,

> (Y: What's the need for a flower in the sky, or moon reflected in water? When the wind passes through, the treetops sway, 何必空花水月. 風過樹頭搖)
>
> (T: If the *dharmakāya*'s not recognized, why care about the National Teacher? 法身不認. 何存國師)

Only Nanyang (Huizhong) could make the most of this role.
Instructing the emperor of China,

> (Y: Such a pity! What's the use of teaching him? What can be accomplished with guidance given by a blind patch-robed monk? 可憐生. 接得堪作何用. 接得瞎衲僧濟什麼事)

To trample the head of Vairocana.

> (T: A sage helping his lord doesn't mean that Suzong grasps the *dharmakāya*, 扶持聖主. 不執法身)

With an iron hammer he smashes Buddha's golden bones,
Between heaven and earth, does anything still exist?

(T: The *dharmakāya*'s absolute, so what else would there be? 法身一絕. 更有什麼)

In three thousand realms, the seas are still and silent all night,
I don't know who'll be able to enter the blue dragon's cave.

(Y: Thirty blows of the staff with nobody left out! He's already brought it up, but do you understand? Nah! Everyone's got their nostrils pierced by Xuedou. Don't mistakenly consider yourself the pure *dharmakāya*, 三十棒. 一棒也少不得. 拈了也. 還會麼咄. 諸人鼻孔被雪竇穿了也. 莫錯認自己清淨法身)

(T: There's clearly an absolute purity, but it's not clear if anyone realizes it, 須然絕點純清. 不知誰能到此)

一國之師亦強名 / 南陽獨許振佳聲 / 大唐扶得真天子 / 曾踏毗盧頂上行 / 鐵鎚擊碎黃金骨 / 天地之間更何物 / 三千剎海夜澄澄 / 不知誰入蒼龍窟.

Comments: The first four lines celebrate Huizhong's reply to the sovereign's query about the Buddha. Xuedou's praise for the National Teacher's prowess seems straightforward but may be subtly yet intentionally undermined, as Hakuin's commentary points out, by the implicit ideal that a Chan adept should remain nameless, without seeking fame or fortune.

Xuedou's ode also relates Huizhong's admirable qualities to his own current teaching situation. The third couplet demystifies and deconstructs the image of the Buddha untainted and removed from the world of everyday concerns. Then, the final lines caution that a true teacher should be able to match a dragon's involvement in turbulent, rather than deceptively calm, waters, but Xuedou seems to remain uncertain whether he himself is capable of such a mission.

Ode 100

Baling's "Each Branch of Coral" 巴陵珊瑚枝枝

Case: In tune with the introduction to case 98, Yuanwu comments here on the pros and cons of his teaching approach, "We sow the causes and reap the effects that are complete from beginning to end. In our meetings, although I haven't kept my views private, I also haven't explained anything. If suddenly someone comes forth and says, 'All summer we've been asking for deeper instruction, why haven't you explained anything,' I'll reply, 'Let's wait until you're awakened, then we'll talk about it' " (收因結果. 盡始盡終. 對面無私. 元不曾說. 忽有箇出來道一夏請益為什麼不曾說. 待爾悟來向爾道).

In the dialogue Baling, also featured in case 13, is asked by a monk, "What's the sword that cuts through a blown hair?" (如何是吹毛劍), which refers to a legendary swordsman whose delicate yet eminently effective martial skills symbolize a Chan adept's ability to help others surpass ignorance but without overwhelming them. Baling replies, "Each branch of coral's sustained by the moon" (珊瑚枝枝撐著月); this could also be rendered, ". . . sustains the moon." As a way of understanding this paradox, modern science has shown that coral reefs, said in Ode 72 to be illumined by the sun, spawn new growths by mysteriously detecting the brightness of the full moon.

Yuanwu writes of the monk's question, "Watch out for the danger!" (嶄嶮), and of Baling's response, "Light swallows myriad forms throughout the land and seas" (光吞萬象. 四海九州). In prose comments Yuanwu says that Baling borrows the saying from Tang poet Chanyue, also cited in remarks on cases 3 and 67 (83), and he included this as a tribute for a departed friend.

Tianqi writes of the query, "He borrows a hidden blade" (借事藏鋒), and of the reply, "He hits the mark" (當央直指). His concluding note says, "Holding and turning a keyword points clearly to directly cutting off all speech and thought" (拈轉話頭. 旨明直截言思); and his wrapping phrase reads, "Twirling it on his fingertips" (信手拈來).

Verse: When trying to bring calm to any disturbance, even a talented teacher may feel unprepared.

(T: The sword must be held with both hands, which is quite a burden. Like trying to play the zither while deaf, isn't this self-defeating? 須是兩手分付. 幾箇全身擔荷. 撫琴與聾. 豈不成拙)

Whether held on fingertips or in the palm, the blade glistens in the sky like freshly fallen snow.

(Y: Stop! If you stare at it, you'll go blind, 斬. 覷着則瞎)

(T: To get the point, respond to circumstances and realize the true self without needing a sharp blade, 若然會得. 隨緣泛應. 得大自在. 無不鋒利)

The most skilled swordsmith can't finish polishing it,
Even a remarkable craftsman won't stop honing it.

(Y: No one could. Even if the famous smith Ganjiang appeared, he, too, would fall back three thousand paces, 人莫能行. 直饒干將出來也倒退三千)

Such an extraordinary saying, "Each branch of coral's sustained by the moon."

(Y: In the third watch of the night the moon descends, its light shining on the cold pond, 三更月落影照寒潭)

(T: Just spit this out; don't try to discuss it, 盡情吐露. 切忌商量)

要平不平. 大巧若拙 / 或指或掌. 倚天照雪 / 大冶兮磨礱不下 / 良工兮拂拭未歇 / 別別. 珊瑚枝枝撐著月.

Comments: Many traditional interpretations generally argue that Baling's saying is deliberately indecipherable and absurd so that, like the weapon, it terminates all delusions. However, Xuedou's verse emphasizes that the hair-cutting sword, emblematic of universal buddha-nature, represents a natural capacity cultivated by human activity that responds to diverse situations when wielded appropriately by an authentic teacher.

By quoting in line four the keyword of the case, Xuedou views the phrase that was initially used by Chanyue as an eloquent expression of the subtleties and profundities of the interconnectedness of all beings. An entity that may appear impervious to moonlight is responsive in a fundamentally vital way, and thereby all that seems darkened or obscure is fully integrated with the brightened and apparent, which also has murky qualities.

As a fitting conclusion to the collection, Yuanwu caps his own comments on the final verse in Xuedou's 100 Odes to Chan cases by offering a disingenuously self-deprecating lyrical remark about the deliberately puzzling interpretations he had been expounding:

A boat filled with ten thousand bushels effortlessly pulls away,
A pot holding a grain of rice entraps a snake.
In bringing up one hundred esteemed gong'an cases,
How much sand have I tossed in everyone's eyes!
萬斛盈舟信手拏 / 却因一粒甕吞蛇 / 拈提百轉舊公案 / 撒却時人幾眼沙.

Notes

Chapter 1

1. Xuedou's text is variously dated 1028 or earlier (1024), but that seems unlikely since it reflects activities during the 1030s.
2. See *Mingjue chanshi yulu* (明覺禪師語錄, T.47.1996, which includes the *Puquan ji* (瀑泉集) and additional works.
3. The text is also known as the *Xuedou Xian heshang Mingjue dashi songgu ji* (雪竇顯和尚明覺大師頌古集); Mingjue, or "Chan Teacher of Clear Enlightenment" (Mingjue Chanshi, 明覺禪師) is Xuedou's title bestowed by the palace along with a purple robe. In letters, Xuedou, named eponymously for his temple location beginning in 1021 on a peak in northeastern Zhejiang province, usually refers to himself as Chongxian (重顯) or Yinzhi (隱之). For a Gozan-ban printing (thirteenth century) of the Song-dynasty edition, plus the collection of prose comments (拈古 *niangu*), the *Puquan ji*, and the *Zuying ji* 祖英集, see Yanagida Seizan and Shiina Koyū, eds., *Zengaku tenseki sōkan*, vol. 2 (Kyoto: Rinsen shoten, 1999). By the way, there are many more German translations of the *Blue Cliff Record* than those in English. Also, I use the term "odes" to distinguish the form of praise or eulogy, which is invariably tinged with a crucial element of irony and skepticism reflecting Xuedou's standpoint emphasizing self-reliance, from other kinds of poetry routinely written by Song-dynasty Chan teachers. This rendering of the key term helps showcase the *Odes* as an independent or stand-alone text presented as such here for the first time in Western scholarship.
4. See *Fenyang Wude chanshi yulu* 汾陽無德禪師語錄, T.47.1992, vol. 2 of 3.
5. See Zhou Yukai 周裕鍇, "Explaining Chan through a Roundabout Path: From Analyzing Chan to Using Poetic Expressions" (繞路說禪:從禪的詮釋到詩的表達), *Wenyì yanjiu* 2 (2000): 50–55. Zhou seems to have based his notion of roundabout on a passage from the *Blue Cliff Record*, T.48.2003.141a; see also Zhou Yukai, *Expressiveness of the Chan School* (禪宗語言, *Chanzong yuyan*) (Taipei: Zongbo chubanshe, rpt. 2002).
6. The medieval Japanese Zen thinker Tetsurō Yoshitoru (徹翁義亨稱, 1295–1369) wrote this tribute after Xuedou's text was transported to Japan. On this and related topics, see "Sichuan and Japan (part 9): "The Premier Chan Text, the *Blue Cliff Record*, in Japan" (四川与日本（九）—禅门第一书《碧岩录》与日本), https://www.163.com/dy/article/F8421A0B05129RFH.html (from March 19, 2020; accessed October 21, 2021).
7. This citation is based on a recent Chinese summary of the passage; for the original see Nukariya Kaiten, *History of the Chinese Zen School* (中國禪宗史, *Chūgoku zenshūshi*) (Tokyo: Genkōsha, 1925).

8. Tianqi also commented on the prominent *songgu* collection by Caodong school master Hongzhi in the *Qiongjue laoren Tianqi zhizhu Tiantong Jue heshang songgu* (煢絕老人天奇直註天童覺和尚頌古, X.67.1306). Moreover, in the early twelfth century, Xuedou's lexicon was examined by Muan Shanqing (睦庵善卿, fl. 1088–1108) in an impactful reference work printed in 1108, *Matters from the Patriarchs' Garden* (祖庭事苑, *Zuting shiyuan*, X.64.1261). This was an important source of information and interpretations consulted by countless commentators during the Song and later periods. Xuedou's works comprise about a third of the twenty-six major topics treated in eight volumes by Muan, with three sections on Yunmen's record and nine on Xuedou. Those include one part on the *Xuedou songgu* in volume 2.3 and the rest on his six other major texts (one of these is divided into two parts, plus there is a section of miscellanea).
9. The *Odes* was occasionally treated as an independent work, such as in *An Appreciation of Master Xuedou's Odes* (雪竇顕禅師頌古称提, *Setchō Ken Zenji juko shōdai*) by one of the leading Sōtō scholastics of the Edo period, Menzan Zuihō (面山瑞方, 1683–1769). Additionally, I refer throughout this book to a critical Japanese edition in *Setchō juko* (雪竇頌古), *Zen no goroku* 15, ed. Iriya Yoshitaka 入矢義高, Kajitani Sōnin 梶谷宗忍, and Yanagida Seizan 柳田聖山 (Tokyo: Chikuma shobō, 1981, rpt. 2018), plus various other modern Japanese commentaries on the *Blue Cliff Record*. See also the independent edition in D.49.8942.2.
10. See *Yuanwu foguo chanshi yulu* (圓悟佛果禪師語錄), T.47.1997, vols. 18 and 19 (of 20). Yuanwu indicates that while he agrees that words are helpful in teaching, he prefers to use a more direct, prose-based approach to language. That technique, referred to as "evaluative examinations" (評唱, *pingchang*), calls into question the standpoints of all parties, including the dialogue partners and also the verse remarks proffered by Xuedou and other interpreters.
11. There are minor but important discrepancies involving the wording and numbering of verses in the stand-alone edition of the *Odes* when compared to the *Blue Cliff Record*'s versions (see Chapter 3). While consulting various traditional and modern versions and annotations of the *Blue Cliff Record* containing Xuedou's *songgu* as the core unit, I mainly cite here the independent version by Tianqi Benrui. In addition, I rely on a crucial modern Japanese edition in the volume, *Setchō juko* (雪竇頌古), Zen no goroku 15, ed. Iriya Yoshitaka (入矢義高), Kajitani Sōnin (梶谷宗忍), and Yanagida Seizan (柳田聖山) (Tokyo: Chikuma shobō, 1981, rpt. 2018), plus various other recent Japanese commentaries. I have also consulted Thomas Cleary and J. C. Cleary, trans., *The Blue Cliff Record*, 3 vols. (Boston: Shambhala, 1977); and Thomas Cleary, trans., *Secrets of the Blue Cliff Record: Zen Comments by Hakuin and Tenkei* (Boston: Shambhala, 2000).
12. The seven parts cover (1) introduction (for seventy-nine cases), (2) case with (3) capping phrases and (4) prose comments, and (5) verse with (6) capping phrases and (7) prose comments; parts 1, 3, 4, 6, and 7 are by Yuanwu.
13. See Ha Jin, *The Banished Immortal: A Life of Li Bai* (New York: Vintage, 2019), 165–166, on the strengths and weakness of the academy in the Tang dynasty according to the views of an eccentric yet greatly admired poet.

14. Xuedou uses the word "gong'an" only one time, in the verse for case 64; this term was borrowed from the legal tradition indicating public (公, *gong*) records (案, *an*). In Xudeou's time the typical designation for a dialogue was simply an "example" or "instance" (則, C. *ze*, J. *soku*).
15. In Ding-hwa Hsieh, "Poetry and Chan 'Gongan': From Xuedou Chongxian (980–1052) to Wumen Huikai (1183–1260)," *Journal of Song-Yuan Studies* 10 (2010): 39–70 (50–51, modified); see also *Sijialu* (四家錄), vol. 2 in D.49.8942.2.77a–80a.
16. T.48.2003.175c.
17. This is a concise summary of numerous categories in Zhou's analysis that also applies to other Northern Song poets, both monks and nonclerical authors deeply influenced by Chan.
18. In the *Canglang shihua* (滄浪詩話), Yan Yu maintains the unity of poetry and Chan based on a novel theoretical framework.
19. Since Chan Buddhism proposes to seek enlightenment in the common and the quotidian, including in trivial objects and physical labor, calligraphy and painting could also be part of Chan practice insofar as they help cultivate concentrated meditativeness, but their materiality is considered more susceptible to forming emotional attachments.
20. T.1996.47.688a.
21. Cited in Juhn Ahn, trans., *Gongan Collection I*, in *Collected Works of Korean Buddhism*, Vol. 7-1 (Seoul: Compilation Committee of Korean Buddhist Thought, 2012), 96–97. Also Xinwen Tanben (心聞曇賁, fl. eleventh–twelfth century) writes critically, "During the reign of Tianxi (1017–1021), Xuedou employed his eloquence and erudition; with good intentions, he changed and manipulated [the Chan tradition] to pursue something new and engage in refinement. He followed Fenyang in writing commentarial verses. He flattered and engaged with contemporary literati. Due to [Xuedou], the style of Chan changed."
22. For an analysis of the connections between Chan and poetry beginning in the Tang dynasty, see Thomas Mazanec, "How Poetry Became Meditation in Late-Ninth-Century China," *Asia Major* 3d ser. 32, no. 2 (2019): 113–151; especially emphasized is the function of *kuyin* (苦吟) or a devotion to composing poetry and reflectively reciting it, often to oneself.
23. According to Zhou Yukai 周裕鍇, the poetry-Chan analogy was used in four ways during the Song: using Chan to classify poetry (以禪品詩); using Chan to produce poetry (以禪擬詩); using Chan to refer to studying poetry (以禪參詩); and using Chan to discourse on poetry (以禪論詩); see Zhou, *The Chinese Chan School and Poetry* (中國禪宗與詩歌, *Zhongguo chanzong yu shige*) (Kaohsiung, Taiwan: Liwen wenhua chubanshe, 1994), 270–296.
24. Joshua Capitanio, "Portrayals of Chan Buddhism in the Literature of Internal Alchemy," *Journal of Chinese Religions* 43, no. 2 (2015): 119–160 (129–131).
25. Note that the title of Fenyang's gong'an collection, 汾陽無德禪師頌古代別卷, includes *songgu* as well as *dai*(*yu*) and *bie*(*yu*).
26. Cited in Jason Protass, *The Poetry Demon: Song-Dynasty Monks on Verse and the Way* (Honolulu: University of Hawaii Press, 2021), 60 (modified); see X.79.1555.622a.

Also, "The gateway of general verse is for teachers past and present to elucidate both inner [Buddhist] and outer [Confucian] learning by composing verses recorded for posterity" (偈頌門. 古今知識, 內外兼明, 唱道篇章, 錄為龜鑒). For Foguo, prose comments on cases function in that, "With great insight they interpret the religious teachings and clarify the awakening of ancestors so that this is accessible for later trainees" (具大知見, 拈提宗教, 抑揚先覺, 開鑿後昆). In addition, Protass's analysis is refreshingly critical of the use of the term "literary Chan" when it is applied too freely or with disregard of appropriate context.

27. Cited in Ronald Egan, "Su Shi's Informal Letters in Literature and Life," in *History of Chinese Letters and Epistolary Culture*, ed. Antje Richter (Leiden: Brill, 2015), 507 (modified).
28. Christopher Byrne, "Poetics of Silence: Hongzhi Zhengjue (1091–1157) and the Practice of Poetry in Song Dynasty Chan *Yulu*," PhD diss., McGill University (2015), 109–120.
29. Byrne, "Poetics of Silence," 111–112.
30. Cited in Yi-hsun Huang, "Chan Master Xuedou and His Remarks on Old Cases in the *Record of Master Xuedou at Dongting*: A Preliminary Study," *Chung-Hwa Buddhist Journal* 22 (2009): 69–95 (90, modified); see *Guzunsu yulu* (古尊宿語錄), X.68.1315.258c–259a.
31. There is no independent version of Xuedou's *Odes* in the *Taishō shinshū daizōkyō* (大正新修大藏經), or in the supplement collection, the *Xuzang jing* (J. *Zoku zōkyō*, 續藏經). However, there are other sources such as the *Sibu Congkan* (四部叢刊) in *Xubian jibu* (續編集部) ser. 2 (Shanghai: Hanfen lou, 1935), v. 370; and the *Setchō Minkaku daishi goroku* (雪竇明覚大師語録) from the Gozan version in *Zengaku tenseki sōkan* (禅学典籍叢刊), ed. Yanagida Seizan (柳田聖 山) and Shiina Kōyū (椎名宏雄) (1999).
32. The nine para-texts indicate that in 1140 Yuanwu's main disciple, Dahui, torched the manuscript because his followers were becoming over-reliant on its verbiage, and it was (partially) reconstructed in the early 1300s; see Steven Heine, *Chan Rhetoric of Uncertainty in the Blue Cliff Record: Sharpening a Sword at the Dragon Gate* (New York: Oxford University Press, 2016).
33. Note that Hongzhi, along with his lineal predecessors, Touzi and Danxia, were from the Caodong school, even though some modern scholarship links the gong'an tradition to the Linji school, which was a distinction valid for later stages of history in China and Japan.

Chapter 2

1. Hsieh, "Poetry and Chan 'Gongan,'" 43.
2. This text, compiled by the monk Daoyuan (道 原, n. d.) in the first decade of the eleventh century, influenced dozens of subsequent representatives of the genre. Yang Yi was appreciative of his own studies with a Chan teacher who helped him resolve underlying uncertainties and doubts; see Albert Welter, "Literati Chan at the Song

Dynasty Court: The Role of Yang Yi in the Creation of Chan Identity," *Journal of Chinese Buddhist Studies* 34 (2021): 91–159 (143). Yang also wrote a preface for the recorded sayings of Fenyang, who was the only still living maser included in the *Jingde Record*.

3. See Peter K. Bol, *"This Culture of Ours": Intellectual Transition in T'ang and Sung China* (Palo Alto, CA: Stanford University Press, 1992), 161–162.
4. See Yu-Chen Tsui, "The Poetic Practices of Hongzhi Zhengjue (1091–1157): Gong'an Commentarial Verses on Old Cases and Verses for Lay Literati," PhD dissertation, University of California at Los Angeles (2018).
5. T.47.1997.613b.
6. T.47.1997.610c.
7. "Characteristics and Forms of Literary Chan: Taking as Examples *Odes to 100 Cases* and the *Blue Cliff Record*" (文字禅的特点与形式: 以《颂古百则》及《碧岩录》为例, *Wenzi Chan de tedian yu xingshi yi: Songgu baize ji Biyanlu weili*), Fenghuang.com Buddhism Compilation (凤凰网佛教综合) (November 2010); accessed February 18, 2023.
8. T.48.2003.175c.
9. T.48.2001.14b.
10. Nagai Masashi 永井政之, "On The Formation of Xuedou's *Songgu*" (雪竇頌古の展開について, *Setchō juko hatten nitsuite*), *Komazawa daigaku Bukkyōgaku kenkyūkai nenpō* 22, no. 1 (1973): 140–141.
11. James J. Y. Liu, *The Art of Chinese Poetry* (Chicago: The University of Chicago Press, 1962), 63–87.
12. Shen Deqian (沈德潛, 1673–1769) formulated a poetic theory by stressing four essential elements: purpose (宗旨), form (體裁), tone (音節), and spiritual resonance (神韻).

Selected Bibliography

Abbreviations

T: *Taishō shinshū daizōkyō* 大正新修大藏經. Edited by Takakusu Junjirō 高楠順次郎 and Watanabe Kaigyoku 渡邊海旭. 85 vols. Tokyo: Taishō issaikyō kankōkai, 1924–1932.
X: *Xuzang jing* (J. *Zoku zōkyō* 續藏經). 150 vols. Taipei: Xinwenfeng chuban gongsi, rpt. 1976.

Main Sources

Biyanlu 碧巖錄. Edited by Huang Xianian 黃夏年and Yang Cengwen 楊曾文. Zhengzhou, China: Zhongzhou guji chubanshe, 2011.
Biyanlu 碧巖錄. T.48.2003.
Foguo Yuanwu Chanshi Biyan lu 佛果圓悟禪師碧巖錄. T.48. 2003.
Hekiganroku 碧巖錄. 3 vols. Edited by Iriya Yoshitaka 入矢義高, Mizoguchi Yūzō 溝口雄三, Sueki Fumihiko 末木文美士, and Itō Fumio 伊藤文生. Tokyo: Iwanami bunko, 1994–1996.
Hekiganroku hisshō 碧巖錄秘抄. By Hakuin Ekaku 白隠慧鶴. Tokyo: Nagata shunyū, 1915.
Hekiganroku kōgi 碧巖錄講義. In *Tenkei Denson Teishō* 天柱傳尊提唱, 10 vols. Tokyo: Kōyūkan, 1903.
Hekiganroku teishō 碧巖錄禅提唱, 10 vols. By Yamada Mumon 山田無文. Kyoto: Zen bunka kenkyūjo, 1985.
Qiongjue laoren Tianqi zhizhu Xuedou Xian heshang songgu 煢絕老人天奇直註雪竇顯和尚頌古, X.67.1302. 2 vols.
Setcho juko 雪竇頌古. Edited by Iriya Yoshitaka 入矢義高, Kajitani Sōnin 梶谷宗忍, and Yanagida Seizan 柳田聖山, *Zen no goroku* 15. Tokyo: Chikuma shobō, 1981, rpt. 2018.
Setchō juko choku 雪竇頌古直註. By Menzan Zuihō 面山瑞方. Tokyo, 1832, rpt. 2021.

Other Primary Sources

Canglang shihua 滄浪詩話. Edited by Guo Shaoyu 郭紹虞. Beijing: Renmin wenxue chubanshe, 1961.
Chanlin sengbao 禪林僧寶. X.78.1560.
Chanyuan qinggui 禪苑清規. X.63.1245.
Chanzong songgu lianzhu ji 禪宗頌古聯珠集. X.65.1295.
Congrong lu 從容録. T.48.2004.
Dafu dingshou lengyan jing 大佛頂首楞嚴經. T.19.945.

Guzunsu yulu 古尊宿語錄. X.68.1315.
Hongzhi chanshi guanglu 宏智禪師廣錄. T.48.2001.
Jiatai pudeng lu 嘉泰普燈錄. X.79.1559.
Jijie lu 擊節錄. X.67.1301.
Jingang bore boluomi jing 金剛般若波羅蜜經. T.8.235.
Jingde chuandeng lu 景德傳燈錄. T.51.2076.
Linjian lu 林間錄. X.87.1624.
Linquan laoren pingchang Danxia Chun chanshi songgu Xutang ji 林泉老人評唱丹霞淳禪師頌古虛堂集. X.67.1304.
Linquan laoren pingchang Touzi Qing heshang songgu Konggu ji. 林泉老人評唱投子青和尚頌古空谷集. X.67.1303.
Mingjue chanshi yulu 明覺禪師語錄. T.47.1996.
Qiongjue laoren Tianqi zhizhu Tiantong Jue heshang songgu 煢絕老人天奇直註天童覺和尚頌古. X.67.1306.
Rentian yanmu 人天眼目. T.48.2006.
Setchō Minkaku daishi goroku 雪竇明覚大師語録. From the Gozan-ban 五山版 version in *Zengaku tenseki sōkan* 禅学典籍叢刊. Vol. 1. Edited by Yanagida Seizan 柳田聖山 and Shiina Kōyū 椎名宏雄. Kyoto: Rinsen shoten, 1999.
Tiansheng guandeng lu 天聖廣燈錄. X.78.1553.
Wansong Xingxiu pingchang Tiantong Jue heshang songgu Congrongan lu 萬 松老人評唱天童覺和尚頌古從容庵錄. T.48.2004.
Weimo jiesuo shuo jing 維摩詰所說經. T.14.475.
Wudeng huiyuan 五燈會元. X.80.1565.
Wumenguan 無門關. T.48.2005.
Xuedou siji 雪竇四集. In *Sibu congkan xubian* 四部叢刊續編. Shanghai: Hanfen lou, 1935.
Xutang Zhiyu chanshi yulu 虛堂智愚禪師語錄. T.47.2000.
Yuanwu Foguo chanshi yulu 圓悟佛果禪師語錄. T.47.1997.
Yunmen Kuangzhen chanshi guanglu 雲門匡真禪師廣錄. T.47.1988.
Zhaozhou lu 趙州錄, in *Guzunsu yulu* 古尊宿語錄. X.68.1315.12–14.
Zutang ji 祖堂集. Taipei: Xinwenfeng chuban gongsi, 1987.
Zutang ji 祖堂集. Edited by Zhang Hua 張華. Zhengzhou: Zhongzhou guji chubanshe, 2001.
Zuting shiyuan 祖庭事苑. X.64.1261.

Secondary Sources

Ahn, Juhn, trans. *Gongan Collection I*. In *Collected Works of Korean Buddhism*, Vol. 7-1. Seoul: Compilation Committee of Korean Buddhist Thought, 2012.
Berling, Judith A. "Bringing the Buddha down to Earth: Notes on the Emergence of 'Yü-lu' as a Buddhist Genre." *History of Religions* 27, no. 1 (1987): 56–88.
Bol, Peter K. *"This Culture of Ours": Intellectual Transition in T'ang and Sung China*. Palo Alto, CA: Stanford University Press, 1992.
Buckelew, Kevin. "Inventing Chinese Buddhas: Identity, Authority, and Liberation in Song-Dynasty Chan Buddhism." PhD dissertation, Columbia University, 2018.
Byrne, Christopher. "Poetics of Silence: Hongzhi Zhengjue (1091–1157) and the Practice of Poetry in Song Dynasty Chan *Yulu*." PhD dissertation, McGill University, 2015.

Byrne, Christopher, and Jason Protass. "Poetry: China (Song and After)." In *Brill's Encyclopedia of Buddhism, Volume One: Literatures and Languages*, edited by Jonathan Silk, 547–553. Leiden: Brill, 2015.

Capitanio, Joshua. "Portrayals of Chan Buddhism in the Literature of Internal Alchemy." *Journal of Chinese Religions* 43, no. 2 (2015): 119–160.

"Characteristics and Forms of Literary Chan: Taking as Examples *Ode to 100 Cases* and the *Blue Cliff Record*" (文字禅的特点与形式: 以《颂古百则》及《碧岩录》为例, *Wenzi Chan de tedian yu xingshi yi: Songgu baize ji Biyanlu weili*), Fenghuang.com Buddhism Compilation (凤凰网佛教综合) (November 2010); accessed February 18, 2023.

Cleary, Thomas, trans. *The Blue Cliff Record*. Berkeley, CA: Numata, 1998.

Cleary, Thomas, trans. *Secrets of the Blue Cliff Record: Zen Comments by Hakuin and Tenkei*. Boston: Shambhala, 2000.

Cleary, Thomas, and J. C. Cleary, trans. *The Blue Cliff Record*. 3 vols. Boston: Shambhala. 1977.

Dumoulin, Heinrich. *Zen Buddhism I: A History, India and China*. Translated by James W. Heisig and Paul Knitter. New York: Macmillan, 1988.

Egan, Ronald. "Su Shi's Informal Letters in Literature and Life." In *History of Chinese Letters and Epistolary Culture*, edited by Antje Richter, 475–507. Leiden: Brill, 2015.

Feng Xuecheng 馮學成. *Birds Dropping Flowers in Front of the Blue Cliff: Fifteen Lectures* (鳥銜花落碧巖前:十五則講記, *Niaoxian hualu Bìyan qian: Shiwuze jiangji*). Guangzhou, China: Nanfang Daily Publishing House, 2013.

Feng Xuecheng 馮學成. *Historical Writings of the Yunmen School* (雲門宗史話, *Yunmen zong shihua*). Chengdu, China: Chengdu wenshu yuan, 2002.

Foulk, T. Griffith. "Myth, Ritual, and Monastic Practice in Sung Ch'an Buddhism." In *Religion and Society in T'ang and Sung China*, edited by Patricia Buckley Ebrey and Peter N. Gregory, 147–208. Honolulu: University of Hawaii Press, 1993.

Geng, Jiyong. "Translation through a Zen Mind: Sam Hamill's Translation of Li Bai's 'Du Zuo Jing Ting Shan.'" *Journal of Global Buddhism* 21 (2020): 117–121.

Gernet, Jacques. *Daily Life in China on the Eve of the Mongol Invasion 1250–1276*. Stanford, CA: Stanford University Press, 1962.

Gill, John, and Susan Tidwell, eds. *After Many Autumns: A Collection of Chinese Buddhist Literature*. Los Angeles: Buddha's Light Publishing, 2011.

Gimello, Robert M. "Mārga and Culture: Learning, Letters, and Liberation in Northern Sung Ch'an." In *The Mārga and Its Transformations in Buddhist Thought*, edited by Robert Buswell, Jr. and Robert M. Gimello, 371–438. Honolulu: University of Hawaii Press, 1992.

Grant, Beata. *Mount Lu Revisited: Buddhism in the Life and Writings of Su Shi*. Honolulu: University of Hawai'i Press, 1994.

Guo Xing. "Metaphorical Imagery and the Fashioning of Caodong Identity in Hongzhi Zhengjue's 宏智正覺 (1091–1157) Commentarial Verses on Old Cases." *Journal of Chinese Buddhist Studies* 33 (2020): 33: 77–119.

Ha Jin. *The Banished Immortal: A Life of Li Bai*. New York: Vintage, 2019.

Heine, Steven. *Chan Rhetoric of Uncertainty in the Blue Cliff Record: Sharpening a Sword at the Dragon Gate*. New York: Oxford University Press, 2016.

Heine, Steven. *From Chinese Chan to Japanese Zen: A Remarkable Century of Transmission and Transformation (1225–1325)*. New York: Oxford University Press, 2017.

Heine, Steven, and Dale S. Wright, eds. *The Kōan*. New York: Oxford University Press, 2000.

Heller, Natasha. *Illusory Abiding: The Cultural Construction of the Chan Monk Zhongfeng Mingben*. Cambridge, MA: Harvard University Press, 2014.

Hongde Zha. "On the Conception of *xingqing* in the Poetics of Yuan Dynasty." *Frontiers of Literary Studies in China* 3 (2009): 547–599.

Hsieh, Ding-hwa. "Poetry and Chan 'Gongan': From Xuedou Chongxian (980–1052) to Wumen Huikai (1183–1260)." *Journal of Song-Yuan Studies* 10 (2010): 39–70.

Huang Jing–Jia. "A Study on Imitating Activities of Hanshan Poems by Chan Buddhist Monks in Song Dynasty." *Journal of Literature and Art Studies* 3/4 (2013): 204–212.

Huang, Yi-hsun. "Chan Master Xuedou and His Remarks on Old Cases in the *Record of Master Xuedou at Dongting*: A Preliminary Study." *Chung-Hwa Buddhist Journal* 22 (2009): 69–95.

Huang Yi-hsun 黃繹勳. "Huayan Thought in a Northern Song Chan Text: The *Zuting Shiyuan*." In *Avataṃsaka* (Huayan, Kegon, Flower Ornament) *Buddhism in East Asia: Origins and Adaptations of a Visual Tradition*, edited by Robert Gimello, Frederic Girard, and Imre Hamar, 109–136. Wiesbaden: Harrasowitz, 2012.

Huang Yi-hsun 黃繹勳. "Reflections on the Life of Chan Master Xuedou Chongxian in his Seven-Work Collection" (雪竇重顯禪師生平與雪竇七集之考, Xuedou chongxian chanshi shengping yu xuedou qijii zhi kaobian). *Taiwan Journal of Buddhist Studies* 1 (2007): 77–117.

Iriya Yoshitaka入矢義高. "Language and Literature of Recorded Sayings" (語録の言葉と文体, Goroku no kotoba to buntai). *Zengaku kenkyū* 68 (1979): 1–19.

Iriya Yoshitaka and N. A. Waddell. "Chinese Poetry and Zen." *The Eastern Buddhist* 6, no. 1 (1973): 54–67.

Ishii Shūdō 石井修道, ed. 3 vols. *Hongzhi's Record* (宏智録, *Wanshi roku*). Tokyo: Meicho Fukyūkai, 1984.

Ishii Shūdō 石井修道. *Stories of the Chinese Chan School History: Studying the Chinese Treasury of the True Dharma Eye* (中国全集史話: 字正法眼蔵に学ぶ, *Chūgoku Zenshūshi wa: Mana Shōbōgenzō ni manabu*). Kyoto: Zen bunka kenkyūsho, 1988.

Keyworth, George Albert. "Transmitting the Lamp of Learning in Classical Chan Buddhism: Juefan Huihong (1071–1128) and Literary Chan." PhD dissertation, University of California at Los Angeles, 2001.

Kirchner, Thomas Yūhō, ed. *The Record of Linji*. Translation and commentary by Ruth Fuller Sasaki. Honolulu: University of Hawaii Press, 2009.

Levering, Miriam. "Dahui Zonggao and Zhang Shangying: The Importance of a Scholar in the Education of a Song Chan Master." *Journal of Sung-Yuan Studies* 30 (2000): 115–139.

Lippit, Yukio. "Apparition Painting." *Anthropology and Aesthetics* 55/56 (2009): 61–86.

Liu, James J. Y. *The Art of Chinese Poetry*. Chicago: The University of Chicago Press, 1962.

Lynn, Richard John. "The Talent Learning Polarity in Chinese Poetics: Yan Yu and the Later Tradition." *Chinese Literature: Essays, Articles, Reviews (CLEAR)* 5, no. 1/2 (1983): 157–184.

Mazanec, Thomas. "How Poetry Became Meditation in Late-Ninth-Century China." *Asia Major* 3d ser. 32, no. 2 (2019): 113–151.

McRae, John. *Seeing Through Zen: Encounter, Transformation, and Genealogy in Chinese Chan Buddhism*. Berkeley: University of California Press, 2003.

Nagai Masashi 永井政之. "On The Formation of Xuedou's *Songgu*" (雪竇頌古の展開について, Setchō juko hatten nitsuite). *Komazawa daigaku Bukkyōgaku kenkyūkai nenpō* 22, no. 1 (1973): 140–141.

Nukariya Kaiten 忽滑谷快天. *History of the Chinese Zen School* (中國禪宗史, *Chūgoku zenshūshi*). Tokyo: Genkōsha, 1925.

Pan, An-yi. *Painting Faith: Li Gonglin and Northern Song Buddhist Culture*. Leiden: Brill, 2007.

Parker, Joseph D. *Zen Buddhist Landscape Arts of Early Muromachi Japan (1336–1573)*. Albany: State University of New York Press, 1999.

Paul, Paramita. "Wandering Saints: Chan Eccentrics in the Art and Culture of Song and Yuan China." PhD dissertation, Leiden University, 2009.

Protass, Jason. "A Geographic History of Song–Dynasty Chan Buddhism: The Decline of the Yunmen Lineage." *Asia Major* 3d ser. 32, no. 1 (2019): 113–160.

Protass, Jason. *The Poetry Demon: Song-Dynasty Monks on Verse and the Way*. Honolulu: University of Hawaii Press, 2021.

Sekida, Katsuki, trans. *Two Zen Classics: Mumonkan and Hekiganroku*. Edited by A. V. Grimstone. New York: Weatherhill, 1977.

Shang Haifeng 商海鋒. "Original and Newer Versions of Xuedou's Record in the Song and Yuan Dynasties" (雪竇錄宋元本舊貌新探, Xuedou lu Song Yuan ben jiumao xintan). *Wenxian* 149, no. 3 (2015): 3–15.

"Sichuan and Japan (part 9): "The Premier Chan Text, the *Blue Cliff Record*, in Japan" (四川与日本（九）— 禅门第一书《碧岩录》与日本), https://www.163.com/dy/article/F8421A0B05129RFH.html (from March 19, 2020; accessed October 21, 2021).

Sterk, Darryl Cameron. "Chan Grove Remarks on Poetry by Wang Shizhen: A Discussion and Translation." MA thesis, University of Toronto, 2002.

Tsuchiya Tasuke 土屋太祐. *The Depth of Thought of the Northern Song Dynasty Chan School* (北宋禪宗思想及其淵, *Beisong chanzong sixiang ji qi yuan*). Chengdu, China: Bashu shushe, 2008.

Tsui, Yu-Chen, "The Poetic Practices of Hongzhi Zhengjue (1091–1157): Gong'an Commentarial Verses on Old Cases and Verses for Lay Literati." PhD dissertation, University of California at Los Angeles, 2018.

Welter, Albert. "Literati Chan at the Song Dynasty Court: The Role of Yang Yi in the Creation of Chan Identity." *Journal of Chinese Buddhist Studies* 34 (2021): 91–159.

Xiao Lihua·蕭麗華 and Wu Jingyi 吳靜宜. "The Influence of Su Shi's Theory of the Unity of Poetry and Meditation on Huihong's "Literary Zen" 蘇軾詩禪合一論對惠洪「文字禪」的影響, Su Shì shi Shan he yi lun dui hui hong "Wenzi Chan" de yingxiang). Xuanzang University Symposium on Buddhism and Literature 玄奘大學「佛學與文學學術研討會」 (April 2003), http://buddhism.lib.ntu.edu.tw/FULLTEXT/JR-NX012/nx115054.html (accessed October 2, 2021).

Xing, Guo. "Metaphorical Imagery and the Fashioning of Caodong Identity in Hongzhi Zhengjue's 宏智正覺 (1091–1157) Commentarial Verses on Old Cases." *Journal of Chinese Buddhist Studies* 33 (2020): 77–119.

Yanagida Seizan 柳田聖山. *Death Poetry in Zen* (禅の遺偈, *Zen no yuige*). Tokyo: Chōbunsha, 1973.

Yanagida Seizan 柳田聖山. *Studies of the Historical Writings of the Early Zen School* (初期禅宗史書の研究, *Shoki zenshū shisho no kenkyū*). Kyoto: Hōzōkan, 1967.

Yanagida Seizan 柳田聖山and Shiina Kōyū 椎名宏雄, eds. *Recorded Sayings of Xuedou Mingjue* (雪竇明覚大師語録, *Setchō minkaku daishi goroku*). In *Zengaku tenseki sōkan* 禅学典籍叢刊, vol. 2. Kyoto: Rinsen shoten, 1999.

Yifa. *The Origins of Buddhist Monastic Codes in China: An Annotated Translation and Study of the* Chanyuan Qinggui. Honolulu: University of Hawaii Press, 2002.

Yu, Gu 于谷. *Language and Literature in the Chan School* (禪宗語言和文獻, *Chanzong yuyan he wenxian*). Jiangsi, China: Jiangsi renmin chubanshe, 1995.

Zengaku daijiten 禪學大辭典. Tokyo: Taishūkan shoten, 1978.

Zhou Yukai 周裕鍇. *The Chinese Chan School and Poetry* (中國禪宗與詩歌, *Zhongguo Chanzong yu shige*). Kaohsiung, Taiwan: Liwen wenhua chubanshe, rpt. 1994.

Zhou Yukai 周裕鍇, "Explaining Chan through a Roundabout Path: From Analyzing Chan to Using Poetic Expressions" (繞路說禪:從禪的詮釋到詩的表達), *Wenyi yanjiu* 2 (2000): 50–55.

Zhou Yukai 周裕鍇. *Expressiveness of the Chan School* (禪宗語言, *Chanzong yuyan*). Taipei: Zongbo chubanshe, rpt. 2002.

Zhou Yukai 周裕鍇. *Literary Chan and Song Dynasty Poetry* (文字禪與宋代詩學, *Wenzi Chan yu Songdai shixue*). Kaohsiung, Taiwan: Liwen wenhua chubanshe, rpt. 2001.

Index

For the benefit of digital users, indexed terms that span two pages (e.g., 52–53) may, on occasion, appear on only one of those pages.

Tables, Figures are indicated by an italic *t* and *f* following the page number.